INDIGENOUS SELF-DETERMINATION IN AUSTRALIA

HISTORIES AND HISTORIOGRAPHY

Aboriginal History Incorporated

Aboriginal History Inc. is a part of the Australian Centre for Indigenous History, Research School of Social Sciences, The Australian National University, and gratefully acknowledges the support of the School of History and the National Centre for Indigenous Studies, The Australian National University. Aboriginal History Inc. is administered by an Editorial Board which is responsible for all unsigned material. Views and opinions expressed by the author are not necessarily shared by Board members.

Contacting Aboriginal History

All correspondence should be addressed to the Editors, Aboriginal History Inc., ACIH, School of History, RSSS, 9 Fellows Road (Coombs Building), The Australian National University, Acton, ACT, 2601, or aboriginalhistoryinc@gmail.com.

INDIGENOUS SELF-DETERMINATION IN AUSTRALIA

HISTORIES AND HISTORIOGRAPHY

EDITED BY LAURA RADEMAKER AND TIM ROWSE

Australian National University

PRESS

ANU PRESS

Published by ANU Press and Aboriginal History Inc.
The Australian National University
Acton ACT 2601, Australia
Email: anupress@anu.edu.au

Available to download for free at press.anu.edu.au

ISBN (print): 9781760463779
ISBN (online): 9781760463786

WorldCat (print): 1191862788
WorldCat (online): 1191862595

DOI: 10.22459/ISA.2020

Cover design and layout by ANU Press

Cover artwork: 'Lightning' (2017), by Noŋgirrŋa Marawili,
Art Gallery of New South Wales

CONTENTS

Part One: Self-determination as a project of colonial authority

Part Two: Self-determination as an Indigenous project

Part Three: Self-determination as principle of international law and concept in political theory

TABLES AND MAPS

ACRONYMS

AACM	Australian Agricultural Consultancy Management Company
AAES	Australian Army Education Service
ABS	Australian Bureau of Statistics
ACA Act	*Aboriginal Councils and Associations Act 1976*
ACCHO	Aboriginal Community Controlled Health Organisation
ACE	Aboriginal Cattle Enterprise
ACG	Aboriginal Consultative Group
ADC	Aboriginal Development Commission
AEDP	Aboriginal Employment Development Policy
AHC	Aboriginal Housing Company
ALCT	Aboriginal Land Council of Tasmania
ALFC	Aboriginal Land Fund Commission
ALP	Australian Labor Party
ALRA	*Aboriginal Land Rights (Northern Territory) Act 1976*
ALS	Aboriginal Legal Service
ALT	Aboriginal Lands Trust
AMS	Aboriginal Medical Service
AnTEP	Anangu Teacher Education Program
ANU	The Australian National University
APY	Anangu Pitjantjatjara Yankunytjara
ARR	Ayers Rock Resort
ASIC	Australian Securities and Investments Commission
ASOPA	Australian School of Pacific Administration

ATSIC	Aboriginal and Torres Strait Islander Commission
ATSIS	Aboriginal and Torres Strait Islander Services
BIITE	Batchelor Institute of Indigenous Tertiary Education
BTEC	Brucellosis and Tuberculosis Eradication Campaign
CAA	Council for Aboriginal Affairs
CAAC	Central Australian Aboriginal Congress
CATSI Act	*Corporations (Aboriginal and Torres Strait Islander) Act 2006*
CDC	Commercial Development Corporation
CDEP	Community Development Employment Projects
CLP	Country Liberal Party
CMS	Church Missionary Society
DAA	Department of Aboriginal Affairs
ECOSOC	Economic and Social Council
FCAA	Federal Council for Aboriginal Advancement
FIAEP	Federation of Independent Aboriginal Education Providers
HREOC	Human Rights and Equal Opportunity Commission
IAD	Institute for Aboriginal Development
IBA	Indigenous Business Australia
ICCPR	International Covenant on Civil and Political Rights
ICESCR	International Covenant on Economic, Social and Cultural Rights
ICJ	International Court of Justice
ILC	Indigenous Land Corporation
LALC	Local Aboriginal Land Councils
LF	Land Fund
LFLF	Literacy for Life Foundation
ML	Mitchell Library
MOM	Methodist Overseas Mission
MPA	Maningrida Progress Association
NAA	National Archives of Australia
NAC	National Aboriginal Conference
NACC	National Aboriginal Consultative Committee

NIC	National Indigenous Council
NLA	National Library of Australia
NSW	New South Wales
NSWALC	New South Wales Aboriginal Land Council
NTA	*Native Title Act 1993*
NTA	Northern Territory Administration
NTAC	Northern Territory Aboriginal Council
NTC	National Tribal Council
NTRS	Northern Territory Records Series
OAA	Office of Aboriginal Affairs
OEA	Office of Evaluation and Audit
ORAC	Office of the Registrar of Aboriginal Corporations
ORIC	Office of the Registrar of Indigenous Corporations
PCIJ	Permanent Court of International Justice
RATE	Remote Area Teacher Education
RCAGA	Royal Commission on Australian Government Administration
RCIADIC	Royal Commission into Aboriginal Deaths in Custody
RDA	*Racial Discrimination Act 1975*
REIT	Real Estate Investment Trust
RLF	Regional Land Fund
SAE	Standard Australian English
SAL	School of Australian Linguistics
SIL	Summer Institute of Linguistics
UAM	United Aborigines Mission
UN	United Nations
UNDRIP	United Nations Declaration on the Rights of Indigenous Peoples
UNESCO	United Nations Educational, Scientific and Cultural Organisation
UNSW	University of New South Wales
UTS	University of Technology Sydney

VET	Vocational education and training
WBACC	Wreck Bay Aboriginal Community Council
WGIP	Working Group on Indigenous Populations

PREFATORY NOTE

This book arose out of a workshop funded by the Academy of Social Sciences in Australia in 2018 at The Australian National University. At that workshop, we arrived at four implications of our findings:

1. That greater public policy attention and funding be directed towards community-controlled adult education and to supporting campaigns and programs aimed at raising adult literacy levels among Indigenous people on a mass scale. Adult literacy is the foundation both for financial literacy and sound governance for Aboriginal incorporations; a rise in literacy is essential to political capacity building and to advocacy of Indigenous interests.

2. That the role of Indigenous interests within governments be expanded. This includes revisiting the recommendations of the Royal Commission on Australian Government Administration that in 1974–76 advocated both greater recruitment of Indigenous public servants and building the capability of Indigenous organisations.

3. That governments actively consider ways to build greater Indigenous control and influence, according to the decisions of Indigenous people, using the various extant capital funds (for instance, Indigenous Business Australia, Aboriginal Benefits Account, Indigenous Land Fund).

4. That Australian governments legislate to ratify the United Nations Declaration on the Rights of Indigenous Peoples so that any future debate about a 'treaty' (at any level of government or region) will know in advance what principles and terms of reference treaty processes would bring into play.

HOW SHALL WE WRITE THE HISTORY OF SELF-DETERMINATION IN AUSTRALIA?

Laura Rademaker and Tim Rowse

The Uluru Statement from the Heart of May 2017 articulated an Indigenous vision for a better relationship between settler and Indigenous Australians: one 'based on justice and self-determination'.[1] The culmination of years of consultation with Indigenous people about constitutional recognition, the statement proposed a referendum in which the Australian people could approve (or not) the formation of an Indigenous deliberative and advisory body – a Voice to Parliament. The government-appointed Referendum Council endorsed this proposal, but the Australian Government quickly dismissed it in October 2017. One prominent advocate of the Uluru Statement and member of the Referendum Council, Megan Davis, seemed to anticipate that response when, back in January 2016, she stated that 'Australia has rejected self-determination – freedom, agency, choice, autonomy, dignity – as being fundamental to Indigenous humanness and development'.[2]

Davis's words are an example of a phenomenon that prompts the writing of this book: the interlacing of historical narratives into the discourse of Indigenous rights. As Bain Attwood has pointed out, Indigenous Australians' political discourse about how they are entitled to be treated has long included a consciousness of history.[3] For both Indigenous and

---

1   Referendum Council, *Uluru statement from the heart*.
2   Davis, 'Listening But Not Hearing'.
3   Attwood, *Rights for Aborigines*, see index entry 'history, Aborigines'.

non-Indigenous Australians, the propositions we exchange about our relationship resonate with frequently retold narratives of how the colonists and the colonised treated each other. Indigenous historical consciousness is rich in accounts of what Indigenous people have done: either to resist or to accommodate the colonists, and to assist (or sometimes to thwart) one another. Telling the truth about history has become so central to Indigenous politics that the Uluru Statement included recommending a truth-telling commission. Non-Indigenous historical consciousness, likewise, has recently become a contested awakening to difficult truths – how authority might have been used better, or perhaps shared through negotiation – pointing to possible paths of national repair.

Davis is not alone in decrying the failure of self-determination. As Patrick Sullivan notes, the failure of past policies for Indigenous Australia is something that 'everybody knows'.[4] Broadly, there are two versions of the failure thesis. One says that from 1973 to the final years of the Howard Government (1996–2007) all governments implemented 'self-determination' but that this failed to empower Indigenous Australians and to reduce the socio-economic 'gap' between Indigenous and non-Indigenous Australians.[5] The other version agrees that socio-economic differences have been stubbornly persistent, but accounts for it by saying that self-determination was never attempted or that, when attempted, it was crippled by underfunding and/or compromised by restraints imposed by Australian laws, policies, institutions and attitudes and/or unjustly terminated (with the Howard Government cast, usually, in the role of terminator). These competing histories of 'failure' not only point to contrasting prescriptions for future action but also marshal different understandings of what 'self-determination' is and could be.

Since both non-Indigenous and Indigenous Australians' senses of political purpose are so saturated with narratives about what happened, what could have happened, and what might yet happen, the question 'how shall we write the history of Indigenous Australian self-determination?' is of more than simply academic interest. Answers to that question are inescapably political in their contribution to non-Indigenous and

---

4   Sullivan, *Belonging Together*, 7.
5   Johns argues that had 'self-determination' not been attempted in Australia the following trends would have continued to create 'more options and choices' for Indigenous Australians: 'movement off the land, intermarriage, general economic and cultural adjustment, and better education'. Self-determination, he claims, has reinforced Aboriginal people's 'inability to adapt'. Johns, *Aboriginal Self-determination*, 66–67.

Indigenous Australians' understandings of their relationship and what that relationship might become. The aim of this book, therefore, is to enrich the historical consciousness in which Indigenous rights advocacy is embedded.

We can thus hear Davis's January 2016 remark as a provocation to historical inquiry, posing the following questions for empirical investigation. How did Australia 'reject self-determination'? Did 'rejection' take the form of specific actions by the state? If so, what were the dates and contexts of these decisive actions? Or was rejection less a set of specifiable state actions and more an entrenched posture of Australian society, manifest in many kinds of actions and attitudes? Before this 'rejection', did 'Australia' ever attempt 'self-determination'? If so, in what forms? And when? Why were they discontinued? Or has Australia never tried self-determination? If that is so, what would be a better description of what governments and people were doing when, in the 1970s, they called the new policy 'self-determination'? Or was Davis's January 2016 statement quite wrong? Perhaps Australia has commenced and continued to apply self-determination, so that the task for the historian is to narrate self-determination's inevitable difficulties (including those bleak moments – such as the extinguishing of the Aboriginal and Torres Strait Islander Commission (ATSIC) in 2004–05, or the Northern Territory Intervention in 2007 – when what was actually happening seemed far from self-determination). Implicit in all these questions is the likelihood that 'self-determination' has meant different things to different people at different times; a history of the contest of the meanings of 'self-determination' is a necessary part of the history of our recent times.

Such are the questions that the authors of this book tackle. In this introduction we seek to distinguish between two approaches to writing the history of self-determination: 'self-determination' as what individuals and organisations actually did when they said they were enabling self-determination, and 'self-determination' as an ideal – derived from international law, political theory and Indigenous demands – against which actions can be judged as succeeding or failing to enable 'self-determination'.

The first approach seeks not to endorse any *a priori* definition of 'self-determination', but to treat 'self-determination' *descriptively* – examining what Australian governments did when they said their policy was self-determination. This immediately raises a question of periodisation. We can say with certainty that on 6 April 1973 Prime Minister Gough Whitlam stated to a conference of Commonwealth and state ministers concerned with Aboriginal affairs in Adelaide that 'the basic object' of his Aboriginal affairs policy 'is to restore to the Aboriginal people of Australia their lost power of self-determination in economic, social and political affairs'.[6] What his government then did can thus be studied as Australia's approach to self-determination. But after the Whitlam Government … ? Has this policy ever been explicitly renounced by subsequent governments and replaced by a policy with a different name and aim? There is no universally agreed answer to this question. In her chapter, Johanna Perheentupa argues that 'self-determination' policy ceased in 1976, when the Fraser Government preferred the label 'self-management' for programs towards Indigenous Australians. In her view, the shift from self-determination to self-management made a real difference to what was possible for Indigenous Australians under Whitlam (1972–75) and then Fraser (1976–83). Conservative governments since Whitlam have been cast as enemies of self-determination, and so many would assent to Jon Altman's opinion that the Australian Government's self-determination policy *de facto* ended in 1996 with Howard's first election and *de jure* with the demise of ATSIC in 2004'.[7] Perhaps 'neoliberalism' has been the nemesis of self-determination? A recent attempt to describe Indigenous public policy in the 'neoliberal age' argues that some features of neoliberalism (such as the vesting of property rights in Indigenous peoples and the promotion of their economic autonomy) are conducive to expressed Indigenous aspirations while other features (the intrusive management of the poor, the insistence that Indigenous organisations compete for government contracts with non-Indigenous providers) have eroded self-determination. Neoliberalism, according to this argument, has done much to promote self-determination as well as much to undermine it.[8]

We doubt that government practices changed significantly when Fraser's 'self-management' replaced Whitlam's 'self-determination', and we note Will Sanders's point that, although the Fraser Government promoted 'self-management' as different, the instances of self-management to which it pointed were the same as those that exemplified the Whitlam Government's self-determination. They were: the formation of the National

6   Whitlam, 'Aboriginals and Society'.
7   Email to the editors, 24 October 2019.
8   Howard-Wagner, Bargh and Altamirano-Jimenèz, 'From New Paternalism'.

Aboriginal Conference in 1977 (as a successor to the National Aboriginal Consultative Committee); 'the influence of Aboriginal organisations such as legal aid and Aboriginal health; the opportunity for Aboriginal councils to provide municipal services in the larger remote settlements; and the opportunity to choose "a traditional lifestyle" by movement to outstations'.[9] The difficulty of deciding when Australian governments ceased to be committed to 'self-determination' is made even more evident if we note that as recently as 2007 one agency of the Howard Government urged 'that any means of protecting Indigenous cultural and intellectual property is based on the principle of self-determination'.[10] In sum, while there is little doubt that the Whitlam Government wanted its programs to be understood as embodying a policy of 'self-determination', the duration of the self-determination policy era remains a matter for interpretation.[11]

As editors, we welcome the approach taken by several of the authors in this book: that what the Whitlam and successor governments did – laws, reports, policies, institutions – can be understood as exemplifying Australia's approach to 'self-determination'. When this approach finds continuities between preceding policies – protection, assimilation – and Australian practices of self-determination, the inference is not necessarily that these residues are flaws in self-determination. In fact, there is no presumption, in this descriptive approach, that 'self-determination' should be a radical rupture with the colonial past. Even if some promoters of self-determination in the early 1970s emphasised the novelty of actions taken in the name of self-determination and celebrated them as the repudiation of a bad past, historians working from what we are calling a descriptive perspective are not obliged to agree. Issues of periodisation, continuity and rupture are open to debate.

---

9   Sanders, 'From Self-determination to Self-management', 8.

10   Australia Council for the Arts, *Protocols*, 8. The protocols declare: 'Indigenous people have the right to self-determination in their cultural affairs and the expression of their cultural material' (p. 12).

11   Just as it remains a matter for debate when 'assimilation' ceased to be Australian Government policy. In the 1960s, critics of 'assimilation' sometimes presented what they considered to be a less coercive policy, which they called 'integration'. What distinguished 'integration' was professed respect for Indigenous choices about the pace and manner of their acculturation to the Australian way of life. 'Integration' recognised value in distinctly 'Aboriginal' or Torres Strait Islander customs, including their senses of shared identity and their social solidarity or 'group life'. Russell McGregor presents a well-documented and thoughtful discussion of the relationship between the terms 'assimilation' and 'integration' in the 1960s. While the advocacy of 'integration' can be seen as paving the way for 'self-determination' to be declared the new policy ideal in 1973, advocates of 'Black Power' were suspicious of 'integration', just as they were adamantly opposed to 'assimilation'. McGregor, *Indifferent*, 177–78.

The second approach to Indigenous self-determination is more explicitly critical, as it measures the practice of self-determination against what Indigenous Australians have said that they wanted (or what the historian infers that they wanted), or what human rights doctrines (in law or in political thought) say they are entitled to. This prescriptive use of 'self-determination' seems to be the perspective that Davis voiced in 2016. This approach views history from the standpoint of an ideal of self-determination that arises from empathy with Indigenous Australians as an imagined subject of history and/or from doctrines of law or concepts in political theory to which the historian assents. The historian then gives a more judgemental account of what actually happened, enabling the reader to see the gap between the ideal and the reality of its flawed Australian practice. Comparison with other settler colonial societies may also inform histories that invoke international law. The historian working in this second perspective may give significance to questions of periodisation, continuity and rupture, arguing, for example, that it is a political indictment of governments and others if elements of 'protection' and 'assimilation' can be detected in practices whose stated intention was 'self-determination'. For example, in her 1977 review of 10 years of Australian policy innovation, Marcia Langton asserted that 'self-determination is a front for assimilation and exploitation'.[12]

In our invitations to participate in our October 2018 workshop, and in our subsequent conversations with authors, we welcomed both descriptive and normative approaches. Indeed, some chapters demonstrate different ways to combine the descriptive and the normative. We do not claim that this book is an Indigenous history of self-determination. Although it is produced in partnership with and includes contributions from leading Indigenous scholars, it does not represent the diverse views, experiences and ambitions of Indigenous people on questions of self-determination. We hope that this book will be useful to Indigenous thinkers and activists, even as we anticipate learning from their insights and critiques. We also hope to see more feminist scholarship around the history of self-determination. We have questions about the gendering of self-determination policies, how they unevenly affected Indigenous men and women and played into (or challenged) existing gender politics of Indigenous and settler communities, that we were unable to address in

---

12   Langton, 'Self-determination as Oppression', 5.

this volume. There is likewise scope for further research in the history of self-determination and the arts as well as the international movements for Indigenous self-determination and their connections to Australia.

Self-determination as what was done

What were the policy innovations that the Whitlam Government called 'self-determination' and that the Fraser Government subsequently endorsed as 'self-management'? While no list is definitive, here is ours:

- establishing a 1973–74 Royal Commission on land rights whose report led to a 1975 Bill and then to the *Aboriginal Land Rights (Northern Territory) Act 1976*
- establishing a national agency, the Department of Aboriginal Affairs, represented by a minister in Cabinet and making grants to Indigenous organisations, including to remote missions and settlements that were evolving into Indigenous townships and to Aboriginal-controlled urban service organisations
- establishing the National Aboriginal Consultative Committee (NACC) as an elected advisory body in 1973, and replacing it with the National Aboriginal Conference in 1977
- establishing the Aboriginal Land Fund Commission, to purchase economic and cultural assets for Aboriginal people to own
- affirming the inherent worth of Indigenous cultures. This included support for bilingual education, and it required the Australia Council, the arts patronage body formed in 1973, to include an Aboriginal Arts Board, made up entirely of Aboriginal and Torres Strait Islander people appointed by the minister for the arts
- outlawing racial discrimination (the *Racial Discrimination Act 1975*), while providing for lawful discrimination in favour of Aboriginal and Torres Strait Islander people
- legislating to facilitate Indigenous Australians to form corporations, to enable their collective action (the *Aboriginal Councils and Associations Act 1976*)
- initiating consultation with Torres Strait Islanders about where to place the border between Australia and Papua New Guinea, and signing a treaty with Papua New Guinea in 1978 that made substantial concessions to Islanders' demands.

Each of these elements of 'self-determination' is dealt with both descriptively and evaluatively in this book.

Continuities with earlier practices

Many of these innovations had continuities with practices under the preceding policy of assimilation. Sana Nakata's chapter reveals that changes to the Census (between the 1966 and 1971 censuses) that acknowledged the social, rather than biological bases of self-identification preceded the government's commitment to self-determination. Sanders shows that the introduction of municipal government in remote regions began as an assimilatory policy and continued as a way to deal with the changes in land title mandated by self-determination. Similarly, as Rademaker demonstrates, the missions in the 1960s were rediscovering the nineteenth-century missiological concept of an 'Indigenous church': 'Aboriginal people taking responsibility for church life, expressed in their own languages, cultures and governance'. The missions also supported moves for Aboriginal political representation, considering all these as consistent with the government's policy of assimilation. Chris Haynes reveals how Northern Territory Welfare Branch officers sought to respond to Aboriginal initiative during the 'assimilation' years, and he dates support for the outstation movement to the mid-1960s.[13] Perheentupa points out that some Aboriginal organisations funded under 'self-determination' policy had been set up to deliver 'welfare' and that what government conceived as the goals of 'welfare' were similar to the aims of 'assimilation'; how to practise 'self-determination' thus became an issue between these organisations and the government. Likewise, Boughton includes within his account of self-determination Aboriginal education collectives, such as Tranby, that date from the 1950s when they were supported as agencies promoting assimilation. Finally, as Simpson shows, mother-tongue education was central to the mission educations at Hermannsburg and Ernabella (admittedly, these missions were in the minority), long before Whitlam.

---

13 This is amply demonstrated by some outstation histories. See Peterson and Myers, *Experiments in Self-determination*.

So what distinguished Australian practices of self-determination from policy approaches before 1973? Was there a core policy logic that marked self-determination as a rupture with previous policy eras? Some would say that giving Indigenous Australians land title (mostly to former reserves) was self-determination's defining rupture from 'assimilation', but against this view we make two observations. First, South Australia, Victoria, New South Wales and Western Australia were already beginning to vest reserve titles in Aboriginal trusts in the years 1966–72, arguably as an adjustment in their tactics of assimilation.[14] Second, as Maria John argues in her chapter, to postulate land rights as self-determination's prerequisite or distinctive feature ignores what urban Indigenous people have said about the struggle for Indigenous health.

As some of our authors note, steps taken in the name of self-determination were sometimes presented as primarily leading to economic independence and the amelioration of disadvantage. Jon Altman reminds us that the goal of 'social and economic equality' underpinned government support for land rights. To Justice Woodward, for instance, land rights were a 'first essential step for people who are economically depressed'.[15] Mike Dillon begins his history of capital funds in 1968, when the Australian Government, in the name of 'assimilation', created the Commonwealth Capital Fund for Aboriginal Enterprises. Some of the Aboriginal Cattle Enterprises supported under self-determination policy, Charlie Ward shows, began as 'assimilation' programs on missions and reserves. The Whitlam Government was 'predisposed to support' what it understood to be Gurindji aspirations to run their own cattle enterprise, giving 'insufficient thought to whether incorporated proprietary companies were appropriate vehicles for remote Indigenous aspirations'. As Ward points out, the increasing availability of welfare payments (according to assimilation's quest for 'equality') contributed to the economic autonomy for individuals of the next generation, frustrating the Gurindji elders' authority as managers. Other contributors suggest that the underlying logic of self-determination policy was to encourage 'responsibility', implying control and self-governance. In his study of the superintendency of John Hunter at Maningrida, Haynes identifies the desire to foster Aboriginal initiative, self-motivation and 'responsibility' as integral to a burgeoning self-determination in Arnhem Land. Rademaker suggests

---

14 Rowse, *Indigenous and other Australians*, 325–28.
15 Woodward, *Aboriginal Land Rights Commission*, 2.

that self-determination and assimilation as applied on Christian missions shared a common interest in Aboriginal people 'taking responsibility', the difference under self-determination being that they were to do so *now* rather than at some future date.

However, what was imagined as 'control' varied. In her chapter outlining the Royal Commission on Government Administration (RCAGA), Elizabeth Ganter explains that, for some, it was mere consultation and 'respect for Aboriginal aspirations', while for others it required Aboriginal involvement in decision-making. In his analysis of the creation of municipal governance on discrete Indigenous communities, Will Sanders suggests we can see the limits of self-determination policy: were discrete communities on Aboriginal land made up of 'self-governing landowners' or merely 'self-servicing landholders'?

The recognition of Indigenous peoplehood was central to the developing body of international law on self-determination, as Asmi Wood's chapter shows. 'Peoples' are not statistically aggregated individuals; they enact their peoplehood as a capacity for collective action by forming institutions. It is therefore significant that one enduring Australian practice of self-determination that distinguishes it from assimilation is to encourage the formation of groups – imagining Indigenous advancement as the work of potent collectives and not just of successful individuals. Katie Curchin and Tim Rowse trace the history of the statutory regulation of Indigenous corporations, arguing that the robust Indigenous sector is the product of self-determination. Mike Dillon also argues that self-determination continues to mean a government preference to engage with Indigenous people as groups, rather than as individuals. Tim Rowse argues that Torres Strait Islanders had long been treated as a collective political entity through Queensland's practices of 'indirect rule'. The Whitlam Government's innovation in 1973 brought the Commonwealth Government into this scene, vying with Queensland as the government that would recognise and reward Torres Strait collectivity.

If 'self-determination' meant recognising Indigenous peoples as collective actors, it also raised the issue of cultural difference: did government policy enable 'groups' only on the condition that their goals and methods depart from 'custom' in order to conform to non-Indigenous Australian norms? Jon Altman's chapter is about the tension between landowners 'becoming equal and remaining different'. At the same time as they have become landowners, the distinct peoplehood of Indigenous Australians in their land *use* has come under pressure. In our two chapters on education (Bob Boughton and Jane Simpson), the recognition of Indigenous people as peoples made for a new urgency in Indigenous control over training and education. No longer focused on educating the individual, the assumption under self-determination was that Indigenous people required language and literacy skills to represent themselves and pursue their interests as peoples.

Yet, well before Australian governments committed to self-determination, they were professing respect for Aboriginal and Torres Strait Islander cultural heritage. Rademaker shows that the protection of Aboriginal cultural life was key to missionaries' re-imagining their role in Aboriginal communities in the 1960s. Self-determination meant that Aboriginal people were to be 'free' to be Christians in their own way. Part of the legacy of the missionisation of these communities, which Simpson identifies, is that Aboriginal people's cultural rights to language received broader recognition from governments than their communication rights. Indigenous health services in both Australia and the United States were, as Maria John reveals, not only sites of Indigenous control but also environments where Indigenous people could be 'proud to be themselves'. Self-governance of these organisations was not an end in itself; it was a means to create urban spaces where Indigenous cultures could flourish.

Given these complexities, as editors, we remain agnostic on the question of whether 'self-determination' had a 'core' that marked it as distinct. Perhaps what most marks the initiatives listed above as a break from the past was the rhetoric of their presentation and the matching enthusiasm and commitment of the Indigenous people who engaged.

Self-determination as Indigenous project

The normative approach to writing the history of self-determination understands self-determination as an ongoing Indigenous ambition within a project of decolonisation. This understanding was reflected in the Uluru Statement and, before it, the Redfern Statement (2008) and Barunga Statement (1988), each demanding Indigenous 'self-determination'. In his 1999 Vincent Lingiari lecture, Pat Dodson claimed that 'Aboriginal peoples have the right to self-determination', that is, the right to 'negotiate our political status and to pursue economic, social and cultural development'.[16] Despite the shortcomings of rights-based discourses (discussed further below), Indigenous people have harnessed the language and visions of self-determination discourses within international law and turned these to their own purposes.

For many Indigenous people, 'self-determination' has meant not only choosing how they will relate to the settler colonial state and economy, but also making choices that would maximise autonomy, driven by a shared memory or imagined ideal of the autonomy they enjoyed before colonisation began. The Whitlam Government's claim to '*restore* to the Aboriginal people of Australia their lost power of self-determination in economic, social and political affairs' reflected this understanding.[17] Many Indigenous Australians understand self-determination to refer to the political realisation of their inextinguishable sovereignty: they never ceded their sovereignty and never could or would cede it. By this understanding, Indigenous 'self-determination', though never entirely lost, was (and is) under continual attack by processes of colonisation. Consequently, for many Indigenous people, 'self-determination' could not be 'bestowed' by governments, it must be asserted, practised and maintained, often despite government policy. As Wiradjuri scholar Robynne Quiggin argued, 'we have a long history of "setting our own course" despite the rejection, confinement and cruelty of colonisation'.[18]

This question of who owns or confers self-determination (and whose interests it ultimately serves), has led some Indigenous thinkers to adopt other frames for Indigenous political mobilisation. As Borrows and Tully[19] recently articulated, Indigenous projects of decolonisation are being conceptualised either as projects of 'reconciliation' with the settler state that might, for instance, include demands for treaties, recognition, return of land, rights and reparations, or as what some call 'resurgence', that is, of reclaiming Indigenous cultures, lands and ways of being without reference to the colonisers. For those seeking resurgence, reconciliatory movements can entail colonising concessions. But where do claims to self-determination fit in relation to these projects? Are claims for self-determination claims of resurgence – because self-determination entails restoring to Indigenous people their authority? Or is demanding Indigenous self-determination

---

16   Dodson, 'Until the Chains Are Broken', 29.
17   Whitlam, 'Aboriginals and Society' (emphasis added). See also Hocking, 'A Transforming Sentiment', S5–S12.
18   Quiggin, 'What Does Democracy and Self-determination Mean', S52–S53.
19   Borrows and Tully, 'Introduction', 1–6.

an act of reconciliation – because it demands concessions from the settler state? The settler state has an incentive to make such concessions: these might give it the moral legitimacy it craves. Stephen Young points out that the state's recognition of Indigenous people, their nationhood and self-determination, also serves to legitimate its own assertions of sovereignty and nationhood.[20] As Noel Pearson recently argued, restoring Indigenous people in Australia their right to 'self-determination' and 'responsibility' would create a 'more complete Commonwealth'.[21]

For some, 'self-determination' is no longer the right way to conceptualise the pursuit of Indigenous interests. Cherokee political scientist Jeff Corntassel argues that the failure of the United Nations Declaration on the Rights of Indigenous Peoples (UNDRIP) to uphold Indigenous peoples' land and water cultural relationships, favouring instead the territorial integrity of the state, is indicative of the false promises of rights-based and state-centred strategies for achieving decolonisation.[22] Quiggin also noted that 'self-determination has its origins in the processes of imperialism and the development of the nation state', that is, the very processes that fuelled the dispossession of Indigenous people.[23] For her, this is not a reason for Indigenous people to reject self-determination but a reason to assert their own self-determination more forcefully in the face of colonising authorities. As Anishinaabe scholar Aaron Mills similarly pointed out, 'self-determination is the language of our settler-colonizer'.[24] Mills argued that self-determination undercuts Indigenous conceptions of selfhood and political community that value interdependence and relationship. For Indigenous people, freedom is not about 'standing apart' but 'standing with' the other.[25] Where Indigenous people mobilise state-centric rights discourses that focus on the supposedly autonomous self, their demands cannot lead to a sustainable self-determination based upon spiritual foundations and on Indigenous peoples' relationships and responsibilities to the natural world. Dene political theorist Glen Coulthard argued in 2007 for Indigenous practices 'less oriented' to attaining 'affirmative [forms] of recognition from the settler state and society, and more about critically revaluating, reconstructing and redeploying culture and

---

20 Young, 'The Self Divided', 195.
21 Pearson, 'A Rightful Place', 72.
22 Corntassel, 'Re-envisioning Resurgence', 92.
23 Quiggin 'What does', S52.
24 Mills, 'Rooted Constitutionalism', 160.
25 Mills, 'Rooted Constitutionalism', 160.

tradition in ways that seek to prefigure, alongside those with similar ethical commitments, a radical alternative to the structural and psycho-affective facets of colonial domination'.[26]

Aileen Moreton-Robinson makes a similar critique while also distinguishing the Indigenous male from the Indigenous female as a self-determining subject. Her Indigenous feminist critique of self-determination as espoused by liberal settler colonial governments argues that Indigenous women give priority to the collective rights of Indigenous people rather than to the individual rights of liberal citizenship. This means that 'Indigenous women's perceptions of self-determination and sovereignty are not consistent with the liberal idea that, through citizenship, self-determination can be realised'.[27] While she does not abandon the language of self-determination, Moreton-Robinson is sceptical of the ability of settler colonial governments' policies of 'self-determination' to empower Indigenous women. Megan Davis has also differentiated the Indigenous subject by gender, arguing that 'the right to self-determination' has 'promoted an impoverished form of self-determination for Aboriginal women in Australia'.[28] Davis's argument is not so grounded in an assumption of Indigenous women's cultural distinction: she draws on Martha Nussbaum's argument that implementing human rights necessitates attention to the practical 'capabilities' of all humans, and she is more optimistic than Moreton-Robinson about the liberal settler colonial state's ability to realise human rights.

For Indigenous activist and public intellectual Noel Pearson, self-determination is best applied on the levels of both individual and community. 'Liberty, responsibility and self-determination' are, to him, 'basically the same'. They are all about 'the freedom and power to choose'.[29] Pearson argued that the right of self-determination includes the ability and 'right' to 'take responsibility'.[30] Notions of 'responsibility' – both individual and collective – are familiar to many Indigenous people who feel a keen sense of responsibility to their country, ancestors and kin.[31] For many Indigenous people, these responsibilities are also the grounds of Indigenous sovereignty. Though Pearson is strongly committed to the idea

---

26 Coulthard, 'Subjects of Empire', 456.
27 Moreton-Robinson, 'Patriarchal Whiteness', 70.
28 Davis, 'Aboriginal Women', 78–88, 79.
29 Pearson, 'A Rightful Place', 43.
30 Pearson, *Up from the Mission*. 167.
31 Corntassel, 'Re-envisioning Resurgence', 93.

that Indigenous Australians are 'peoples', he does not use the language of 'sovereignty'. Pearson argues that an obsession with 'self-determination and international law' and 'concepts of autonomy and sovereignty' have distracted from the 'practical realities of self-determination'.[32] By 'practical realities' he means the financial and social capital that would enable Indigenous people to make decisions about their lives. Decisions about how to take responsibility might even lead to 'assimilation', a possibility raised by Mike Dillon in this volume (considering the forms that Indigenous 'wealth' can take) as well as by Michael Mansell. Mansell identifies three political options for Indigenous Australians under self-determination: 'to form a new state through secession, agree to autonomy or association in a federal state, or to integrate or assimilate in a single unitary state'.[33]

But elsewhere 'sovereignty' has risen to prominence in Indigenous political discourse since it emerged in the 1960s.[34] Sovereignty and self-determination are often used together, presented as two approaches to or conceptualisations of a single struggle, as John's chapter points out.[35] While critiquing both 'sovereignty' and 'self-determination' as European imports to Indigenous political discourses,[36] Taiaiake Alfred described 'the two most important strategies' for Indigenous people as 'assertion of prior and coexisting sovereignty' and 'the assertion of a right of self-determination', describing these strategies as 'woven together'.[37] To Leroy Little Bear, sovereignty is 'about making your own decisions, following your own mind, being self-determining' without forgetting our interdependence; sovereignty is 'qualified by your dependence on other people'.[38] In Australia, Michael Mansell explained that 'sovereignty' underpins other Indigenous ambitions, including self-determination.[39] In 2003, Larissa Behrendt described 'recognition of sovereignty as an expression of distinct identity and a starting point for the exercise of self-determination as a way of achieving empowerment, autonomy and equality'.[40] In 2013 she distinguished 'self-determination' ('when Indigenous people are involved

---

32 Pearson, *Up from the Mission*, 168.
33 Mansell, *Treaty and Statehood*, 165.
34 Moreton-Robinson, 'Introduction', 3.
35 Strelein, 'Missed Meanings', 85, 89.
36 Alfred, 'Sovereignty', 40.
37 Alfred, 'Sovereignty', 37.
38 Little Bear, 'An Elder Explains Indigenous Philosophy', 7.
39 Mansell, *Treaty and Statehood*, 74.
40 Behrendt, *Achieving Social Justice*, 115.

in the setting of priorities within their community, the development of policy, the delivery of services, and the implementation of programs') from 'sovereignty' ('when control is given centrally to Aboriginal people without constraint'). Indigenous Australians have sometimes practised both self-determination and sovereignty: 'many successful programs ... [have been] developed by community members, often without government assistance, such as night patrols, dry-out areas, and safe houses'.[41]

Non-Indigenous Australians have sometimes responded defensively to Indigenous claims of 'sovereignty', despite its close association with self-determination (which is seen as less threatening) and notwithstanding that sovereignties can be understood as multiple and overlapping.[42] Tim Rowse's chapter is a caution against assuming that the Indigenous assertion of sovereignty necessitates the rejection of Australian sovereignty. When Torres Strait Islanders asserted their customary interest in the social and ecological relations of the border between Australia and Papua New Guinea, they insisted that their lands and seas be protected by continuing to remain under Australian sovereignty. Indigenous claims to sovereignty do, however, expose the fragility of the settler state's own claims. As Asmi Wood explains, in law 'there is no doctrinal answer to the question of how [non-Indigenous or colonial] sovereignty was acquired'. There is, therefore, 'both an opportunity and a space for negotiations and discussions on self-determination without preconditions', and 'the principle of *uti possidetis* puts Indigenous Australians in a position to negotiate under international law'. Perhaps the growing appeal of the language of sovereignty to Indigenous activists is that they believe self-determination to have failed: they are looking for new ways to make settler colonial society pay attention to their claims.

Self-determination and international law

Dylan Lino has summarised what extant international law offers to Indigenous Australians:

> First, the established international law is very specific, entailing a limited number of legal remedies, for example decolonisation, that have no applicability to Indigenous peoples in settler-colonial

---

41   Behrendt, 'Aboriginal Sovereignty', 171–72.
42   Behrendt, *Achieving Social Justice,* 115; Strelein, 'Missed Meanings', 85.

states like Australia. Second, despite the presently limited nature of the established law on self-determination, the law is continuing to develop. It is true that legal rules applying the right of self-determination to Indigenous peoples are yet to crystallise into a clear and cogent body of law, but there is certainly a space in international law – especially post-UNDRIP – in which to flesh out an Indigenous right of self-determination. Third, the direction in which the nascent law on Indigenous self-determination is developing is moving away from secession and independence and towards internal, intra-state configurations.[43]

Three chapters of this volume engage with international law as a resource for Indigenous political thought.

Asmi Wood points out that self-determination began to circulate as a concept of international law when Woodrow Wilson and Vladimir Ilyich Lenin enunciated it, in their different ways, in 1918. The Charter of the United Nations in 1945 mentions 'self-determination', and the concept has been the focus of discussion and development in UN forums ever since. In 2007, the UNDRIP included:

> Article 3.
>
> Indigenous peoples have the right of self-determination. By virtue of that right they freely determine their political status and freely pursue their economic, social and cultural development.
>
> Article 4.
>
> Indigenous peoples, in exercising their right to self-determination, have the right to autonomy or self-government in matters relating to their internal and local affairs, as well as ways and means for financing their autonomous functions.[44]

As Maria John observes in her chapter, the UNDRIP was deliberately unspecific about the scope of Indigenous peoples' self-determination. It references only internal matters and 'local affairs', and it does not allow territorial sovereignty as a basis of Indigenous self-determination. Self-determination as a norm of international law has disappointed some Indigenous people who see it as too vague and imprecise to serve as a foundation for Indigenous claims.[45] Wood argues that Australian

---

43   Lino, 'The Politics of Inclusion', 850.
44   United Nations, *United Nations Declaration on the Rights of Indigenous Peoples*.
45   Mansell, *Treaty and Statehood*, 194.

Indigenous people should nevertheless continue to press for Australia to legislate to ratify the UNDRIP. This would compel Australian courts to adjudicate disputes around Indigenous self-determination with regard to international law and literature, giving Indigenous people greater opportunity to exercise their peoplehood under the law, as well as laying the ground for treaty negotiations.

Sana Nakata also refers to self-determination as a concept in international law, alluding – like Wood – to the UN Charter, the International Covenant on Civil and Political Rights and the International Covenant on Economic, Social and Cultural Rights. In her reading of the history of 'self-determination', there is a deep connection between the right of an individual to identify with a 'people' and the right of that 'people' to self-determination; that is, both rights make appeal to the values of 'Autonomy. Freedom. Sovereignty ... concepts that attach as much to individual human beings as they attach to nations and states'. Nakata then argues that the institutional form of peoplehood can be evaluated according to its practice towards the autonomy of the individual.

Nakata and others are therefore troubled by the way that the state has delegated the adjudication of individuals' claims to be 'Aboriginal' to the Indigenous sector. In Australia, she argues, the colonial sovereign's criteria for recognising a people are likely to result in the mis-recognition of some individuals. Nakata draws on Bronwen Carlson's ethnography *The Politics of Identity* to illustrate Indigenous experiences of mis-recognition that seem to have become increasingly common in the early twenty-first century – that is, of having one's identity claims rejected by Indigenous organisations. If the purpose of 'recognition' is 'justice', then mis-recognition (rejecting a person's claim to be Aboriginal) is injustice, Nakata argues. The injustice of such mis-recognition is compounded where the state empowers Indigenous organisations to give or withhold recognition. She also raises the possibility that, as Indigenous Australian claims give emphasis to *constitutional* recognition of peoplehood, there will be less need for any authority to judge an individual's claim to be Indigenous. Nakata insists that Indigeneity is too dynamic historically to be contained by official criteria, not least because both colonisation and the pursuit of rights are ongoing disruptors of Indigeneity.

Failure narratives and self-determination

Many accounts of self-determination have argued true 'self-determination' (variously defined) was never really attempted in Australia because, in valuing the preservation of Indigenous cultural difference, the policy set limits to Indigenous choices to change. Pearson, for instance, argued that self-determination failed because the 'preservation of some kind of imagined cultural purity' trumped giving Indigenous people real choices about 'how to reconcile their cultures with the demands of development'.[46] In Peter Sutton's view, the new rights of the self-determination era were not matched with measures 'designed to assist people through the crises of occupation, discipline, motivation, conflict management and community trauma that soon erupted and by the 1990s had reached a crescendo, especially in the remoter regions'.[47] Likewise, according to conservative commentator Gary Johns, self-determination was never really tried, because a commitment to an idealised version of Aboriginal cultures, together with an incoherent pursuit of both Aboriginal separatism and integration, prevented Aboriginal people from pursuing their own interests.[48] Moreover, Johns argues that Aboriginal people lacked the capacity to manage their own affairs and to make decisions, meaning that they 'won their freedom and lost their livelihood': self-determination as practised in the 1970s was never true freedom.[49]

Refuting Johns and reviewing policy from 1972 to 2005, Stuart Bradfield argued that self-determination enacted 'a logic of "domestication", which acts to manage and curtail Indigenous separatism, rather than give expression to it'.[50] Aboriginal political identities were 'contained' via 'impotent representative bodies' from the 1970s. Land rights were granted, but were always managed by the state.[51] Even ATSIC, supposedly exemplary of self-determination, remained subject to federal control and was eventually dismantled, as Aileen Moreton-Robinson, Elizabeth Strakosch and Will Sanders also note.[52] Moreton-Robinson argues that

---

46   Pearson, 'A Rightful Place', 47.
47   Sutton, *The Politics of Suffering*, 58.
48   Johns, 'The Failure of Aboriginal Separatism', 18.
49   Johns, 'The Failure of Aboriginal Separatism', 12.
50   Bradfield, 'Separatism or Status-Quo?', 82.
51   Bradfield, 'Separatism or Status-Quo?', 84.
52   Bradfield, 'Separatism or Status-Quo?', 88; Moreton-Robinson, 'Introduction', 4; Strakosch, 'The Technical Is Political', 126; Sanders, 'Missing ATSIC', 113–30.

so-called 'self-determination' policy was only ever 'self-management'.[53] This position is also reflected by some authors in this volume. Perheentupa, for instance, argues that the Department of Aboriginal Affairs never intended to give Aboriginal organisations the autonomy they claimed and that the 1975 shift to 'self-management' further undermined Aboriginal autonomy.

Many Indigenous intellectuals insist that Indigenous demands were not heard under self-determination. Gary Foley, for instance, lamented that Indigenous leaders were quickly disappointed by the gap between the Whitlam Government's promises to Indigenous people and its actions, particularly its failure to enact its stated principle that Aboriginal people should run their own affairs (which Foley calls 'sovereignty').[54] Ian Anderson traced a state of 'chronic crisis' in Indigenous policy and politics, dating back to the removal of barriers to citizenship for Indigenous Australians (presumably in the late 1960s).[55] The perpetual crisis, Anderson argued, is attributable in part to institutional structures of our parliamentary system that have never required consultation with Indigenous people or representation of Indigenous interests.[56] There was no structural mechanism to ensure self-determination for Indigenous people.

Numerous scholars from an anthropological background have pointed to cultural barriers to self-determination. As Cowlishaw argued, under self-determination the 'bourgeois ideal of autonomous, self-willed subjects' drove policies and governance of Aboriginal people. Aboriginal communities were to learn to value independence, self-management and autonomy, whether these represented Aboriginal values or not.[57] Tatz objected to the artificial formation of these 'autonomous' communities. These had previously been ruled as 'total institutions' (i.e. as missions or settlements), often consisting of tribal and language groups with conflicting interests, frequently rivalries, but were made to become 'communities', 'regardless of whether or not there was an actual *communitas*'.[58] The forms of governance these communities were made to adopt bore little resemblance to Indigenous peoples' own ways of governing themselves.

---

53 Moreton-Robinson, 'Introduction', 4.
54 Foley, 'The Australian Labor Party', 125.
55 Anderson, 'The Crisis of Australia's Indigenous Policy', 54.
56 Anderson, 'The Crisis of Australia's Indigenous Policy', 59.
57 Cowlishaw, 'Erasing Culture and Race', 150.
58 Tatz, *Aboriginal Suicide*, 27.

Others suggest that self-determination was attempted, but later undermined. The shift in government focus towards 'reconciliation' in the 1990s, followed by the Howard Government's emphasis on 'practical reconciliation' and the policy of 'closing the gap', have eroded policies of self-determination by deliberately avoiding and undermining Indigenous claims to sovereignty and self-determination.[59] Under the Abbott Government's Indigenous Advancement Strategy, funding for non-Indigenous organisations with 'Reconciliation Action Plans' and 'philanthrocapitalism' 'replaced self-determination as the path to modernisation', argues Davis. What some call 'neoliberal' commitments reframed Aboriginal polities simply as the 'Indigenous sector', along with the 'business sector' or 'education sector'. When understood as a mere 'sector', Davis argues, Indigenous Australians are denied the right to self-determination.[60] With the return of a conservative national government in 1996, governments showed greater antipathy to rights-based policy agendas for Indigenous people. Indigenous services were instead to be 'mainstreamed' and 'normalised' within a broader 'neoliberal' agenda.[61] As noted above, one of the effects of the 'neoliberal age' is a return to government intrusion in Indigenous peoples' private lives.[62] Chapters by Altman and Boughton are instances of this failure narrative, arguing that 'neoliberal' reforms beginning in the 1990s undermined previous gains for Aboriginal people. According to this understanding, the 'deficit discourse' that accompanied 'practical reconciliation' and the 'closing the gap' agenda further discredited self-determination. As Laurie Bamblett argued, describing and defining Indigenous people only in terms of disadvantage and deficit 'makes it easier to deny Aboriginal communities self-determination on the grounds of incapability'.[63]

---

59   Ladner, 'Proceed with Caution', 250.
60   Davis, 'Gesture Politics'.
61   Lovell, 'Languages of Neoliberal Critique', 223.
62   Howard-Wagner, Bargh and Altamirano-Jiménez, 'From New Paternalism to New Imaginings', 14–15.
63   Bamblett, 'Serious Whitefella Stuff', 81.

Self-determination as a concept implicit in Indigenous action

The historian who wishes to compare the actual practice of self-determination to what Indigenous Australians wanted (or to what, in the historian's opinion, they were entitled) may search for statements by Indigenous people and/or by authorities concerned with formulating Indigenous rights or at least human rights. However, historians might also infer Indigenous conceptions of 'self-determination' from actions and from words that do not include the phrase 'self-determination'.

The fact that Indigenous Australians have been a colonised people is, for some historians, sufficient basis for attributing to them a strong desire for self-determination. According to this approach, the task for the historian is to discover the contingent expressions of that desire in what Indigenous Australians said (or did not say) and what they did (or did not do) in specified times and places. Anthropological research has sometimes deciphered political messages in Indigenous Australians' ritual innovation. Ronald Berndt, for instance, interpreted the Yolngu decision to display secret objects in 1958 as expressing a desire for a 'greater measure of control over their own affairs, politically and religiously, and especially in relation to education and employment'.[64] Berndt, however, did not call this a claim to 'self-determination'; that concept in international law had not yet acquired the 'domestic' meaning it later gained. In some contexts, explicit programmatic statements by Indigenous Australians are discoverable in the archive and easy to interpret (some even use the word 'self-determination'). In other contexts, however, the historian engages in reasoned attribution, finding what he/she considers to be 'self-determination' in certain words and actions. For example, Tim Rowse presents certain actions and words of Torres Strait Islanders in the 1970s as 'self-determination', notwithstanding their explicit demand to remain within Australian sovereignty. What the historian considers 'self-determination' to mean is, therefore, an important question for historians' practice, an aspect of the question that animates this book: 'How shall we write the history of Australian Indigenous self-determination?'

---

64   Berndt, *An Adjustment Movement*, 87.

Haynes's account of Hunter is grounded in the view that Aboriginal people were 'self-determining' when they first came to the settlement at Maningrida and when they left for outstations. By characterising Indigenous agency this way, Haynes is able to describe the space that was open to Hunter's prefiguring of self-determination, that is, a space defined by people sometimes *not* taking up what governments offered. The gap between white official (assimilationist) expectations and actual Aboriginal behaviour is sometimes described as Aboriginal 'resistance' to assimilation, and this indeed is the term Haynes chooses. In the story as Haynes tells it, the historian does not need to find evidence of an articulate Aboriginal concept of self-determination; 'self-determination' was prefigured in Hunter's practice to the extent that he acknowledged and bent to realities (geographical, human) that were beyond government control.

If Indigenous agency is to be treated historically, the story of the emergence of Indigenous points of view will include discursive gaps, silences and hesitations. For example, reviewing gains made by Indigenous Australians in the period 1967–77, Nugget Coombs (chair of the Council for Aboriginal Affairs, 1967–76) celebrated Arnhem Land's outstation movement as self-determination in action, before commenting that in several other domains of public policy – education, health and housing – self-determination had not yet displaced assimilation.[65] By way of explanation, he mentioned government inertia, as well as Indigenous Australians not yet having had time to consider and to articulate their distinctive needs for education, health and housing. The point should not be missed by historians: willingness and capacity to speak programmatically has developed unevenly across Australian regions and across policy domains. Not every instance of Indigenous aspiration is as articulate as the statements from the Tent Embassy, cited by Jon Altman.

Elizabeth Ganter's chapter exemplifies another way to attribute Indigenous conceptions of 'self-determination'. The term 'self-determination' is nowhere in the 1977 Royal Commission on Australian Government Administration (RCAGA) report, yet Ganter shows how we might find it implicit. Some recommendations of the report were a (neglected) stimulus to 'self-determination', as she understands that concept. Ganter is explicit in deriving her conception of self-determination from recent political theories of representation that urge democratic states to recruit public

---

65   Coombs, *Australia's Policy Towards Aborigines*.

servants diversely. A state committed to Indigenous self-determination would ask: how can Indigenous public servants be 'both grounded … in their communities and empowered … in government decision-making'? Ganter argues that certain RCAGA recommendations in effect addressed that question: they looked positively on the possibility that Indigenous individuals would be mobile between public service employment and working in the Indigenous sector, thus 'building relationships between Indigenous administrators on the inside and their communities and organisations on the outside'. Ganter reports from her own interviews with Indigenous officers of the Northern Territory Government that many of her interviewees were mobile between government and Indigenous sector employment, just as the RCAGA recommendations had imagined. Her task as historian is thus to theorise these peoples' careers as an emergent practice of self-determination.

Mike Dillon's chapter is a third example of the possibility of inferring Indigenous conceptions of 'self-determination' from the practices of Indigenous people. His question is: in what ways could public sector capital funds have contributed to Indigenous self-determination? Writing from a normative standpoint, Dillon's history of Indigenous Business Australia and the Indigenous Land Corporation and its associated Land Fund affirms a *procedural* notion of self-determination: that decision-making about the use of funds should maximise Indigenous participation at the highest level. When considering whether these investment decisions have achieved greater self-determination, he is more cautious. Noting that Indigenous people have different views about the forms that capital might take, he declines to say which uses of the capital funds *he thinks* would lead more to 'assimilation' than to outcomes more distinctively Indigenous. Instead, he alludes to ongoing debates among Indigenous Australians about how best to invest these funds. Such debates were crucial in defining what we might refer to as the Indigenous vision of self-determination, but little is yet known of them.

The limits of the settler colonial liberal nation-state

Some narratives of the historical failure of self-determination in Australia are grounded in a theory of the limited ability of settler colonial states to enable Indigenous autonomy. Gillian Cowlishaw argued that self-determination in Australia created only 'a semblance of autonomous governmental structures' that were always subject to state strictures and regulations: 'self-determination did not mean laissez-faire or autonomy from the state at all'.[66] In fact, self-determination policies had more to do with the settler colonial state repositioning itself as 'the liberator from past oppression' and disavowing its racist past than about eradicating racial inequalities.[67] Francesca Merlan concluded that, under self-determination, the state replaced 'overt coercion' with a mode of seeking to 'elicit from Aboriginal people … their own modes of organisation' in order to 'recast the management of Aboriginal affairs in what are seen to be indigenous terms'.[68] That is, the state did not and perhaps cannot cease to authorise (or disallow) versions of Indigenous tradition.

It remains unclear whether the Australian case illustrates deep limits to the settler colonial state's sympathetic recognition of Indigenous difference. If there were such limits, then self-determination would be marked by contradiction and failure. For Peter Sutton, clashes between custom and corporate accountability under self-determination were symptomatic of a deeper contradiction between 'modernism and cultural traditionalism' within the very idea of self-determination.[69] Self-determination pursued Indigenous sameness in some ways and Indigenous difference in others, but the rationale for when or why one or the other was preferred was never articulated. In an influential critique of Australian multiculturalism, Elizabeth Povinelli has argued that the settler colonial state's approach to culture – liberal multiculturalism – asserts the sovereign right to selectively approve differentiated aspects of Indigenous culture: there was no scope for Aboriginal practices that were contrary to governments' agenda.[70] Anthropologist Emma Kowal also argued that the contradictory pursuit of sameness *and* difference is inherent to liberal multiculturalism. The 'postcolonial logic' that 'prevailed in the self-determination era' sought to eliminate inequality (which she calls 'remedialism') while also maintaining essential difference ('orientalism').[71] Altman, in this volume, describes the 'twin logics' of the *Aboriginal Land Rights (Northern Territory) Act 1976*, namely 'justice by returning ancestral lands' while

---

66 Cowlishaw, 'Helping Anthropologists, Still', 53.
67 Cowlishaw, 'Erasing Culture and Race', 147.
68 Merlan, *Caging the Rainbow*, 150.
69 Sutton, *The Politics of Suffering*, 59.
70 Povinelli, *The Cunning*; Cowlishaw, 'Helping Anthropologists, Still', 53.
71 Kowal, 'The Politics of the Gap', 338.

also 'improving socio-economic marginality'. These clashing logics mirror the 'postcolonial logic' that Kowal identifies. For Altman, these tensions within self-determination were exacerbated by recent Australian Government policies.

In this perspective, Australia, as a settler colony, must fail its projects of self-determination. A settler colonial state must continually contain and erase Indigenous sovereignty if it is to uphold its own legitimacy. In one version of this view, self-determination rhetoric was window-dressing for a new iteration of colonising policies. Elizabeth Strakosch refers to an unresolved 'foundational sovereign conflict'; that is, an underlying clash of sovereignties between the settler colonial state and Australia's Indigenous people. Although Indigenous policy may appear to pursue 'self-determination', it does not and cannot address the underlying structures. Quite the opposite: by acting unilaterally on Indigenous people (treating them as legitimate subjects of the state), and by representing Indigenous people as problems for the settler colonial state to address, Indigenous policy entrenches the colonial relationship.[72] This was also true 'despite the rhetoric of the self-determination era'.[73]

It follows from this perspective that the settler state's apparent concessions to forms of Indigeneity are always only ever strategic and that they render, eliminate or erase Indigenous people. In Patrick Wolfe's theory, settler colonies are 'premised on the elimination of native societies'.[74] For him, 'a range of historical practices' that 'might otherwise appear distinct' can all be understood through this lens.[75] These practices include, more recently, Australian Government policies that appear to celebrate Indigeneity: these are 'strategic pluralism'.[76] According to this theory, government policies of self-determination, despite any benevolent appearances, further processes of elimination. It would, in fact, be impossible for the settler colonial state to genuinely pursue Indigenous self-determination as this would threaten its claim to legitimate sovereignty. It follows from this view that Indigenous self-determination can only ever be a project in opposition to the settler state.

---

72 Strakosch, 'The Technical Is Political', 116, 120.
73 Brigg and Maddison, 'Unsettling Governance', 6.
74 Wolfe, *Settler Colonialism*, 2.
75 Wolfe, *Settler Colonialism*, 163.
76 Wolfe, *Settler Colonialism*, 167.

This theory of the settler colonial state presents the relationship between Indigenous and settler authorities in zero-sum terms, such that Indigenous engagement with policies of self-determination is destined to fail and/or be self-deluding. We feel wary of this theoretical framework because it supposes reconciliation to be impossible, a process of mutual self-delusion. What is the historian to say of Indigenous people who have sought to work with and gain concessions from the settler colonial state (as many still do), not seeing their gains as merely illusory? As Borrows and Tully comment in their critique of the limits of settler colonial theory, 'independence and interdependence have characterised Indigenous–settler relationships for centuries'.[77] We read the history of settler–Indigenous relationships as shaped by historical particularities, interdependence and political agency on each side, even as these can be understood within a broader colonial structure. We favour histories that offer Australians a broader range of political resources and possible futures as they pursue their interests.

The successes of self-determination

Thus we question the thesis that self-determination has failed entirely. Of course, Indigenous people have consistently asserted sovereignty and have been 'self-determining' in their resistance to and engagement with colonising powers; this form of self-determination has persisted under all kinds of policy agendas and continues today. In addition to this, we can identify some ways in which the policy suite introduced by the Whitlam Government enabled Indigenous people wider choices and greater control for themselves and their communities.

Phillip Falk and Gary Martin point out the multiple ways in which Indigenous people today have rights to 'self-determination and self-management'.[78] While they concede that there are always limits on Indigenous control, disputes and policy failures, they argue that Indigenous people are exercising authority across many domains in which, 50 years ago, they had little control. On territorial sovereignty, there is lands rights legislation, native title land and land granted through the Indigenous Land Corporation. In health, there are now Indigenous medical centres and Indigenous health professionals. In education there are Indigenous

---

77   Borrows and Tully, 'Introduction', 8.
78   Falk and Martin, 'Misconstruing Indigenous Sovereignty', 40.

pre-primary, primary and secondary schools, and Indigenous student support centres in TAFEs and universities as well as Indigenous education institutes. Indigenous people are now co-managers of some national parks and involved in land and water management beyond parks. The federal *Aboriginal Councils and Associations Act 1976* has also enabled Indigenous people a degree of self-government on the local level.[79] Moreover, on the level of the individual, many Indigenous people have more options in their lives than ever before. But, as Stan Grant remarked, Indigenous successes such as these are ignored in the face of an overwhelming narrative of failure:

> 65 per cent of Indigenous people in Australia (360,000) are employed and living lives, materially and socio-economically, like those of other Australians ... There is a story here, a story largely untold. It is a story of success and how it is spurned like an unwanted child.[80]

Such achievements, on the individual and communal level, must have a historical explanation. We suggest they can be explained historically by the operation of three strands of self-determination identified in this book: international law, Indigenous political ambition and the policy suites that issued from the 1960s and were declared as 'self-determination' in the 1970s.

Of course, the achievements of self-determination have also been uneven. This very unevenness has, perhaps, contributed to the widespread view that self-determination failed entirely. On the level of the individual, many of those who were best able to take advantage of self-determination were those who had experienced policies of assimilation most intensely. We see this in the ways that mission and church leaders rose to positions of secular leadership under self-determination. We also see this in the ways that skills some gained under assimilation policies, particularly literacy in English, became useful and politically potent. Indigenous women have, perhaps, been better positioned to take advantage of self-determination on an individual level, despite their marginal role in some formal institutions of self-determination. The gendering of assimilation around feminine domesticity in some ways created employment opportunities for Indigenous women under the economic changes of 1980s as well as kinds

---

79 Falk and Martin, 'Misconstruing Indigenous Sovereignty', 41.
80 Grant, 'The Australian Dream', 68.

of jobs in demand (particularly in administration, health and education) under self-determination.[81] It is also true, however, that women bore the brunt of what are often identified as self-determination's failures: drug and alcohol abuse, family violence and community disorder. The gendering of self-determination is an area that requires further research.

In linking assimilation and self-determination in this way we are presenting a contestable history of 'assimilation'. We would argue that, in many ways, assimilation policies created a class of people ready to take advantage of self-determination policies. But this was not because they were assimilated; on the contrary, many of them had already joined together to denounce and oppose assimilation. The political experience of resistance to assimilatory policies and the creation of pan-Aboriginal identities in opposition to assimilation laid the ground for even greater gains in the 1970s. As Grant put it:

> Assimilation was about how government tried to control this 'problem', but it was also about how we negotiated this new reality … It is a mark of the strength of Aboriginal people that they not only endured this, but responded with renewed demands for equality and rights. The Aboriginal political movement found its voice, campaigning for full citizenship and jobs.[82]

It was not necessarily easy for Indigenous people who were most acculturated to settler colonial society to adopt the empowered positions that self-determination policies created. Often these very people faced new challenges of legitimation to their communities under self-determination. They were sometimes seen as too 'Aboriginal' for the state, but too 'white' for many Indigenous activists. As Francesca Merlan points out, in the 1970s, the very people who were 'marching in the front ranks towards assimilation' became, in some contexts, 'marginal to a policy that now valorised Aborigines' cultural continuity'.[83]

---

81   Haebich, *Spinning the Dream*, 124.
82   Grant, 'The Australian Dream', 77.
83   Merlan, *Dynamics of Difference*, 163–64.

The future of self-determination

Self-determination continues as a topic for Indigenous Australian political theory.[84] We conclude by pointing to two questions faced in such theoretical work.

First, the federal structure of the settler colonial state provides opportunities. As Will Sanders's survey of local government reminds us, it is not only at the national level that significant policy decisions are made: Australian federalism also makes sub-national governments effective shapers of the processes through which Indigenous Australians are governed and through which they may govern themselves. At the time of writing, two jurisdictions (Victoria and the Northern Territory) are considering agreements with the Aboriginal people whose countries fall within their borders. Both jurisdictions will create models from which the other six sub-national jurisdictions will learn.

Second, the relationship between the individual 'self' and the collective 'self' is becoming problematic as people enact the right to self-identification. Mick Dodson declared in 1994 that 'the right to control one's own identity is part of the broader right to self-determination; that is, the right of a people to determine its political status and to pursue its own economic, social and cultural development'.[85] In this formulation, the dual meaning of 'one' (a person, a people) presents a question of identity that remains to be resolved by Aboriginal communities.

The roots of this second problem are found in one of the policy changes that blurs the temporal boundary between 'assimilation' and 'self-determination' policy eras. Australian practices of self-determination include a census questionnaire, reformed between the 1966 and 1971 censuses, that allows a person to identity as 'Aboriginal' without the respondent having to consider whether he or she is 'half' or 'one-quarter' Aboriginal (as he/she was obliged to do in the 1966 Census). In confidential responses to the census, the claim to be Aboriginal or Torres Strait Islander is not subject to any qualifying 'blood' test: the individual is truly autonomous in self-identification. However, Indigenous identity is also a public matter in that policy regimes attach finite, palpable benefits to successful assertions of Indigenous identity. Those who consider themselves

---

84 For example Vivian et al., 'Indigenous Self-government'.
85 Dodson, 'The Wentworth Lecture the End in the Beginning', 5.

entitled, as Aboriginal or Torres Strait Islander persons, have an interest in policing the boundary between who can have the benefit and who cannot. Nakata is critical of the Australian Government's identification protocol for conferring on Indigenous 'community' organisations a responsibility to inspect and verify (or not) an individual's public assertion of Aboriginal or Torres Strait Islander status.

Alexis Wright recently asked: 'What kind of people are we?' She answered: 'We are becoming more complicated. Were we ever more individualistic in spirit than we are today?'[86] One recent ethnographic inscription of 'Indigeneity' highlighted the individual as the unit of 'self-determination'. According to a study of cultural practice in the Melbourne home of an Indigenous woman named Maree: 'Culture-making occurs *in a self-determined place* where Maree has curated safety and belonging for informal, intercultural exchanges exemplifying decolonising co-production in contemporary, cosmopolitan Melbourne'.[87] As well, Elizabeth Watt and Emma Kowal have used recently collected interview data to illustrate the terms in which 'an increasing number of Australians are identifying as Indigenous later in life' – terms that may not persuade invigilating Indigenous organisations.[88] The question of who is the 'self' of Indigenous self-determination, it seems, will become more complex with more possible answers in coming years.

References

Alfred, Taiaiake. 'Sovereignty'. In *A Companion to American Indian History*, edited by Philip Deloria and Neal Salisbury, 33–50. Malden: Blackwell, 2002.

Anderson, Ian. 'The Crisis of Australia's Indigenous Policy'. *Meanjin* 74, no. 3 (2015): 54–59.

Attwood, Bain. *Rights for Aborigines*. Crows Nest, NSW: Allen and Unwin, 2003.

Australia Council for the Arts. *Protocols for Producing Indigenous Australian Writing* (second edition). Strawberry Hills: Australia Council for the Arts, 2007.

---

86 Wright, *Tracker*, 1.
87 Thorner et al., 'Maree's Backyard', 281 (emphasis added).
88 Watt and Kowal, 'To be or not to be Indigenous?', 76.

Bamblett, Laurie. 'Serious Whitefella Stuff: When Solutions Become the Problem in Indigenous Affairs [Book Review]'. *Australian Aboriginal Studies*, no. 2 (2018): 80–81.

Behrendt, Larissa. 'Aboriginal Sovereignty: A Practical Roadmap'. In *Sovereignty: Frontiers of Possibility*, edited by Julie Evans, Ann Genovese, Alexander Reilly and Patrick Wolfe, 163–77. Honolulu: University of Hawai'i Press, 2013. doi.org/10.1515/9780824865764-009.

Behrendt, Larissa. *Achieving Social Justice: Indigenous Rights and Australia's Future.* Alexandria, NSW: Federation Press, 2003.

Berndt, Ronald. *An Adjustment Movement in Arnhem Land, Northern Territory of Australia*. Paris: Mouton, 1962. Reissued as Oceania Monograph, no. 54. Sydney: University of Sydney, 2004.

Borrows, John and James Tully. Introduction to *Resurgence and Reconciliation: Indigenous-Settler Relations and Earth Teachings*, edited by Michael Asch, John Borrows and James Tully, 3–28. Toronto: University of Toronto Press, 2018. doi.org/10.3138/9781487519926-002.

Bradfield, Stuart. 'Separatism or Status-quo?: Indigenous Affairs from the Birth of Land Rights to the Death of ATSIC'. *Australian Journal of Politics & History* 52, no. 1 (2006): 80–97. doi.org/10.1111/j.1467-8497.2006.00409a.x.

Brigg, Morgan and Sarah Maddison. 'Unsettling Governance: From Bark Petition to YouTube'. In *Unsettling the Settler-State: Creativity and Resistance in Indigenous-Settler State Governance*, edited by Sarah Maddison and Morgan Brigg, 1–15. Alexandria: Federation Press, 2011.

Coombs, H. C. *Australia's Policy towards Aborigines 1967–1977*. Report (Minority Rights Group), no. 35. London: Minority Rights Group, 1978.

Corntassel, Jeff. 'Re-envisioning Resurgence: Indigenous Pathways to Decolonization and Sustainable Self-determination'. *Decolonization: Indigeneity, Education & Society* 1, no. 1 (2012): 86–101.

Coulthard, Glen S. 'Subjects of Empire: Indigenous Peoples and the "Politics of Recognition" in Canada'. *Contemporary Political Theory* 6, no. 4 (2007): 437–60.

Cowlishaw, Gillian. 'Erasing Culture and Race: Practising "Self-determination"'. *Oceania* 68, no. 3 (1998): 145–69. doi.org/10.1002/j.1834-4461.1998.tb02663.x.

Cowlishaw, Gillian. 'Helping Anthropologists, Still'. In *Culture Crisis: Anthropology and Politics in Aboriginal Australia*, edited by Jon Altman and Melinda Hickson, 45–60. Kensington, NSW: UNSW Press, 2010.

Davis, Megan. 'Aboriginal Women: The Right to Self-determination'. *Australian Indigenous Law Review* 16, no. 1 (2012): 78–88.

Davis, Megan. 'Gesture Politics'. *The Monthly*, December 2015. Accessed 29 May 2019. www.themonthly.com.au/issue/2015/december/1448888400/megan-davis/gesture-politics.

Davis, Megan. 'Listening But Not Hearing'. *Griffith Review*, 51 (2016). Accessed 29 April 2019. griffithreview.com/articles/listening-but-not-hearing/.

Dodson, Michael. 'The Wentworth Lecture the End in the Beginning: Re(de)finding Aboriginality'. *Australian Aboriginal Studies*, no. 1 (1994): 2–13.

Dodson, Patrick. 'Until the Chains Are Broken: Aboriginal Unfinished Business (Excerpts from the Vincent Lingiari Memorial Lecture 1999)'. *Arena Magazine*, no. 45 (2000): 29–31.

Falk, Phillip and Gary Martin. 'Misconstruing Indigenous Sovereignty: Maintaining the Fabric of Australian Law'. In *Sovereign Subjects: Indigenous Sovereignty Matters,* edited by Aileen Moreton-Robinson, 33–46. Sydney: Allen & Unwin, 2007.

Foley, Gary. 'The Australian Labor Party and the Native Title Act'. In *Sovereign Subjects: Indigenous Sovereignty Matters,* edited by Aileen Moreton-Robinson, 118–39. Sydney: Allen & Unwin, 2007.

Grant, Stan. 'The Australian Dream: Blood, History and Becoming'. *Quarterly Essay*, no. 64. Carlton, Vic.: Black Inc., 2016.

Haebich, Anna. *Spinning the Dream: Assimilation in Australia 1950–1970.* Fremantle, WA: Fremantle Press, 2008.

Hocking, Jenny. '"A Transforming Sentiment in This Country": The Whitlam Government and Indigenous Self-determination'. *Australian Journal of Public Administration* 77, no. S1 (2018): S5–S12. doi.org/10.1111/1467-8500.12353.

Howard-Wagner, Deirdre, Maria Bargh and Isabel Altamirano-Jiménez. 'From New Paternalism to New Imaginings of Possibilities in Australia, Canada and Aotearoa/New Zealand: Indigenous Rights and Recognition and the State in the Neoliberal Age'. In *The Neoliberal State, Recognition and Indigenous Rights: New Paternalism to New Imaginings*, edited by Deirdre Howard-Wagner, Maria Bargh and Isabel Altamirano-Jiménez, 1–42. Canberra: ANU Press, 2018. doi.org/10.22459/caepr40.07.2018.01.

Johns, Gary. *Aboriginal Self-determination: The White Man's Dream.* Ballan, Vic.: Connor Court, 2011.

Johns, Gary. 'The Failure of Aboriginal Separatism'. *Quadrant* 45, no. 5 (2001): 9–18.

Kowal, Emma. 'The Politics of the Gap: Indigenous Australians, Liberal Multiculturalism, and the End of the Self-determination Era'. *American Anthropologist* 110, no. 3 (2008): 338–48. doi.org/10.1111/j.1548-1433. 2008.00043.x.

Ladner, Kiera. 'Proceed with Caution: Reflections on Resurgence and Reconciliation'. In *Resurgence and Reconciliation: Indigenous-Settler Relations and Earth Teachings*, edited by Michael Asch, John Borrows and James Tully, 245–64. Toronto: University of Toronto Press, 2018. doi.org/10.3138/9781487519926-010.

Langton, Marcia. 'Self-determination as Oppression'. Preface to *Australia's Policy towards Aborigines 1967–1977*, by H. C. Coombs. Report (Minority Rights Group), no. 35. London: Minority Rights Group, 1978.

Lino, Dylan. 'The Politics of Inclusion: The Right of Self-determination, Statutory Bills of Rights and Indigenous Peoples'. *Melbourne University Law Review* 34 (2010): 839–69.

Little Bear, Leroy. 'An Elder Explains Indigenous Philosophy and Indigenous Sovereignty'. In *Philosophy and Aboriginal Rights: Critical Dialogues*, edited by Sandra Tomsons and Lorraine Mayer, 6–18. Oxford: Oxford University Press, 2013.

Lovell, Melissa. 'Languages of Neoliberal Critique: The Production of Coercive Government in the Northern Territory Intervention'. In *Studies in Australian Political Rhetoric*, edited by John Uhr and Ryan Walter, 221–42. Canberra: ANU Press, 2014. doi.org/10.22459/sapr.09.2014.11.

Mansell, Michael. 'Mixed Ironies in Aboriginal Issue'. *The Australian*, 17 June 2004. Accessed 29 May 2019. www.kooriweb.org/foley/resources/pearson/aust17jun2004.html.

Mansell, Michael. *Treaty and Statehood: Aboriginal Self-determination*. Alexandria: Federation Press, 2016.

McGregor, Russell. *Indifferent Inclusion: Aboriginal People and the Australian Nation*. Canberra: Aboriginal Studies Press, 2011.

Merlan, Francesca. *Caging the Rainbow: Places, Politics, and Aborigines in a North Australian Town*. Honolulu: University of Hawai'i Press, 1998. doi.org/10.1515/9780824861742.

Merlan, Francesca. *Dynamics of Difference in Australia: Indigenous Past and Present in a Settler Country*. Philadelphia: University of Pennsylvania Press, 2018. doi.org/10.9783/9780812294859.

Mills, Aaron. 'Rooted Constitutionalism: Growing Political Community'. In *Resurgence and Reconciliation: Indigenous-Settler Relations and Earth Teachings*, edited by Michael Asch, John Borrows and James Tully, 123–74. Toronto: University of Toronto Press, 2018. doi.org/10.3138/9781487519926-006.

Moreton-Robinson, Aileen. Introduction to *Sovereign Subjects: Indigenous Sovereignty Matters*, edited by Aileen Moreton-Robinson, 1–14. Sydney: Allen & Unwin, 2007.

Moreton-Robinson, Aileen. 'Patriarchal Whiteness, Self-determination and Indigenous Women: The Invisibility of Structural Privilege and the Visibility of Oppression'. In *Unfinished Constitutional Business? Rethinking Indigenous Self-determination*, edited by Barbara Hocking, 61–73. Canberra: Aboriginal Studies Press, 2005.

Pearson, Noel. 'A Rightful Place: Race, Recognition and a More Complete Commonwealth'. *Quarterly Essay*, no. 55. Carlton, Vic.: Black Inc., 2014.

Pearson, Noel. *Up from the Mission: Selected Writings*. Carlton, Vic.: Black Inc., 2009.

Peterson, Nic and Fred Myers (eds). *Experiments in Self-determination*. Canberra: ANU Press, 2016. dx.doi.org/10.22459/ESD.01.2016.

Povinelli, Elizabeth. *The Cunning of Recognition: Indigenous Alterities and the Making of Australian Multiculturalism*. Durham: Duke University Press, 2002.

Quiggin, Robynne. 'What Does Democracy and Self-determination Mean for Indigenous Australians?' *Australian Journal of Public Administration* 77, no. S1 (2018): S52–S58. doi.org/10.1111/1467-8500.12359.

Referendum Council. *Uluru statement from the heart*, 2017. Accessed 15 August 2020. www.referendumcouncil.org.au/sites/default/files/2017-05/Uluru_Statement_ From_The_Heart_0.PDF.

Rowse, Tim. *Indigenous and other Australians since 1901*. Kensington, NSW: UNSW Press, 2017.

Sanders, Will. 'From Self-determination to Self-management'. In *Service Delivery to Remote Communities*, edited by Peter Loveday, 4–10. Darwin: North Australia Unit, 1982.

Sanders, Will. 'Missing ATSIC: Australia's Need for a Strong Indigenous Representative Body'. In *The Neoliberal State, Recognition and Indigenous Rights: New Paternalism to New Imaginings*, edited by Deirdre Howard-Wagner, Maria Bargh and Isabel Altamirano-Jiménez, 113–30. Canberra: ANU Press, 2018. doi.org/10.22459/caepr40.07.2018.06.

Strakosch, Elizabeth. 'The Technical Is Political: Settler Colonialism and the Australian Indigenous Policy System'. *Australian Journal of Political Science* 54, no. 1 (2019): 114–30. doi.org/10.1080/10361146.2018.1555230.

Strelein, Lisa. 'Missed Meanings: The Language of Sovereignty in the Treaty Debate'. *Arena Journal* 20 (2002): 83–96.

Sullivan, Patrick. *Belonging Together: Dealing with the Politics of Disenchantment in Australian Indigenous Affairs Policy*. Canberra: Aboriginal Studies Press, 2011.

Sutton, Peter. *The Politics of Suffering: Indigenous Australia and the End of the Liberal Consensus*. Melbourne: Melbourne University Press, 2009.

Tatz, Colin. *Aboriginal Suicide Is Different: A Portrait of Life and Self-destruction*. Canberra: Aboriginal Studies Press, 2005.

Thorner, Sabra, Fran Edmonds, Maree Clarke and Paola Balla. 'Maree's Backyard: Intercultural Collaborations for Indigenous Sovereignty in Melbourne'. *Oceania* 88, no. 3 (2018): 269–91. doi.org/10.1002/ocea.5206.

United Nations. *United Nations Declaration on the Rights of Indigenous Peoples*. *United Nations*, 2008. Accessed 15 August 2020. www.un.org/esa/socdev/unpfii/documents/DRIPS_en.pdf.

Vivian, Alison, Miriam Jorgensen, Alexander Reilly, Mark McMillan, Cosima McRae and John McMinn. 'Indigenous Self-government in the Australian Federation'. *Australian Indigenous Law Review* 20 (2017): 215–42.

Watt, Elizabeth and Emma Kowal. 'To be or not to be Indigenous?' *Ethnic and Racial Studies* 42, no. 16 (2019): 63–82.

Whitlam, Gough. 'Aboriginals and Society'. Press statement no. 74, 6 April 1973. Accessed 29 May 2019. pmtranscripts.pmc.gov.au/release/transcript-2886.

Wolfe, Patrick. *Settler Colonialism and the Transformation of Anthropology: The Politics and Poetics of an Ethnographic Event*. London: Cassell, 1999.

Woodward, A. E. *Aboriginal Land Rights Commission: Report*. Canberra: Australian Government Publishing Service, 1973–74.

Wright, Alexis. *Tracker: Stories of Tracker Tilmouth*. Artarmon, NSW: Giramondo, 2017.

Young, Stephen M. 'The Self Divided: The Problems of Contradictory Claims to Indigenous Peoples' Self-determination in Australia'. *International Journal of Human Rights* 23, nos 1–2 (2019): 193–213. doi.org/10.2139/ssrn.3487235.

PART ONE: SELF-DETERMINATION AS A PROJECT OF COLONIAL AUTHORITY

1

SELF-DETERMINATION IN ACTION

How John Hunter and Aboriginal people
in Arnhem Land anticipated official
policy in the late 1960s and early 1970s

Chris Haynes

Introduction

The central figure of this chapter, John Hunter, was superintendent of the Maningrida Settlement on the Liverpool River estuary in Arnhem Land for most of the period between 1963 and 1973. Only 25 years old when first appointed in an acting capacity, a decade later he left Maningrida as a polarising figure. As Dan Gillespie, with whom I worked at both Maningrida and, later, Kakadu National Park, noted:

> Though shy and retiring Hunter had a strong personality, a fine wit and a huge capacity for work of all kinds; the Aboriginal people of Maningrida looked on him with respect and affection; [and] the European population's reaction to him varied from considerable respect to an intense dislike.[1]

---

1   Gillespie, 'John Hunter and Maningrida', 2.

Respect and affection for him were commonly expressed by Aboriginal people around Maningrida when I conducted interviews there during 2013; Wulaki man Ngaraidj Morogopina, for example: 'He was the one … who helped us, always [to do what we wished to do]. He worked day and night and would always do what he said'.[2]

Gillespie went on to remark that 'Hunter's support in word and deed for Aboriginal people's right to basic equalities' generated the ire of the European population.[3] Gillespie's informed opinion, based on several years as a teacher and art and craft outlet manager at Maningrida in the early 1970s, takes us to major issues of this chapter: (1) the playing out of official policy, determined in Canberra, in this remote setting; (2) the issues that so polarised the 'balandas', that is, the European population; (3) the agency of a relatively junior, albeit locally powerful, official working in partnership with local Aboriginal people; and (4) Aboriginal people's pursuit of 'basic equalities', but as they, not policymakers in Canberra or other balandas, perceived them. This last point is linked to the first, my argument being that Maningrida's Aboriginal people, assisted by Hunter, expressed their self-determination through their decision to establish outstations. In this chapter we will see how Aboriginal people and Hunter's actions together anticipated formalisation of self-determination as policy under the Whitlam Government; and that such actions made for structural change, affecting large groups of people. Before exploring these issues, I turn first to the historical background of the town and the forces that brought it to where it was in Hunter's time.

Making Maningrida and its part in the assimilation program

It is difficult to imagine how remote Maningrida was when Hunter became acting superintendent in 1963; these days it is possible to drive from the Northern Territory capital, Darwin, to Maningrida in a matter of hours. Although a very rough exploratory track from Oenpelli had been cut in the dry season of that year, the settlement (as it was called back then) was reached only by boat or light aircraft. For many years after, the road trip from Darwin to Maningrida would take two or more days.[4]

---

2   Recently deceased people are identified here, and later, by subsection and clan names.
3   Gillespie, 'John Hunter and Maningrida', 2.
4   Long, *The Go-Betweens*, 130.

The state established a permanent presence in 1957 when the first Government Manager, David Drysdale, sailed into the Liverpool River estuary with his wife, Ingrid, and two patrol officers, Ted Egan and Trevor Milikins.[5] The details of Maningrida's early years are well described by Ingrid Drysdale and, more recently, by a Darwin-based historian, Helen Bond-Sharp.[6] They depict the evolution of a tiny bush camp into a settlement, as it was officially proclaimed by the Director of Welfare, Harry Giese, in the Northern Territory Administration (NTA), in 1961.[7]

By 1961 Giese had articulated a coherent role for the settlements as a practical way of enacting the Commonwealth's assimilation policy in places where more traditionally based Aboriginal people lived, as expressed in the Welfare Branch Annual Report for 1958–59:

> The main purposes of these establishments are:
>
> i. to bring natives together into a community and to teach them the habits and skills of living in such a community;
>
> ii. to provide welfare services fitted to their needs and to their stage of social development;
>
> iii. to provide the means whereby training may be given, particularly to children and adolescents;
>
> iv. to introduce the general concept of 'work' as a worthwhile aim in life; and
>
> v. to develop in the younger and middle age-groups an attitude that the settlements and mission statements are there to provide health and education services for their children, so that the latter may be prepared for a future life as adults living in a wider community than the tribe.[8]

By the standards of today, these objectives were blatant social engineering that, as we will see, met with increasing resistance – at Maningrida and elsewhere. Yet they set the framework under which Hunter and other superintendents were required to work, especially in the early years. And so, consistent with such policy, by 1961 Maningrida had a 'town plan', with built up roads laid out on a grid. Tracks spidered out from the settlement into surrounding country and there had been considerable building and other development: a health clinic, school, government

---

5   Drysdale and Durack, *The End of Dreaming*, 79.
6   Bond-Sharp, *Maningrida*, 52–95.
7   Drysdale and Durack, *The End of Dreaming*, 77.
8   NTA, Welfare Branch, *Annual Report 1958–59*, 30.

offices, housing for government officers, a 4-hectare fruit and vegetable garden and a sawmill, for example. There was even a kitchen to provide meals for those people considered unable to fend for themselves. Out of town, a project to develop local forests was getting underway.

The NTA's original vision for Maningrida did not materialise as intended. Consistent with the detailed strategies that had been developed before the Second World War by the NTA's parent department, the Department of the Interior, and its minister, John McEwen, the initial intention had been to allow Aboriginal people on reserves such as Arnhem Land to remain undisturbed and the lands to be protected from exploitation.[9] Arnhem Land had been made an Aboriginal reserve in 1931 and, although there had been a few patrols around Maningrida before and after the war, policymakers still considered it to be a very wild and untamed part of Australia in the early 1950s. Hence it seemed wise for the state to tread cautiously; besides, both financial resources and manpower in that postwar period were scarce. The small trading post that had been set up by patrol officers Syd Kyle-Little and Jack Doolan in 1949, although considered successful, was abandoned at the end of that year because these men were needed elsewhere.[10]

Yet, there were other aspects of the McEwen policy that called for intervention; for example, provision for the immediate medical and physical needs of all Aboriginal people, wherever they were.[11] Patrol officers reported widespread chronic diseases, notably yaws and leprosy, among the hundreds of people living in the vicinity of the Liverpool River. Their treatment required frequent nursing care that could not be provided from Darwin or even Goulburn Island and Millingimbi missions. By 1956 Harry Giese had decided the time was right to establish Maningrida as a station and, with the strong support of the Minister for Territories, Paul Hasluck, pushed ahead with its establishment the following year. Their intention had been to make a more permanent version of what Kyle-Little and Doolan had done in 1949; people from the bush could come in to trade crocodile skins and artefacts, receive healthcare and return to their homelands. Almost immediately, however, in an act of self-determination, they stayed around the new station, returning to homelands only for hunting and ceremonies.

---

9   McEwen, 'The Northern Territory', 5.
10   Kyle-Little, *Whispering Wind*, 172–74; Long, *The Go-Betweens*, 85–88.
11   McEwen, 'The Northern Territory', 1, 11.

The more or less permanent movement of the Aboriginal people to the station broadened the state's ambition for Maningrida. The transition from trading post and health service provision to proclaimed settlement took place within very few years. With the permanent settlement of Aboriginal people it became possible for Maningrida to become a site for the implementation of the assimilation policy as articulated in the Welfare Branch's 1958–59 policy on settlements, discussed above. Thus, very soon Maningrida was to see not only the small enterprises that Aboriginal people themselves had developed (sales of crocodile skins and artefacts) but also Western style (mostly primary) industries that could be undertaken by people without formal education. As can be seen from the annual reports of the Welfare Branch through the late 1950s and early 1960s, there was an almost formulaic approach to primary industries.[12] Thus, nearly all settlements had gardens, piggeries, poultry, cattle runs and dairies. Maningrida, with its good rainfall and soils, seemed to offer much greater opportunity than many other settlements: big, ambitious projects in fisheries, forestry and sawmilling.

Hasluck had been pursuing forestry as a potential industry for the Northern Territory from when he took office in 1951. He got the scent of its possibilities after hearing mildly positive reports from foresters serving there during the war. The Commonwealth Forestry and Timber Bureau, the government's official source of forestry advice, had sent a professional forester, Bill Bateman, to evaluate the prospects of forestry. His report was, to Hasluck's disappointment, equivocal.[13] It indicated only limited potential for commercial development of existing forests and urged caution about the possibilities of plantations. Notwithstanding Hasluck's impatience for a positive story, G. J. Rodger, Director General of the bureau, followed up with blunt advice to the head of Hasluck's department, C. R. Lambert, in February 1958. His opening sentence, 'there are no forests of consequence of economic value in the Territory at the present day and, at the best, the climate and soils are marginal for the growth of trees in forest', set the tone for a critical appraisal of what Hasluck was pursuing.[14]

---

12   See, for example, NTA, Welfare Branch, *Annual Report 1963–64*.
13   Bateman, *Forestry*.
14   Memo from G. J. Rodger, Director General, 19 February 1958, National Archives of Australia (hereafter NAA) A452, 1957/82 Part 1.

Despite the advice, Hasluck pushed a forestry program for the Northern Territory through Cabinet later that year.[15] The program was modest and 'experimental' but was the basis of a start to forestry operations at Maningrida in 1961. Operated initially by the Forestry and Timber Bureau itself and, after 1968, as a branch of the NTA – not under the Welfare Branch, as Hasluck himself emphatically, but quite incorrectly, claimed in his autobiography – it was (like fisheries) to prove a major cause of frustration and anguish for Hunter later in the 1960s.[16] Although Hasluck had pushed the program largely as a means to benefit local Aboriginal people, the foresters took almost exclusive charge and, as we will see, not even Giese was able to influence their approach.[17] The conceptualisation and management of both the forestry and fisheries programs were completely outside the experience of local Aboriginal people; and that had much to do with the ultimate failures of these programs some years later.

Hunter as the Welfare Branch man

One of the 1939 McEwen policies was to establish a cadre of patrol officers to bring some cohesion to contact between the state and Aboriginal people throughout the Northern Territory. By the time Giese started as director in 1954, a handful of such officers were in place, but there were not nearly enough of them to do what Giese considered necessary. Again, backed by Hasluck, Giese set about negotiating training for recruits to the service through the Australian School of Pacific Administration (ASOPA), already doing such work for Papua New Guinea. Recruitment was initiated at the same time but with disappointing results. Interest among the kinds of men he hoped to recruit was patchy and most of the applicants did not meet the high standards that Giese expected.[18] Although feminist critics of Commonwealth policies in the 1930s have since pointed to the advantages of appointing female protectors, neither McEwen nor his successors recruited women as patrol officers, and none had been recruited by the time the service was discontinued in 1973.[19]

---

15   NAA Cabinet papers, A4926, decision 1557.
16   Hasluck, *Shades of Darkness*, 114.
17   Hasluck, *Shades of Darkness*, 114.
18   NAA F1, 1956/557; NAA F1, 1956/2663.
19   Holland, *Just Relations*, 239–41.

Raised on a small farm with oyster leases near Bega, New South Wales, Hunter knew many Koori kids as he grew up, contributing to his interest in working with Aboriginal people. Unusual for someone of a rural background at that time, he passed his Leaving Certificate and was thus immediately able to take up a clerical position in the Welfare Branch in Darwin, arriving only a few months after Giese in 1955. Too young to be a patrol officer, he waited 18 months before being selected to undertake the year-long Australian School of Pacific Administration (ASOPA) course in 1958. He passed only moderately well, but well enough to be sent to Alice Springs where he remained for most of the time until the late 1963 appointment to Maningrida. Although he had spent several months as superintendent at Areyonga, it was a big step for someone so young. He left the post after about 18 months, in April 1965. It is not clear whether he was pushed out or asked to be relieved. Perhaps it was by mutual agreement. He told me years later, 'I made a mess of it, just too young for the responsibilities of the job'.[20] In any event he went back to patrol work and a period as acting superintendent at Bamyili (now Barunga) before returning to Maningrida in September 1966. At first he was acting superintendent before he was confirmed in the position about a year later. He was still only 27.

Following assimilationist policy

By the time Hunter arrived, more than 400 Aboriginal people were living in the settlement. Their more or less permanent residence made it easier to give people medical attention, but the continuing presence of such a large number of people in a small area created many social and administrative problems. Inter-clan tensions that were aggravated by the relatively cramped spaces of the settlement would often escalate into mass spear fights, for instance.[21] Hunter and his predecessors seemed to take these in their stride, able to mobilise their experience as patrol officers and the clear authority vested in the position of superintendent. In a popular article in the *National Geographic*, journalist Kenneth MacLeish gives us a glimpse of how Hunter dealt with such an issue in 1971 or 1972, towards the end of his term there:

---

20   The conversations to which I refer mostly took place either as we drove together in the bush around Maningrida or in one or the other's houses between 1972 and 1977. I had got to know Hunter when, as a junior forester for the NTA, I approached him about ways in which the Forestry Branch could work better with Maningrida's Aboriginal people in 1972.

21   Drysdale and Durack, *The End of Dreaming*, 102–4.

> After dark, superintendent John Hunter returned to his house looking tired and carrying three spears. 'Family troubles again,' he told his colleague [Assistant Superintendent] Wilders. 'Brian's mob were getting ugly. They're Rembarnga. One of their women wouldn't stay with her husband, who belongs to another tribe and speaks another language. He protested, and the Rembarnga got their spears. I had to take them away. What's for tea?'[22]

The article captures the tiredness resulting from Hunter's long days in the field and from the additional work after dark; it also conveys Hunter's confidence in carrying out his tasks. Such fights, and domestic conflicts, were almost routine. From the point of view of the government, there was no doubt that settlement residents must follow the white man's law. That was a matter Aboriginal people everywhere accepted only reluctantly.

The inter-clan tensions were accompanied by the not so well-known tensions among an already large population of balandas – nurses (who were present at the start of the settlement), schoolteachers, managers and foremen. Managers and foremen were there to teach and supervise tasks that required only minimal training for the industries discussed above. The balandas were also there to build and service the material apparatus of assimilation: the school, the clinic, public offices, houses (all for other balandas in those early days), the garden and all the rest. Some of these functions, for example, teaching, forestry and health, were performed by people who did not report to the superintendent; the officers in charge of such units sometimes having to deal with social and disciplinary problems that arose beyond Hunter's responsibility and even, sometimes, his knowledge. All the same, the superintendent and the other balanda authorities needed to liaise – and Hunter had to deal with social tensions that were an inevitable feature of a colonial outpost, especially among those balandas who reported to him directly.

The petty disputes that challenged his predecessors were an ever-present feature of Hunter's tenure and they were among the reasons he left the post in 1965.[23] Such disputes were still there when he returned in 1966, but he was now more confident about handling them. He often told me he did not expect to be backed by his superiors on matters of staff discipline, and he learnt to ignore all but the most serious trouble among

---

22 MacLeish, 'The Top End', 171.
23 See, for example, Report on dispute by M. Ivory, 10 October 1961, NAA E460, 1976/460 Part 1.

the balandas.[24] Gillespie's observation at the beginning of this chapter that 'the European population's reaction to him [Hunter] varied from considerable respect to an intense dislike' reflects a population polarised before Hunter's time.[25] A minority were, like Hunter, seriously interested, even at times enchanted, by what we now call the 'otherness' of the local Aboriginal people, but most found relationships with Aboriginal people awkward and stilted, often expressing barely concealed attitudes of white superiority. Some even referred to Aboriginal people as 'rock apes' or used similarly outrageous terms. We might note that while Giese was very discerning in his selection of patrol officers, he did not scrutinise all settlement employees in the same way. The increasing polarisation in balanda attitudes was strikingly evident in the local paper, *The Maningrida Mirage*, through the late 1960s and early 1970s.[26] In what I have called 'separate group discourse', Europeans talked among themselves about Aboriginal people (and vice versa) and about the other Europeans who held alternative world views.[27] Hunter's understanding of this difficult sociality was more sophisticated than the rest of us held at the time; indeed, it is only much more recently that the outlooks of isolated populations of balandas have been the subject of academic study.[28]

The industrial arm of assimilation

Returning to the statement about the purpose of settlements, we see how major effort was being made to re-form Aboriginal social organisation around Western institutions. The logics of words and phrases like 'teaching' and 'the general concept of "work"' flowed seamlessly into phasing out traditional hunting and gathering, for example, to be replaced by locally produced Western food. Such modes of production were to be taught and it was assumed that Aboriginal people would adopt them. When Hunter arrived, the settlement boasted a 4-hectare garden and arrangements were well underway for a cattle herd, poultry yard and some dairy cows, these being delivered soon afterwards. He dutifully kept all these activities propped up against considerable logistical and technical

---

24   See also NAA F941, 1966/13.
25   Gillespie, 'John Hunter and Maningrida', 2.
26   'Newsletters (*Maningrida Mirage*)', AIATSIS, accessed October 2019, aiatsis.gov.au/collections/collections-online/digitised-collections/maningrida-mirage-newsletters/newsletters-maningrida-mirage.
27   Haynes, 'The Value of Work'.
28   See, for example, Kowal, 'The Politics of the Gap'; Lea, *Bureaucrats*.

difficulties. These included maintaining a cadre of balanda managers and other technical experts, and the social problems associated with this group that I have already discussed; but there were also problems in simply getting systems to work productively. A major technical issue emerged in 1964, early on Hunter's watch, when the water supply for the settlement failed and much of the garden that had offered so much promise had to be abandoned.[29]

Giese originally had ambitious plans for even more projects that would lead to Western style self-sufficiency. Just before Hunter arrived in 1963, he set out a manifesto for the development of projects that included the beef cattle herd mentioned above.[30] Considerable work went into building fences, sowing pasture grasses and the introduction of a herd from Bamyili. By 1968, despite Hunter's own particular interest in this endeavour, it was clear that the cattle were failing to thrive and the project would have to be abandoned. In what turned out to be a good example of fertile collaboration between the superintendent and the director, Hunter recommended that they find another location, well south of Maningrida, at Bulman. This is a story that we pick up again in a later section where I discuss Hunter's capacity to turn assimilationist projects to ends that suited the Aboriginal people themselves. Meanwhile, this example also demonstrates that Giese was prepared to listen and adapt, an aptitude for which he has not always been given credit.

Good as he was at garnering resources for the settlements, Giese was often frustrated by the lack of technical expertise within the Welfare Branch, no more so than when confronted with the major projects located at Maningrida: forestry, sawmilling and fisheries. Notwithstanding Hasluck's belief that forestry was under the Welfare Branch's control, others had decided that these three projects would be controlled from other NTA branches. A sawmill was originally built and staffed by Welfare Branch personnel, but two years after the original mill burnt down in 1967, NTA Assistant Administrator Martyn Finger transferred control of the new mill to the Forestry Branch. Giese argued hard to retain control of the sawmill but was overruled.[31] Hunter protested to Giese that at Maningrida he had no power to supervise the increasing band of local forestry people, let alone their superiors visiting from Darwin. To Hunter's list of

---

29   Bond-Sharp, *Maningrida*, 85–86.
30   NAA F1, 1962/287.
31   NAA F1, 1975/2181.

complaints about the mill (over issues such as location and size) were added a growing number from out in the bush. Aboriginal people were increasingly distraught at the Forestry Branch invading sacred sites and ceremonial grounds and at branch attempts to stop fires that Aboriginal people considered part of traditional practice and 'right' for the country.[32] Ignoring these complaints, the Forestry Branch acted as if it had no need to consult people at Maningrida, continuing to offend both Hunter and the Aboriginal people whom he was attempting to represent.

Hunter also objected to the way that the administration promoted fisheries. In 1965, the government built a supposedly pilot fisheries factory. Like the sawmill, the factory was soon proven, in Hunter's assessment, to be inappropriate for purpose, and it was hardly used. Although the potential Aboriginal fishers were keen and capable, the project was seriously underfunded by the NTA Primary Industries Branch, an important consequence of which was that the fisheries officer was at Maningrida for only half the time. This had a further consequence: that leadership and supervision of the project were inadequate.[33] Moreover, the first boats were totally unsuitable, being too big and unwieldy for the local conditions, and they fell into disuse very quickly.

In 1969 the superintendent, exasperated by lack of meaningful response to his many memos to Giese, found a new way to express himself. Recently elected as first president of the newly formed Maningrida Progress Association (MPA), he used his new hat to approach William Charles Wentworth, minister with special responsibilities for Aboriginal affairs, appointed by Prime Minister Gorton earlier that year.[34] Wentworth's presentations to Cabinet often clashed with the Minister for the Interior, Peter Nixon (Country Party), who considered the Northern Territory a Country Party domain and resented Wentworth's advocacy of new policy.[35] Hunter was not to know that his representations to Wentworth would be just one of many issues already causing considerable tension between Wentworth and Country Party ministers.

---

32   Haynes, 'Submission'; Haynes, 'The Pattern'.

33   NAA F1, 1967/1674.

34   In the early 1960s a group of welfare officers and others had formed a cooperative society, mainly to help them buy stores at cheaper rates from Darwin. Over the decade they opened a store which proved popular with Aboriginal people as well and by 1968 it was decided to broaden its franchise and reincorporate as the MPA.

35   Rowse, *Obliged to be difficult*, 42–46.

Hunter's letter targeted both forestry and fisheries, expressing frustration that while these projects showed promise for economic independence, they paid too little attention to the needs of Aboriginal people.[36] He invited Wentworth to come and see for himself. The letter caused a major stir because Hunter had sent a courtesy copy to Giese and it was passed up the line much faster than usual. Before Wentworth had read it he received a 'warning off' letter from Doug Anthony, Acting Minister for the Interior. Wentworth punched back, telling his ministerial colleague that he would go and see whatever he wanted and, in due time, he went to Maningrida. Simultaneously, embarrassed senior officers in the Department of the Interior intended to charge Hunter with a breach of the Public Service Regulations. Although eventually heeding the advice of their legal counsel that the charge would not succeed, they remained irritated by this junior officer's cheeky intervention. When Giese reminded Hunter of the need to keep him informed, Hunter replied with another blast from the field:

> The inability, or unwillingness, of the Forestry to play their part in our work at Maningrida is a source of great disappointment to me. ... [T]he timber development and the advancement of Maningrida people are well and truly bound together ... but this is not being done to the fullest advantage. ... In regard to fisheries the same comments will apply. I could not attempt to express the bitterness I have felt at being associated with such a monumental example of a good thing gone wrong. The plant is there, the fish are available, the people are enthusiastic, but the Government has been weak. If ever the spirit of the N.T. Administration were epitomised in one manifestation, then the Maningrida Fishery is just that.[37]

In the years following this episode Hunter told me (and anyone else willing to listen) that he saw forestry as a key part of Maningrida's development, but 'it was [also] a good thing gone wrong'. Although the enterprise employed (and trained) people and much of the roading done by forestry was widely appreciated, there was no consultation with Aboriginal people until much later. This is what Hunter meant by the project 'not being done to the fullest advantage'. Regarding fisheries, Hunter found less cause for complaint when the government opted out of its failed enterprise and the MPA took over fishing. The MPA had the flexibility to better match technology with Aboriginal aspirations.

---

36 Maningrida Progress Association to Wentworth, 10 June 1969, NAA F1, 1967/1674.
37 Hunter to Giese, memo, 23 December 1969, NAA F1, 1967/1674.

Self-determination Maningrida style

Just as whole groups of people settling in Maningrida in the late 1950s were an act of Aboriginal self-determination, so were the choices of those who chose to remain in their homelands, living more or less as their forbears had for millennia. In deciding to eschew the settlement, these leaders made the tough decision to remain self-sufficient and relatively independent. Recognising and admiring these characteristics early in his tenure, Hunter made and maintained contact with these small groups for the whole time he was at Maningrida. He also admired the way hundreds of people would leave Maningrida to celebrate the Kunipippi and other ceremonies in their homelands. Right from his earliest days, back in 1963, when occasionally visiting people out at the ceremonies he noticed a remarkable change in demeanour in the very people who, in the settlement, would gather in supplication outside his office day after day. Here those same people were totally independent, going about the business in hand without a sideways look at the superintendent.

The opportunity to put the increased amenity afforded in the settlement together with the much greater energy and vigour that went with self-reliance on the homelands came in 1968. The failures of the settlement water supply in 1964 and 1965 made it clear that the gardens were not a viable proposition in the long term. Hunter had begun an investigation of the country surrounding Maningrida from the time he had arrived, sometimes with other welfare staff and sometimes with Aboriginal guides alone.[38] Sometime in the mid-1960s Aboriginal guides led him to a large waterhole on the Cadell River, about 50 kilometres from Maningrida, Gochan Giny-jirra, a central place for the Gun-nartpa language people.[39] Hunter persuaded Giese that this site, with its good deep loam and adequate water supply, would be ideal for a larger commercial proposition and, as Giese well recognised, an outstation.[40] Access was aided by the expansion of the forestry road network in 1968, and in 1970 the newly formed MPA under the leadership of an energetic new manager, Glen Bagshaw, took over its running. (Later Senator) Bob Collins, the first on-site manager, set up a garden that was as productive as the Maningrida

---

38   See, for example, Long, *The Go-Betweens*, 130; England et al. *Gun-ngaypa rrawa*, 96–106.

39   I am following the orthography of England et al., *Gun-ngaypa rrawa*, for all Gun-nartpa language names.

40   NAA E460, 1983/487.

garden had been years earlier. Its progress was accompanied by an almost complete exodus of Gun-nartpa people from Maningrida. Some, both men and women, worked for wages but, arguably as important, Gochan Giny-jirra was now a focus of decentralisation. A self-determining people had voted not with words or a ballot box, but with their feet.

In that same period (1968–71), Hunter took advantage of the failure of beef cattle husbandry at the settlement, discussed earlier. The fact that Bulman, where he found fertile soils, good water supplies and potential for both cattle and buffalo, was nearly 200 kilometres south did not worry Giese, who authorised good levels of funding for the trial.[41] Ultimately that project lapsed, but it provided the opportunity for members of the group that Hunter considered troublesome, 'Brian's mob' of the *National Geographic* article, to decentralise and live more independently.[42] Both this group and those at Gochan Giny-jirra received minimal services that helped smooth the way back into bush living. Both cases represent a team effort: between the Aboriginal people themselves, who had to accept responsibility for their actions; Hunter, who acted as their intermediary, formulating plans that would be palatable to Giese; and Giese, who found the funds to support the enterprises. Giese's decision implies that, by 1968 at least, the harshness of the settlement policy was softening and, incidentally, foreshadowed changes in policy under the McMahon Government in 1971.

The momentum towards this form of self-determination was unstoppable, with many other groups following the Gun-nartpa and Bulman groups back to homelands. As Jon Altman records in detail for the Kuninjku language group, many did not wait for financial assistance, simply going out with limited material benefits to build traditional bark huts and make use of traditional food and 'stay on country'.[43] They went for many reasons: to escape the constant inter-clan tensions noted earlier; to get beyond the constant gaze of the balandas who by 1968 were flooding into the settlement to drive the assimilatory apparatus there; to keep a necessary watchful eye on Forestry Branch balandas and the miners who were, in those days, starting to go wherever they liked within their untrammelled exploration licences; and, perhaps most of all, to gain succour from being on the country of their ancestors.

---

41   NAA F1, 1973/4731.
42   Most of them ultimately resettled in outstations closer to Maningrida.
43   Altman, 'Imagining Mumeka', 283–87.

It would be wrong to say Hunter and the movement around Maningrida were unique in this period. Missionaries to the east and west were supporting similar decentralisation movements. They did not have to report to the director in the same detail as the welfare superintendents, however. Nor did they contend with the antagonisms of balandas in the settlement who regarded the movement as a 'step back into the stone age', as I often heard. It would also be wrong to say that Hunter battled those balandas and many senior officers in the Welfare Branch on his own. As Gillespie notes, Hunter was encouraged by the continuous fieldwork of archaeologists-anthropologists, Rhys Jones and Betty Meehan, in 1972 and 1973 with the Anbara Gidjingali people who had established an outstation at Gopanga on the mouth of the Blyth River.[44] The Cadell is a tributary of the Blyth and it was possible to use the landing near the new gardens at Gochan Giny-jirra to gain access to the new outstation. Despite the hostility of the majority of balandas, Hunter was always supported from the time of his first arrival by Rev. Gowan Armstrong, the United Church of North Australia minister. From the late 1960s the list of supporters grew: Assistant Superintendent John Wilders; Progress Association manager Glen Bagshaw; Dan Gillespie himself and about a dozen teachers and others.

H. C. Coombs's visit in 1972 also encouraged Hunter from the highest levels of government. Chair of the three-person policy advising group, the Council for Aboriginal Affairs, Coombs included Maningrida in his frequent travels to Aboriginal communities. The independence and demeanour of people living in the outstations, introduced to him by Hunter, made a strong impression.[45] For Hunter, the contact with Coombs was very different from what he experienced within his own department and he told several people happily: 'I'm on Nugget terms now!' Coombs relished meeting outsiders. 'I like people who *don't* conform', he had told the world on his retirement as governor of the Reserve Bank in 1967.[46] Hunter was content to be included in their number, and content also to have the admiration and encouragement of the relatively few balandas who were prepared to watch and learn from him. But, in the end, he was driven by the steely logic of the message he told anyone who was prepared to listen: 'In all my years of working with Aboriginal people this [the outstation movement] is the only thing that has been initiated by

---

44 Gillespie, 'John Hunter and Maningrida', 5.
45 Coombs, *Kulinma*, 65–66.
46 Rowse, *Obliged to be Difficult*, 3.

them.[47] The regular visits to the outstations he was making after about 1968 gave him the satisfaction of witnessing palpable independence and energy in self-determining groups. All the other industries and activities were dependent on initiative and supervision by the balandas who were increasingly dominant around the settlement.

Hunter finished at Maningrida in December 1973. The government had changed and 'self-determination' became the new government's Aboriginal affairs policy. Although Hunter told me he welcomed the policy, that welcome was qualified because, like all the other superintendents, he was taken away from Maningrida for much of that year to attend reorientation courses for the 'old welfare' staff. He felt constrained by his enforced absences. Nevertheless, he was able to push through many requests that came from Aboriginal people, including those from the traditional owners of Maningrida itself, the Gunividji, who often complained to Hunter (and anyone else prepared to listen) that their country was being overrun by outsiders, both balandas and other Aboriginal people:

> The Gunividji group at Maningrida are having more than their fair share of culture break-down problems being experienced at Maningrida. This is showing up particularly in child delinquency; e.g. petrol sniffing, minor crime, vandalism and promiscuity … I am afraid that the group are suffering an accelerated rate of breakdown because of impingement on their area by other Aboriginals and Europeans.[48]

He was gratified that most of the arguments he advanced (like this one) were accepted and that his requests were approved. But time was short, exacerbated by his promotion to a position in Darwin at the end of the year. He used that position to make great changes at Maningrida in 1974, but he left frustrated and disappointed at not being able to do more to assist Aboriginal people – at the very time that the self-determination they had all so courageously pursued in previous years now had the backing of the new government.[49]

In his parting message in *The Maningrida Mirage*, Hunter reflected, among many other issues, on the richness of Aboriginal culture, how we balanda had failed to listen and take note, and how Maningrida was a piece of

---

47   Personal communication to author.
48   NAA E460, 1976/1108.
49   Bond-Sharp, *Maningrida*, 162–77.

colonialism over which Aboriginal people had no say, concluding that his taking leave was encumbered by a sense of personal failure.[50] With Gillespie, my view is that he achieved a great deal, much of which carried on in later years. He made structural changes that go to much more than individual choice. True, the passage of the *Aboriginal Land Rights (Northern Territory) Act 1976* allowed Aboriginal custom more influence, but I argue here the work of Hunter and his Aboriginal partners paved the way for self-determination by whole groups of people, not just individuals. The final words about him should be from an Aboriginal voice, the late Bangardi Mildjingi, who worked closely with Hunter:

> He was a good man, you know, he was helping people, talk about land, everything, take you back home, where you belonging, you out from [the] Maningrida yard, like bulliki … and you go home, to make your own stations and that's why this work, Hunter's work, made everything good, you know, like go back to your outstation, establish your home, everything. And we did, yo, from him.[51]

References

Archival sources

National Archives of Australia (NAA)

A452, 1957/82 Part 1, Forestry Policy – Northern Territory

A4926, 1310, Northern Territory forestry programme – Decision 1557(GA)

E460, 1976/460 Part 1, Maningrida – Reports on Community Development

E460, 1976/1108, Movement of Gunavidji people to Juda Point

E460, 1983/487, Maningrida policy and development

F1, 1956/557, Patrol Officer in Training – Welfare Division – Darwin

F1, 1956/2663, Patrol Officers and Cadet Patrol Officers at School of Pacific Administration 1957 and 1958

F1, 1962/287, Maningrida Settlement Policy and Development

F1, 1964/2231, Welfare Branch – Leichhardt district – Maningrida contact area – Native peoples

F1, 1967/1674, Maningrida Progress Association

---

50 Hunter, 'A Confession!'
51 Bangardi Mildjingi, interview with author, July 2013.

F1, 1973/4731, Bulman cattle project – Maningrida

F1, 1975/2181, Maningrida Settlement Forestry & Timber Project

F941, 1966/13, Maningrida Staff

Other sources

Altman, Jon. 'Imagining Mumeka: Bureaucratic and Kuninjku Perspectives'. In *Experiments in Self-determination: Histories of the Outstation Movement in Australia*, edited by N. Peterson and F. Myers, 279–99. Canberra: ANU Press, 2016. doi.org/10.22459/esd.01.2016.14.

Bateman, W. *Forestry in the Northern Territory*. Leaflet no. 72. Canberra: Forestry and Timber Bureau, 1955.

Bond-Sharp, Helen. *Maningrida: A History of the Aboriginal Township in Arnhem Land*. Darwin: Helen Bond-Sharp, 2013.

Coombs, H. C. *Kulinma: Listening to Aboriginal Australians*. Canberra: Australian National University Press, 1978.

Drysdale, Ingrid and Mary Durack. *The End of Dreaming*. Adelaide: Rigby, 1974.

England, Crusoe Batara, Patrick Muchana Litchfield, Raymond Walanggay England and Margaret Carew. *Gun-ngaypa rrawa: My Country*. Batchelor, NT: Batchelor Press, 2014.

Gillespie, Dan. 'John Hunter and Maningrida – a Chorus of Alarm Bells'. In *Service Delivery to Outstations*, edited by P. Loveday, 1–7. Canberra: Australian National University Press, 1981.

Hasluck, Paul. *Shades of Darkness: Aboriginal Affairs 1925–1965*. Carlton, Vic.: Melbourne University Press, 1988.

Haynes, Chris. 'Submission and Evidence'. In *Joint Select Committee on Aboriginal Land Rights in the Northern Territory (subcommittee A)*, 753–80. Canberra: Commonwealth of Australia. Parliament, 1977.

Haynes, Chris. 'The Pattern and Ecology of *munwag*: Traditional Aboriginal Fire Regimes in North Central Arnhemland'. *Proceedings of the Ecological Society of Australia* 13 (1985): 203–14.

Haynes, Chris. 'The Value of Work and "Common Discourse" in the Joint Management of Kakadu National Park'. *Australian Journal of Anthropology* 28 (2017): 72–87. doi.org/10.1111/taja.12169.

Holland, Alison. *Just Relations: The Story of Mary Bennett's Crusade for Aboriginal Rights*. Crawley: University of Western Australia Press, 2015.

Hunter, John. 'A Confession!', *Maningrida Mirage*, no. 217, 14 December 1973, 1.

Kowal, Emma. 'The Politics of the Gap: Indigenous Australians, Liberal Multiculturalism and the End of the Self-determination Era'. *American Anthropologist* 110 (2008): 338–48. doi.org/10.1111/j.1548-1433.2008. 00043.x.

Kyle-Little, Syd. *Whispering Wind: Adventures in Arnhem Land*. London: Hutchinson, 1957.

Lea, Tess. *Bureaucrats and Bleeding Hearts: Indigenous Health in Northern Australia*. Sydney: UNSW Press, 2008.

Long, J. P. M. *The Go-Betweens: Patrol Officers in Aboriginal Affairs Administration in the Northern Territory 1936–1974*. Darwin: North Australia Research Unit, 1992.

MacLeish, Kenneth. 'The Top End of Down Under'. *National Geographic* 142 (1973): 145–74.

McEwen, John. 'The Northern Territory of Australia: Commonwealth Government's Policy with Respect to Aboriginals'. Manuscript, 12 pp. Canberra: Department of the Interior, 1939.

'Newsletters (*Maningrida Mirage*)', AIATSIS. Accessed October 2019, aiatsis.gov. au/collections/collections-online/digitised-collections/maningrida-mirage-newsletters/newsletters-maningrida-mirage.

Northern Territory Administration (NTA). Welfare Branch. *Annual Report 1958–59*. [Darwin]: Northern Territory Administration, 1959.

NTA. Welfare Branch. *Annual Report 1963–64*. [Darwin]: Northern Territory Administration, 1964.

Rowse, Tim. *Indigenous Futures: Choice and Development for Aboriginal and Islander Australia*. Sydney: UNSW Press, 2002.

Rowse, Tim. *Obliged to be Difficult: Nugget Coombs' Legacy in Indigenous Affairs*. Cambridge: Cambridge University Press, 2000. doi.org/10.1017/cbo97805 11552199.

2

AN EMERGING PROTESTANT DOCTRINE OF SELF-DETERMINATION IN THE NORTHERN TERRITORY

Laura Rademaker

Australia's introduction of self-determination policy under the Whitlam Government in 1973 is often portrayed as the end of both the 'assimilation era' and 'mission era'. Yet Christian missionaries, while holding various views about the Whitlam Government's policy, also formulated and instituted their own visions of self-determination for Aboriginal people over the 1960s and 1970s. In many cases, the key planks of what became known as the self-determination policy (e.g. forms of Aboriginal representation and self-governance, Aboriginal-controlled industries and mother-tongue education) were present or developing on Christian missions before the 1970s. Focusing on discussions at the Northern Territory's Missions Administration conferences and drawing on the mission archives, this chapter tracks the missions' shift over the 1960s and early 1970s from assimilation to self-determination.

Elsewhere, I have explored the changing approaches of Anglican missionaries to assimilation in the 1960s, arguing that change was forced upon them by financial and political circumstances.[1] The assimilation program on missions was becoming financially, politically and intellectually unviable by the mid-1960s. In this chapter I focus on the

---

1   Rademaker, '"Only Cuppa Tea"'; Rademaker, *Found.*

intellectual bases of the missions' innovations, arguing that the seeds of a Christian self-determination were present within the Protestant missionary conceptions of assimilation as these included the establishment of an 'Indigenous church'.[2] Rather than a revolution in missionary theory and practice, I find a gradual shift in emphasis on the question of how the 'Indigenous church' would be realised.

This chapter also brings 'secular' and 'spiritual' visions of self-determination together, placing the missionaries' visions for self-determination in their wider context, but also revealing the ways in which missionaries' distinctly Christian missiologies of self-determination flowed into 'secular' spaces. Most research into Aboriginal self-determination has neglected mission histories; however, there are exceptions. Miranda Johnson noted the Australian Council of Churches' calls in the early 1970s for Aboriginal land rights and argued that the churches considered self-determination and Aboriginal land rights more as spiritual than economic concerns.[3] With regard to the missions, Noel Loos argued there was a gradual shift in approach of the Australian Board of Missions over the 1960s and a devolution of responsibilities for Aboriginal communities to governments in Queensland. In 1967, its new policy 'Acceptance: The Next Step Forward' envisaged cultural pluralism.[4] John Kadiba, in his study of the Methodist Overseas Mission (MOM), argued that missionaries deemed their traditional 'Indigenous church' principle impossible in Arnhem Land until the 1970s due to their concerns to achieve assimilation.[5]

In the Northern Territory, Christian missions were the Australian Government's agent for implementing a policy of assimilating Aboriginal people into white Australia. According to the Director of Welfare, Harry Giese, this partnership between Christian missions and government was special and 'unique in the world'.[6] Missions were almost entirely dependent on governments for financial support and selectively engaged with various funding schemes. The missions received an annual government subsidy.

---

2   The Catholic missions did not subscribe to this theory of mission, due to their different ecclesiology. Following the *Nostra Aetate* Declaration of the Second Vatican Council in 1965, they too made moves towards celebrating Aboriginal cultures and promoting Aboriginal leadership. *Nostra Aetate*'s teaching on the good in all cultures enabled what became known as 'incarnating' and 'inculturating' the liturgy. While taking a different theological route, the Catholic missions reached similar practical conclusions to the Protestants. See Rademaker, 'Going Native'.

3   Johnson, *The Land*, 52.

4   Loos, *White Christ*, 139.

5   Kadiba, 'The Methodist Mission', 214.

6   Northern Territory Archives Centre, Northern Territory Records Series (hereafter NTRS) 53, box 3.

From 1942, Child Endowment payments were made available by the Commonwealth for children in institutions, so missions with dormitories began receiving 10 shillings per week per child in their care (the MOM's rejection of dormitories, therefore, came at a considerable financial cost). Over the course of the 1950s, there was heavy investment by the Northern Territory Administration's Welfare Branch in the development of missions. Missions were eligible for capital grants that covered the costs of purchasing livestock, equipment, buildings and vehicles (although the Missionaries of the Sacred Heart refused capital grants, believing these entangled church and state). The Welfare Branch also covered the costs of individual mission staff in particular roles. The range of government subsidies for missionary staff expanded over the 1950s, from covering only teachers and nurses in 1951 to many other roles by the 1960s, including agriculturalists, mechanics and hygiene assistants. Missions then pooled the funds from their subsidised positions to cover the costs of unsubsidised roles, particularly their chaplains.

The first Missions Administration Conference was held in 1948. From 1953 they were held biennially and hosted by the Welfare Branch with representatives from various mission societies and government departments working in the Territory. By 1961, government delegates present included representatives from the departments of Social Services, Civil Aviation and Health, the Crown Law Office and Welfare Branch (including Harry Giese and Jeremy Long).[7] On the mission side, delegates represented the Missionaries of the Sacred Heart and Catholic Diocese of Darwin, the Church of England Diocese of Carpentaria, Church Missionary Society (CMS), Aborigines Inland Mission, MOM, Baptist Union Home Mission and Finke River Mission of the United Evangelical Lutheran Church.[8] At the conferences, delegates discussed overarching Aboriginal policy, mission funding and responsibilities as well as questions around Aboriginal employment, industry and education. These biennial gatherings were the primary site for discussion across mission organisations as well as for airing missions' concerns to government; the conference was, in Lutheran missionary Paul Albrecht's words, 'one of the best venues for a round the table type discussion of the differences' between missions and the Welfare Branch on 'the whole question of helping Aboriginals find their place in the Australia of today'.[9]

---

7   National Archives of Australia (hereafter NAA) F1, 1959/3380.
8   NAA F1, 1959/3380.
9   Paul Albrecht to Harry Giese, 17 May 1971, NTRS 56, box 7.

Aboriginal choice and hasty assimilation

Missionaries often expressed frustration at the vagueness of government policy around assimilation and what it meant for the long-term prospects of the communities in which they operated. After consulting the MOM, the CMS's Acting Secretary for Aborigines, Bishop Clive Kerle, wrote to Giese with what would seem basic questions about the policy for clarification at the 1961 conference: 'what is the Government policy concerning the future of the mission stations?' and 'where in their plan for assimilation does the Missions fit?'[10]

The answer caused a stir. At the 1961 conference, Paul Hasluck presented a paper informing missionaries that their days were numbered. Although missions had always presumed that in the distant future they would withdraw and hand their authority to Aboriginal people, mission representatives were shocked when Hasluck suggested this might happen in only 20 years time (although Hasluck anticipated that the final 'completing of assimilation' would take 'two generations' or 60 years). Hasluck stated that missions and settlements should 'work ourselves out of a job' because their objectives were to 'help [Aboriginal people] become self-respecting and self-supporting members of the Australian community, living and working wherever they choose to live and work'.[11]

Missionaries had long expressed concern over the 'pace' of assimilation. Hasty assimilation, they argued, was against the wishes of Aboriginal people themselves, so could never create the self-standing citizens for which it supposedly aimed. If assimilation were to enable Aboriginal people to become 'responsible' citizens, rather than 'pauperised' persons, missionaries argued, then surely the desire to change must come from Aboriginal people themselves. In 1953, the MOM's Arthur Ellemor was already raising concerns that assimilation would be impossible because Aboriginal people did not want to assimilate.[12] Again, in 1955, he called for missions to have 'much more discussion with the Aborigines concerning their own future'.[13] The fear that assimilation might be 'forced' mirrored missionaries' fears that they might be forcing Christian conversion and that, consequently, Aboriginal expressions of

---

10   Clive Kerle to Harry Giese, 10 July 1961, NAA F1, 1959/3380.
11   Hasluck, 'The Future', 6.
12   NAA A452, 1955/368 Part 1.
13   NAA F1, 1954/1025.

faith were inauthentic.[14] The question of Aboriginal choice (especially for evangelicals) was a sensitive issue. In 1959, the conference resolved that it 'refutes any suggestion that compulsion is exerted upon aborigines on missions to enforce acceptance of Christianity' and that the missions sought 'voluntary acceptance of Christianity'.[15] Through the 1950s and early 1960s, missions continued to assert that, although assimilation was merely a temporary phase, it should be a slow, almost imperceptible process that moved at a pace of Aboriginal people's own choosing. At the 1953 conference, for example, Catholic Bishop O'Loughlin anticipated that missions might even continue for another century.[16]

Hasluck's 1961 announcement of an accelerated timeframe was therefore especially concerning. In response, F. H. Leske from the Finke River mission, commented that even 60 years was 'optimistic'. Paul Albrecht also thought that 'things are getting pushed rather fast' and that 'if you push the process of assimilation too quickly … people may revert to their primitive way of life'. To prevent a 'throwback', a degree of autonomy must be given to Aboriginal people and 'take it at the pace which the people themselves develop'; that is, assimilation depended on a kind of autonomy. Laurie Reece of the Warrabri mission argued for Aboriginal people to be 'given a sense of responsibility and a part in [their] own destiny', and Leske queried 'whether aborigines had any say in their destiny'. Ted Milliken, the Northern Territory Administration's representative, responded that, 'if free choice were there, the result would be extinction'; at this stage, missionaries were more concerned than the administration about the degree to which Aboriginal people were conceded 'choice'.[17] By 1963, in a paper circulated among both Methodist and Presbyterian missionaries, Stuart Fowler of the United Aborigines Mission (UAM) concluded that assimilation was impossible to impose externally but could occur only through social forces from within a community.[18]

14　Rademaker, '"Only Cuppa Tea"'.
15　NAA F1, 1959/3380.
16　NAA A452, 1955/368 Part 1.
17　NAA F1, 1961/2151.
18　Fowler, 'Apostolic'.

The crisis of assimilation on missions

Given these concerns about Aboriginal 'choice' and the realisation that missions' existing relationship with and support from governments would not continue forever, the question of withdrawing from the Northern Territory became a pressing concern for missions in the early 1960s.

Missionaries knew that the assimilation program was becoming unviable, as the scope of activities required on missions in pursuit of assimilation increased. Assimilation required not only schoolteachers and nurses, but now also builders, home management instructors, hygiene workers and preschool teachers. Though these positions were increasingly subsidised by governments, missions struggled to find recruits. With drastic changes in Australians' religious participation and practice in the 1960s, missionary societies were facing difficulties attracting not only donations but also new missionary staff.[19] Meanwhile, missionaries who had been drawn to their vocation for spiritual and evangelistic reasons found themselves overwhelmed by the administrative and practical concerns of running a small community. They often became disillusioned with the day-to-day work of assimilation and frustrated by the seeming lack of spiritual fruit. Aboriginal people, so far as many could see, were not interested in assimilating, nor were they converting to Christianity in the numbers hoped. As one missionary wrote in 1964, 'there is little evidence of any "break through" and, as far as I can see, not much sign of an Indigenous Church'.[20] Worse still, some suspected that their approaches were actively harming Aboriginal societies by undermining Aboriginal communities' own existing authority structures.[21]

Meanwhile, although the government was increasing the breadth of subsidies available, these did not match the increasing costs of assimilation, nor growing demands from Aboriginal people to manage their own money. When Aboriginal people insisted that they be paid pensions (available from 1959) and Child Endowment directly and in cash, missions acknowledged that Aboriginal people's money could not be withheld for much longer. Some gave in to this demand. The CMS Roper River mission, for instance, began paying all subsidies, endowments and pensions to Aboriginal people in 1966. But without that income,

---

19   Cole, *A History*, 31.
20   Mitchell Library (hereafter ML) MSS 6040/6.
21   Albrecht, 'The Finke River Mission', 10.

the mission could not survive; all but its 'spiritual ministry' was handed over to Welfare Branch in 1968.[22] As missions made greater moves to Aboriginal responsibility (understood as achieving the objectives of assimilation), these moves undercut their ability to continue assimilatory policies. Therefore, assimilation through missions, at least as envisaged at the time, seemed a social, spiritual and financial impossibility.

In the early 1960s, both the CMS and MOM commissioned inquiries into their work in the Territory, investigating the relationship of their work to the policy of assimilation. The CMS terms of reference were to recommend whether CMS should 'continue its work as at present' or 'hand over the work to the government'.[23] When it asked its missionaries if the 'policy of assimilation is capable of fulfilment under existing levels of government support', all but one thought not.[24] Its Federal Council resolved in 1964 to downscale and refocus the work. Rather than continuing the 'industrial' work, the CMS's resources 'should be concentrated on the pastoral, evangelistic and educational work'. For the Federal Council, 'the demands of assimilation require that the civil administration be gradually assimilated to the common pattern of the Australian life': that is, assimilation itself required that civil authorities replace church authorities in Indigenous communities. They would hand over mission administration to government.[25]

The MOM 1965 inquiry's terms of reference were more focused on what they considered the paradox of assimilation and Aboriginal cultural identity. They sought:

> To assess the proper relationship between the presentation of the Gospel, the life of the Church, education and social assimilation on the one hand and a continuing Aboriginal culture and language on the other.[26]

Like the CMS, the MOM commission recommended missionaries be relieved of 'administrative details' to free them for 'evangelistic and pastoral ministry' and that administration be passed to 'local governing bodies'. It also recommended 'active recognition of a universal truth' that mission 'is only effective … if it is taken up by the indigenous church'.[27]

---

22 ML MSS 6040/5.
23 ML MSS 6040/6.
24 CMS South Australia/Northern Territory office (hereafter CMS SA) Box 19.
25 ML MSS 6040/5.
26 NTRS 53, box 1.
27 NTRS 53, box 1.

Assimilation and the Indigenous church

This rediscovery, or reimagination, of an old missiological vision of the establishment of the 'Indigenous church' was common across denominations in this time of reassessing missions. Protestant missionary thinking had long been shaped by the theory of nineteenth-century CMS missionary Henry Venn. He defined the 'Indigenous church' by what became known as the 'three selves': it was self-funding, self-propagating and self-governing, thereby embodying the culture and thought of the people. The marks of an 'Indigenous church', as opposed to a mission, would be that it was led by Indigenous clergy and governed and funded by Indigenous people. Missions would be 'self-euthanising', that is, they would eventually hand over all controls to local people, becoming a church, not a mission.[28] This theory was revived by missiologist Roland Allen in the early twentieth century and gained new popularity in international mission circles in the 1960s.[29] In Australia, UAM missionary Stuart Fowler argued in 1963 that the 'indigenous church' theory was 'enjoying tremendous popularity in missionary circles', it was time that 'we who are involved with the Australian Aborigines … catch up with world trends'.[30]

The Indigenous church concept implied that mission churches would become self-determining as local people replaced missionaries. Yet the establishment of the 'Indigenous church' was not, at first, considered contrary to assimilation. Indeed, the development of an Aboriginal Christianity or 'Indigenous church' was, at first, to be an essential component of assimilation, as it bore a strong resemblance to Hasluck's language of 'self-respecting' and 'self-supporting' Aboriginal communities and of missionaries 'working themselves out of a job'.[31] Of course, the implications of assimilation were open to different understandings and it was possible to see assimilation as overwhelming all vestiges of Aboriginal autonomy. For example, one CMS missionary doubted whether, in the face of what he considered to be the imminent and inevitable white settlement of the Northern Territory, the establishment of an 'Aboriginal church' was a worthwhile objective. He believed there could be 'no separate future for Aboriginal people'.[32] Most missionaries,

---

28   Tippett, *Introduction*, 85.
29   Allen, *Missionary Methods*; Allen, *Spontaneous Expansion*.
30   Fowler, 'Apostolic', 2.
31   Hasluck, 'The Future', 6.
32   CMS SA Box 19.

however, saw no contradiction between assimilation and the planting of an Indigenous church. For Fowler, the Indigenous church would be a 'training ground' to 'prepare believers for assimilation'.[33] In 1961, one chaplain described the CMS's 'immediate objective' as 'to train, teach and prepare the Aborigines for Assimilation in accordance with present Government policy' as part of a long-term objective of 'the establishment of an Indigenous Church'.[34] Another commented that missions 'should aim at establishing an indigenous church as soon as possible', but in the same document he explained the necessity of preparing Aboriginal people for assimilation.[35]

In such visions of assimilation, it remained possible and, in fact desirable, for the world view of Aboriginal Christians to remain distinct from the world view of other Australians, both Christian and non-Christian. From the mid-1960s missionaries insisted that the Indigenous church had, so far, failed to develop in the Northern Territory due to their own failure to allow for authentic Aboriginal choice and cultural expression. This self-criticism was part of a broader cultural moment that emphasised the need for personal authenticity.[36] If Aboriginal people were allowed the freedom to be authentically themselves and to choose their own path of development, the Indigenous church would soon emerge. Beulah Lowe, a MOM linguist and teacher, for instance, added 'self-expression' to Venn's original 'three selves' when she wrote:

> The indigenous church is self-supporting, self-propagating, self-expressing and self-governing … Regarding self-expression. Firstly there is self-expression in worship patterns. These follow the indigenous culture and are not imposed from without.[37]

The version of assimilation missionaries articulated at the Missions Administration conferences in the early 1960s likewise reflects a greater concern for Aboriginal self-expression and cultural identity, in line with the 'Indigenous church' principles. Missionaries insisted in 1963 that assimilation should not mean any loss of cultural distinctiveness or peoplehood:

---

33 Fowler, 'Apostolic', 8.
34 CMS SA Box 19.
35 CMS SA Box 19.
36 Taylor, *A Secular*, 473.
37 NTRS 871, box 127.

> Some groups are resisting assimilation because it has been
> presented to them as implying absorption and obliteration.
> A fundamental provision ... is the full recognition that Aborigines
> are a distinctive ethnic group within the Commonwealth and have
> the right to remain as such.[38]

The 'Indigenous church' model also required that missionaries engage
with Aboriginal languages to enable 'self-expressing' worship. The 1963
conference was a watershed for the question of language. The CMS's George
Pearson raised the language question and, for the first time, convinced
government authorities that missionary linguistics could be of secular use.[39]
Language, he explained, was 'part of the people's cultural and spiritual
inheritance' and vital to 'their status as a people, with a say in their own
affairs'.[40] The conference therefore resolved that since language 'is part of
their heritage and a factor of social and cultural importance' governments
must fund linguistic research and mother-tongue literacy programs.[41]

On the question of Aboriginal preparedness for leadership, the 'Indigenous
church' model meant that missionaries were to trust that the Holy Spirit
would guide Aboriginal people as leaders. Barry Butler, from the CMS,
wrote in 1969 that 'Missionaries must let Aboriginal Christians develop at
their own pace as the Holy Spirit leads them'.[42] Fowler made willingness
to hand over authority to Aboriginal people a test of faith:

> Faith would not require local skills before handing over – We are
> walking by sight and not by faith while ever we say 'When I see
> sound local leadership operating I will be prepared to pull out.'
> This is simply not the way of faith.[43]

Accordingly, across the missions there were moves to greater Aboriginal
representation in leadership bodies (to varying degrees) and attempts
to consult with Aboriginal people even at the Missions Administration
conferences themselves. In 1961, Cecil Gribble from the MOM proposed
that Aboriginal leaders from missions be invited to future conferences.[44]
Giese suggested that Aboriginal representatives come as observers only, and
that they be excluded from some sensitive discussions. Gordon Symons

---

38 NAA A452, 1963/2353.
39 NAA F1, 1963/1989.
40 NAA F1, 1963/1989.
41 NAA F1, 1963/1989.
42 Butler, 'Relationship', 1.
43 Fowler, 'Apostolic', 2.
44 NAA F1, 1961/2151.

from the MOM agreed with this arrangement.[45] But Jack Langford from the CMS insisted that excluding Aboriginal people 'would be a barrier to full cooperation of the Aboriginal representatives' and 'cause ill feeling'.[46] Aboriginal representatives were then invited in 1963 as full delegates.

On the issue of representation, the pace of change was markedly slower than what Aboriginal people themselves desired. The conference became a site where Aboriginal people from across the missions expressed demands to have a voice in government. The delegates – Nandjiwarra Amagula, Michael Tipungwuti, Deimbalibu, Harry Jagamara and Denis Daniels – were expected to 'indicate quite clearly the thoughts and feelings of their own people in regard to the assimilation programme'. Jagamara told the conference that this move was insufficient: 'it was no good sending two or three representatives like this'. He proposed a conference in which Aboriginal people formed the majority, but he was ultimately ignored.[47] His idea was discussed again at the 1967 conference.[48] In 1969 the conference proposed the establishment of 'regional conferences of representatives of the Aborigines' and a 'Northern Territory wide conference of representatives of Aborigines'.[49] These did not take place.

Still, the Missions Administration Conference made gradual moves to increase Aboriginal control over missions (under white overseers). The Welfare Branch's Senior Research officer, Jeremy Long, urged superintendents to be more 'democratic'. Most missions developed some form of form Aboriginal leadership structure – a Village Council or Town Council – in the early 1960s.[50] Aboriginal representatives on these bodies tended to be Christian converts who were also offered leadership roles in mission churches (again, according to the principles of establishing the 'Indigenous church'). At the 1963 conference, the CMS representative proposed that, given Aboriginal people had made valuable contributions in mission management on station councils, Aboriginal people should also be represented on the Northern Territory Legislative Council; there was some sense that Aboriginal people should be represented as a people, not only as individual citizens. Giese responded that Aboriginal people could be elected 'like anyone else' now that they had voting rights.[51]

45 Symons to Giese, 14 December 1962, NAA E460, 1974/773/33.
46 Langford to Giese, 31 December 1962, NAA E460, 1974/773/33.
47 NAA F1, 1963/1989.
48 NAA A452, NT1967/4400.
49 NAA F1, 1969/6123.
50 Long, 'Some Problems', 2.
51 NAA F1, 1963/1989.

These moves were nonetheless considered consistent with assimilatory visions by both missionaries and government officials. Aboriginal participation and leadership in town councils, sports and social clubs, for instance, were to be 'education for citizenship', according to the ideals of assimilation.[52] In 1965, the conference urged missions and governments to plan for Aboriginal people 'to take increasing control of their own affairs as they are able'.[53] It also resolved during this process that 'mixed personnel' (i.e. both public servants and missionaries) be employed on missions so that 'Aboriginals may be better prepared for the inevitable encounter with the world which must be faced in years ahead'; missionaries still imagined themselves to be preparing Aboriginal people to meet (secular) white Australia, even in this process of devolution of authority.[54] In this vein, the 1965 conference resolved that the words 'missions' and 'settlement' be abandoned and replaced with 'suitable Aboriginal names'.[55] By 1969, the conference resolved that the word 'mission' be replaced with 'community'.[56] Missionaries also used the conferences to urge government towards measures that might increase Aboriginal people's ability to manage their own affairs. In 1961, Bishop Matthews suggested that Aboriginal people on missions could be made eligible for unemployment benefits. Bishop O'Loughlin agreed.[57] By 1969, the conference proposed a kind of training allowance scheme: 'a special grant of funds be made to missions to allow special projects to be commenced or developed ... to occupy those employable Aborigines who cannot find gainful employment'.[58]

On the question of land rights, missionaries were more ambivalent. Arthur Ellemor, from the MOM, had been an early supporter of land rights. In a paper presented to the 1955 Missions Administration Conference he argued that, since the 'actual land robbery has not yet occurred' in much of the Northern Territory, there was still time to prevent it. Using the language of assimilation, he argued that land rights were essential to 'fit [Aboriginal people] for citizenship' because 'attachment to their traditional territories' was a 'prerequisite for stability' and could be the starting point for 'newer concepts of land rights for agricultural, pastoral

---

52 Long, 'Some Problems', 1.
53 NAA F1, 1965/3502.
54 NAA A452, 1965/8518.
55 NAA A452, 1965/8518.
56 NAA F1, 1967/3401.
57 NAA F1, 1961/2151.
58 NAA A452, 1965/8518.

and home-building'.[59] Yet, when Nabalco proposed a bauxite mine on Yolngu land near the Yirrkala mission, the MOM agreed to the mine in 1958 without consulting Yolngu people. The missionaries reacted to Yolngu concerns in diverse ways. Some joined the Yolngu in their protest (notably the superintendent of the mission, Edgar Wells, who the MOM later dismissed for his involvement).[60]

At the 1963 Missions Administration Conference, delegates debated the question of consultation and land. Giese 'stressed' that there had been 'full discussions' between government, mining interests and mission authorities but conceded that 'there should have been earlier consultation with the people'. Gribble, from the MOM, argued that it was missions' responsibility to 'consult with local people'. Pearson from the CMS suggested determining a date for the 'eventual transfer of ownership of mission leases to the people' to remove missions from negotiations around future land use.[61] Yet, that year, the Groote Eylandt Mining Company also began operations, after negotiating with the CMS to pay royalties into a trust for Aboriginal people. The Aboriginal landowners were consulted, but only after the mission had already reached this agreement.[62] For the missionaries, the mine was an answer to their prayers. Given the mission's uncertain future, the jobs that mining would provide meant the community (and its 'Indigenous church') might survive into a post-mission future.

The Missions Administration Conference reached few resolutions on land rights. The 1965 conference recommended that a 'commission be established to examine claims by individuals or groups of Aborigines to ownership of land'.[63] A resolution of the 1971 conference recommended that where mining leases are granted on Aboriginal reserves there be mandatory 'special conditions after consultation with local Aborigines' to protect Aboriginal interests.[64] The United Church in North Australia, however, eventually changed its position from the MOM's earlier approach.[65] In 1972, it challenged Prime Minister McMahon's Australia

---

59   NAA A452, 1955/368 Part 2.
60   Wells, *Reward and Punishment*, 25–26.
61   NAA F1, 1963/1989.
62   ML MSS 6040/5.
63   NAA F1, 1965/3502.
64   NTRS 56, box 4.
65   The United Church in North Australia was a union of Methodist and Presbyterian churches that developed in Darwin during the Second World War and preceded the formation of the Uniting Church in 1977.

Day statement, urging the government to 'continue its examination of its policies' and calling for 'legislation to grant a proprietary right to any Aboriginal clan which can demonstrate "cogent feeling of obligation to the land"'.[66]

The conference's failure to establish a position on land rights was partly because the 'Indigenous church' model did not give missionaries any direction on questions of customary land tenure. Whereas local governance and cultural programs were easily understood as in the interests of 'self-governing' and 'self-expressing' churches, land rights were not. Missionaries had long sought to uphold the spatial isolation of Aboriginal communities as they believed it aided community cohesion and cultural vitality and gave Aboriginal people a degree of protection from influences missionaries deemed 'undesirable'. But they also wanted Aboriginal people to have jobs. It was never clear how maintaining isolation could be consistent with the long-term goals of assimilation. Mining was attractive because, missionaries believed, it would offer a source of income for remote communities, without requiring people to leave. The expectation that the Indigenous church be 'self-supporting' also pushed missionaries towards mining, as mining might make these communities economically viable. While missionaries expressed concern that Aboriginal people be given a 'choice' about the use of their land, they presumed that Aboriginal people would choose economic development. Missionaries were eager that Aboriginal people live on their country but many had a limited vision of Aboriginal land rights. It was only after the Yolngu made their protest heard that missionaries argued that land was vital, not only for economic and social reasons, but also cultural survival, and land rights were integrated into missionary visions for the authentic Indigenous church.

Abandoning assimilation

By the late 1960s, missionaries increasingly felt that 'assimilation' could not capture their objectives for Aboriginal people because it did not allow for 'choice'. By 1969, the government line was that assimilation meant that Aboriginal people 'will choose' to live like other Australians.[67] At that year's conference, Fr Leary commented that difficulties with Aboriginal

---

66   NTRS 55, box 10.
67   NAA F1, 1967/3401.

'social development' were due to Aboriginal 'failure to accept the responsibilities that must be accepted'. The solution was 'to aid him with his willing cooperation'; Leary was still thinking that Aboriginal people might be encouraged to 'choose' assimilation.[68] Most other delegates thought otherwise. At the 1971 conference Paul Albrecht circulated two papers.[69] He objected to the 'imposition' of assimilation and warned that 'social change' must come from 'within' or else 'it can lead to complete social disorganization'.[70] He considered the government's expectation that Aboriginal people 'will choose' assimilation disingenuous:

> Although the present wording of the policy – 'seeks that all persons of Aboriginal descent will choose to attain a similar manner and standard of living to that of other Australians and live as members of a single Australian community' … the policy does not envisage Aborigines exercising this option, nor does it make any provision for them in case they wish to opt out of the assimilation programme.[71]

Albrecht proposed returning judicial authority to Aboriginal communities and instituting executive councils of both Aboriginal and non-Indigenous staff on each settlement to take over management from missions.[72] The missions' evangelistic and pastoral roles would nonetheless continue; churches would still be heavily involved in 'proclamation of the Gospel' and social and economic programs in these communities.[73]

The United Church in North Australia also clarified its objectives for the 1971 conference. It saw itself as an adviser, advocate and mediator. Importantly, the church's role of 'preparing' Aboriginal people – the purported reason Aboriginal people had been segregated from white Australia under assimilation – was dropped, as they acknowledged Aboriginal people might not wish to 'become involved' with white Australia at all:

> The aim of such development is to ensure that Aboriginal communities have the opportunity to make true and free choices as to their place within the Australian society … It is their right to decide whether they wish to become involved in

---

68   Leary, 'Developing', 3.
69   Albrecht, 'Social Change'; Albrecht, 'Aboriginal Advancement'.
70   Albrecht, 'Social Change', 62.
71   Albrecht, 'Social Change', 51.
72   Albrecht, 'Aboriginal Advancement', 64.
73   Albrecht, 'Aboriginal Advancement', 8.

> the wider community. It is their right to decide the extent and form that involvement should take should they decide to belong to the wider community ... Real decisions can only be made on adequate knowledge of what is possible and an appreciation of the implications involved in their decisions. It is the task of the Church to offer this help and to persuade the larger community to recognise the issues involved in Aboriginal development.[74]

At the 1971 conference, missions confirmed that the only way Aboriginal free choice could be ensured would be a full devolution of authority from missions and governments to local Aboriginal organisations and government agencies. Yet, contrary to Hasluck's 20-year timeframe of 1961, the conference resolved that 'no timetable [could] be set' for this devolution as this was a matter for Aboriginal people.[75] Now that missions were no longer conceived as urgently 'preparing' Aboriginal people for 'inevitable' contact with (secular) white Australia, there was no need to estimate a timeframe for change. Of course, this also effectively allowed missions to reserve the right to remain and continue indefinitely (many are still operating in some form today), claiming to do so according to the wishes of Aboriginal people.

The following year (1972), however, the Finke River mission did set an end date in a statement for the Lutheran General Synod. Perhaps this was in reaction to the Missions Administration Conference's resolution that there could be no timetable and the fear that missionaries might linger longer than necessary:

> There has been a marked emergence of the Aboriginal people in the spiritual and material spheres of life. This would indicate that the present policy of helping the Aboriginals to regain their lost dignity by encouraging them to make their own responsible decisions is meeting with success. These developments challenge the Church to recognise that the Finke River mission has reached that stage in its history when the aim of all mission work is being achieved, namely to establish an indigenous church. This means that ultimately functions and work carried out by white staff must be transferred to the Aboriginal people themselves ... In the centenary year of 1977 it may be possible to hand over the major proportion of the work at Hermannsburg and on the Run to the Aboriginal people.[76]

---

74 NTRS 56, box 4.
75 NTRS 56, box 4.
76 Albrecht, *From Mission*, 42.

Linking Aboriginal people's self-determination in secular matters to their progress in the spiritual realm, they suggested that the achievement of the Indigenous church was so imminent that full authority in the community could be given to Aboriginal people by 1977 (though even this short-term target was not achieved).

The Indigenous church and the self-determination era

The final Missions Administration Conference took place in 1971. In September 1972, it was replaced by the Church and Mission Authorities Advisory Conference. From 1973, this conference was held quarterly with the Department of Aboriginal Affairs and various churches and other territory and federal government departments.[77] Aboriginal representatives were no longer invited to contribute. Ironically, the formal arrival of 'self-determination' as a Commonwealth Government policy in 1973 meant that Aboriginal people on missions lost the conference as a site for airing grievances and raising their concerns. Rather than this single channel, they were instead to consult with a plethora of government agencies while the mission agencies continued their close relationship with the Northern Territory Administration.

The churches continued their efforts towards establishing authentic, self-determining 'Indigenous churches'. Building on the relationships established through the Missions Administration Conferences, in 1973 the MOM, CMS, Anglican Diocese and United Church in North Australia co-founded Nungalinya College in Darwin (later joined by the Catholics) to develop an Indigenous leadership.[78] Its first principal, Keith Cole, described its objective in terms of the Indigenous church theory: training Aboriginal people for 'ministries within the indigenous church' and the precursor to 'the final move in [Aboriginal parishes'] evolution from missions to churches'.[79] In 1974, the United Church in North Australia compiled its most comprehensive statement on self-determination in a report entitled *Free to Decide*, based on discussions with Aboriginal leaders across its missions. Its conclusions resonated with

---

77   NTRS 559, box 78; NTRS 56, box 4.
78   Emilsen, 'The United', 16.
79   Cole, *A History*, 143.

the missions' fresh concern for authenticity; it claimed Aboriginal people had told them 'we do want help, but not on terms which deny us the freedom to be Aboriginal people in an Aboriginal environment'.[80] The official histories of the Finke River mission and the CMS in the Northern Territory are both titled *From Mission to Church,* reflecting the prominence of the Indigenous church theory to their authors' understanding of the mission.[81] As Albrecht explained in the foreword, the movement from 'mission to church' meant Aboriginal people taking responsibility for church life, expressed in their own languages, cultures and systems of governance.[82]

This Christian self-determination policy grew out of a Christian assimilation policy conceived as a movement towards an Indigenous church. It focused primarily on the mission churches but flowed into 'secular' spaces. Missionaries shaped 'self-determination' towards Christian and evangelistic ends. Yet their concern, first and foremost, for the local and 'authentic' Indigenous church, meant that their 'self-determination' was often limited to local Indigenous groups and privileged Aboriginal people who had embraced the missionary faith. Missionaries often rejected pan-Aboriginal movements associated with self-determination (some expressing frustration that Aboriginal people with non-Indigenous heritage might represent local communities in the Northern Territory). They also resented the coming in of consumer goods and alcohol to communities, seen as destructive of traditional culture. Many expressed nostalgia for a pre-assimilation mission time, which they saw as marked by authentic relationships, cultural richness and freedom from bureaucratic interventions. Missionaries' Christian self-determination could, in some ways, be understood as a kind of Christian neo-protectionism, with missionaries envisaging their role as protectors of Aboriginal culture and local communities, and as mediators between Aboriginal people and outsiders, much as they had done in an earlier protectionist era.

---

80   United Church, *Free to Decide,* 45.
81   Albrecht, *From Mission;* Cole, *From Mission.*
82   Albrecht, *From Mission,* x.

References

Archival sources

National Archives of Australia (NAA)

A1734, NT/1971/889, Missions Administration Policy, Albrecht, 1971

A452, 1955/368 Part 1, Missions – Administration Conference – Northern Territory, 1953

A452, 1961/3786, Missions Administration Conference – Northern Territory, July 1961

A452, 1963/2353, Missions and Administration Conference NT, 1963

A452, 1965/8518, Northern Territory Missions Administration Conference, 1965

A452, NT/1967/4400, Missions Administration Conference, 1967

E460, 1974/773, Missions Administration Conference Policy and Procedures, 1957–1970

F1, 1954/1025, Missions Administration Conference, 1955

F1, 1959/3380, Missions Administration Conference, 1961

F1, 1961/2151, Missions Administration Conference, 1963

F1, 1963/1989, Missions Administration Conference Proceedings, 1963

F1, 1965/3502, Missions Administration Conference, 1965

F1, 1967/3401, Missions Administration Conference, 1939

F1, 1969/6123, Action arising from Missions Administration Conference, 1969

NT, 1971/1/899, Missions Administration Conference Resolutions on Albrecht Paper, 1971

Northern Territory Archives Service (NTAS)

NTRS 53, Records relating to the Methodist Overseas Mission, 1961–1978

NTRS 55, Records relating to [Uniting Church] Northern Synod and Joint Planning Committee, 1966–1983

NTRS 56, Records relating to Aboriginal Affairs, 1959–1981

NTRS 559, General correspondence files [Church Missionary Society of Australia], 1970–1973

NTRS 871, General records of the Numbulwar (Rose River) Community, 1942–1984

Mitchell Library (ML)

ML MSS 6040/5, Aborigines Committee Minutes 1950–1968

ML MSS 6040/6, Aborigines Policy Committee of Inquiry 1964–1969

Church Missonary Society South Australia Office Adelaide (CMS SA)

CMS SA Box 19

Other sources

Albrecht, Paul. 'Aboriginal Advancement, Thoughts on Objectives & Methods'. 22 June 1971, NAA A1734, NT/1971/889. National Archives of Australia.

Albrecht, Paul. 'The Finke River Mission Approach to Mission Work among Aborigines in Central Australia'. *Lutheran Theological Journal* 32, no. 1 (May 1998): 7–15.

Albrecht, Paul. *From Mission to Church, 1877–2002: Finke River Mission.* Hermannsburg, NT: Finke River Mission, 2002.

Albrecht, Paul. 'Social Change and the Aboriginal Australians of Central Australia'. 1970, NAA A1734, NT/1971/889. National Archives of Australia.

Allen, Roland. *Missionary Methods: St. Paul's or Ours?* [1912]. Grand Rapids: Eerdmans, 1962.

Allen, Roland. *The Spontaneous Expansion of the Church: And the Causes Which Hinder It* [1927]. Grand Rapids: Eerdmans, 1962.

Butler, Barry. 'Relationship between Christianity and Aboriginal Ceremonies'. *Arnhem Land Epistle*, March 1969, 1.

Cole, Keith. *A History of the Church Missionary Society of Australia.* Melbourne: Church Missionary Historical Publications, 1971.

Cole, Keith. *From Mission to Church: The CMS Mission to the Aborigines of Arnhem Land, 1908–1985.* Bendigo, Vic.: Keith Cole Publications, 1985.

Emilsen, William. 'The United Church in North Australia: Australia's Other Experiment in Ecumenism'. *Uniting Church Studies* 8, no. 2 (2002): 1–22.

Fowler, Stuart. 'Apostolic Foundations'. September 1963, NTRS 871, box 126. Northern Territory Archives Service.

Hasluck, Paul. 'The Future of the Missions'. 17 July 1961, NTRS 56, box 4, Missions Administration Conference. Northern Territory Archives Service.

Johnson, Miranda. *The Land Is Our History: Indigeneity, Law and the Settler State*. Oxford: Oxford University Press, 2016.

Kadiba, John. 'The Methodist Mission and the Emerging Aboriginal Church in Arnhem Land 1916–1977'. PhD thesis, Northern Territory University, 1998.

Leary, John. 'Developing Social Responsibility among the Aboriginals'. 1969, NAA F1, 1967/3401. National Archives of Australia.

Long, Jeremy. 'Some Problems of Village Councils on Missions and Settlements'. 1961, NAA A452, 1961/3786. National Archives of Australia.

Loos, Noel. *White Christ Black Cross: The Emergence of a Black Church*. Canberra: Aboriginal Studies Press, 2007.

Rademaker, Laura. *Found in Translation: Many Meanings on a North Australian Mission*. Honolulu: University of Hawai'i Press, 2018.

Rademaker, Laura. 'Going Native: Converting Narratives in Tiwi Histories of Twentieth-Century Missions'. *Journal of Ecclesiastical History*, online (2018): 1–21. doi.org/10.1017/s0022046918000647.

Rademaker, Laura. '"Only Cuppa Tea Christians": Colonisation, Authentic Indigeneity and the Missionary Linguist'. *History Australia* 13, no. 2 (2016): 228–42. doi.org/10.1080/14490854.2016.1185999.

Taylor, Charles. *A Secular Age*. Cambridge: Harvard University Press, 2009.

Tippett, Alan Richard. *Introduction to Missiology*. Pasadena: William Carey Library, 1987.

United Church in North Australia. *Free to Decide: The United Church in North Australia Commission of Enquiry, Arnhem Land, March–April 1974*. Darwin: The Church, 1974.

Wells, Edgar. *Reward and Punishment in Arnhem Land, 1962–1963*. Canberra: Australian Institute of Aboriginal Studies, 1982.

3

THE ABORIGINAL PASTORAL ENTERPRISE IN SELF-DETERMINATION POLICY

Charlie Ward

Introduction

This chapter describes the origins, development and operation of Aboriginal Cattle Enterprises (ACEs) as efforts by governments to assist Aboriginal self-determination in the Northern Territory of Australia. Few ACEs satisfied their Indigenous participants and bureaucratic champions. I draw on agronomist Stuart Phillpot's study of Northern Territory ACEs in the period 1972–96 and on my own thesis research.[1] After contextually assessing two ACEs (the Puraiya Cattle Company at Ti Tree and the Ngarliyikirlangu Pastoral Company at Yuendumu), Phillpot found that government support did not allow for ACEs' multiple land use aspirations and that this led to those organisations' decline. While Phillpot explains this outcome by pointing to poor communication, misunderstood and undiscerned cultural assumptions, and the inflexibility and variability of government funding, he does not assess the effects of the internal social dynamics of the Aboriginal groups involved in ACEs. I will argue that the growing gap between generations was also significant in determining the sector's long-term viability. Drawing on analyses of social

---

1   Phillpot, 'Black Pastoralism'; Ward, 'Gurindji people'.

change among Aboriginal groups beyond the Territory, I will suggest that the lessons drawn by Phillpot and myself are of wider relevance in northern and Central Australia.

Origins

When the Labor Government, on the advice of the Council for Aboriginal Affairs, announced in 1972 that it would 'restore to the Aboriginal people of Australia their lost power of self-determination in economic, social and political affairs', a novel economic and geographic problem faced thousands of Aboriginal people in Australia's remote centre and north.[2] During colonial settlement, Europeans had occupied Aboriginal people's lands for the purposes of farming cattle and sheep. For decades prior to the mid-1960s, pastoralists relied on the presence on their leases of a pool of labour made up of Aboriginal traditional owners. Aboriginal people subsisting on pastoral leases had gained little or no cash income, as they were paid in rations or in small wage payments held in trust. It was rare, however, for their employment to exceed 30 weeks per year.[3] In the 1950s, the Australian Government increasingly took responsibility for Aboriginal people, resulting in the award of invalid, aged and nursing pensions to Aboriginal adults in 1959.[4] Although pastoralists and missionaries continued to supply goods rather than pass on the entire benefit as cash, people were exposed to money from this time in the form of a small proportion of the government allowances and a low cash wage for employees. By the early 1960s in the Northern Territory, the amount paid to Aboriginal workers was still approximately only 20 per cent of the *Cattle Station Industry (Northern Territory) Award 1951*.[5]

By the late 1960s, this situation was changing, as investment in the beef industry reduced the demand for labour and as Aboriginal people explored opportunities to live in new ways on missions, government settlements and in towns. In line with assimilation policy, both the North Australia Workers' Union and the Commonwealth Government argued that Aboriginal workers should get the same protection of their living standards that other employees enjoyed and, in March 1966, after

2   See Whitlam, 'Statement'.
3   Peterson, 'Capitalism', 90.
4   Hamilton, 'Aboriginal Women', 174; Rowse, *White Flour*, 133.
5   Berndt and Berndt, *End of an Era*, 71.

weighing union and government submissions against the pastoralists' warnings of dis-employment, the Commonwealth Conciliation and Arbitration Commission decided to include male Aboriginal workers in the Cattle Station Industry (Northern Territory) Award (while authorising lower wages for those classified as 'slow workers').

The 'equal wages' decision, as it became known, contributed to a decline in employer demand for labour and thus to a fall in the number of Aboriginal people employed and/or residing on Northern Territory pastoral leases. According to government figures, 4,676 Aboriginal people resided on pastoral properties in 1965, and by 1969 this figure had declined to 4,305.[6] In the opinion of policymakers, the weakening attachment of many Aboriginal people to the pastoral industry created both problems and opportunities for them. Some people moved off leases, at either their own or the lessee's initiative. Those station camps that persisted did so with great uncertainty about their future as a labour force entitled to unemployment benefits and as resident communities entitled to basic services (health, housing and education). Some Aboriginal groups that were reluctant to terminate their involvement with the pastoral industry wished to recast their pastoral activities on their own terms. As well, growing political support for the idea that Aboriginal people had customary rights to own land raised the question of the tenure of Aboriginal groups still resident on pastoral leases that included some or all of their traditional country.

To consider the future of Indigenous people on Northern Territory pastoral communities, in December 1970 the Gorton Government commissioned a team of experts, chaired by Cecil Gibb, Professor of Psychology at The Australian National University. The committee's terms of reference included:

- To survey the situation of Aborigines on pastoral properties in the Northern Territory so as to identify problems and special needs;
- To examine ways by which [their] economic and social conditions may be improved;
- To see whether new or additional steps need to be taken to give effect to existing policies for Aboriginal communities on pastoral properties.[7]

6   Gibb, *The Report*, 34.
7   Gibb, *The Report*, 2.

The Gibb Committee predicted that many Aboriginal people would in future have to find employment outside the pastoral industry, and it recommended strengthening 'a wider ranging employment service to Aborigines to encourage and assist their training and placement in work in other areas as well as on pastoral properties'.[8] For those who would remain on pastoral properties, the Gibb Committee proposed that land should be excised from pastoral holdings for residential and small-scale subsistence-type activities. Recognising the aspirations of some Aboriginal people to own, manage and be employed by their own cattle enterprises, the committee recommended that the government:

- [Encourage and help Aborigines financially] to establish enterprises in activities serving the cattle industry e.g. contract trucking, mustering, fencing and yard building, bore sinking, share farming etc (with experienced managers).
- [W]herever a coherent group of Aborigines indicates effective interest in establishing a group-owned enterprise it should be encouraged if the enterprises possesses reasonable prospects of success; [government grants] together with technical and managerial expertise could be justified.[9]

The committee also recommended that the government legislate to 'enable an Aboriginal Community Society to be loosely incorporated', leading to the *Aboriginal Councils and Associations Act 1976*. Thus, the ACE became possible as legislation, and government land purchases and operational funding facilitated the participation of Aboriginal people in the pastoral industry through novel, hybrid enterprises. I argue that their (usually unanticipated, misunderstood and/or inadequately resolved) hybridity made them largely unsuccessful vehicles of self-determination policy.

The Aboriginal pastoral sector

The Gorton Government had established the Commonwealth Capital Fund under the *Aboriginal Enterprises (Assistance) Act 1968* to assist Aboriginal people to establish business enterprises; this was the source of the government's first land purchases for Aboriginal groups. In October 1971, the McMahon Government was persuaded to allocate funds for the

---

8   Gibb, *The Report*, 72–77.
9   Gibb, *The Report*, 72–77.

purchase of pastoral leases for both economic and social purposes. Senior bureaucrats in the Department of the Interior and Liberal–Country Party Coalition politicians impeded grants to Aboriginal individuals and/or groups of individuals (rather than families, clan groups or 'communities').[10]

Among the Aboriginal groups frustrated by government resistance to arguments for Aboriginal land rights were the Gurindji, employed on Wave Hill Station in the Victoria River District of the Northern Territory. In the years 1966–72, Gurindji elders and their activist supporters had generated much publicity for their quest to own land on which they could make a living by raising beef cattle. On coming to power, the Whitlam Government favoured such aspirations and passed the *Aboriginal Land Fund Act 1974*, implementing a decision made in 1972 by the McMahon Government (following a Gibb Report recommendation). This established the Aboriginal Land Fund Commission (ALFC) – an expert statutory body to manage the purchase of pastoral land for Aboriginal people. The ALFC worked in liaison with the Department of Aboriginal Affairs (DAA).

Under the policy of self-determination, government consulted groups such as the Gurindji and sought to adapt the laws and policies of the settler state to assist the realisation of their aspirations. I argue that the government gave insufficient thought to whether incorporated proprietary companies were appropriate vehicles for remote Indigenous aspirations. In the period of the Whitlam Government, the ALFC purchased three pastoral properties or parts of pastoral properties. One was made on behalf of the Gurindji: Wattie Creek, or Daguragu, which was then part of Wave Hill Station. These purchases by the Whitlam Government were the first of many. By 1993, 20 pastoral leases had been purchased, and cattle enterprises had continued or been initiated on a further 13 properties contained within former reserve land, now held under 'Aboriginal freehold' title granted through the *Aboriginal Land Rights (Northern Territory) Act 1976* (ALRA). During the period of the Fraser Government (1975–83), the ALFC's land-buying passed in 1980 to the new Aboriginal Development Commission (ADC). In 1990, during the period of the Hawke and Keating governments (1983–96), the land-buying program passed from ADC to the Aboriginal and Torres Strait Islander Commission (ATSIC). Such grants and purchases are summarised in the table below:

---

10   Palmer, *Buying Back*, 21–23.

Table 3.1: Northern Territory Aboriginal communities with Aboriginal Cattle Enterprises (ACEs) on Aboriginal freehold or leasehold land with date of title (granted or purchased) prior to 1993.

Communities with Cattle Enterprise	Year Freehold Granted or Lease Purchased
Murwangi	ALRA 1976*
Gulin Gulin	ALRA 1976*
Oenpelli/Gunbalunya	ALRA 1976*
Croker Island	ALRA 1976*
Yugal	ALRA 1976*
Daly River	ALRA 1976*
Lajamanu	ALRA 1976*
Yuendumu	ALRA 1976*
Santa Teresa	ALRA 1976*
Haasts Bluff Land Trust	ALRA 1976*
Palumpa	Pastoral Lease 1976
Peppimenarti	Pastoral Lease 1976
Beswick (Jimboingal)	Pastoral Lease 1976
Amanbidji	Pastoral Lease 1973
Yarralin	Pastoral Lease 1973
Willowra	Pastoral Lease 1973
Daguragu	Pastoral Lease 1975
Ti Tree	Pastoral Lease 1975
Yuelamu	Pastoral Lease 1976
Utopia	Pastoral Lease 1976
Robinson River	Pastoral Lease 1980
Mt Barkly	Pastoral Lease 1981
Eva Valley	Pastoral Lease 1984
McLaren Creek	Pastoral Lease 1985
Atula	Pastoral Lease 1989
Tanami Downs	Pastoral Lease 1989
Hodgson Downs	Pastoral Lease 1990
Elsey	Pastoral Lease 1991
Fitzroy	Pastoral Lease 1991
Muckaty	Pastoral Lease 1991
Mistake Creek	Pastoral Lease 1992
Loves Creek	Pastoral Lease 1992
Alcoota	Pastoral Lease 1993

*ALRA 1976: In these communities, cattle enterprises were operated by mission or government authorities on land that was 'reserve' until the *Aboriginal Land Rights Act 1976* converted the tenure to Aboriginal freehold title.

Source: Adapted from Hanlon and Phillpot, 'Rural Development', 38–40.

To benefit from gaining title (either by purchase or as an effect of the ALRA), Aboriginal cattle enthusiasts were obliged to incorporate. Charles Rowley, founding chair of the ALFC, later reflected that 'the transfer of land or other property to a group long dispossessed brings a new upheaval, as new problems of its use, of leadership, and distribution of profit, are thrashed out'.[11] Government policy was to vest grantees with the responsibility of a lessee. For instance, the Daguragu Pastoral Lease granted to Gurindji people in 1975 by the Whitlam Government (as codified by the *Northern Territory Crown Lands Ordinance 1971*) determined the tenure and terms, and thus the nature and timing, of the Muramulla Company's improvements. It was a condition of ACEs' funding that the grantees seek profit by selling beef. When government-contracted consultant agronomists predicted that ACEs would be able to return a net profit with requisite monitoring and financial and 'technical' (practical) support, governments only committed to provide ACEs with financial support until they made a profit.

ACEs were typically led at a local level by a coterie of Aboriginal former stockmen, guiding the involvement of their families or clans. Those elders were commonly responsible to a much larger group of kin and other groups comprising the landholding body. Usually these groups were thoroughly proficient in all the physical operations of a cattle station, with comprehensive ecological knowledge of their leasehold. They did not usually possess the knowledge required to manage the businesses that they were funded to run, however. In most cases, they had been deliberately denied the opportunity to gain managerial knowledge during their earlier experiences as pastoral industry subordinates.

The governmental rationale for support

While the Whitlam Government rushed to support remote incorporated Aboriginal groups with funding on the basis of its self-determination and Aboriginal land rights policies, in 1975 the DAA applied six criteria to assess eligibility to receive large developmental grants: precedents for government assistance, benefits to the community, consultation, implications of the request *not* being met, eligibility and economic feasibility. In Table 3.2, these criteria are presented (in bold); to illustrate

---

11   Rowley, 'Aboriginal Land Fund', 259.

their operational meaning in regard to the Gurindji, I have quoted the responses to each of a DAA Project Officer regarding the Gurindji's Muramulla Company.

Table 3.2: DAA 'Report on Application for Funds', 1975, Aboriginal cattle project funding assessment, Muramulla Cattle Company.

1. **Precedents for Government Assistance:** The Government has previously supported pastoral projects for Aboriginal community enterprises e.g. the Murin, Unia and Yugal cattle projects. In addition, the Government has accepted the Gurindji claim to the land and has promised to support the project;

2. **Benefits to the community:** The project will provide both regular and substantial employment and also provide significant long-term financial benefits, [such as] improved services for the community, resulting from the generation of funds from the pastoral project;

3. **Consultation:** Departmental officers have been in close liaison with the Daguragu Community, and the proposal is in accordance with the desires and ambitions of the community;

4. **Implications of the request *not* being met** [emphasis mine]: If the government did not provide funds to develop this area, the community would be most disappointed and perhaps even feel betrayed. There would undoubtedly be national publicity;

5. **Eligibility:** The Muramulla Company has nine Gurindji people as directors, each holding a one dollar share in trust for the Muramulla Gurindji Association, which represents the full Aboriginal community at Daguragu. Thus the Muramulla Company is eligible to receive assistance from the government;

6. **Economic feasibility:** The area involved was formerly part of the Wave Hill Station and this country is suitable for a pastoral property. Wave Hill Station has operated successfully for a number of years and the only factor that would vary the viability of the Muramulla Gurindji project from that of Wave Hill Station is its size. … The fact that the Department has divided Wave Hill Station lease may be construed as indicating that they consider the Muramulla Gurindji lease as being sufficient for a viable pastoral project.

Source: NAA E460, 1975/137.

The project officer's responses suggest a Whitlam Government predisposition to support the Gurindji's Muramulla operation on flimsy or assumed grounds, as we see below:

1. **Precedents for government assistance:** The use of government assistance 'precedents' to justify the provision of further government assistance is largely self-supporting.

2. **Benefits to the community:** The 'benefits to the community' perceived by the DAA are listed without any evidence. They are apparently justified by the assumption that a private company (Muramulla) should or could legally fulfil a (municipal?) service provision role within a 'community'.

3. **Consultation:** Records show that prior consultation by departmental officers had not reflected 'close liaison with the Daguragu Community', and neither had it successfully identified the actual nature of 'the desires and ambitions' of the 'community'. Instead, extremely rushed consultations conducted in 1973 had focused on determining whether the land sought by the Gurindji might possibly be converted into a conventionally managed, profitable cattle station.[12]

4. **Implications of the request *not* being met:** While Wattie Creek had been the object of the ALP (Australian Labor Party)'s remedial intentions for eight years (1967–75), the bureaucracy was under pressure to resolve the Gurindji's situation as quickly as possible.

5. **Eligibility:** In light of the intergenerational tension affecting many Aboriginal groups in the period (discussed below), any claim that an organ derivative of the elders' Muramulla Company (or any other incorporated body) was representative of a 'full Aboriginal community' is highly suspect.

6. **Economic feasibility:** The claim that the Gurindji leasehold was 'suitable for a pastoral property [because] Wave Hill Station has operated successfully [on it] for a number of years' fails to take into account both the larger size of the station and the variability of country within a financially viable pastoral lease. The area excised by the Vestey company for the Gurindji comprised the poorest pastoral country of Wave Hill Station.

The origins of many ACEs' misfortunes can be gleaned from the DAA's justification of the Muramulla Company's initial funding. In 1975 the government believed that the use to which the Gurindji would put their lease had already been decided by the Gurindji and the government, and that this understanding had been developed with the Gurindji's full knowledge and participation. By such means, pronounced contradictions and elisions characterised ACEs' structure and operations.

The government's confidence that the Gurindji knew what they wanted and that the government could provide it matched the new rhetoric of self-determination policy, but it was disingenuous to claim that the legal and financial terms of the Muramulla 'proposal is in accordance with the desires and ambitions of the community'. While it was true that the entire

---

12   'Visit of AACM Representatives … to Wave Hill Station, Libanungu and Daguragu', 13–16 June 1973, NAA F985, 1972/1049.

Muramulla Board had signed a statement requesting 'a big station … same as other people have got it', there is no evidence that the full financial management, property development and corporate governance implications of such statements had been explained to this group of Aboriginal elders; nor is there evidence that the Gurindji grasped the extent to which the industry itself had changed in the decade since they had terminated their routine employment in it.[13] In conversations with the Muramulla proponents, DAA and Australian Agricultural Consultancy Management (AACM) staff had proposed a conventional pastoral station business model, yet these conversations did not include the time-consuming, expert-facilitated process required to develop a shared understanding of what this might mean for the Gurindji.[14] Wishing to minimise perceptions of financial indiscretion and profligacy, the Whitlam Government and its successor had also promoted a mainstream 'non-Aboriginal' model of animal husbandry. In 1973, DAA staff had opined that 'the manner in which the Gurindji [operate] the project will … *depend on the terms of the Government* making finance available for securing the lease and establishing the project [emphasis added]'.[15] For such officials, consultation about ACEs' 'manner' of operation was ultimately unnecessary. According to its internal reasoning, the government could create an 'Aboriginal' project for the Gurindji simply by giving that label to a project designed on the government's terms. Further, according to the DAA:

> *The basis of costing and income estimation are* [sic] *determined as for a non-Aboriginal project.* It is probable that the income of an Aboriginal-operated project will be less and the costs greater if professional management is not provided [emphasis added].[16]

By requiring that the Muramulla enterprise be supervised by two literate, management-experienced, pastoral industry advisers, the government imposed a 'non-Aboriginal project' model on the Gurindji and other groups. For the DAA and the various governments that would deal with ACEs, financial accountability and profit-maximisation were paramount. How these were achieved and the extent of Aboriginal management was functionally unimportant.

---

13   Committee of Muramulla Gurindji Company to Managing Director of Vestey, [12 December 1970], Oke Personal Collection.

14   'Visit of AACM Representatives … to Wave Hill Station, Libanungu and Daguragu', 13–16 June 1973, NAA F985, 1972/1049.

15   'Muramulla Gurindji Co Pty Ltd – Directors Report', 1 June 1977, NAA F1, 1975/4091.

16   'Muramulla Gurindji Co Pty Ltd – Directors Report', 1 June 1977, NAA F1, 1975/4091.

Unarticulated and contrasting Aboriginal visions

In addition to lacking financial and governance knowledge, the Aboriginal leaders of ACEs pursued goals at cross-purposes with, and sometimes unknown to, government officials. They intended that any of their language group who sought food and/or an income from their cattle operations would be provided for, yet the companies they ostensibly managed were designed to employ fewer than a dozen individuals on each station, with negligible profits. Anthropologist Gillian Cowlishaw describes a common situation: the government-employed cattle adviser and consultant working with the Jandi cattle company at Jimboingal near Katherine were ignorant of the aims, priorities and social structure of the Aboriginal group that nominally led the enterprise.[17] Officials were more indifferent to Indigenous cattle goals than the rhetoric of self-determination policy purported them to be, and it is questionable whether governments would have regulated ACEs more flexibly and/or subsidised them more generously had they known Aboriginal cattle aspirations better.

As board members of proprietary companies, Aboriginal elders were required to contribute to organisational governance, but their past experience had not equipped them to provide financial oversight. The implementation of self-determination policy therefore required apparent mistruths and elisions from them, solicited by those working in their name and resulting in implausible 'Directors' Reports', which included statements from old Indigenous stockmen, lacking formal education such as the following:

> The Directors submit the accounts of the Company and report as follows: [We have taken] reasonable steps, before the profit and loss statement and balance sheet were made out, to ascertain what action had been taken in relation to the writing off of bad debts and the making of provisions for doubtful debts [etc.].[18]

For such statements to be true, their signatories would have required training in English literacy and business. Rather than explain matters to Indigenous board members, non-Indigenous members of the enterprises'

---

17 See Cowlishaw, 'Blackfella Boss'.
18 'Muramulla Gurindji Co Pty Ltd – Directors Report', 1 June 1977, NAA F1, 1975/4091.

advisory, funding, staffing and operational arms frequently attempted to retain their authority over what they perceived as their areas of operation. Very few individuals within the Gurindji enterprises or in the 'support' organisations of their interlocutors possessed the local, financial, entrepreneurial, pastoral, ecological and Aboriginal/social knowledge required, yet the sectoral need for such training was not acted on until the 1980s.[19]

Even in domains in which Aboriginal workers believed themselves to be highly skilled, such as the management of herds, there were conflicts between 'white'/'modern' and 'Aboriginal' approaches. Gurindji cattlemen, for instance, vowed that their enterprise would never muster by plane, despite sustained pressure from the Muramulla Company's funding bodies, often relayed through the consultant agronomist they had been forced to employ.[20] Their resolute refusal can be interpreted in different ways: as their failure to appreciate economic imperatives and as a public 'statement' affirming the elders' own abilities and their strong belief in the value of cattle work for their sons and nephews – whatever the cost. It is not clear whether the DAA's officers appreciated that the elders' true motives in 'running cattle' were more about the continuation of a certain culture of work than about the creation of a business enterprise.

Cowlishaw points out that the non-Indigenous protagonists of ACEs frequently failed to realise or underplayed the fact that conflicts within ACEs took place in a context of unequal power that '[was] created by, and effectively protects, the wider economic and political structures'.[21] The conflicts that plagued ACEs were not, in other words, only 'between cultures, but between groups of people with different access to resources'.[22] ACEs' non-Indigenous intermediaries either did not understand that they embodied Anglo-European governmental values or did not wish to question those values; rarely did they explain or question the regulations, statutes, social conventions and laws in which these values were encoded. Rather, the encoding of these cultural principles revealed to the Aboriginal people that their own values and knowledge were of limited importance. This recognition frequently hastened the withdrawal of Aboriginal people from what they saw as essentially 'whitefella' operations.

---

19 Lovegrove [DAA] to Muramulla, 3 March 1976, NAA E460, 1981/256, Part 2.
20 'Report and Financials ...', September 1978', NAA E629, 1978/7/7581.
21 Cowlishaw, 'Blackfella Boss', 68.
22 Cowlishaw, 'Blackfella Boss', 61.

In addition to being somewhat handicapped by their hybridity, ACEs could not control global beef prices or governments' policies and financial support. The Fraser Government (elected 13 December 1975) reduced funds to the entire Aboriginal Affairs portfolio, and a phase of increasing emphasis on profitability by funding bodies began.[23] This increasingly adversarial political and ideological environment was exacerbated when the Australian Parliament granted self-government to the Northern Territory in July 1978.[24] More challenging to ACEs was the federal Brucellosis and Tuberculosis Eradication Campaign (BTEC), however.

Brucellosis and Tuberculosis Eradication Campaign

BTEC required that all pastoralists in the nation would capture and test every beast on their land (a feat never achieved before), destroy any infected animals, and build any fencing required to properly manage their herd in the future.[25] Although the federal government assisted landholders with the costs of de- and re-stocking, the Commonwealth reported that, 'as the campaign proceeds into the difficult parts of northern Australia, the costs of eradication rise rapidly, raising doubts about the ability of cattle producers to meet these costs and remain viable'.[26] Experts described BTEC as 'undoubtedly the most significant factor to impact on the industry since World War II'.[27] At the time, one experienced consultant warned that it might 'destroy' the Aboriginal pastoral sector.[28] According to an expert:

> BTEC's approach to disease eradication forced the modernisation of the pastoral industry, with disproportionate impact on the Aboriginal sector. The historical mode of pastoralism in the NT was deemed no longer adequate to meet the demands of the modern international cattle market. Until the 1970s, cattle control in Northern and Central Australia had been sporadic and incomplete. The owners of most properties had made their living from irregular harvests of what were essentially feral populations. Other stations

---

23 Lovegrove [DAA] to Muramulla, 3 March 1976, NAA E460, 1981/256, Part 2.
24 Jaensch and Loveday, *Under One Flag*, 5.
25 Department of Agriculture, Fisheries and Forestry, 'Eradication Success'.
26 Stoneham and Johnson, 'Australian Brucellosis', 2.
27 Hanlon and Phillpot, *Rural Development*, 28.
28 Hanlon, 'Aboriginal Pastoral', 187.

had generally mustered once a year, with no expectation that all cattle would be accounted for. Very few stations had the yards, races and crushes needed for branding; stockmen lassoed the calves and pulled them to the ground. Even on company-owned stations in the most productive cattle country, there had been virtually no separation of different classes of cattle.[29]

Corporations owning multiple properties had already modernised before the BTEC. According to Graeme Fagan, the manager of Wave Hill Station, by the early 1980s the station's wealthy owner had ensured that:

[Cattle] were mustered twice a year, regardless of BTEC. … We did four rounds a year of branding and weaning. We had paddocks where we could isolate cattle – 'tail-tag' paddocks they were called. You could have three or four [such paddocks, and] cattle couldn't move out of them … until you tested them.[30]

Such standards remained far beyond the reach of the Muramulla Company and most ACEs. Instead, their board members were increasingly marginalised and alienated by the industry's growing, technologised managerialism – a characteristic of the 'new pastoralism' of which they had no previous experience.

Generally, the position of Aboriginal cattle operations in a marginal industry was more tenuous than that of their competitors. They were usually new and relatively undeveloped leaseholds, and were thus required to do more work to meet the campaign's requirements. Their proponents also had little or no experience with the financial aspects of long-term herd management on which they could rely to 'ride out' the effects of BTEC. Nonetheless, unlike other 'mandatory' conditions placed on pastoralists by the state, non-compliance with BTEC was not an option. The primary condition of an approved plan was that a lessee be able to reliably test their entire herd. When the lessee was unable to do so, the government killed untested animals and paid the lessee compensation for their loss.[31] Unable to commit themselves to an approved disease eradication plan, all but three of the ACE leases in the Northern Territory were fully or partially destocked during BTEC.[32]

---

29 Lehane, *Beating the Odds*, 230.
30 Graeme Fagan interviewed by Charlie Ward, September 2012, NTRS 3609, BWF 42, Northern Territory Archives Service, Darwin.
31 Lehane, *Beating the Odds*, 196.
32 Phillpot, 'Black pastoralism', 338–39.

We should not assume that BTEC affected all ACEs in the same way. Like the Daguragu lease, the holdings of the Puraiya Cattle Company were destocked under BTEC during 1980–83. By 1996 it had recovered sufficiently to achieve some commercial viability, albeit on the basis of substantial subsidies. According to Phillpot, while the terms under which the company was established and its leasehold purchased were inimical to the Anmatyere people's self-determination and self-management, the shareholders of the company (six Anmatyere families) received ongoing material benefit.[33] In contrast, the Ngarliyikirlangu Pastoral Company at Yuendumu met BTEC requirements. Despite this success, its variable funding arrangements, staffing issues and a lack of training combined with poor markets and climatic conditions to render it unviable by 1996.[34]

Intergenerational dissociation

Regardless of the significantly 'European' composition of their cattle operations, ACEs' elderly Aboriginal leaders commonly intended to transfer the management of their enterprise to their descendants. Complicating this process was a combination of economic, social and technological factors that combined to hasten processes of intergenerational social dissociation, however. To understand how these disaggregative social processes impacted ACEs and other government-funded Aboriginal organisations, it is necessary to describe the clash between the structure and social norms cohering Aboriginal societies and the social policies of the Whitlam Government that were then integrating remote Indigenous Australians into Australia's economy. Increasing monetary income of Aboriginal people from wages and social welfare enfranchised and individualised them as consumers. Many remote Aboriginal people, especially the young, embraced aspects of this social change with enthusiasm, while the older cohort were commonly resistant.

A disaggregative impulse had been present within remote groups such as the Gurindji for decades. Anthropologists in the 1930s–50s observed that young Gurindji men and women were reluctant to fully participate in the ceremonial life valued by their elders.[35] Another significant source of intergenerational tension was the monopolisation of young women's

33 Phillpot, 'Black Pastoralism', 237.
34 Phillpot, 'Black Pastoralism', 280.
35 Berndt, *Women's Changing*, 63.

sexuality by older men, according to Aboriginal societies' systems of kinship. Polygyny was practised, and kinship systems – mostly as interpreted and enforced by male elders – determined which man a woman might marry. Anecdotal evidence and ethnographic research across remote regions of Australia suggest that, increasingly in the post-contact era, many young women harboured resentment towards male elders for forcing them into unwanted unions, and many young men likewise resented the same elders for 'taking' their potential partners.[36] Catherine Berndt believed such tensions were so widespread that she described 'young people who were enticed by the prospect of brighter lights and greener pastures' as the 'Trojan Horse' compounding the difficulties of older Aboriginal people in resisting what they saw as the damaging effects of their society's engagement with the settler mainstream.[37] Anthropologist Les Hiatt argued that the inequitable distribution of power within Aboriginal society made it 'vulnerable to external challenge and susceptible to internal collapse'.[38] Similar tensions within Gurindji society were paralleled in hundreds of other Indigenous groups across Australia.

Rapid dissociation among members of Aboriginal societies occurred in the 1970s–80s, exacerbated by the payment of award wages to Aboriginal male pastoral workers from December 1968. More jobs outside the pastoral industry were available in the 1970s, mostly in the new 'Aboriginal' organisations, and unemployment benefits were also easier to obtain. The increasing availability of cash had powerful equalising and destabilising effects on remote societies, which were unaccustomed to regular surplus. Notwithstanding the obligations of remote Indigenous people's kinship-based, demand sharing economies, this equalisation of income empowered young adults in relation to their powerful elders.[39] According to anthropologist David Martin, among the Wik people in North Queensland, 'having an independent income allowed individuals – if they so choose – to obtain basic necessities such as food outside the network of reciprocal rights and obligation of the Wik domain'.[40] These changes greatly facilitated young people's independence from their parents' generation and bolstered their ability to resist the demands of their elders regarding their employment and much else.

---

36 McKnight, *Going the Whiteman's*, xix–xxvi.
37 Berndt, 'Out of the frying pan', 403.
38 Hiatt, *Arguments About*, 98.
39 Sansom, *The Camp*, 254; Rowse, 'From Houses', 56.
40 Martin, 'Autonomy', 117.

Intergenerational transfer of leadership within ACEs was also undermined in other ways. Young Aboriginal men who worked or who may have wished to work in the industry found that mainstream cattle stations paid better than ACEs subsidised by the federal government's Community Development Employment Projects (CDEP) scheme. By the early 1980s, Muramulla employed their Indigenous staff via participation in Daguragu Council's CDEP scheme. Under CDEP arrangements, a subsidised allowance was paid to company staff via Daguragu Council, but even with 'top-up' from Muramulla, the amount was short of the award paid on mainstream commercial stations. In addition, Aboriginal youth, increasingly influenced by Western values and by their long-term occupation of housing, were less interested in pastoral work.[41]

Conclusion

In 1986, members of the Muramulla Board conceded privately that the Gurindji's cattle enterprise – and their property – was getting away from them. Muramulla remained a 'strictly European legal animal', and by the time governance training – its board members' first – was planned, cattle work had become an occasional, recreational pursuit.[42] When Muramulla was liquidated in the late 1980s after being destocked by BTEC, the elders' most valued 'pillar' of Gurindji self-determination collapsed. Other ACEs also declined, as Phillpot describes. In 1980, 28 ACEs were operating in the Northern Territory; by 1988, there were 12.[43] By the mid-1990s, there were only six subsidised ACEs functioning in the Territory. In combination with drought, lower beef prices and BTEC, funding bodies' exclusive criterion of commercial viability made an increasing number of ACEs unviable.

Although ACEs were created to cater to the cattle-related aspirations of Aboriginal leaders, they were corporate entities built on unstable and incongruous foundations. ACEs were designed by government officers and their advisers to function, if need be, without the input or labour of their Aboriginal protagonists and intended beneficiaries. The regulatory and funding framework for ACEs differed little from that guiding their mainstream competitors. What distinguished ACEs from the rest of the

---

41 Graeme Fagan interviewed by Charlie Ward, September 2012, NTRS 3609, BWF 42, 110–14.
42 Eames [CLC] to Muramulla, 19 January 1977, NAA E242, K9/2/3.
43 Phillpot, 'Black Pastoralism', 350.

pastoral industry was their greater engagement with government, by virtue of their reliance on government funding. While governments intended to build Aboriginal capacity and accountability under self-determination policies, ACEs' often experienced government intervention as directly inimical of their own decision-making and authority. The social policies of the era and the internal dynamics of the remote Indigenous social order also forced the gerontocratic authority of ACEs' leadership into further decline.

References

Archival sources

Oke Personal Collection

National Archives of Australia (NAA)

NAA E242, K9/2/3, Libanungu Daguragu [Department of Aboriginal Affairs]. NAA, Darwin

NAA E460, 1975/137, Muramulla Gurindji Company – Pastoral, 1975–79

NAA E460, 1981/256 Part 2, Muramulla Gurindji Co. Pastoral Project

NAA E629, 1978/7/7581, Department of Aboriginal Affairs – Project documentation – Murumulla [Muramulla] Gurindji – cattle project

NAA F1, 1975/4091, Cattle mustering venture – Aboriginal Co – Wave Hill/ Wattie Creek – Muramulla Gurindji Co

NAA F985, 1972/1049, Wave Hill Station – Matters Affecting Aborigines

Northern Territory Archives Service (NTAS)

NTRS 3609, BWF 42

Other sources

Berndt, Catherine H. 'Out of the Frying Pan...? Or, Back to Square One?' In *Aborigines and Change: Australia in the 70s*, edited by R. M. Berndt, 402–11. Canberra: Australian Institute of Aboriginal Studies, 1977.

Berndt, Catherine H. *Women's Changing Ceremonies in Northern Australia*. Paris: Hermann, 1950.

Berndt, Ronald and Catherine Berndt. *End of an Era: Aboriginal Labour in the Northern Territory*. Canberra: Australian Institute of Aboriginal Studies, 1987.

Cowlishaw, Gillian. 'Blackfella Boss: A Study of a Northern Territory Cattle Station'. *Social Analysis*, no. 13 (May 1983): 54–69.

Department of Agriculture, Fisheries and Forestry. 'Eradication Success Story: Australia Is Free of *Brucella Abortus*'. Accessed 6 January 2020. www.agriculture. gov.au/sites/default/files/sitecollectiondocuments/animal-plant/animal-health/ pet-food-safety/brucella-abortus-colour.docx.

Gibb, Cecil (chair). *The Report of the Committee to Review the Situation of Aborigines on Pastoral Properties in the Northern Territory*. Canberra: Commonwealth Government Printer's Office, 1973.

Hamilton, Annette. 'Aboriginal Women: The Means of Production'. In *The Other Half: Women in Australian Society*, edited by Jan Mercer, 167–79. Ringwood, Vic.: Penguin Books, 1975.

Hanlon, David. 'The Aboriginal Pastoral Industry: A Conflict of Development Objectives'. In *Ecology Management of the World's Savannas*, edited by J. C. Tothill and J. J. Mott, 85–189. Canberra: Australian Academy of Science, 1985.

Hanlon, David and Stuart Phillpot. *Rural Development Skills: Can We Meet the Challenge? Volume 2*. Report prepared for Department of Employment, Education and Training by R. C. S. Hassall. Springhill, Qld: R.C.S. Hassall Pty Ltd, 1993.

Hiatt, L. R. *Arguments about Aborigines: Australia and the Evolution of Social Anthropology*. Melbourne: Cambridge University Press, 1996.

Jaensch, Dean and Peter Loveday. *Under One Flag: The 1980 Northern Territory Election*. North Sydney: Allen & Unwin, 1981.

Lehane, Robert. *Beating the Odds in a Big Country: The Eradication of Bovine Brucellosis and Tuberculosis in Australia*. Collingwood, Vic.: CSIRO Publishing, 1996. doi.org/10.1071/9780643100756.

McKnight, David. *Going the Whiteman's Way: Kinship and Marriage among Australian Aborigines*. Aldershot, England: Ashgate, 2004.

Martin, David. 'Autonomy and Relatedness: An Ethnography of the Wik People of Aurukun, Western Cape York Peninsula'. PhD thesis, The Australian National University, 1993.

Palmer, Ian. *Buying Back the Land: Organisational Struggle and the Aboriginal Land Fund Commission*. Canberra: Aboriginal Studies Press, 1988.

Peterson, Nicolas. 'Capitalism, Culture and Land Rights: Aborigines and the State in the Northern Territory'. *Social Analysis: The International Journal of Social and Cultural Practice*, no. 18 (December 1985): 85–101.

Phillpot, Stuart. 'Black Pastoralism: Contemporary Aboriginal Land Use – the Experience of Aboriginal-Owned Pastoral Enterprises in the Northern Territory, 1972–1996'. PhD thesis, The Australian National University, 2000.

Rowley, Charles. 'The Aboriginal Land Fund Commission: 1974–1980'. In *Aboriginal Land Rights: A Handbook*, edited by Nicolas Peterson, 254–66. Canberra: Australian Institute of Aboriginal Studies, 1981.

Rowse, Tim. 'From Houses to Households? The Aboriginal Development Commission and Economic Adaptation by Alice Springs Town Campers'. *Social Analysis* 24 (1988): 50–65.

Rowse, Tim. *White Flour, White Power: From Rations to Citizenship in Central Australia*. Melbourne: Cambridge University Press, 1998. doi.org/10.1086/ahr/104.4.1283-a.

Sansom, Basil. *The Camp at Wallaby Cross: Aboriginal Fringe Dwellers in Darwin*. Canberra: Australian Institute of Aboriginal Studies, 1980. doi.org/10.1017/s0047404500010435.

Stoneham, Gary and Joe Johnston. 'The Australian Brucellosis and Tuberculosis Eradication Campaign: An Economic Evaluation of Options for Finalising the Campaign in Northern Australia'. *Bureau of Agricultural Economics: Occasional Paper*, no. 97. Canberra: Australian Government Publishing Service, 1987.

Ward, Charlie. 'Gurindji People and Aboriginal Self-Determination Policy, 1973–86'. PhD thesis, Western Sydney University, 2017.

Whitlam, Edward Gough. 'Aboriginals and Society – Statement by the Prime Minister, the Hon. E. G. Whitlam, Q.C., M.P., to the Ministerial Australian Aboriginal Affairs Council in Adelaide on 6 April 1973'. Press Statement no. 74, Department of the Prime Minister and Cabinet, 6 April 1973.

4

UNMET POTENTIAL

The Commonwealth Indigenous managed capital funds and self-determination

M. C. Dillon[1]

Introduction

Since the late 1960s, a strand of Indigenous policy has focused on the establishment of separate capital funds for a number of related, but conceptually distinct purposes. This chapter focuses on the development, rationales and operations of two longstanding and largely Indigenous managed Commonwealth entities: Indigenous Business Australia (IBA); and the Indigenous Land Corporation (ILC) and its associated Land Fund (LF).[2] There are similar entities operating in state and territory jurisdictions, and Indigenous interests have themselves established a number of capital funds in different contexts.

---

1   I wish to acknowledge the helpful comments of Tim Rowse, Laura Rademaker, Neil Westbury and Jon Altman on earlier drafts of this chapter. Of course, responsibility for the content is entirely mine.

Declaration of interest: The author was personally involved in a number of the matters discussed in this paper: he worked on the development of the ATSIC legislation, including the Commercial Development Corporation (CDC), and on the development of the *Native Title Act* and the subsequent LF legislation. He worked for three federal ministers responsible for Indigenous affairs at various times between 1986 and 2011, and worked for the ILC from 2013 to 2015.

2   Each of these entities has undergone various name changes. IBA was originally named the Aboriginal and Torres Strait Islander Commercial Development Corporation. While this book was in press, the ILC was renamed the Indigenous Land and Sea Corporation. The LF, which was originally named the Aboriginal and Torres Strait Islander Land Fund and is currently titled the Aboriginal and Torres Strait Islander Land Account was, as of 1 July 2019, renamed the Aboriginal and Torres Strait Islander Land and Sea Future Fund.

This chapter explores the effectiveness of IBA and the ILC/LF in contributing to Indigenous self-determination to identify approaches that may operate more generally to advance self-determination in public sector capital funds.

Capital funds and self-determination

For almost 50 years, the notion of self-determination has been at the heart of Indigenous policy in Australia. Facilitating Indigenous citizens to make choices about the ways in which they engage with the wider Australian society has been a key driver for policy design and policymakers' rhetoric since the establishment of the Council for Aboriginal Affairs in 1967.[3] Self-determination through increased involvement in decision-making at all levels has been a longstanding aspiration of Indigenous people.

The salience of self-determination for both policymakers and Indigenous people has varied, but the idea of self-determination retains significant normative force throughout this period, notwithstanding the varying definitional interpretations, emphases and levels of commitment that infuse any discussion of the concept. While the policy of self-determination replaced policies directed to assimilation, in substantive terms, self-determination does not rule out Indigenous choices to assimilate. In addition, the 'shadow' of assimilationist policy continued well into the era of self-determination, embedded in institutions both formal and informal. For present purposes, therefore, assimilation ought not to be seen as the opposite of self-determination.

In tracing the evolution of IBA and the ILC/LF over the past half-century, the present analysis identifies the policy intentions behind the multiple innovations and reforms wherever possible, but is more concerned to identify their actual outcomes against the yardstick of strengthening self-determination.[4] The specification of such a yardstick is itself open to multiple formulations. The broad approach adopted here focuses on substance rather than rhetoric and, following Wilson and Selle, emphasises two complementary elements of self-determination: degrees of autonomy

---

3   Rowse, *Obliged*, 30.
4   Because most policy innovations are the product of negotiation and iterative development processes, it is extremely rare for there to be a single policy intention involved. As well, most policy innovations have unintended consequences both positive and negative. These factors reinforce the utility of focusing on outcomes over intention.

or self-rule, and levels of participation and influence over decisions on matters that affect Indigenous people.[5] While these elements can operate at local, regional or national levels (both IBA and the ILC/LF are Commonwealth entities with nationwide remits) the yardstick is applied at a national level.

There are at least two ways in which government-established capital funds might facilitate self-determination of Indigenous citizens. The first, and potentially most significant, emerges if the funds raise the economic and/or political status of Indigenous peoples generally. Even an ostensibly compensatory fund such as the ILC/LF can have the effect of advancing Indigenous interests economically and politically (and thus advancing self-determination) through the restitution of expropriated assets. This focus on the achievement of substantive and formal policy aims could be termed the 'outcomes perspective' on self-determination. Implicit in it are assumptions regarding Indigenous world views and choices that may not in fact be accurate for all Indigenous groups or individuals.

The second way these funds might facilitate self-determination is by enabling Indigenous representatives to make decisions related to each capital fund's operations and, in particular, the disbursement of investment income. This might be termed the 'process perspective' on self-determination. Government-appointed boards, which comprise a majority of Indigenous members, govern both IBA and the ILC, raising fundamental questions regarding self-determination. But who do those appointed represent, to whom are they accountable, and how independent can they be from ministers and the government (even if legislation provides for formal independence)? Importantly, the LF was originally conceptualised as holding funds in trust for Indigenous interests, akin to a fiduciary relationship. The statute establishing the LF specified automatic drawdowns of funds from the LF to the ILC that were not subject to ministerial discretion. Nonetheless, the executive arm of government, assisted by an advisory committee that included ILC representation, retained control over the LF's investment policy.

The 'outcome' and 'process' senses of self-determination are often in tension, so that IBA and the ILC/LF have needed to trade off desired 'outcomes' against adherence to ideal 'process'.

---

5   Wilson and Selle, 'Indigenous', 8–12.

Indigenous Business Australia

The genesis of IBA is the *Aboriginal Enterprise (Assistance) Act 1968*. This law established a fund to which Aboriginal people could apply for business related loans.[6] Tim Rowse describes this legislation as one of the Council for Aboriginal Affairs's (CAA) 'few political victories of 1968'.[7] He documents the role of the CAA in advocating for 'programs to develop and strengthen the capacity of Aboriginal people to manage their own affairs' and notes that this terminology was soon referred to by others as 'self-determination'.[8] From the very beginning, the capital fund policies were intended by the CAA to advance self-determination broadly defined. This capital fund was rolled into the Aboriginal Loans Commission in 1974, which in turn was subsumed within the Aboriginal Development Commission (ADC) in 1980.

The continuing policy thread or rationale weaving through each of these institutional iterations was to help Indigenous business operators to access capital. A deeper, and questionable, policy assumption that emerged over time was that Indigenous economic development must involve the development of Indigenous-owned or controlled commercial enterprises, rather than merely raise Indigenous income levels. This assumption has its origins in assimilationist or anti-communal ideas as well as in progressive ideas linked to self-determination and Indigenous aspirations for autarky (at least in economic terms). The increased focus on Indigenous procurement policies over the last decade is the most recent embodiment of this assumption. A parallel issue (discussed below) is the tension between communally based land acquisitions and more individualised support for housing loans and finance.

In 1985, the *Report of the Committee of Review of Aboriginal Employment and Training Programs* (the Miller Report), which included Mick Miller as chair and Dr H. C. Coombs as a key member, provided the first major policy assessment of federal government economic programs in Indigenous affairs. The Miller Report was explicitly critical of the ADC for prioritising the funding of housing over enterprise development. The report recommended that the government transfer responsibility

---

6   I will refer to IBA as a 'fund' because it comprises a significant and growing financial asset embedded within a statutory corporation with a remit to use its resources for Indigenous benefit.

7   Rowse, *Obliged*, 40.

8   Rowse, *Obliged*, 107.

for the support of commercially viable small businesses from the ADC to a new unit in the Commonwealth Development Bank.[9] While this recommendation was never adopted, the analysis fed into the momentum for a new approach to supporting Indigenous economic development.

In 1989, the Hawke Government established the Aboriginal and Torres Strait Islander Commercial Development Corporation (CDC) at the same time as it legislated the Aboriginal and Torres Strait Islander Commission (ATSIC). Breaking from the previous approach, the CDC was a largely Indigenous-led corporation with a statutory remit to invest and take up equity positions in commercial projects relevant to Indigenous interests. A small capital base ($10 million (m) per annum over four years plus the transfer of ADC assets of around $10m) funded these investments. The rationale for this new approach was less to provide access to capital for Indigenous businesses (an autonomy focus) and more to build Indigenous political and economic influence at local and regional levels (a participation focus). CDC sought to make strategic investments in key businesses within regional economies, and thus gain access to the business and political networks that had excluded Indigenous interests. The prototype was an Indigenous-owned corporation, Centrecorp, that invested a proportion of royalty revenues in businesses that would particularly benefit Indigenous residents of Central Australia.

In 2001, the Howard Government renamed the CDC 'Indigenous Business Australia'. In 2005, the abolition of ATSIC led to further legislative change. ATSIC's enterprise loan function, and the housing loan function that ATSIC had inherited from the ADC, transferred to IBA.[10] These changes added programs, funded by budget appropriations, that duplicated, albeit in concessional terms, a private sector bank's lending operations. They were therefore a reversion to the earlier 'access to capital' policy rationale. While IBA's investment remit was not affected, the 2005 changes returned IBA – at least in some years – to the annual budget appropriation process. Since its lending capability was based on funds appropriated by government, IBA was more beholden to government.

9   Miller, *Report*, 303–11.
10   *Aboriginal and Torres Strait Islander Amendment Act 2005* (Cth).

In practice, IBA continued to favour housing over enterprise. By June 2017, IBA controlled net assets of $1.33 billion (bn), up from $987m in 2008–09 and $81m in 2003. Over half ($679m) were concessional home loans, only $30m (or 2 per cent) were enterprise loans, with the balance in a range of investments and cash, term deposits and an unspecified category termed 'other'.[11] Thus, IBA ignored the Miller Report's critique of underinvestment in enterprise support. Furthermore, while these lending decisions built an asset base, they also made IBA primarily a housing loan provider, changing and undermining IBA's character. Notwithstanding this emphasis on housing finance, IBA continues to support Indigenous entrepreneurs and small business owners and also invests directly in commercial opportunities via partial or full ownership of around 20 active subsidiary corporations.[12]

In recent years, IBA has also become a fund manager. In 2013, it established an Indigenous Real Estate Investment Trust (REIT), and in 2015 it established a number of 'prosperity funds'. IBA's intention in each case was to provide a secure vehicle for Indigenous investors to invest in a diversified and actively managed portfolio. The minimum investment is set at $500,000, suggesting that IBA is primarily seeking to support Indigenous landowners and native titleholders who gain money from agreements with resource developers. According to the IBA website, as at June 2016, the IBA REIT was invested in six commercial properties and had a value of $102m; the prosperity funds comprise separate growth, income and cash funds, and have a gross asset value of $78m. According to its 2017 Annual Report, IBA provided investment support to 109 Indigenous organisations, and co-invested with 36 Indigenous investors holding a total of $129m in equity.[13] This suggests that the IBA equity contribution to the funds is $51m ($129m minus $78m).

How should we assess the performance of IBA in relation to its statutory remit, and the overarching policy challenge of Indigenous economic development?

---

11 Indigenous Business Australia, *Annual Report 2016–17*, 105.
12 Indigenous Business Australia, *Annual Report 2016–17*, 156.
13 Indigenous Business Australia, *Annual Report 2016–17*, 9.

IBA's three major programs are all worthwhile, and its design is fundamentally sound. However, over its 30-year history, IBA has made only a marginal contribution to improving Indigenous economic status and it has not increased significantly the political and economic influence of regional Indigenous interests. Not only has IBA been under-capitalised, but also its boards have concentrated on concessional home loans at the expense of making strategic commercial investments. While concessional home loans do build Indigenous wealth, it is unclear whether the same quantity of home loans could have been provided by private sector institutions. If IBA home loans are merely substitutes for loans that could be obtained from other lenders, then perhaps it would have been better for IBA to give priority to strategic investments. However, governments have encouraged the IBA Board's emphasis on concessional home loans, and this may also be what Indigenous Australians prefer IBA to do, as the benefits of home ownership accrue in much more targeted ways than the more abstracted political benefits of increased commercial engagement. An Indigenous constituency favouring IBA home loans over strategic commercial investment may be growing as the Indigenous population in south-eastern Australia grows.[14]

While IBA continues to give priority to home lending, it has also renewed focus on the investment portfolio and on managed funds. The Indigenous corporations that face the challenge of managing their financial assets sustainably welcome both. However, IBA and its predecessor the CDC have never been funded sufficiently to lift the economic status of the Indigenous population generally (around 650,000 individuals in the 2016 Census). Moreover, the impact of IBA's strategic investments in changing the structural underpinnings of Indigenous economic and commercial exclusion has been slight, given the magnitude of the challenges facing Indigenous Australians. In terms of self-determination, IBA has been unsuccessful in driving major improvements in Indigenous autonomy and has been unable to increase substantially Indigenous influence within mainstream decision-making.

---

14   Markham and Biddle, 'Indigenous', 2017.

Indigenous Land Corporation and the associated Aboriginal and Torres Strait Islander Land Account

The antecedent of the ILC and the associated Land Fund was the Aboriginal Land Fund Commission (ALFC), established in 1975.[15] Notwithstanding its name, and the formal creation of a 'fund', the ALFC got its money from annual appropriations of the Australian Government Budget. While there was a commitment to make $50m available over 10 years,[16] even in its first year the ALFC was allocated only $2m. Palmer outlined the ALFC's five-year struggle for funding: when the Department of Aboriginal Affairs (DAA) decided in 1976 to offer up $1m of the original allocation as savings, the ALFC refused to repay the funds.[17] In this dispute, the DAA and the ALFC were in conflict over policy. A series of ministerial directives constrained the ALFC's ability to acquire properties without consulting the department and gaining the minister's approval.

The ADC replaced the ALFC in 1980. Four functional responsibilities came together within the ADC: enterprise support, housing, training and land acquisition. Because of the ADC's commitments to enterprises and housing – inherited from the Department of Aboriginal Affairs – ADC funds for land acquisition were limited. The Miller Report lamented that in the transition from ALFC to ADC the concept of a fund dedicated to supporting land acquisition had been lost. The need for land was even greater than when first noticed in 1972 and the report argued that the economic status of Aboriginal people had continued to deteriorate: 'We therefore recommend that immediate action be taken to re-establish a specific land fund vote within the ADC'.[18]

The overarching pressure of recurrent housing needs and the significant funding and policy effort involved in making even small land acquisitions pushed the ADC away from capital acquisitions and towards investment in a recurrent housing program. From 1980 to 1985, ADC expenditures totalled $279m. Of this, $178.7m or 64 per cent was allocated to housing

---

15 Ian Palmer's book *Buying Back the Land* recounts in detail the establishment of the ALFC and the bureaucratic policy struggles which dogged the ALFC's short lifespan (1975–79). Palmer, *Buying*.
16 Miller, *Report*, 318.
17 Palmer, *Buying*, 50–56.
18 Miller, *Report*, 319.

loans and grants, $38.2m or 13.6 per cent to enterprises, and only $9.5m or 3.4 per cent to land acquisition.[19] The Miller Report noted that, against the 1972 commitment to allocate $50m to land acquisition over 10 years, actual expenditure had been merely $17.5m.[20]

In 1989, the establishment of ATSIC effectively absorbed the ADC. Sections 14 and 15 of the Commonwealth *Aboriginal and Torres Strait Islander Commission Act 1989* empowered the commission to purchase and grant land. In addition, Section 68 established a Regional Land Fund (RLF) that enabled the regional councils that were constituent parts of ATSIC to accumulate funds for land acquisition. The RLF provisions were largely not utilised. ATSIC's major programs were the Community Development Employment Projects (CDEP) program, the community housing and infrastructure program and the law and justice program, and it continued the ADC approach of allocating little for land acquisition. In 1994–95, from a budget of around a billion dollars ATSIC spent $22m on the acquisition of 21 properties and on 282 land management projects.[21]

Following the High Court of Australia's Mabo no. 2 decision in 1992, the Commonwealth legislated to respond to the implications of 'native title'. The Keating Government's response to the High Court's recognition of 'native title' was intended to provide greater certainty for all interests, whether native title claimants, Indigenous landowners or third parties with potentially invalid titles. Certainty was no problem for most titles issued by the Crown, because the High Court had found that native title was entirely vulnerable to actions by the Crown that resulted in the issue of a title to a third party. However, titles granted by the Crown over native title since the enactment of the *Racial Discrimination Act 1975* (RDA) were now suspect. Any title issued since the RDA came into force on 31 October 1975 would be invalid because – without the Crown compensating for native title loss – such acts of extinguishment were inconsistent with the RDA's requirement that governments not act in a racially discriminatory way. This new obligation primarily affected titles issued by the states and territories since 31 October 1975, as the states and territories are primarily responsible for land administration and the Commonwealth Parliament has the power to amend or override

---

19   These figures were calculated from data provided in Palmer, *Buying*, 157. The balance of 19 per cent presumably related to administrative costs of the ADC.
20   Miller, *Report*, 319.
21   ATSIC, *Annual Report 1994–95*, chapter 4.

the RDA. One purpose of the *Native Title Act 1993* (NTA) was to set up a process that would validate any grants of title by the Crown that might be suspect, subject to the provision of 'just terms' compensation. However, the NTA offered nothing to native title owners whose native title right had been extinguished *prior to the commencement of the* RDA. By law, no compensation was due to these owners, because the High Court's judgement was that the Crown's extinguishment of native title had always been lawful. However, it was arguable that the difference between the native title holders who had to be compensated and those who did not have to be compensated was essentially arbitrary.[22]

The Keating Government agreed with Indigenous negotiators that governments had a moral and political obligation to purchase land for those legally dispossessed. Accordingly, Section 201 of the NTA established a Land Fund to assist Indigenous peoples to acquire land and to manage the acquired land in a way that provides economic, environmental, social and cultural benefits to the new owners. The Act effectively made clear that the purpose was not a narrowly defined focus on economic development. The operational details and quantum of funding allocated were to be set out in subsequent regulations. Within two years, the parliament enacted the *Land Fund and Indigenous Land Corporation (ATSIC Amendment) Act 1995*, which repealed and replaced Section 201 of the NTA. The process of parliamentary consideration was both long and contentious.[23]

The Keating and Howard governments built up the LF over 10 years, beginning with a payment of $200m and followed by payments of $121m (indexed) in each of the subsequent nine years. After 10 years, the value of the LF stood at $1.4bn. In the following 14 years, it has grown to just over $2bn. The establishment of the LF (which was renamed the Land Account in 2005) has raised three issues.

The first is how quickly the LF can accumulate funds and thus spending power. At the insistence of the Department of Finance, the legislation limited LF investments to a range of very conservative options – term deposits, government bonds and the like – that severely restricted the fund's potential growth. The ILC Board under each of the last three chairs (Shirley Macpherson, Dawn Casey and Eddie Fry) requested

---

22   Dillon, 'Emerging'.
23   Tickner provides a detailed account of the legislation's contentious passage. See Tickner, *Taking*, 221–36.

the government of the day to broaden the LF's investment parameters. The boards' persuasive arguments were that the Commonwealth Future Fund had performed well without such restrictions on its portfolio, over a period of strong performance since the 2007 global financial crisis, and most recently that the Commonwealth had found it necessary in its 2016 Budget to include a package rescuing the ILC from its debts. In early 2018, Prime Minister Turnbull announced that the government would widen the Land Account's investment parameters. It did so in November 2018 by transferring the Land Account and its management to the Future Fund, with broader investment parameters.[24] While the change in investment parameters will enable the LF to grow faster, this improvement is arguably 23 years too late. The Commonwealth has not compensated the LF for the foregone revenues over the past quarter century. Moreover, in a global economic environment in which growth rates are slowing, there is no guarantee that the Future Fund managers will achieve the levels of return enjoyed since 2007. When Prime Minister Turnbull predicted that the changed arrangements would make Indigenous interests 'better off' to the tune of $1.5bn over 20 years, he was optimistically assuming that global economic growth would be so high as to enable a real rather than a merely nominal improvement in the fund's growth.

The second policy issue is how much money the LF is allowed to transfer to the ILC so that the ILC can acquire lands, divest them to Indigenous Australians and then support Indigenous owners in their land management. Policymakers have struggled to devise a workable formula that both protects the capital base (the LF) and allows 'drawdowns' to the ILC that are not subject to wide fluctuations. Drawdowns were previously determined by a formula, but the most recent amendments provide for ministers to control the drawdowns on an ad hoc basis. This will diminish the scope for the ILC to plan its program strategically over several years.

The third, and least obvious, policy issue is the question of the underlying purpose of the LF. The legislative intention in 1995 was clearly to give a government agency, rather than Indigenous interests, the responsibility for managing the LF's assets, while providing for the ILC's majority Indigenous board to decide what lands to acquire and what land management projects to support. A Consultative Forum that included ILC Board members advised the LF on its investment policy.

---

24 This was effected by amending the *Aboriginal and Torres Strait Islander Act 2005* (Cth) and by enacting the *Aboriginal and Torres Strait Islander Land and Sea Future Fund Act 2018* (Cth).

While there was no explicit statutory requirement that the government limit itself to the role of fiduciary trustee, it is clear that the intention of the LF's architects was that the ILC Board have wide scope to make decisions. The Commonwealth, as fiduciary trustee, took a back seat. Yet the transfer of the LF into the Commonwealth Future Fund not only failed to acknowledge this fiduciary intention, but also further diluted that relationship by embedding the LF more deeply within the Commonwealth's financial architecture.

Taking into consideration the ways that the Australian Government has dealt with the three issues discussed – investment portfolio, drawdown decisions and the role of the ILC Board – it is apparent that, since 1995, the original intentions underpinning the creation of the LF have been progressively diluted. The tension between whether the ILC exists to fulfil the purposes of the compensatory LF, or the LF exists to fulfil the remit of the government-influenced ILC, has increasingly been resolved in favour of the latter. The ILC is now conceived by policymakers as just another Commonwealth statutory corporation (nominally independent, but in practice subject to substantial ministerial influence) rather than an independent statutory mechanism to deliver compensation within a fiduciary policy context. In fact, to align with the original policy intentions, both entities ought to be considered intertwined strands of the same independent institution.[25]

Finally, the operations of the ILC require brief assessment. The ILC has, over 20 years, acquired hundreds of properties, large and small, for Indigenous groups and communities and provided significant and innovative assistance towards the management of Indigenous lands, including path-breaking work on carbon farming in northern Australia. A recent ILC media release indicated that the ILC had invested $1.0bn in the Indigenous estate over the life of the ILC (1995–2018) and purchased 257 properties totalling 6 million hectares.[26] However, the ILC has slowed the pace of its property acquisitions. In its first eight years, the ILC had acquired 151 properties totalling over 5 million hectares.[27] In the following 12 years, it acquired only another 75.[28] The slowdown

25   Michael Dillon, 'The Devil in the Detail: The Government's Proposed Indigenous Land Fund Legislation', *A Walking Shadow* (blog), 2 April 2018, accessed 24 October 2019, refragabledelusions. blogspot.com/2018/04/the-devil-in-detail-governments.html.
26   Indigenous Land Corporation, 'Indigenous Land Corporation Welcomes New Era'.
27   Indigenous Land Corporation, *Improving*, 8.
28   Indigenous Land Corporation, *Land*, 15.

can be attributed to a number of factors. First, there has been an increased demand for land management as native title claims came to fruition and as the ILC's own former acquisitions have sought assistance. Second, the ILC has focused more on the operations of its own subsidiaries. Third, the financial commitments arising from the 2010 purchase of the Ayers Rock Resort (ARR) have been huge. The second and third of these factors are arguably strategic mistakes by successive ILC boards.[29]

Under its statutory remit, the ILC must consider land not only as an income-generating asset but also as meeting an Indigenous need to hold land in accordance with broader social and cultural aspirations.[30] In considering land as an income-generating asset, the ILC has used its power to establish subsidiaries to build a commercial portfolio on its own behalf (rather than in partnership with landowners as was originally intended). By establishing and operating subsidiaries in pastoral operations, tourism and cultural support, the ILC has sought to create jobs and economic opportunities. As Sullivan persuasively argues, the architects of the ILC's initial and amended legislation intended that any subsidiaries would work in partnership with Indigenous groups of landowners.[31]

The most egregious example of the ILC's misplaced confidence in operating unilaterally via its subsidiaries has been the $300m acquisition of the ARR. The ILC paid a price above commercial valuation for this asset and borrowed significant sums to finance the acquisition. Servicing this debt has effectively crippled the ILC's ability to fulfil its primary legislative remit. Even if the ARR eventually becomes commercially successful, and the ILC's outstanding bank borrowings are repaid, there will have been an effective 20-year hiatus in land acquisition and management across the nation, with all the opportunity costs which that entails.

The ILC has also faced problems in its relationship with pastoral operations. Contrary to its statutory obligations, the ILC has not always divested acquired pastoral leases in cases where it wished to directly

29   In a related vein, a 2010 Strategic Review of Indigenous Expenditure commissioned by Cabinet noted that the ILC's then current emphasis had been on employment and training (effected through its subsidiaries) rather than land acquisition. While noting the ILC's independence, the review recommended a reorientation towards support for the management of land acquired under native title settlements. Department of Finance, *Strategic Review*, 278.

30   Altman and Pollack, 'The Indigenous', 77.

31   Sullivan, 'Policy Change'.

manage the enterprise. This has antagonised local groups whose lands were acquired but not divested to the traditional owners. More recently, the ILC has changed tack and is now in the process of withdrawing from direct involvement in pastoral operations. That is, it is divesting those pastoral stations it retains to their traditional owners, selling its substantial cattle herd (which less than six years ago was among the 15 largest herds in the country) and returning management of pastoral operations to local communities, notwithstanding that they will face significant challenges given low economies of scale. The ostensible reasons for this process of divestment include the high capital costs of operating a national business and the pressure of local Indigenous communities.

It is a mistake to retreat from managing a national pastoral enterprise that returns economic benefits to local communities. While the ILC has a statutory obligation to divest land it acquires to local Indigenous groups within a 'reasonable period', there is nothing to stop the ILC leasing the lands back on a commercial basis to build a single integrated enterprise managed in cooperation with local communities that has economies of scale and access to the ILC's expertise and capital. Most successful pastoral operations in northern Australia operate across multiple properties and have access to professional management and adequate capital. One effect of the divestment of the national pastoral enterprise is that substantial ILC capital is freed up: the ILC herd of around 68,000 head is worth around $38m. However, the sale of the cattle herd has reduced the value of the herd by almost $18m.[32] The ILC's desire to free up funds through asset sales is a direct result of the financial pressures flowing from the misguided acquisition of the ARR.

Perhaps the ILC would not have made (or would not be making) these strategic mistakes were its boards more accountable to broader Indigenous interests such as land councils and other peak bodies. The process of Indigenous self-determination is compromised by the power of ministers to appoint directors. This opens up risks of politicised appointments and, ultimately, inappropriate or informal interference.

From this review of risks and failures we can draw three conclusions relevant to the quest for greater Indigenous control over the ILC and related institutions.

---

32   Indigenous Land Corporation, *Annual Report 2017–18*, 102.

First, the tension between acquiring land for economic development and acquiring land in order to compensate dispossessed people is ongoing. While both goals are important and intertwined, there is also a history – and thus ongoing risk – of ministers and bureaucrats substituting a focus on economic development that is invariably interpreted in narrow terms focused on individual entrepreneurship (or worse, a focus on the rhetoric of economic development) for an ongoing substantive policy of compensation via the operations of the ILC. Both prospectively focused economic development and retrospectively focused compensation for dispossession (if the quantum aligns with the prior loss) will contribute to Indigenous self-determination. They will facilitate both Indigenous autonomy and the capacity to participate in wider decisions from a position of greater strength and resilience. It seems likely that uncompensated loss of identity, culture, land and political agency is a core factor in the creation of intergenerational deep-disadvantage and the high-level policy failure seen in the failure of successive governments to make progress in 'closing the gap'.[33] If so, the failure to pursue substantive and effective policies focused on compensation risks undermining policy efforts across the breadth of the Indigenous affairs domain. This failure is a potential contributor to the ongoing high-level policy failure in Indigenous affairs over recent decades.

Second, the establishment of the ILC/LF within the public sector has clear drawbacks for self-determination: in setting policy for the LF, governments have wound back Indigenous influence and increased government control. The obvious alternative is to establish the ILC/LF outside the public sector as a truly independent and self-determining entity.

Third, accountability between government, ILC directors and the broader Indigenous community has been a systemic problem. The operation of the LF and the ILC has lacked transparency, and this has contributed to strategic missteps that have disadvantaged Indigenous interests and led to both sub-optimal outcomes and processes in terms of advancing Indigenous self-determination. The missteps have weakened Indigenous autonomy and reduced Indigenous capacity to influence mainstream decision-making.

---

33   Morrison, *Closing*, 2019.

Conclusion

This chapter has examined two models of statute-based Indigenous capital accumulation – IBA and the ILC/LF. Neither led to a leap from capital accumulation to broadly based self-determination, either in terms of greater autonomy or in terms of greater political influence for Indigenous interests. Nor does it appear likely that, either separately or together, they have the capacity to make this leap. While each has a majority Indigenous board and Indigenous chair, board members have not been accountable to the wider Indigenous community. Reasons include the 'light touch' regulatory oversight of all Commonwealth statutory corporations, the informal control exercised by ministers derived from their powers of appointment and reappointment, and the variable quality of boards over time arising from the political lens applied to board appointments by ministers. In addition, in the case of the LF, government control over investment strategy and, in the case of IBA, governments' use of budget appropriations as an incentive to shape board decisions, have militated against Indigenous self-determination.

Both IBA and the ILC/LF have been starved of start-up capital and revenue flows. Each has confronted management and governance challenges that are a systemic source of under-performance. Strategic mistakes by both organisations have constrained their long-term impact. Importantly, each has been the subject of serious and sustained bureaucratic and political pushback. Statutory land rights and native title have had more impact than the capital fund institutions. Legislation to recognise land rights (including 'native title') has returned very substantial areas of land to Indigenous ownership and control and this has increased the political and social leverage of Indigenous interests vis-a-vis other interest groups and governments at all levels.

However, to compare policies related to capital funds and land rights in this way ignores the synergies between land and capital. We should assess the impact of the array of economic, social, cultural and political institutional frameworks established since 1966 as a systemic whole, each element contributing to the extent and quality of the Indigenous domain. It is likely that these capital funds do contribute to increased self-determination through their synergistic and largely intangible supplementation of the value of land rights and native title to Indigenous interests.

In the medium term, these capital funds would contribute more to self-determination – in terms of both increased autonomy and greater capacity to influence public policy – were governments to give them more money and to transfer control to an appropriate Indigenous ownership structure outside the public sector.[34] Clearly, such a policy turnaround would require a shift in public sentiment and strong political commitments at a government level.

References

ATSIC (Aboriginal and Torres Strait Islander Commission). *Annual Report 1994–95*. Canberra: ATSIC, 1995. Accessed 24 October 2019. pandora.nla. gov.au/pan/41037/20050516-0000/www.atsic.gov.au/About_ATSIC/Annual _Report/Previous_Annual_Reports/default.html.

Altman, Jon C. and David Pollack. 'The Indigenous Land Corporation: An Analysis of Its Performance Five Years On'. *Australian Journal of Public Administration* 60, no. 1 (2001): 67–79. doi.org/10.1111/1467-8500.00242.

Department of Finance. *Strategic Review of Indigenous Expenditure*. Canberra: Department of Finance, 2010.

Dillon M. C. 'Emerging Strategic Issues in Native Title: Future Political and Policy Challenges'. *CAEPR Discussion Paper*, no. 292/2017. Canberra: Centre for Aboriginal Economic Policy Research, ANU, 2017.

Indigenous Business Australia (IBA). *Annual Report 2016–17*. Canberra: IBA, 2017.

Indigenous Land Corporation. *Annual Report 2017–18*. Canberra: Commonwealth of Australia, 2018.

Indigenous Land Corporation. *Improving Outcomes from Indigenous Land Purchases*. Canberra: Indigenous Land Corporation, 2003.

Indigenous Land Corporation. 'Indigenous Land Corporation Welcomes New Era'. Media release. Canberra, 28 November 2018. www.ilsc.gov.au/home/ news/indigenous-land-corporation-welcomes-new-era/.

Indigenous Land Corporation. *Land: 20 years of the Indigenous Land Corporation*. Canberra: Indigenous Land Corporation, 2015.

---

34   Dillon, 'Emerging', 12.

Markham, F. and N. Biddle. 'Indigenous Population Change in the 2016 Census'. *CAEPR 2016 Census Paper*, no. 1. Canberra: Centre for Aboriginal Economic Policy Research, ANU, 2017.

Miller, M. (chair). *Report of the Committee of Review of Aboriginal Employment and Training Programs*. Canberra: Australian Government Publishing Service, 1985.

Morrison, S. (Prime Minister). *Closing the Gap: Report 2019*. Canberra: Department of the Prime Minister and Cabinet, 2019.

Palmer, I. *Buying Back the Land: Organisational Struggle and the Aboriginal Land Fund Commission*. Canberra: Aboriginal Studies Press, 1988.

Rowse, T. *Obliged to be Difficult: Nugget Coombs' Legacy in Indigenous Affairs*. Cambridge: Cambridge University Press, 2000. doi.org/10.1017/cbo9780511 552199.

Sullivan, P. 'Policy Change and the Indigenous Land Corporation'. *AIATSIS Research Discussion Paper*, no. 25. Canberra: AIATSIS, 2009.

Tickner, R. *Taking a Stand: Land Rights to Reconciliation*. Crows Nest, NSW: Allen & Unwin, 2001.

Wilson, Gary N. and Per Selle. *Indigenous Self-determination in Northern Canada and Norway*. IRPP Study, no. 69. Montreal, Canada: Institute for Research on Public Policy, 2019. doi.org/10.26070/jc5j-5162.

5

AFTER RESERVES
AND MISSIONS

Discrete Indigenous communities
in the self-determination era[1]

Will Sanders

Introduction

Growing up in the northern suburbs of Sydney in the 1960s, my interactions with Indigenous Australians were few. Passing Purfleet community as we drove the Pacific Highway to our annual north coast beach holiday was one minor regular encounter; buying sandworms for fishing from the small group of Aboriginal houses at our destination of South West Rocks was another. In the 1970s, family beach holidays moved to the south coast of New South Wales, to a house near Jerrinja community, formally known as Roseby Park reserve or mission. While I did not come to know Indigenous Australians personally through these fleeting encounters, I did come to appreciate that there were small discrete Indigenous communities scattered across New South Wales. Known in the past as reserves and missions, these communities seemed to be changing

---

1   My research for this paper draws on conversations with many public officials in Indigenous land councils, local governments and their associations, and state and territory governments. I thank them all for sharing their time and knowledge with a researcher from The Australian National University who just approached them out of the blue. You have maintained my faith in open public administration. My ANU colleague Ed Wensing must also be acknowledged for sharing his encyclopaedic knowledge of land law and local government. This paper's interpretations and inaccuracies are of my own making, but the knowledge on which it is based has been generously shared by others.

during the Whitlam Government years of my adolescence. New housing and related infrastructure started appearing at Purfleet, Jerrinja and other discrete Indigenous communities funded by the Commonwealth Government.

The land rights and self-determination era in Australian Indigenous affairs offered new potentialities for discrete Indigenous communities. From restrictive reserves and tutelary missions under 'protection' and 'assimilation', these places were becoming small self-servicing settlements, and some new discrete Indigenous communities were developing, as I became aware when attending the University of Sydney in the mid-1970s. The Block in Redfern, owned by the Aboriginal Housing Company, was then newly emerging as an urban centre of services and residence for Indigenous people.

This paper surveys discrete Indigenous communities during the first half-century (c. 1970–2020) of the self-determination era in Australian Indigenous affairs. It begins with the changing Commonwealth role as infrastructure funder for these communities nationwide. Developments in each state and territory are then discussed separately. While there is no single clear story nationally, there are commonalties in what has emerged conceptually from different policy histories. Discrete Indigenous communities have everywhere become 'self-servicing corporate landholders'. Note that I do not use the terms 'landowners' or 'self-governing', though in some jurisdictions these terms may be justified. Some discrete communities have formed local governments, while others have adopted more 'private' corporate forms. How and why this has occurred will emerge during the survey of jurisdictions.

Commonwealth benevolence and withdrawal

The Commonwealth funded infrastructure for discrete Indigenous communities from 1972, first through the Department of Aboriginal Affairs and then via the Aboriginal and Torres Strait Islander Commission (ATSIC) established in 1990. Programs with the words infrastructure, community and housing in their titles funded water, electricity, roads and housing in both long-established and new discrete Indigenous communities across Australia. Commonwealth authorities also developed surveys of these communities to scope the task and identify priorities.

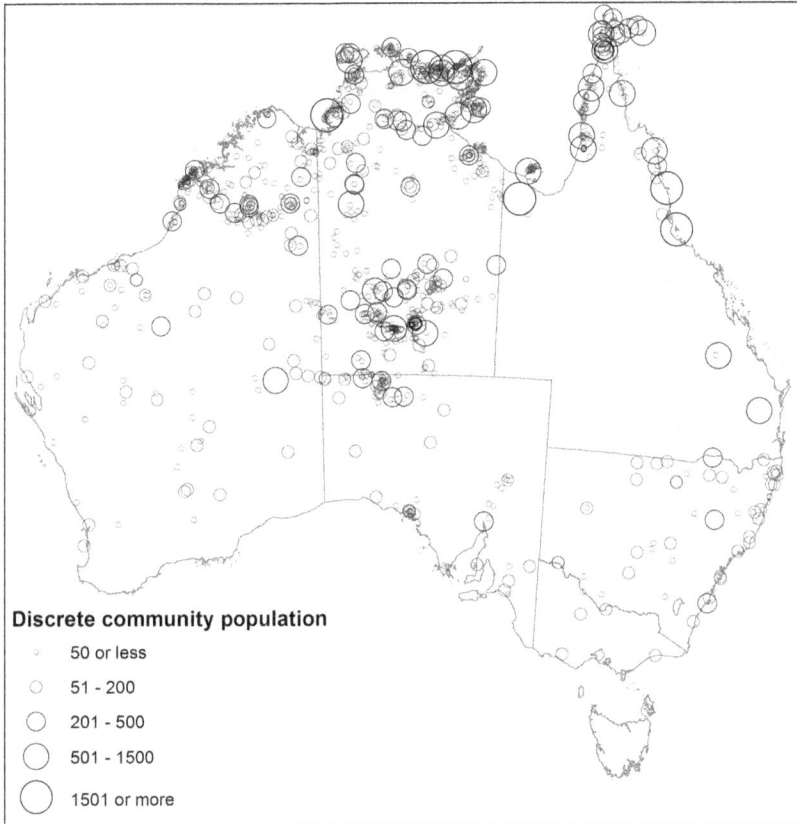

Discrete community population

- 50 or less
- 51 - 200
- 201 - 500
- 501 - 1500
- 1501 or more

Map 5.1: Geographic distribution of 1,187 discrete Indigenous communities by population size, 2006.

Source: Francis Markham (Centre for Aboriginal Economic Policy Research, The Australian National University), using data from the ABS 2006 Community Housing and Infrastructure Needs Survey.

Table 5.1 shows findings from three surveys conducted by ATSIC and the Australian Bureau of Statistics (ABS) in 1992, 1999 and 2006. In the four south-eastern jurisdictions, numbers of discrete Indigenous communities were relatively stable, around 70, or possibly slightly in decline. In the four more sparsely settled jurisdictions, numbers of discrete Indigenous communities and their populations were more substantial and growing, at least in the first half of these 15 years. Somewhere between 1,100 and 1,200 communities with between 90,000 and 100,000 residents was the finding around the millennium for South Australia, Queensland, the Northern Territory and Western Australia combined.

Table 5.1: Numbers and populations of discrete Indigenous communities, 1992–2006.

	1992 No.	1992 Pop.	1999 No.	1999 Pop.	2006 No.	2006 Pop.
New South Wales	65	7,930	67	9,103	57	5,082
Australian Capital Territory	1	240				
Victoria	1	165	2	320	2	270
Tasmania	1	38	1		1	76
South Australia	94	4,549	106	5,254	91	4,567
Queensland	77	23,885	149	29,440	124	27,446
Northern Territory	489	36,299	681	48,716	641	41,681
Western Australia	178	15,342	285	17,161	271	13,838
Australia	**906**	**88,448**	**1,291**	**109,994**	**1,187**	**92,960**

Source: Australian Construction Services, *1992 National Housing*; Australian Bureau of Statistics, *Housing and Infrastructure 1999*; Australian Bureau of Statistics, *Housing and Infrastructure 2006 (Reissue)*.

Table 5.2: Numbers of discrete Indigenous communities reporting resident populations <50, 50–199 and 200+ in four jurisdictions, ATSIC and ABS Survey, 1999.

	Pop. <50	Pop. 50–199	Pop. 200+
South Australia	79	18	9
Queensland	105	9	35
Northern Territory	550	67	64
Western Australia	200	65	20

Source: Australian Bureau of Statistics, *Housing and Infrastructure 1999*.

Table 5.2 divides the 1999 survey findings in the four more sparsely settled jurisdictions by size of population in discrete Indigenous communities. There were eight to 10 times as many 'small' Indigenous communities (population <50) as 'large' ones (population 200+) in the Northern Territory (550/64), South Australia (79/9) and Western Australia (200/20), while the ratio in Queensland was a lesser factor of three (105/35). Queensland's relative preponderance of large communities reflects its practices of the 'protection' and 'assimilation' eras that moved many Indigenous people far off their land into large, consolidated and isolated Indigenous settlements. This relative concentration in a few, large discrete Indigenous communities has continued under Queensland's approach to land rights and self-determination.[2]

---

2   Queensland policy has long distinguished strongly between Aboriginal and Torres Strait Islander circumstances. While Islanders have remained in small, discrete communities, Aboriginal people were moved during the early decades of the twentieth century into just a few, large consolidated communities.

While jurisdictional differences will emerge further in later analysis, an important commonality is the withdrawal of Commonwealth support for infrastructure in discrete Indigenous communities after the abolition of ATSIC in 2004–05. Since 2006, the Commonwealth has pressured state, territory and local governments to take responsibility for infrastructure in these communities. Responses have varied and have been complicated by a 10-year Commonwealth commitment to public housing in remote Indigenous communities under the 2008 National Partnership Agreement on Remote Indigenous Housing. Commonwealth withdrawal has stopped the surveys of discrete Indigenous communities and their infrastructure needs since 2006, so no more recent comparative data exists across the eight sub-national jurisdictions.

New South Wales: Conflict over local government rates

Aboriginal land rights reform in New South Wales occurred in two stages over a decade. In 1973, a Liberal–Country Coalition Government legislated to establish an Aboriginal Lands Trust (ALT) that would hold title to Aboriginal reserves.[3] In 1983, after six years preparatory work, the Wran Labor Government legislated a new structure of Aboriginal land councils. The landholders of former reserves and other claimed land would now be 120 Local Aboriginal Land Councils (LALCs), overseen by the New South Wales Aboriginal Land Council (NSWALC) that would be divided into nine regions for purposes such as the election of representatives.

In 60 established reserve communities across New South Wales on the edges of towns or cities or in more isolated locations, the land rights reforms meant that LALCs began receiving rates bills from encompassing local governments – a surprise to some of them. The argument that they should be exempt wholesale from rates has been resisted, both by local governments and by the New South Wales Government.[4] While Aboriginal land deemed 'vacant' and/or of 'cultural or spiritual significance' can be exempted from rates, Aboriginal land used for residential or commercial purposes incurs

3   Peterson, *Aboriginal Land Rights,* 16–27.
4   Sanders, 'Local Governments'.

the obligation to pay rates.[5] When providing 'social housing', LALCs can also gain exemptions from local government rates as 'public benevolent institutions', though they must still pay for water and sewerage.[6]

What infrastructure services could discrete Indigenous communities expect from local governments in return for rates? The question arose in 1987 when strained relations between Toomelah community and the Moree Plains Shire Council were the subject of a report by the Commonwealth's Human Rights and Equal Opportunity Commission (HREOC). After noting that the 'reserve era for Toomelah ended only in 1977 when the last manager left' and that 'in the decade since, the community has had to come to terms with a vast array of new rights and responsibilities', the report found that:

> The Toomelah community of five hundred Aboriginal people endures appalling living conditions which amount to a denial to them of the most basic rights taken for granted by most other groups in society, and by other Australian communities of a similar size.[7]

The report compared Toomelah with Boggabilla, a town 25 kilometres away, where the shire provided infrastructure services in return for rates. The shire argued not only that resource constraints prevented such servicing at Toomelah, but also that it was a 'private settlement' on a single communal block of land.[8]

Conflict over rates and services at Toomelah in 1987 pointed to unresolved policy issues in New South Wales. Local governments had not provided services to discrete Indigenous communities when they had been 'reserves' managed by the state government; in the 1980s, they were still coming to grips with their new responsibilities to Indigenous landholders as rate payers, and to the LALCs acting on behalf of discrete Indigenous communities. As well as resource constraints, there were some legal impediments to local governments providing infrastructure services on land held by others.

While conflict over rates has settled, the abolition of ATSIC threw into high relief the resources it had contributed to infrastructure in the discrete Indigenous communities in New South Wales. In 2008, NSWALC

---

5   'Rate Exemptions', NSW Government, Aboriginal Affairs, 2018, accessed 1 January 2020, www.aboriginalaffairs.nsw.gov.au/pdfs/land-rights/Rates-Exemptions-July-2018.pdf.

6   New South Wales Aboriginal Land Council, *Submission*, 7–8.

7   Human Rights and Equal Opportunity Commission, *Toomelah Report*, 3, 61.

8   Human Rights and Equal Opportunity Commission, *Toomelah Report*, 34.

entered into a partnership with the New South Wales Government called the Aboriginal Communities Water and Sewerage Program. Overseen by that government's Industry department, this program aimed to invest $200 million over 25 years in 62 eligible Aboriginal settlements.[9] Other programs developed in conjunction with the state's Planning and Environment authorities attend to waste management and other infrastructure issues in these discrete Indigenous communities.[10]

This new model for resourcing infrastructure in discrete Indigenous communities in New South Wales recognises that, under the land rights system introduced in 1983, LALCs are independent landholders, overseen and supported by NSWALC.[11] These statutorily independent Aboriginal land interests now partner with New South Wales Government agencies and, to some extent, with local governments, to sustain infrastructure. While responsibility remains shared and unclear, infrastructure services in the former reserves and missions are being managed through these partnerships, albeit at lower standards than in urban areas.

The number of discrete Indigenous communities in New South Wales seems stable during the self-determination era. Apart from the Block in Redfern, Sydney, which lasted for about 40 years from the mid-1970s, before being reduced to vacant land in the 2010s, the 60 or so discrete Indigenous communities, having once been reserves and missions, are longstanding.[12] The physical infrastructure of such settlements does not quickly spring into existence or disappear, and it is likely that the variation for New South Wales shown in Table 5.1 reflects changing survey procedures as much as actual growth or decline.

---

9   'Aboriginal Communities Water and Sewerage Program', NSW Government, accessed 1 January 2020, www.industry.nsw.gov.au/water/water-utilities/infrastructure-programs/aboriginal-communities.
10   'Aboriginal Community Lands and Infrastructure Program', NSW Department of Planning, Industry and Environment, updated 14 June 2019, accessed 1 January 2020, www.planning.nsw. gov.au/About-Us/Our-Programs/Aboriginal-Community-Lands-and-Infrastructure-Program; 'Aboriginal Communities Waste Management Program', NSW Environment Protection Authority, updated 22 February 2019, accessed 1 January 2020, www.epa.nsw.gov.au/working-together/grants/ illegal-dumping/aboriginal-communities-waste-management-program.
11   One indication of independence from government is the web domain of the NSW Aboriginal Land Council, accessed 1 January 2020, alc.org.au/. A 15-year levy on land tax from 1983 also gave NSWALC considerable financial independence.
12   The Block in Redfern has been vacant land for the last few years. The Aboriginal Housing Company has been seeking approval for a major residential redevelopment. The Block may yet re-emerge as a discrete Indigenous community, but this is far from certain.

Victoria and Tasmania

In the ATSIC/ABS surveys reported in Table 5.1, Victoria had two discrete Indigenous communities and Tasmania had one. These are readily identifiable, of longstanding and remain to this day as self-servicing corporate landholders.

Lake Tyers and Framlingham were reserves, until Victoria's *Aboriginal Land Act 1970* made them into statutory trusts and self-servicing landholding communities. Each was included in a local government area and pays rates, as a single landholder, to that local government. This has not led to conflict, as in New South Wales, perhaps because, along with ATSIC, the Victorian Government has always contributed significantly to the two trusts for community self-servicing. But both the Lake Tyers and the Framlingham Aboriginal Trusts have had periods of imposed administration, when Victoria's minister for Aboriginal affairs intervened to safeguard public resources. Nevertheless, the basic model of a statutory trust that is a landholder and responsible for internal community servicing is well established in Victoria. Thus, two former missions have survived to become modern discrete Indigenous communities.

In Tasmania, the long-recognised discrete Indigenous community is Cape Barren Island, declared a reserve under the *Cape Barren Island Reserve Act 1912*. Title over most of Cape Barren Island was transferred to the Aboriginal Land Council of Tasmania in 2005. However, the Aboriginal residents of Cape Barren Island live on land that had been alienated to Housing Tasmania (for public housing) and to some private owners of residences. The Cape Barren Island Aboriginal Association, established in 1975, owns a civic/cultural centre and service assets through which its annual turnover has been $1.8 million in recent years.[13] These landholders pay local government rates to Flinders Council, which conducts most of its service activities on the adjacent Flinders Island. Rates on Cape Barren Island are set lower than on Flinders Island, in recognition of differences in service levels and of landholder self-servicing. The Aboriginal Land Council of Tasmania (ALCT) pays rates for the airstrip on Cape Barren Island, but not for the vast majority of its landholding. This larger portion

---

13   'Cape Barren Island Aboriginal Association Incorporated', Australian Charities and Not-for-profits Commission, accessed 1 January 2020, www.acnc.gov.au/charity/d266a6e09e89b603b9f48 aaee45bc21f#overview.

of the ALCT landholding is seen as 'land used principally for Aboriginal cultural purposes' and is exempt from local government rates under Section 19(c) of Tasmania's *Land Tax Act 2000*.

Wreck Bay and Australian Capital Territory

Originally a reserve community in New South Wales, Wreck Bay was transferred to the Australian Capital Territory in 1915 and became part of the Commonwealth's responsibility in Indigenous affairs. The Commonwealth returned land at Wreck Bay to the Aboriginal community in two stages under the *Aboriginal Land Grant (Jervis Bay Territory) Act 1986*. First was the village settlement of 403 hectares, then second, in 1995, a much larger area of land to be co-managed with the Commonwealth as a national park. The Wreck Bay Aboriginal Community Council (WBACC) was established as a Commonwealth statutory authority in 1986 as the governance structure to service the community. Since 1995, WBACC has also undertaken land management services for the national park, at an annual turnover of $4 million, according to recent annual reports.[14] While laws of the Australian Capital Territory apply at Wreck Bay, WBACC has power to make by-laws and is, in practice, a small separate local, or even territory, government for this land area.[15] This village settlement of some 200 people is possibly the most autonomous and self-governing discrete Indigenous community in Australia.

Northern Territory: Challenging Commonwealth land rights by encouraging local government

In 1978, the Northern Territory was granted limited self-government by the Commonwealth. One matter over which the Commonwealth maintained clear control was the Aboriginal land rights regime instituted just two years earlier. The new Country Liberal Party (CLP) Government

14 'Publications', Wreck Bay Aboriginal Community Council, accessed 1 January 2020, www.wbacc. gov.au/publications/.
15 'Jervis Bay Territory Governance and Administration', Australian Government Department of Infrastructure, Transport, Cities and Regional Development, accessed 1 January 2020, regional.gov. au/territories/jervis_bay/governanceadministration.aspx.

in the Territory fought against this limitation, including challenging particular land claims and pushing for statehood, which it envisaged would give the Territory government control over land. As well, the Northern Territory Government challenged the land rights regime by promoting local government across the Territory.

Under direct Commonwealth administration up to 1978, formal local government in the Territory had been restricted to Darwin, Alice Springs, Katherine and Tennant Creek. The new Northern Territory Government began to offer local government incorporation to smaller urban centres and to remote communities under its *Local Government Act 1978*, which provided for flexible schemes of 'community government'.

The Northern and Central land councils, established under the Commonwealth's land rights statute, resisted this offer of local government. Their academic consultant argued that, by giving too much control to the Northern Territory minister for local government, community government schemes 'subverted' the authority of 'traditional owners' under Commonwealth land rights legislation.[16] A visiting Canadian academic agreed, suggesting that the 'objective' of community government was the extension of the Northern Territory Government's 'jurisdictional authority'; she advised Aboriginal communities to exercise 'caution' and to consider 'more autonomous and self-determining forms of government'.[17] The land councils' consultant argued that more powerful forms of incorporation for Indigenous communities were available through the Commonwealth's *Aboriginal Councils and Associations Act 1976*.

Despite these criticisms, Aboriginal communities across the Territory adopted community government schemes, so that by 2000 there were 32 community governments in the Northern Territory: five in small open highway towns and 27 in discrete Indigenous communities, either singly or in small regional groups.[18] These were in addition to the Northern Territory's six municipalities and 29 'association councils'. Association councils were community associations that had been recognised since the late 1980s as performing some functions of local government; as such, they received local government funding, though they did not have formal authority over a land area. By 2000, 80–90 per cent of Territorians were

---

16   Mowbray, *Black and White*; Mowbray, 'Subverting', 12.
17   Wolfe, *'That Community Government Mob'*, 171.
18   Sanders, *Local Governments*, 3.

covered by 67 local governing bodies, though only 10 per cent of the Territory's land area was. Of these, 56 were Aboriginal-majority councils governing discrete Indigenous communities.[19] Among the Territorians not covered by local governments were pastoral leaseholders who provided their own housing and infrastructure and many homeland Aboriginal communities that relied on 'resource agencies'.[20]

In the first decade of the twenty-first century, Northern Territory governments reformed local government arrangements for small, Indigenous-majority communities. Initially, CLP and Labor governments encouraged amalgamations to create larger regional groupings, of which two emerged in 2001 and 2003. Judging progress too slow, the inaugural Territory Labor Government under Clare Martin abandoned persuasion and announced in late 2006 that the government would amalgamate remote area local governments into shires covering about 5,000 people. During 2007, nine potential shires were identified, alongside the Territory's six municipalities. Under pressure from urban fringe settlers, Labor dropped its plan to create a shire on the outskirts of Darwin, but proceeded with amalgamations that created eight shires in more remote areas in 2008. While the new shires still had Aboriginal-majority constituencies and were focused primarily on governing discrete Indigenous communities, many also embraced an unprecedented mix of non-Aboriginal interests, such as pastoralists and open highway towns.[21] The critics of community government in the 1980s had been prescient in pointing to the power of the Northern Territory minister for local government. Indigenous Territorians felt betrayed and overridden as they lost the small local governments they had been encouraged to develop over the previous 30 years.[22] The new shires were local governments not only for discrete Indigenous communities, but also for large tracts of land between communities and for settler interests as well.

---

19   Sanders, *Local Governments*, 3.
20   Altman, Gillespie and Palmer, *National Review*, 23.
21   Sanders, 'Changing Scale'.
22   Sanders, 'Losing Localism'.

Queensland: Becoming local governments to challenge Commonwealth policy, then as part of state policy

In Queensland's discrete Indigenous communities we see both parallels and contrasts with the Northern Territory from the 1970s to the 2010s. When the Whitlam and Fraser Commonwealth governments were exploring practices of Indigenous self-determination and self-management, Queensland, under National Party Premier Joh Bjelke-Petersen, offered the most resistance. The Australian Parliament passed two laws focused on Queensland: the *Aboriginal and Torres Strait Islanders (Queensland Discriminatory Laws) Act 1975* and the *Aboriginal and Torres Strait Islanders (Queensland Reserves and Communities Self-Management) Act 1978*. In the latter the Fraser Coalition Government sought to support new councils of residents in two discrete Aboriginal communities that had been missions on reserve land: Aurukun and Mornington Island. The Queensland Government's response was to de-gazette the two reserves and to pass the *Local Government (Aboriginal Lands) Act 1978*, creating local government shires at Aurukun and Mornington Island, thus moving the two communities outside the terms of the Commonwealth legislation.[23]

In the 1980s, the Bjelke-Petersen Government changed the status of reserves and created small local governments in another 32 discrete Indigenous communities. Community Services legislation in 1984 established 15 Aboriginal councils and 17 Island councils. A change from 'reserves' to 'trust areas' was enabled by amendments to the *Land Act* in 1982 and 1984 and then, in 1986, Deeds of Grant in Trust (DOGITs) were issued to most of the 32 Aboriginal and Island councils.

Three aspects of the Queensland National Party's approach to discrete Indigenous communities drew criticism: the maintenance of reserve by-laws until the new councils made new ones, the exclusion of residents of trust areas from participation in the larger local government areas surrounding DOGITs, and the closer oversight of Aboriginal and Island councils compared to Queensland local governments more generally.[24] Responding to some of these criticisms became part of land rights reform under the Goss Labor Government in the early 1990s.[25] Although

---

23   Tatz, *Race Politics,* 66-81; Lippmann, *Generations,* 84-89.
24   Human Rights Commission, *Community Services (Aborigines) Act 1984.*
25   Brennan, *Land Rights,* 121–68.

Aboriginal people and commentators such as Frank Brennan remained critical of the Goss Government for not pushing land rights further, it was generally acknowledged by 1991 that the councils in Queensland's 34 officially recognised, discrete Indigenous communities had secure titles to land and, as local governments, were establishing a greater presence in Queensland public life.[26]

After the millennium, the Beattie Labor Government made further changes to local government in Queensland's discrete Indigenous communities. The *Local Government (Community Government Areas) Act 2004* instituted a four-year transition period through which the 15 Aboriginal and 17 Island councils were to become more fully included in and compliant with the general *Local Government Act 1993*. As this transition was coming to an end, Beattie established a Local Government Reform Commission to make a case for amalgamations. This commission argued that Queensland's 157 local governments should be reduced to 73, and this happened in 2008.[27] Two of the 34 community governments – the Aurukun and Mornington Island local governments – remained, but the other 32 (known as Aboriginal and Island Councils) were reduced to 14 in the following ways. Fifteen Island councils were combined into one Torres Strait Island Regional Council.[28] Two Island councils on the tip of Cape York were combined with three Aboriginal councils to become a single unit, the Northern Peninsula Area Regional Council.[29] Twelve other Aboriginal councils with unchanged borders were renamed shires.[30] In short, in 2008, Queensland's 34 Indigenous community governments reduced to 16.

---

26 Brennan, *Land Rights*, 173.

27 Four amalgamations were reversed in 2013 under the Newman Liberal National Party Government, taking the total number of Queensland local governments up to 77. Queensland, Local Government Reform Commission, *Report*.

28 This new local government under Queensland legislation should not be confused with the Torres Strait Regional Authority that was created in 1994 as part of ATSIC. This regional elected Commonwealth Indigenous statutory authority survived the abolition of ATSIC in 2005, more by good luck and distance than strategy. Nonetheless, its survival is important and worth understanding, though that would be another paper.

29 This was effected by the *Local Government and Other Legislation (Indigenous Regional Councils) Amendment Act 2007* passed by the Queensland Parliament in November 2007. The previous Acts from 1978 and 1984 were much reduced at this time and renamed the *Aurukun and Mornington Island Shire Leases Act 1978* and the *Aboriginal and Torres Strait Islander Communities (Justice, Land and Other Matters) Act 1984*. A rewrite of legislation at this time also produced a new *Local Government Act 2009*, which applied to all local councils across Queensland.

30 Longland described these 'donut' arrangements of Aboriginal shires within the land areas of larger encompassing shires as having 'inherent structural inefficiencies', and only argued against their amalgamation on the grounds of unresolved issues relating to DOGITs land and 'additional responsibilities undertaken by Aboriginal local governments'. This was a rather weak defence of the discrete Aboriginal shires. Local Government Reform Commission, *Report*, vol. 1, 64.

It should also be noted that Queensland has about a dozen discrete Indigenous communities that have *not* become local governments. For example, Mossman Gorge sits on two parcels of land, one of which is still a reserve held by a Queensland Government department and the other a block of private freehold held by an Aboriginal corporation. Just 80 kilometres from Cairns, Mossman Gorge has a successful tourism operation. The Aboriginal corporation delivers infrastructure services to around 30 households in the settlement, with funding assistance from the Queensland Government, and pays rates to Douglas Shire on its freehold block. The corporation and the encompassing local government work in collaboration on rates and services. In other parts of Queensland, however, there have been tensions between these discrete Indigenous communities and local governments over rates and services.

South Australia: Land rights leads to some local governing bodies and some self-servicing settlements

In South Australia, pushes for land rights, rather than reactions against it, have resulted in discrete Indigenous communities becoming local governing bodies.[31] In the early 1980s, parliament legislated title to reserves in the north-west of the state: the *Pitjantjatjara Land Rights Act 1981* and the *Maralinga Tjarutja Land Rights Act 1984*. Each law raised the question of whether the resulting Aboriginal landholding corporation was also a local governing body. In 1987, amendments to the 1981 legislation gave the body corporate, Anangu Pitjantjatjara, the power to make by-laws.[32] In later years by-law-making power was extended to Maralinga Tjarutja and to the renamed Anangu Pitjantjatjara Yankunytjatjara.

These policies of the 1980s built on an earlier wave of reform: a 1966 law creating the ALT, a statutory authority holding title to reserves in the south and east of South Australia. This led to the emergence of eight Aboriginal community councils in discrete Indigenous communities on these reserves in the 1970s.[33] Three of these community councils emerged *outside*

---

31   South Australia maintains a distinction between local governments under the *Local Government Act*, of which there are 68, and some other organisations recognised as local governing bodies.
32   Tedmanson, *Shifting State,* 73–76.
33   See Peterson, *Aboriginal Land Rights,* 117. Also Rowse, *Rethinking,* 62–79.

existing incorporated local government areas; they provided for their own internal infrastructure and public order in conjunction with the ALT, the Commonwealth DAA and later ATSIC. Five others fell *within* existing incorporated local government areas but did not pay local government rates. These five, too, have attended to their own internal public order and infrastructure services in conjunction with the trust, Commonwealth funders and, sometimes, encompassing local governments on a negotiated contract or fee-for-service basis. Although these arrangements continue to the present day, the Commonwealth has reduced its funding in the last decade.

Conceptually these 10 sets of governance arrangements for discrete Indigenous communities in South Australia push strongly towards the status of local government, particularly when considered in conjunction with the resources and authority of the ALT.[34] This is reflected in the three community councils on ALT land *outside* existing local government areas (Gerard, Nepabunna and Yalata) having been members of the Local Government Association of South Australia since the early 1990s. They are notably identified on the association's website along with Anangu Pitjantjatjara Yankunytjatjara and Maralinga Tjarutja.[35] In contrast, the five ALT communities and community councils *within* existing local government areas are not listed as members of the association, but they do still function as self-servicing corporate landholders and somewhat like local governing bodies.

Western Australia: Self-servicing settlements searching for resources

Like South Australia and New South Wales, Western Australia in 1972 created an ALT to hold title to lands reserved for Aboriginal use.[36] Unlike other jurisdictions, Western Australia went no further with land rights. Aboriginal reserves, covering about 10 per cent of this large jurisdiction, have remained outside the rateable land base of local governments though formally within their incorporated land areas. This has meant that Western

---

34   Sanders, 'Local Governments', 171. The ALT of South Australia has powers to make regulations for these communities and has done so in a number of instances, in consultation with community councils.

35   'Council Maps', Local Government Association of South Australia, accessed 15 August 2020, www.lga.sa.gov.au/sa-councils/councils-listing.

36   *Aboriginal Affairs Planning Authority Act 1972* (WA), section 10.

Australia's many discrete Indigenous communities have developed little relationship with their encompassing local governments and have looked to other public authorities to assist them with infrastructure and public order.

Western Australia's *Aboriginal Communities Act 1979* gave by-law-making power to councils of residents in reserve communities. Together with program resources from the Commonwealth DAA and later ATSIC, this enabled councils on reserve land to service themselves with basic infrastructure and public order. Since 2005, these arrangements have become fractious and contested. The new Commonwealth Indigenous affairs authorities have demanded that state and local government authorities pay for infrastructure services, and these authorities have typically argued that they cannot afford to do so.

In a 2016 report, the Western Australian Government insisted that it could not provide infrastructure services for all 305 identified discrete Indigenous communities. The government differentiated two groups of communities by location and policy 'direction'. One was '37 town-based reserves across 20 towns' with 'up to 3,000 Aboriginal residents'. For these, the policy 'direction' was to 'receive the same service opportunities, and share the same payment responsibilities, as other residents of the relevant town'.[37] The other group was 274 'remote communities' (each with about '12,000 Aboriginal residents'), 'about 165' of which the government claimed to have 'been supporting [with] essential and municipal service delivery' since 2015. In these communities, the policy 'direction' was 'progressively to meet minimum standards for essential and municipal services in larger remote Aboriginal communities'.[38] While cast positively, this was in fact a threat to withdraw infrastructure support by the Western Australian Government for most of the remote communities it then identified (274) or claimed to help service (165). Only 50 of these communities with over 50 permanent residents were clearly admitted to the 'larger' category, and beyond this the Western Australian Government's commitment was weak.

On public order in reserve communities, Brady has recently documented how a 2005 Law Reform Commission inquiry in Western Australia initially argued for abolition of the *Aboriginal Communities Act 1979*, but later supported its retention in light of Aboriginal community support

---

37   Regional Services Reform Unit, *Resilient Families*, 18.
38   Regional Services Reform Unit, *Resilient Families*, 16.

for its by-law-making power. The by-laws were, in the words of one council chair, 'our law in that we requested it for the protection of our well-being'.[39]

Because Western Australia did not progress land rights in the 1980s, it is now experiencing land reform through the implementation of the Commonwealth *Native Title Act 1993*. Discrete Indigenous communities are slowly being recognised as having native title over the reserve lands on which they sit, and their prescribed bodies corporate are being recognised as landholders within the Australian land governance system. Discrete Indigenous communities in Western Australia are becoming self-servicing corporate landholders searching for resources to support their infrastructure and public order. Conceptually, such communities push towards a parallel, but impoverished Indigenous local government system. They have by-law-making power under the *Aboriginal Communities Act 1979* and some corporate authority under the Commonwealth *Native Title Act 1993*, but no secure resource or fiscal base like general local governments.

One regional group of discrete Indigenous communities on reserve lands in the central desert in the far eastern parts of Western Australia managed to become a general local government in 1993. This process commenced in 1984, when Aboriginal residents were included in the local government franchise in Western Australia. Ngaanyatjarra residents in 10 discrete communities with a total population of around 1,000 used this new voting right to gain representation on the Shire of Wiluna, first as a minority of councillors and then as a majority in 1987.[40] Their leadership then resulted in a move to form the Shire of Ngaanyatjarraku as a 'community of interest' distinguishable from the predominantly pastoral Wiluna Shire.[41] Twenty-five years on, Ngaanyatjarraku is the only instance of discrete Indigenous communities in Western Australia being able to use electoral power to establish a local government under general legislation.

---

39   Brady, 'Law Reforming', 44.
40   Fletcher, *Aboriginal Politics*, 114–38.
41   McLean, 'Aboriginal Local', 139–46.

Conclusion

While Commonwealth governments of the last half-century have sometimes been ambivalent about applying the term self-determination to Indigenous policy, Indigenous people around the world have been adamant that this right of peoples in international law applies to them. The resounding 2007 vote in the United Nations General Assembly in favour of the Declaration on the Rights of Indigenous Peoples has confirmed this stance. It is now possible to talk of the self-determination era in Indigenous policy as established fact, as much as hopeful claim. Together with developments in land rights and native title, this right of peoples in international law is slowly opening new potentialities for Indigenous people in Australia, both in discrete Indigenous communities and beyond.

My brief history of the eight sub-national jurisdictions demonstrates the diversity and the commonalities in the developing potentialities for discrete Indigenous communities. In three south-eastern jurisdictions, New South Wales, Victoria and Tasmania, about 70 discrete Indigenous communities have become 'private' corporate landholders, paying rates to encompassing local governments and seeking resource partnerships with parts of government to sustain internal community infrastructure. In the fourth south-eastern jurisdiction, Wreck Bay Aboriginal Community Council has developed partnerships with Commonwealth authorities that give it the status of a local government or small territory government operating under the laws of the Australian Capital Territory.

In the four more sparsely settled jurisdictions, over 1,000 discrete Indigenous communities have been left outside the rateable land base of existing local governments. As newly recognised corporate landholders, these discrete Indigenous communities have sought ways to sustain their infrastructure and public order and this has often been through becoming local governments, or quasi local governing bodies. This is not a settled solution, as major local government restructuring showed in Queensland and the Northern Territory in 2008. But it does create a public corporate form in which majority Indigenous populations can lead to Indigenous participation and influence, as voters and elected members.

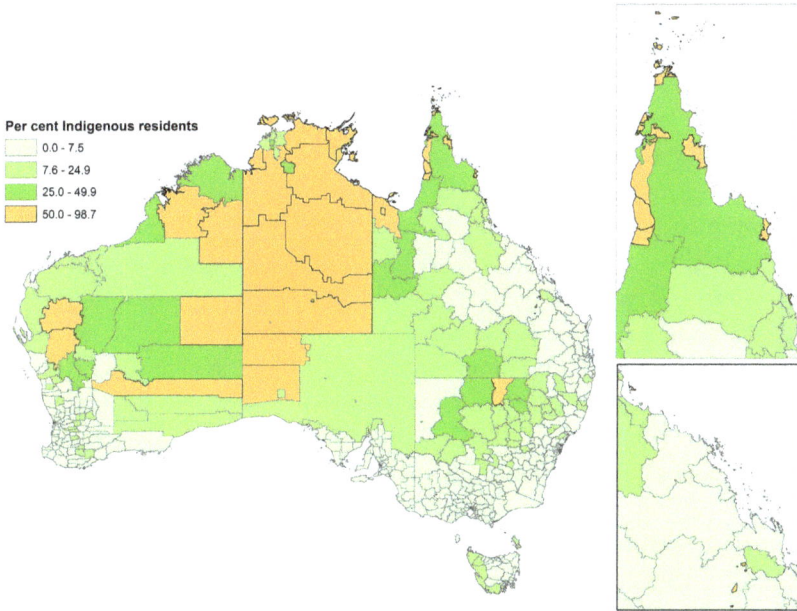

Map 5.2: Local government areas by percentage Indigenous residents, 2016 Census.

Source: Heather Crawford (Centre for Aboriginal Economic Policy Research, The Australian National University), using data from the ABS 2016 Census of Population and Housing.

Using 2016 Census data, a map of local government areas differentiated by Indigenous proportion of residents (Map 5.2) shows that, of the 539 recognised local government areas in Australia, 37 have Indigenous-majority populations, 18 in Queensland, 10 in the Northern Territory, 6 in Western Australia, 2 in South Australia and 1 in New South Wales.[42] The majority of these are instances in which discrete Indigenous communities have become recognised as local governments. In others, Indigenous majorities have emerged demographically in long-established local government areas. In both cases, Indigenous voters can hopefully use this demographic fact to both stand for public office and influence local government policies. While this is not Indigenous self-determination per se, these local governments should be acknowledged as public governance contributors towards that goal.

---

42   None of the Aboriginal Land Trust of South Australia communities is included in this ABS categorisation. Neither is Wreck Bay, which like the rest of the Australian Capital Territory is treated in this ABS categorisation as 'unincorporated' in a local government area.

I began by noting that as a child my first encounters with Indigenous affairs were through occasional observations of discrete Indigenous communities. Known as reserves and missions in past policy eras, these residential concentrations of Indigenous Australians appeared, in my adolescence, to be developing new potentialities in the emerging policy era of land rights and self-determination. After four decades of professional involvement in Indigenous affairs, these early impressions still strike me as having merit, though my faith in a benevolent Commonwealth has been strongly tested in the last 15 years. Under the combined influences of market liberalism, contractualism, new public management and a less centralist federalism, the Commonwealth has withdrawn resources for the infrastructure services of discrete Indigenous communities. To discrete Indigenous communities, the Commonwealth must now look fickle and unpredictable, rather than a benevolent provider. Indigenous corporate landholders, emerging in all jurisdictions across Australia, need assured financial resources to be self-servicing providers of infrastructure and public order in their discrete settlements. This is the big missing element in current arrangements, and has been since the abolition of ATSIC.[43]

Residents of discrete Indigenous communities are probably a declining proportion of the total Indigenous population. We do not know for sure because the Commonwealth has not surveyed discrete Indigenous communities since 2006. My guess, as a professional observer, is that the number of discrete Indigenous communities and their populations have remained constant or declined just slightly. Meanwhile, the national Indigenous population has increased significantly from 455,028 in 2006 to 649,171 in 2016.[44] This means that the proportion of Indigenous people living in discrete Indigenous communities has probably declined from one in five to one in seven. Despite this relative decline in proportion of Indigenous population, discrete Indigenous communities are still an important part of Indigenous policy and politics. Their continuing physical dominance of even small portions of the Australian landmass is suggestive of Indigenous peoplehood and the right to self-determination.

---

43   This point was made quite strongly in Queensland Productivity Commission, *Service Delivery*.
44   See Time Series Profile at '2016 Census Community Profiles', Australian Bureau of Statistics, updated 12 July 2019, accessed 1 January 2020, quickstats.censusdata.abs.gov.au/census_services/get product/census/2016/communityprofile/036?opendocument.

References

Altman J. C., D. Gillespie and K. Palmer. *National Review of Resource Agencies Servicing Indigenous Communities, 1998.* Canberra: Aboriginal and Torres Strait Islander Commission Office of Public Affairs, 1998.

Australian Bureau of Statistics. *Housing and Infrastructure in Aboriginal and Torres Strait Islander Communities: Australia 1999,* ABS Catalogue No. 4710.0. Canberra: Australian Bureau of Statistics, 2000.

Australian Bureau of Statistics. *Housing and Infrastructure in Aboriginal and Torres Strait Islander Communities: Australia 2006 (Reissue).* ABS Catalogue No. 4710.0. Canberra: Australian Bureau of Statistics, 2007.

Australian Construction Services. *1992 National Housing and Community Infrastructure Needs Survey: Final Report, Stage 1.* Brisbane: Aboriginal and Torres Strait Islander Commission, 1993.

Brady, M. 'Law Reforming Lawyers and Aboriginal Social Control: The Case of the Western Australian Aboriginal Communities Act'. *Australian Indigenous Law Review* 17, no. 1 (2013): 38–46.

Brennan, F. *Land Rights Queensland Style: The Struggle for Aboriginal Self-management.* St Lucia, Qld: University of Queensland Press, 1992.

Fletcher, C. *Aboriginal Politics: Intergovernmental Relations.* Carlton, Vic.: Melbourne University Press, 1992.

Human Rights and Equal Opportunity Commission (HREOC). *Toomelah Report: Report on the Problems and Needs of Aborigines Living on the New South Wales–Queensland Border.* Sydney, The Commission, 1988.

Human Rights Commission. *Community Services (Aborigines) Act 1984.* Report no. 9. Canberra: Australian Government Publishing Service, 1985.

Lippmann, L. *Generations of Resistance: The Aboriginal Struggle for Justice.* Melbourne: Longman Cheshire, 1981.

Local Government Reform Commission. *Report of the Local Government Reform Commission. Volume 1.* Chaired by B. Longland. Brisbane: Queensland Parliament, 2007. www.parliament.qld.gov.au/documents/TableOffice/Tabled Papers/2007/TP1809-2007.pdf.

McLean, D. 'Aboriginal Local Government Power in Western Australia'. In *Aboriginal Self-determination in Australia,* edited by C. Fletcher, 139–46. Canberra: Aboriginal Studies Press, 1994.

Mowbray, M. *Black and White Councils: Aborigines and Local Government in the NT,* Report to the Central and Northern Land Councils. Kensington, NSW: University of New South Wales, 1986.

Mowbray, M. 'Subverting the Aboriginal Land Rights (NT) Act 1976: The NT Local Government Act 1993'. *Indigenous Law Bulletin* 4, no. 10 (1998): 12–16.

New South Wales Aboriginal Land Council. *Submission to the Independent Pricing and Regulatory Authority Review of the Local Government Rating System.* October 2016.

Peterson, N., ed. *Aboriginal Land Rights: A Handbook.* Canberra: Australian Institute of Aboriginal Studies, 1981.

Queensland Productivity Commission. *Service Delivery in Queensland's Remote and Discrete Indigenous Communities: Final Report.* Brisbane: The Commission, 2017. www.qpc.qld.gov.au/inquiries/service-delivery-in-queenslands-remote-and-discrete-indigenous-communities/.

Regional Services Reform Unit. *Resilient Families, Strong Communities: A Roadmap for Regional and Remote Aboriginal Communities.* [Perth]: Regional Services Reform Unit, Department of Regional Development, July 2016. www.regional servicesreform.wa.gov.au.

Rowse, T. *Rethinking Social Justice: From 'Peoples' to 'Populations'.* Canberra: Aboriginal Studies Press, 2012.

Sanders, W. 'Changing Scale, Mixing Interests: Generational Change in Northern Territory Local Government'. *Australian Journal of Political Science* 47, no. 3 (2012): 473–90. doi.org/10.1080/10361146.2012.704008.

Sanders, W. 'Local Governments and Indigenous Australians: Developments and Dilemmas in Contrasting Circumstances'. *Australian Journal of Political Science* 31, no. 2 (1996): 153–74. doi.org/10.1080/10361149651166.

Sanders, W. *Local Governments and Indigenous Interests in Australia's Northern Territory.* Discussion Paper, no. 285. Canberra: Centre for Aboriginal Economic Policy Research, ANU, 2006.

Sanders, W. 'Losing Localism, Constraining Councillors: Why the Northern Territory Supershires are Struggling'. *Policy Studies* 34, no. 4 (2013): 474–90. doi.org/10.1080/01442872.2013.822704.

Tatz, C. *Race Politics in Australia: Aborigines, Politics and Law.* Armidale, NSW: University of New England Publishing Unit, 1979.

Tedmanson, D. 'Shifting State Constructions of Anangu Pitjantjatjara Yankunytjatjara: Changes to the South Australian Pitjantjatjara Land Rights Act 1981–2006'. PhD thesis, The Australian National University, 2016.

Wolfe, J. *'That Community Government Mob': Local Government in Small Northern Territory Communities.* Darwin: The Australian National University, North Australia Research Unit, 1989.

6

'TAXPAYERS' MONEY'? ATSIC AND THE INDIGENOUS SECTOR

Katherine Curchin and Tim Rowse

Introduction

Funding organisations controlled by Indigenous Australians and dedicated to serving them, in the name of 'self-determination', has created risks both for governments (who must satisfy the public that 'taxpayers' money' is being well spent) and Indigenous leaders (who must not only meet service expectations of Indigenous Australians but also acquit funding according to government criteria). This chapter compares two experiments in governance: the Indigenous sector (thousands of Aboriginal and Torres Strait Islander corporations) and the Aboriginal and Torres Strait Islander Commission (ATSIC).

Australian governments have encouraged Indigenous Australians to form corporations in order to hold title to Indigenous property, advocate, deliver services and manage employment programs. The federal (conservative, led by Malcolm Fraser) government passed the *Aboriginal Councils and Associations Act 1976* (henceforth ACA Act) in 1976. The Howard (conservative) Government replaced the ACA Act in 2007 with the *Corporations (Aboriginal and Torres Strait Islander) Act 2006* (henceforth CATSI Act). Both Acts authorised the Registrar of Aboriginal/Indigenous Corporations to report publicly on Indigenous corporations' financial accountability and organisational integrity. At the same time, Australian governments created national, elected Indigenous representative

143

organisations: the National Aboriginal Consultative Committee (NACC, 1973–76), the National Aboriginal Conference (NAC, 1977–85) and the Aboriginal and Torres Strait Islander Commission (ATSIC, 1989–2005).

ATSIC, unlike its predecessors, administered programs – mostly infrastructure, housing and employment, but not health, education and security programs. Under the Howard Government (1996–2007), the increasing political embarrassment of ATSIC led to a 2002–03 review and then ATSIC's abolition in 2004–05. Critical attention to the Indigenous sector took the form of amendments of the ACA Act in 1992, reviews of the Act in 1996–97 and 2001–04 and new legislation (the CATSI Act) in 2005–06. Why was one experiment in the delegation of public expenditure to Indigenous Australians (ATSIC) terminated while the funding of Indigenous organisations has continued as a permanent adaptation of Australian government to Indigenous political mobilisation?

Expectations of the ACA Act

Although some Aboriginal and Torres Strait Islander people had formalised their collective action before the 1960s (sometimes in the context of long-lasting missions), we begin our story in 1970 with Charles Rowley's suggestion that the Aboriginal 'group' would no longer be treated by governments as a 'disappearing liability' (as assimilation policy tended to assume), but as 'an asset, to be endowed, by its own efforts, with enduring legal personality'.

The 'fringe group' was 'the raw material for a corporation in perpetuity'.[1] When Prime Minister McMahon spoke on Aboriginal policy in January 1972, he promised to investigate 'a simple flexible form of incorporation for Aboriginal communities'.[2] Justice Woodward's advice to the Whitlam Government on land rights in 1973 included recommending that an incorporation statute be easy to understand, flexible enough to meet the needs of a variety of situations in which Aboriginal people would find themselves, not liable for taxation of its income, open to Aboriginal customs of decision-making and open to government intervention 'if things go wrong … through corruption, inefficiency, outside influences or for other reasons'.[3]

1   Rowley, 'Outcasts', 425.
2   McMahon, *Australian*, 12.
3   Woodward, *Aboriginal*, para. 332, p. 65.

Barrie Dexter, Secretary of the Department of Aboriginal Affairs from 1973, recalled in 2015 that Aboriginal-controlled incorporated bodies were 'crucial to so much we were trying to do'.[4] However, as they came under scrutiny, 'Parliament and the community at large seemed to have become more interested in correct, detailed accounting than in the outcome of programs', making the Department of Aboriginal Affairs 'more reluctant to fund Aboriginal groups and let them learn by making mistakes, since we would certainly be further roasted by Parliament and our critics for any failures'.[5] An incorporation statute designed to empower Indigenous Australians would also have to be a means of accountability and tuition.

Introducing a Bill for Aboriginal Councils and Associations in September 1975, the minister for Aboriginal affairs (Lesley Johnson) linked it to land rights in the Northern Territory; the Act was to provide 'a method of incorporation that would safeguard Aboriginal tenure of land'. He went on to list ways that the Act would also enable collective action not related to land tenure: receiving grants, holding and disposing of real and personal property, contracting, operating enterprises, and 'generally to conduct their affairs in an orderly manner' so that Indigenous Australians could fulfil their 'obligation to acknowledge responsibility for the consequences of their actions'. The Act would be especially helpful to 'remote, tradition-oriented communities where the understanding of Western European legal concepts is very limited'; for such people, Johnson believed, the existing corporations laws were not helpful.[6] Speaking in support, Manfred Cross remarked that 'Aborigines do not have the sophistication and business experience to comply with many of the complex and technical requirements of State laws'.[7] In establishing the Registrar of Aboriginal Corporations, the government intended to 'advise and assist Aboriginal corporations and to supervise their activities in much the same way as a Registrar of Companies supervises the affairs of companies'.[8] Johnson's bill lapsed when parliament dissolved in November 1975, but the Fraser Government saw the ACA Act through the parliament in 1976.

---

4   Dexter, *Pandora's Box*, 336.
5   Dexter, *Pandora's Box*, 336.
6   Johnson, *Commonwealth Parliamentary Debates*, House of Representatives (*CPD* HoR), 30 September 1975, 1410.
7   Cross, *CPD* HoR, 4 November 1975, 2762.
8   Johnson, *CPD* HoR, 30 September 1975, 1410–11.

We note several themes in the justification of the ACA Act: to acknowledge overlooked Indigenous political capacity by giving it a formal vehicle, to acknowledge cultural difference in Indigenous ways of associating, to bring order and transparency to group life, to make Aboriginal collective actions legally and fiscally accountable, and to spare Aboriginal people the burden of understanding complex legislation.

An emerging sense of political risk

Incorporation was not only a means to Indigenous political development, it also became a resource for political elites (Indigenous and non-Indigenous) to manage a new political risk that arose partly from different views about what Australia owed Indigenous Australians. For some Aboriginal people in the 1970s, as Johanna Perheentupa has shown in her chapter, government grants were compensation for dispossession and ill-treatment, so that Aboriginal people were not accountable to anyone but themselves in their spending of such funds. This view persisted among many Aboriginal people. In 1981, the NAC – the Fraser Government's representative, elected assembly – called for the compensatory payment of 5 per cent of Australia's gross national product to Aboriginal people to meet Aboriginal needs.[9] Such claims were sympathetically acknowledged in 1991 in the *National Report* of the Royal Commission into Aboriginal Deaths in Custody:

> What, to non-Aboriginal people, is a citizens' right (which is subject to assessment, monitoring and may be taken away if the citizen fails to meet administrative and other criteria) should be available for them on a basis rather like that which might apply if compensation payments were made for past injustices. Given that sense of injustice, many Aboriginal people regard it as an added insult that payments made, either directly or through Aboriginal organizations, to meet basic needs should be subjected to the minute and suspicious scrutiny which accompanies such payments. At this level, Aboriginal people would see the whole process of delivery of such services as being one of further control of their lives and not one which offers autonomy.[10]

---

9 'Aborigines Want Land, Self-Rule', *West Australian*, 23 September 1981.
10 Royal Commission into Aboriginal Deaths in Custody (RCIADIC), *National Report*, vol. 2, 525–26.

The national commissioner's impression was that Indigenous Australians 'have accepted the concept of representation through organizations', and he predicted that they would come to trust their organisations more, allowing their leaders more scope for decision-making.[11] For trust to develop, he advised, governments would have to moderate or cease their close inspection of organisations' use of public money.

By then, the minister for Aboriginal affairs had initiated discussion of the Act, circulating a review paper in February 1990.[12] There were 1,024 corporations registered under the ACA Act and supported by government grants. The registrar proposed amendments to the ACA, resulting in the Keating Government's *Aboriginal Councils and Associations Amendment Act 1992*. The changes were intended to strengthen the rights of ordinary members and to improve public accountability. Governing committees could no longer include bankrupts or certain categories of persons sentenced to imprisonment; members of governing committees would disclose financial interest in matters before the committee; the registrar would arbitrate internal disputes and enforce dissenting members' right to request that governing committees convene a special meeting; the registrar could now issue statutory notices, seek injunctions, appoint administrators and petition for a corporation's wind-up. In June 1993, the Keating Government tabled further amendments that would have increased state discipline.[13]

These changes addressed perceptions that Aboriginal corporations might use grants improperly if not more closely monitored. Adding to the perception that public money was at risk, there was now another layer of Indigenous control over money, as ATSIC assumed responsibility for programs that had been administered from 1973 to 1990 by the Department of Aboriginal Affairs (DAA). While ATSIC officials, like DAA officials, were Commonwealth public servants, ATSIC policies were set by elected Indigenous Australians. The Aboriginal and Torres Strait Islander electorate voted in regions (at first 60, but reduced to 36 in 1993) to select regional councillors, and regional councils formulated development plans. To select ATSIC's national leadership, regional councillors were grouped into 17 electoral zones, each zone electing one commissioner. The government appointed three commissioners

---

11   RCIADIC, *National Report*, vol. 2, 525–26.
12   Office of the Registrar of Aboriginal Corporations (ORAC), *Annual Report 1989–90*.
13   Mantziaris, 'Beyond'.

(including the chair), to make a board of 20. Regional Councils had discretion over grants to Indigenous organisations delivering housing, infrastructure and employment, subject to policies set by the commissioners. ATSIC was thus a hybrid of two previously distinct kinds of agency: program delivery (formerly DAA's responsibility) and the work of political representation and policy advice previously carried out by the NAC and its predecessor the NACC.

Debating the *Aboriginal and Torres Strait Islander Commission Act 1989*, conservative members of parliament had doubted that an agency controlled by elected Indigenous Australians would handle public money responsibly. The shadow minister for Aboriginal affairs (Warwick Smith) criticised ATSIC as excessively centralised, adding:

> This integration of representative and administrative functions [would leave the commissioners] torn between doing the best for their constituents and administering hundreds of millions of dollars for grants with bureaucratic impartiality. That is a fundamental conflict, a conflict in which lie the seeds of ATSIC's destruction.[14]

Conservative misgivings about ATSIC went even deeper than this. The very idea of a distinct Indigenous institution seemed wrong in principle to John Howard. On 11 April 1989, before the bill's 'first reading', he warned that:

> If the Government wants to divide Australian against Australian, if it wants to create a black nation within the Australian nation, it should go ahead with its Aboriginal and Torres Strait Islander Commission (ATSIC) legislation and its treaty.[15]

The Hawke Government did not yield to Howard's point, but it did address the worry that elected persons might use public money to ingratiate Indigenous constituents. The Act prescribed an Office of Evaluation and Audit (OEA) within ATSIC. The intended functions of the OEA paralleled those of the Registrar of Aboriginal Corporations.

---

14 Smith, *CPD* HoR, 23 May 1989, 2714.
15 Howard, *CPD* HoR, 11 April 1989, 1328.

The registrar becomes active

Though not obliged to issue annual reports, the Registrar of Aboriginal Corporations began to do so in 1989–90, ATSIC's first financial year, listing corporations subject to the new regime of 'enforcement' enabled by the 1992 amendments to the ACA Act. Registrar Nourredine Bouhafs (appointed in January 1993, after two periods 'acting' in 1991 and 1992) justified his powers:

> When the Act was originally drafted in the 1970s, the emphasis was on keeping the incorporation process simple, allowing for the flexible operation of Aboriginal Corporations and keeping the ongoing reporting requirements to a minimum. The Act was particularly oriented towards the needs of remote communities receiving one-off grants for special purposes. Legislators at the time could not have foreseen the size and range of funding now flowing to Aboriginal Corporations, the complex business activities in which many are now involved and the considerable assets accumulated by Corporations over the past 16 years.[16]

Bouhafs advised further amendments to the ACA Act, finding the Keating Government receptive. When ATSIC was asked to comment in 1994, the commissioners persuaded the minister to defer amendments, pending a review of the ACA Act to be conducted by ATSIC. The review (by Dr James Fingleton for the Australian Institute of Aboriginal and Torres Strait Islander Studies) recommended relaxation of restrictions on the design of Indigenous corporations, to align them better with Indigenous custom.[17] Fingleton's 1996 recommendations did not persuade the Howard Government to change the ACA Act.

While Fingleton was conducting his review, the election of the Howard Government in March 1996 brought to power members of parliament still sceptical about whether Indigenous people other than public servants should be spending public money. Publicised instances of dishonesty and/or incompetence illustrated for many Australians that public money allocated to elected Indigenous Australians could bankroll political patronage by an emerging Indigenous political class. Accordingly, there was an audience for Bouhafs's continuing reports. Enforcement statistics for July 1994 to June 2000 (the period in which Bouhafs was Registrar) are shown in Table 6.1:

---

16   ORAC, *Annual Report 1993–94*, vii.
17   See Rowse, 'Culturally' for a discussion of the Fingleton Report.

Table 6.1: Acquittal lapses and corrective actions, ORAC, 1994–95 to 1999–2000.

Year	1994–95	1995–96	1996–97	1997–98	1998–99	1999–2000
Administrators appointed	9	15	15	10	17	13
Not submitting financial statement	803	1,015	Not reported	700 ('for last three years')	'a high proportion'	388 ('for last three years')
Examinations completed	90	56	70	65	35	47
Issue of compliance notice	48	30	22	44	14	32
Subject to winding up	13	18	28	26	34	57
Total corporations registered	2,389	2,654	2,816	2,999	2,853	2,703

Source: ORAC, *Annual Reports 1994–95, 1995–96, 1996–97, 1997–98, 1998–99, 1999–2000*.

Examinations enabled the registrar to provide 'feedback', usually in the form of a letter detailing a list of required improvements. Corporations in serious trouble were sent a formal notice requiring them to 'show cause' why ORAC (Office of the Registrar of Aboriginal Corporations) should not appoint a 'special administrator' to take temporary control of the corporation. Administration did not usually include liquidating the corporation's assets, negotiating a plan to pay its debts and winding it up. More often, 'administration' sought to enable an Indigenous corporation to continue on a more sustainable financial footing, so that the surviving Indigenous corporation could be handed back to its directors.

The registrar continued to press for reform, noting significant changes in the Act's environment in the 1990s: Australian lawmakers at the state and the national levels had been forced by a High Court ruling in 1990 to engage in a major reconstruction of corporate regulation, resulting in the *Corporations Act 2001*; and the implementation of the *Native Title Act 1993* was giving rise to many prescribed bodies corporate, as title-holding entities. In November 2000, the registrar commissioned a review of the ACA Act by a multidisciplinary team headed by Corrs Chambers Westgarth, Lawyers. The review's consultation paper asked whether a specific Indigenous incorporation statute was still necessary, and (if so) whether it should be for all Indigenous corporations, regardless of size. Consultations found widespread support for such a statute with no restriction on the size of the organisations to which it would apply; as well, according to the registrar, supporters wanted the Act to be both 'more flexible' about the design of corporations and more consistent with the *Corporations Act*, while enabling the registrar's office to focus more on 'capacity building and assistance'.[18] The final report and recommendations of the Corrs review were released in December 2002. Before we describe the legislation that flowed from the report, it is necessary to note what was happening to ATSIC.

ATSIC's demise, 2002–05

From the inception of ATSIC, its leaders had faced a problem of legitimacy in the eyes of Indigenous Australians, as the first appointed chair of ATSIC, Lowitja O'Donoghue, acknowledged in 1995:

> Certain Indigenous organisations have also been critical of ATSIC's role and representativeness. They have challenged its decisions or sponsored challenges in public debate, in courts or tribunals or through the Ombudsman. To a great extent these challenges should not be regarded as surprising or necessarily reflecting on ATSIC's competence. It is only natural that other organisations may have agendas that differ from the Commission's. It should not be assumed that indigenous Australia will always speak with one voice. But ATSIC as the only national structure of indigenous representation will endure. Above all, ATSIC represents a challenge for Indigenous Australians, a challenge to get involved, to make processes work for them.[19]

On assuming office, the Howard Government modified but did not extinguish the Hawke government's and Keating government's defining Indigenous policies: ATSIC and native title. In April 1996, the Howard Government appointed a special auditor to ATSIC. Before grants or loans to organisations could be made, a clearance from the special auditor would be required. ATSIC disputed the legality of this innovation and the Federal Court ruled that the government was not empowered to direct the commission in this way. By the time this judgement was announced,

---

18   ORAC, *Annual Report 2001–02*, 3.
19   ATSIC, *Annual Report 1994–95*, 34.

the special auditor had already examined 1,122 organisations, clearing 95 per cent of them for further funding. ATSIC was pleased to report the opinion of the special auditor that many accountability problems related not to dishonesty but to the small size of the organisations and to their lack of training.[20] In its first budget (1996–97), the Howard Government reduced ATSIC's funding by 6 per cent.

Constrained by the new national ideology of 'reconciliation' (which Howard described as 'an unstoppable force'), the Howard Government seemed cautiously to explore what legacies of Labor to reject and what to 'live with', pragmatically.[21] Affording ATSIC greater autonomy, the government in 1999 allowed that the chair of ATSIC be elected by the Board of Commissioners. In December 1999, the board elected Geoff Clark, whose commitment to Indigenous rights made him one of many critics of the Howard Government's 1998 amendments to the *Native Title Act*. Howard and Clark were thus on opposite sides of a 1990s debate about whether recognising distinct Indigenous rights was essential for reconciliation.[22] While both agreed that 'reconciliation' included reducing Indigenous Australians' socio-economic 'disadvantage', ATSIC (and Clark) argued that the key to overcoming disadvantage was greater government recognition of Indigenous Australians as self-determining peoples within the Australian nation. The Howard Government dismissed distinct Indigenous rights as a distraction from the interests of Indigenous Australians: the 'practical reconciliation' that would result from government programs in housing, health, education, security services, employment and Indigenous enterprise formation.

Clark, like O'Donoghue, sensed that ATSIC was politically vulnerable. At ATSIC's policy conference in April 2002 he reminded his audience that, even though ATSIC spent less than half of the Commonwealth's Indigenous program budget, it was conspicuous (to the public) as the paramount Indigenous agency, and easily blamed for not achieving socio-economic equality ('practical reconciliation').[23] Exacerbating ATSIC's problem were the diminishing reputations of Clark and his Deputy Chair Ray Robinson. In July 2002, police in Victoria decided not to prosecute Clark for rape, after 12 months of investigating well-publicised

---

20 ATSIC, *Annual Report 1996–97*, 25.
21 Howard, *Howard*, 252.
22 For a content analysis of federal MPs' uses of the 'reconciliation' see Pratt, *Practising*.
23 'Systemic Ignorance over ATSIC Budget: Clark', *National Indigenous Times*, 22 May 2002, 9.

accusations. He was also being prosecuted for 'riotous behaviour' after a fight in a hotel. Some observers questioned the political judgement of ATSIC's Board of Commissioners for covering the costs of his defence by a top Melbourne QC. In Queensland, Ray Robinson began legal proceedings against the *Courier Mail* for alleging his improper financial dealing, while the Office of Evaluation and Audit investigated the claim.[24]

Without referring to these problems of individual standing, in June 2002 the minister (Philip Ruddock) announced a review of ATSIC. He justified the inquiry as a response to Indigenous disquiet, quoting Marandoo Yanner describing ATSIC as a 'hopeless, powerless, useless organisation'. While that was harsh, the minister commented, it 'speaks of the sort of frustrations that are there'.[25] Two weeks later, the *National Indigenous Times* reported a young Aboriginal man, Joe Hedger, saying that ATSIC was in the newspapers 'for the wrong reasons' and that young people such as himself were not attracted to it for a political career.[26] In July 2002, Clark acknowledged that some Indigenous Australians were so alienated from ATSIC that they might not participate in its fourth election (scheduled to be held on 19 October 2002). Voter registration, he acknowledged, was a test of ATSIC's significance to Indigenous Australians.[27] Clark and John Ah Kit (an Indigenous member of the Northern Territory Legislative Assembly) were quoted as saying that, while they respected the choice not to vote, Indigenous Australians should vote.[28] The October election produced a new board and, in December, Clark and Robinson persuaded commissioners that they should continue as chair and deputy chair.

Criticism of ATSIC came from Indigenous people whom the minister could not ignore. At the time of the election, Patrick Dodson (former chair of the Council for Aboriginal Reconciliation) was reported as calling for ATSIC to be phased out; ATSIC was tarnished, he reportedly said, by

---

24   Chris Graham, 'ATSIC Launches Inquiry; Robinson Claims Innocence', *National Indigenous Times*, 31 July 2002, 1, 4.
25   Chris Graham, 'Ruddock Calls for Debate on ATSIC's Future', *National Indigenous Times*, 5 June 2002, 1, 4.
26   Chris Graham, 'A Fiery Political Welcome for Young "Warrior"', *National Indigenous Times*, 19 June 2002, 1, 9.
27   Chris Graham, 'ATSIC Enters Election Mode', *National Indigenous Times*, 31 July 2002, 1, 17.
28   Chris Graham, 'To Vote or Not to Vote? That Was the Question', *National Indigenous Times*, 9 October 2002, 1, 4. Table 8 in Sanders, Taylor and Ross, 'Participation', 508 shows that voter turn-out, as a proportion of voting age Indigenous population, was 23.7 per cent in 1993, 24.1 per cent in 1996 and 22.9 per cent in 1999.

the actions of its leaders.[29] At the same time, newspapers reported a court case in which Clark's predecessor as chair, Gatjil Djerrkura, was accused of sexual harassment. Commissioner Jenny Pryor was quoted as saying that a woman should lead ATSIC, given the behaviour of its male leaders.[30] In November 2002, Minister Ruddock announced rules that would allow him to remove a commissioner 'for a variety of behavioural offences, including causing public embarrassment to an Aboriginal organisation, seriously disrupting meetings and sexual harassment in or out of the workplace'.[31] In December the new CEO of ATSIC, Wayne Gibbons, was quoted as saying that:

> A lot of what you hear about ATSIC is not too favourable. There's a perception of poor administration and of waste. That's got to be dealt with or ATSIC does not have a future.[32]

Lowitja O'Donoghue wrote to Ruddock asking him to state his reasons for not sacking Clark.[33]

Meanwhile, on 12 November 2002, the minister had announced the ATSIC inquiry's terms of reference and the panel that would conduct the review: Bob Collins, John Hannaford and Jackie Huggins. Within weeks, he had pre-empted their recommendations in one respect. In order to deal with perceptions of conflict of interest, he announced on Christmas Eve 2002 that ATSIC could no longer fund organisations of which ATSIC full-time officeholders were directors or in which they had a controlling interest.[34] The review recommendations were further pre-empted, in April–June 2003, by a ministerial command that radically redesigned ATSIC: removing nearly all staff and almost the entire budget from the control of the Board of Commissioners and handing them over to a new body, the Aboriginal and Torres Strait Islander Services (ATSIS). ATSIS was to be made up of former ATSIC public servants, answerable to the minister and making all decisions about individual grants (within policy guidelines formulated by ATSIC's Board of Commissioners). Debating this change in April 2003, Ruddock and Clark had been unable

---

29   Chris Graham and AAP, 'Dodson Comments Sour Grapes: Sugar', *National Indigenous Times*, 23 October 2002, 1.

30   'Pryor Says ATSIC Needs a Woman at the Helm', *National Indigenous Times*, 23 October 2002, 10.

31   Chris Graham, 'Tough New Rules for ATSIC Board', *National Indigenous Times*, 20 November 2002, 1, 11.

32   Chris Graham, 'ATSIC Needs an Overhaul: CEO', *National Indigenous Times*, 18 December 2002.

33   'ATSIC under Fire', *National Indigenous Times*, 30 April 2003, 4.

34   ATSIC, *Annual Report 2002–03*.

to agree on a model that would deal – to the government's satisfaction – with perceptions that persons elected to ATSIC had a conflict of interest if they participated in grant decisions.[35] In the formation of ATSIS, the minister had asserted his authority – 'a gun pointed at our head', as Clark later described it.[36] ATSIS commenced on 1 July 2003.

The Howard Government received the report of the ATSIC review in November 2003. Explaining Indigenous Australians' estrangement as an effect of ATSIC's concentration of power at the national level, the panel sought more power for elected regional councils. At the national level, the Board of Commissioners should be split into a deliberative, policymaking body of 38 that would delegate day-to-day leadership to a 'national executive' of up to 10 members, serviced by policy committees. Seeking to reduce expectations of ATSIC, the review pointed to the small role assigned to ATSIC in relieving Indigenous Australians' immense problems. Finally, the panel suggested that the elected and administrative arms (ATSIC and ATSIS) be reintegrated, but with a clearer delineation of their roles.[37]

The federal Opposition (the Australian Labor Party) contributed to the debate about these reforms by announcing on 30 March 2004 that it would abolish ATSIC if it won the 2004 election and replace it with a directly elected national Indigenous body. This emboldened the government to announce (on 15 April 2004) that it would abolish ATSIC, appoint a National Indigenous Council (NIC), devolve Indigenous-specific programs to mainstream departments, establish forums (Ministerial Taskforce, Secretaries Group, Indigenous Coordinating Centres) for intergovernmental and cross-agency cooperation, and negotiate agreements on service delivery with communities. Invoking their right to self-determination, around 200 Indigenous leaders gathered in Adelaide from 11 to 14 June to call for a new national Indigenous representative body, though they did not specify how representatives should be chosen. The Howard Government's response in November 2004 was to appoint a small, advisory NIC. Chaired by Aboriginal magistrate Sue Gordon, the NIC was not a representative but an 'expert' body, advising the Ministerial Taskforce on Indigenous affairs.

---

35   Chris Graham, 'A Painful Separation for ATSIC', *National Indigenous Times*, 16 April 2003, 6.
36   Brian Johnstone interview with Geoff Clark, 'An Assault on Me Is an Assault on Us All: Clark', *National Indigenous Times*, 23 July 2003, 7.
37   Review of the Aboriginal and Torres Strait Islander Commission, *Report*.

What caused ATSIC's downfall? Perhaps ATSIC demonstrated the limits of Australian governments' commitment to self-determination. Australian governments could have funded ATSIC more generously, broadened its program responsibilities and secured its seat in the higher forums of federated government so that it could call other federal and state/territory agencies to account. Against that view, we note that it was in response to Indigenous criticism (by Aboriginal community-controlled health services) that the Keating Government had removed health program funding from ATSIC (in which regional councils had much say about money for health programs) to the Commonwealth Department of Human Services and Health in July 1995. Another explanation of ATSIC's demise was that its inception was 'a classic pre-emption of Aboriginal choice' – that is, a national institution imposed on a political culture in which affiliations are local and in which mobilisation is necessarily episodic.[38] Yet another explanation is to point to cynicism (the venality and naivety of certain individuals who had been empowered by national structures) and naivety (unrealistic expectations by Indigenous voters about what ATSIC's programs could achieve and how quickly). A fourth explanation points to genuine philosophical differences about what it means to represent and serve 'your mob', with resulting unclarity of norms about ethical dealing ('conflicts of interest'). Here we note the novelty – within Australia's settler colonial political culture – of the very idea of Indigenous rights in governance. Whereas Indigenous property rights have been relatively easy to encode in legislation (though never without controversy), it has not been so clear how 'Indigenous rights' in governance should be operationalised. As well, the norms relevant to government funding (compensation or 'taxpayers' money'?) have been contested. The dispute about what counted as a 'conflict of interest' in ATSIC's processes had little to do with the criminality (real or alleged) of this or that individual and more to do with unresolved issues of jurisdiction and political culture.

---

38   Wootten, 'Self-determination', 17–18.

The CATSI Act[39]

According to the 2002 Corrs review, the rationale for an Indigenous-specific incorporation statute was that most Indigenous corporations had social rather than commercial objectives. The review sought to recognise greater diversity among those social purposes, acknowledging the possibility of different constitutions and reporting requirements, and it recommended that the registrar have discretion to modify the latter.[40] Meanwhile, the responsibilities of directors and officers could more closely align with the *Corporations Act 2001*. The Howard Government's legislation largely followed these recommendations, and members of parliament from Labor and the Coalition had few differences to debate. Some Opposition speakers recalled that the Fingleton review had criticised the ACA Act for being too prescriptive of the internal structure of registered corporations. While they welcomed the new legislation's expanded options, they called for vigilance, so that actual Indigenous control did not slip away: improved corporate practices, they warned, should not be effected by 'experts' supplanting Indigenous people. Another reservation expressed by Labor speakers was that the registrar should be obliged to obtain a court order before ordering appointment of an administrator.

The *Corporations (Aboriginal and Torres Strait Islander) Act 2006* is a special measure for the advancement and protection of Aboriginal peoples and Torres Strait Islanders under Paragraph 4 of Article 1 of the Convention for the Elimination of Racial Discrimination and the *Racial Discrimination Act 1975*. The Act sets out rules about membership, elected office-holding, meeting procedures and record-keeping; it specifies corporate obligations about the timing and content of reports to the Office of the Registrar of Indigenous Corporations (ORIC); it defines ORIC's powers of enforcement and specifies offences; it demarcates the jurisdiction of courts as allies of the registrar in enforcement, enabling ORIC to prosecute. Thus empowered, ORIC has provided formal training in corporate governance to members and directors of Indigenous corporations and information and advice to members who have grievances about their corporation. In 2017–18 ORIC completed examinations of 53 corporations (out of

---

39   In October 2006 parliament considered a package of bills: the Corporations Amendment (Aboriginal and Torres Strait Islander Corporations) Bill 2006; the Corporations (Aboriginal and Torres Strait Islander) Consequential, Transitional and Other Measures Bill 2006, the transitional bill; and the Corporations (Aboriginal and Torres Strait Islander) Bill 2005, the amendment bill.
40   Corrs Chambers Westgarth et al., *Modern Statute*.

3,046 registered corporations at 30 June 2018). On 5 July 2017 the Australian Government announced additional funding of $4 million over four years for ORIC (roughly a 12 per cent increase in ORIC's budget, each year) for additional training, examinations and investigations.

The CATSI Act focuses on organisational soundness and financial transparency, but Indigenous organisations are also subject to *program accountability* to the government departments that fund them. Departments influenced by new public management have moved away from funding not-for-profits through block grants, instead contracting with not-for-profits for the delivery of services in accordance with precise program expectations. Many Indigenous corporations rely on income from programs administered by more than one department, making reporting complex and demanding advanced English literacy. Curchin's interviews with corporations elicited concern about the time diverted from service delivery to reporting. In 2010, the Commonwealth Ombudsman Allan Asher warned that 'promising Indigenous programs in rural and remote communities risk failure due to complex and onerous government reporting requirements'.[41]

The abolition of ATSIC also created problems insofar as mainstream departments that took over ATSIC's programs were reluctant to continue funding small highly localised Indigenous organisations. They encouraged the formation of larger regional Indigenous organisations or made contracts for the delivery of Indigenous services with non-Indigenous organisations including international non-government organisations. In 2012, ORIC reported that the 'move towards mainstreaming and regionalisation of service delivery for remote communities and away from funding for community organisations is affecting the solvency and long-term viability of many community-based Aboriginal and Torres Strait Islander organisations'.[42] ORIC was called on to assist in the restructuring and winding up of many organisations that had lost their most important funding stream.[43] At times, government departments were clawing back control of assets that had originally been funded by government programs, assets that Indigenous people see as belonging to the Indigenous community.

---

41   Commonwealth Ombudsman, 'Red Tape Causes Indigenous Programs to Fail', Media Release, 10 December 2010, www.ombudsman.gov.au/media-releases/media-release-documents/commonwealth-ombudsman/2010/146.
42   ORIC, *Yearbook 2011–12*, 6.
43   ORIC, *Yearbook 2011–12*, 6.

Conclusion

Indigenous organisations have been crucial to 'self-determination', and ATSIC and the Indigenous sector (made up of thousands of Indigenous corporations) have been experiments in governments' funding of Indigenous Australians to administer services to other Indigenous Australians. Within 15 years (1990–2005), ATSIC acquired and lost political support for reasons both structural and contingent. If the Indigenous sector has proved comparatively robust, it is not only because the benefits of local service organisations have been more obvious to Indigenous Australians than the benefits of national representative institutions, but also because the Australian state has been tutelary and disciplinary, providing a statutory environment that facilitated the Indigenous sector in three ways: enabling the exit of organisations that fell into disuse or into irreparable dysfunction, encouraging the formation of new organisations (including many formed as prescribed bodies corporate pursuant to the *Native Title Act*), and submitting organisations to oversight and training in what Australian governments and many Indigenous Australians considered good governance. The ACA and CATSI Acts both enabled and constrained the autonomy of Indigenous collectives. While the regulatory regime that has evolved since 1976 still sees persisting Indigenous communality in a positive light, it demands good governance.[44] Much of the CATSI Act mirrors the *Corporations Act 2001*, so that directors of Indigenous corporations must meet expectations derived from Western corporation law.

Among Indigenous leaders who see a governance gap that must be closed by encouraging Indigenous Australians to run corporations in better ways, we find Mick Dodson. In 2003, he and Diane Smith evoked an ethical culture that would result in profitable Indigenous enterprises

---

44   The embrace by some Indigenous public figures of the concept of good governance followed recognition by international financial institutions in the 1990s that good governance promotes economic growth and hence that international development assistance should be made conditional on good governance. 'What is Good Governance?' United Nations Economic and Social Commission for Asia and the Pacific, 10 July 2009, www.unescap.org/resources/what-good-governance; 'The IMF's Approach to Promoting Good Governance and Combating Corruption – A Guide: Why Does the IMF Care So Much about Good Governance?', International Monetary Fund, last updated 20 June 2005, www.imf.org/external/np/gov/guide/eng/index.htm#care; World Bank, *Governance and the Law*, World Development Report 2017 (Washington, DC: World Bank, 2017), www.worldbank.org/en/publication/wdr2017.

and 'political and business stability'.[45] They proposed 'a clear separation between the powers and responsibilities of leaders and boards, and the daily management of community businesses and services'.[46] They listed core ingredients and principles of good governance, including respect for the 'rules of the game', such as those found in publications of the Australian Stock Exchange; commitment to procedures of appeal and dispute resolution; and ability to explain financial management systems to governing boards.[47] They hoped that Indigenous organisations could grow in size without losing effectiveness – scaling up beyond the local.[48] Based on his empirical investigation of Aboriginal community councils, Limerick considered that the conventional Western-derived practices and principles of good governance 'are not only relevant in the unique cultural context of Indigenous governance, but perhaps have even greater importance in this context'.[49] In his view, Indigenous governance must be especially robust to survive members' and directors' family-oriented cultural values.

The Australian regime enacts protectionist and assimilationist policy logics. Sanders has noted the return of 'protection' and 'guardianship' to Indigenous affairs in the Howard era.[50] Indeed, protectionist logic has been evident in the regulation of Indigenous corporations since the 1970s. Indigenous collectives have been viewed as especially vulnerable, requiring a conscientious guardian (the registrar) against threats internal and external. However, Indigenous Australians are not unique in their subjection to protective and civilising powers, as we can see in the similarities of ORIC's functions with those of the Australian Securities and Investments Commission (ASIC). Both ORIC and ASIC protect corporations' creditors by preventing corporations from trading while insolvent, and both have the power to investigate and prosecute directors and senior officers of corporations. ORIC is far more tutelary, setting limits to acceptable customary difference; it can supervise problematic organisations more closely than ASIC, in what Sullivan calls the larger

---

45   Dodson and Smith, 'Governance', 15, 20.
46   Dodson and Smith, 'Governance', 15.
47   Dodson and Smith, 'Governance', 14–17.
48   Dodson and Smith, 'Governance', 19.
49   Limerick, 'What Makes', 424.
50   Sanders, 'Ideology'.

'attempt to normalize Aboriginal people by concentrating on Aboriginal deficit'.[51] ASIC possesses no power equivalent to ORIC's authority to examine Indigenous corporations' books.

Do protection and assimilation, persistent in this regime, compromise self-determination? One of this chapter's authors has argued that:

> Self-determination, no less than assimilation, implies Indigenous acculturation. Capacities are not culturally neutral. Self-determination affords new pressures and opportunities for Indigenous Australians to be more like non-Indigenous Australians, in many ways. This does not demand the surrender of Indigenous identity (quite the opposite), but it stimulates changes in Indigenous ways of reckoning their obligations to one another.[52]

But what if the 'Indigenous identity' of a corporation includes norms and practices that amount to a 'polity', a colonised 'jurisdiction' not yet extinguished and demanding recognition? Indigenous political theorists, encouraged by 'mounting evidence of Indigenous polities increasing their authority over their Country and citizens', implicitly challenge Rowse's view.[53] They argue that, since the 1970s, Indigenous polities have adopted incorporation as a legal device to deal with the settler colonial state and civil society, an 'accommodation to colonizer law' that 'can create confusion between the governance of Indigenous community organisations and the governance of Indigenous communities'. Indigenous collectives need 'to transition from "corporate governance" (management of community organisations) to "political governance" (governing of polities)' a shift that 'might also be described as a transition from self-management to self-determination'.[54] Indigenous commentary on the CATSI Act is, therefore, ambivalent. Speaking at a forum convened by ORIC, Harold Furber complained of 'the imposition of Western systems upon an existing governance process ... I think ORIC is attempting to do it, and doing it to a certain extent well, but in the end what it is talking about is Western systems of governance and in the end it's an imposition'.[55]

---

51   Sullivan, 'Disenchantment', 354.
52   Rowse, *Indigenous*, 231.
53   Vivian et al., 'Indigenous', 220. For an older (1996) Indigenous critique see Widders, 'On the Dreaming'.
54   Vivian et al., 'Indigenous', 227.
55   Harold Furber speaking at an ORIC forum on Indigenous Corporate Governance in Alice Springs in 2010, Curchin field data.

The Indigenous sector has enacted Rowley's vision of (what Batty calls) 'linkages between the mechanisms of government and a collective Aboriginal subjectivity or agency' such that Aboriginal people would 'incorporate the administrative procedures of government into their own sense of communal personhood'.[56] Aboriginal 'communal personhood' has bent to fit the mechanisms of government, far more than the mechanisms of government have bent to fit with Aboriginal 'communal personhood'.

References

Aboriginal and Torres Strait Islander Commission (ATSIC), *Annual Report, 1994–95*.

Aboriginal and Torres Strait Islander Commission (ATSIC), *Annual Report, 1996–97*.

Batty, Philip. 'Private Politics, Public Strategies: White Advisers and Their Aboriginal Subjects'. *Oceania* 75, no. 3 (March–June 2005): 209–21. doi.org/10.1002/j.1834-4461.2005.tb02881.x.

Commonwealth Ombudsman. 'Red Tape Causes Indigenous Programs to Fail'. Media Release, 10 December 2010. www.ombudsman.gov.au/media-releases/media-release-documents/commonwealth-ombudsman/2010/146.

Corrs Chambers Westgarth, Anthropos Consulting, Mick Dodson, Christos Mantziaris and Senator Brennan Rashid. *A Modern Statute for Indigenous Corporations: Reforming the Aboriginal Councils and Associations Act*. Sydney: Corrs Chambers Westgarth, 2002.

Dexter, B. *Pandora's Box: The Council for Aboriginal Affairs 1967–1976*. Edited by Gary Foley and Edwina Howell. Southport: Keeaira Press, 2015.

Dodson, Mick and Diane Smith. 'Governance for Sustainable Development: Strategic Issues and Principles for Indigenous Australian Communities'. *CAEPR Discussion Paper*, no. 250. Canberra: Centre for Aboriginal Economic Policy Research, ANU, 2003.

Howard, John. *Howard: The Art of Persuasion Selected Speeches 1995–2016*. Edited by David Furse-Roberts. Redland Bay, Qld: Jeparit Press, 2018.

---

56 Batty, 'Private', 213.

Limerick, Michael. 'What Makes & Aboriginal Council Successful?: Case Studies of Aboriginal Community Government Performance in Far North Queensland'. *Australian Journal of Public Administration* 68, no. 4 (December 2009): 414–28. doi.org/10.1111/j.1467-8500.2009.00648.x.

McMahon, William. *Australian Aborigines: Commonwealth Policy and Achievements (Statement by the Prime Minister the Rt Hon. William McMahon, C.H., M.P. 26 January 1972)*. Canberra: Government Printer, 1972. indigenousrights.net.au/__data/assets/pdf_file/0006/384333/f61.pdf.

Mantziaris, Christos. 'Beyond the Aboriginal Councils and Associations Act? Part 1'. *Indigenous Law Bulletin* 4, no. 5 (August–September 1997): 10–14.

Office of the Registrar of Aboriginal Corporations (ORAC), *Annual Report 1989–90*.

Office of the Registrar of Aboriginal Corporations (ORAC), *Annual Report 1993–94*.

Office of the Registrar of Aboriginal Corporations (ORAC), *Annual Report 1994–95*.

Office of the Registrar of Aboriginal Corporations (ORAC), *Annual Report 1995–96*.

Office of the Registrar of Aboriginal Corporations (ORAC), *Annual Report 1996–97*.

Office of the Registrar of Aboriginal Corporations (ORAC), *Annual Report 1997–98*.

Office of the Registrar of Aboriginal Corporations (ORAC), *Annual Report 1998–99*.

Office of the Registrar of Aboriginal Corporations (ORAC), *Annual Report 1999–2000*.

Office of the Registrar of Aboriginal Corporations (ORAC), *Annual Report 2001–02*.

Office of the Registrar of Indigenous Corporations (ORIC), *Yearbook 2011–12*.

Pratt, Angela. *Practising Reconciliation: The Politics of Reconciliation in the Australian Parliament, 1991–2000*. Canberra: Department of Parliamentary Services, 2005.

Review of the Aboriginal and Torres Strait Islander Commission. *In the Hands of the Regions – a New ATSIC: Report of the Review of the Aboriginal and Torres Strait Islander Commission.* Canberra: The Review Panel, 2003.

Rowley, Charles D. *Outcasts in White Australia.* Canberra: Australian National University Press, 1970.

Rowse, Tim. 'Culturally Appropriate Indigenous Accountability'. *American Behavioural Scientist* 43, no. 9 (1999): 1514–32. doi.org/10.1177/0002764 0021955900.

Rowse, Tim. *Indigenous Futures.* Sydney: UNSW Press, 2002.

Royal Commission into Aboriginal Deaths in Custody (RCIADIC). *National Report. Volume 2.* Canberra: Australian Government Publishing Service, 1991.

Sanders, Will. 'Ideology, Evidence and Competing Principles in Australian Indigenous Affairs: From Brough to Rudd via Pearson and the NTER'. *Australian Journal of Social Issues* 45, no. 3 (2010): 307–31. doi.org/10.1002/ j.1839-4655.2010.tb00182.x.

Sanders, Will, John Taylor and Kate Ross. 'Participation and Representation in ATSIC Elections: A 10 Year Perspective'. *Australian Journal of Political Science* 35, no. 3 (2000) 493–513. doi.org/10.1080/713649344.

Sullivan, Patrick. 'Disenchantment, Normalisation and Public Value: Taking the Long View in Australian Indigenous Affairs'. *Asia Pacific Journal of Anthropology* 14, no. 4 (2013): 353–69. doi.org/10.1080/14442213.2013.804871.

Vivian, Alison, Miriam Jorgensen, Alexander Reilly, Mark McMillan, Cosima McCrae and John McMinn. 'Indigenous Self-government in the Australian Federation'. *Australian Indigenous Law Review* 20 (2017): 215–42.

Widders, Terry. 'On the Dreaming Track to Citizenship: Indigenous People and the Ambivalence of Citizenship'. In *Martung Upah: Black and White Australians Seeking Partnership*, edited by Anne Pattel-Gray, 212–29. Blackburn: HarperCollins, 1996.

Woodward, A. E. *Aboriginal Land Rights Commission: Second Report April 1974.* Canberra: Australian Government Publishing Service, 1974.

Wootten, Hal. 'Self-determination after ATSIC'. *Dialogue* 23 (2/2004): 16–25.

PART TWO: SELF-DETERMINATION AS AN INDIGENOUS PROJECT

7

ADULT LITERACY, LAND RIGHTS AND SELF-DETERMINATION

Bob Boughton

Self-determination can be understood as a policy of the Australian settler state, in a particular period. But it is also a key demand of the social movement for Indigenous rights, and a set of practices within the organisations that comprise that movement. This chapter outlines a view of that movement's history based on my work within it as a non-Indigenous activist, and as a practitioner and academic in the field of adult education and development. I began my activism in Sydney in the 1970s as a member of the New South Wales Aboriginal Land Rights Support Group. In the 1980s I worked for Tangentyere Council and the Institute for Aboriginal Development (IAD) in Alice Springs, and in the 1990s for Tranby Aboriginal College and the Federation of Independent Aboriginal Education Providers (FIAEP). Currently, I work with the Literacy for Life Foundation (LFLF), an Aboriginal organisation established in 2013 by three Aboriginal education leaders, Pat Anderson, Donna Ah Chee and Jack Beetson, to lead a national adult literacy campaign across Aboriginal Australia.[1]

The achievement of self-determination involves the collective exercise by Aboriginal peoples of a high degree of control over their social, political and economic development. This has entailed a long political struggle in

---

1   The Foundation's website is at www.lflf.org.au.

and with the apparatus of the Australian colonial settler state, a struggle to mobilise and engage the Indigenous population in the process of retaking control of the conditions of their existence. It included the struggle to establish an independent economic base, since political independence requires a degree of economic independence to sustain it; and so the history of self-determination in NSW, the focus of this paper, is inseparable from the struggle for land rights and compensation. At the same time, the colonial state on which these demands are being made is also not autonomous, but must to some extent serve its economic base, by taking responsibility for the institutions of social reproduction that sustain the settler-capitalist economy, including the formal education system.

Indigenous peoples, the 'self' in self-determination, constitute themselves as a collective historical subject through the actions of the social movement for Indigenous rights. As E. P. Thompson said of the English working class, they are present at their own making. Moreover, like the working class of classical Marxism, while they are making history, it is not in conditions of their own choosing. Each generation struggles to achieve, and to practice, self-determination under conditions and within limits inherited from the past. Most importantly for this chapter, these inherited conditions include the 'level' and type of education to which people have had access. In New South Wales (NSW), while the formal education system has served the settler economy well for generations, it has, over the same period, left the majority of the Aboriginal peoples of rural and remote areas with minimal education levels, and with minimal understanding of their rights, as peoples.[2] This has been despite the best efforts of Indigenous peoples themselves, through their organisations and with their allies, to make it do otherwise.[3]

'Closing the gap' in enrolments and outcomes from *existing* education institutions is not enough. Education for Indigenous self-determination can only be provided when Indigenous people are themselves exercising control over that education. How could it be otherwise? The reproduction (and in the case of a colonised people, the reconstruction) of all societies requires them to control their own systems of educating future generations. This is why community-controlled education plays a central role in the movement for land rights and self-determination. In NSW, the intimate connection between community-controlled education and

---

2   Audit Office of NSW, *Improving the Literacy.*
3   Fletcher, *Clean.*

the achievement of the right of self-determination is demonstrated most clearly through the role of Tranby Aboriginal College.[4] However, Tranby College and its courses were central parts of a 'system' that extended well beyond the walls of its classrooms in inner-Sydney Glebe, including the social and political activities of the wider movement as an integral part of its 'curriculum' and pedagogy.

Since reaching a high point in the late 1990s, Aboriginal community-controlled education has suffered a series of defeats, part of the wider neoliberal roll back of the social democratic self-determination/land rights model legislated in 1983 by the NSW Labor Government.[5] Two decades on from those defeats, this still-emerging system of 'education for self-determination' is now addressing one of its most significant challenges, a challenge common to decolonising movements all over the world – namely, how to raise the level of literacy among the majority adult population, especially in rural communities.

Adult education, adult literacy and self-determination

In Australia, as in much of the world, adult education has several traditions. From the universities sprang a liberal tradition of adult education, sometimes called 'extension studies', dating back to the late nineteenth century. In recent decades, this tradition has become less prominent, as more people entered university education directly from school. A second tradition that began with working men's colleges and mechanics institutes eventually became what we now know as the vocational education and training (VET) system. This includes public TAFE colleges and, increasingly, private and not-for-profit registered training organisations. In the 1950s, these two traditions, liberal and vocational, combined to provide a model of adult education for countries of the Global South, in the field known as adult education and development, which is strongly supported by United Nations Educational, Scientific and Cultural Organisation (UNESCO). A third, more radical variant of adult education originated with the Chartist movement in Britain and was taken up by socialist and communist tendencies within the labour

---

4   Goodall, *Invasion to Embassy*; Cook and Goodall, *Making Change*.
5   Austin-Broos, 'Brewarrina'.

movements of the Global North, and by anti-colonial movements in the Global South. Originally known as independent working-class education, this is today more commonly referred to by its Latin American name, as popular education,[6] or as social movement learning.[7]

In this popular education tradition, the right of self-determination became part of the 'curriculum' of the Aboriginal rights movement in the early years of the twentieth century,[8] and it first appeared in policy statements of the communist and socialist workers' movement in the 1930s.[9] University adult education did not seek to develop leadership for self-determination until much later. According to Rowse, Indigenous Australians were 'not visible as political agents' to the university-based historians and political scientists of the 1950s and 1960s.[10] He cites Charles Rowley, writing in *Oceania* in 1962:

> We cannot produce leadership; what we can do, in situations where it is not too late, is to provide some of the conditions in which it becomes possible; and to provide assistance on request to potential leaders.[11]

Rowley's background was in liberal adult education. He was an adult educator in the Australian Army Education Service (AAES) and, in 1949, he was a member of the Australian delegation to the first UNESCO CONFINTEA, a world conference on adult education.[12] In 1950, he wrote about his experiences as an army educator, and took part in debates at that time about the 'tasks of adult education'. He was among the first adult educators in Australia to promote 'community development' as integral to adult education.[13] In 1962, as principal of the Australian School of Pacific Administration in Sydney, he was still an adult educator, training patrol officers to work in Papua New Guinea, the Northern Territory and the Pacific.

---

6   Boughton, 'Does Popular'.
7   Choudry, *Learning Activism*.
8   Maynard, *Fight for Liberty*.
9   Boughton, 'The Communist Party'.
10 Rowse, 'The Reforming State', 66.
11 Rowley, 'Aborigines', 263.
12 The AAES was under the command of Bert Madgwick, who, before the war, was a Sydney University Extension lecturer. He became the first vice-chancellor of my university, the University of New England (UNE), and Founding President in 1961 of the Australian Association of Adult Education. Dymock, *Sweet Use of Adversity*.
13 Inglis, 'Charles Dunford Rowley'.

Although Rowley looked to adult education agencies in 1962 to overcome 'peculiar difficulties in urban areas' for Aboriginal development, he did not mention an active adult education agency in inner Sydney that was already developing Indigenous leadership courses to help people take more control of development in their communities. In 1958, Tranby Aboriginal Cooperative College had opened in the Sydney suburb of Glebe, pioneering structured education for Aboriginal leaders in how to use cooperatives to take over economic and social development on reserves and missions. Cooperatives were a product of the independent working-class education tradition, initially promoted by nineteenth-century English Chartists and taken up by the early socialist movement. Their adoption in Australia at this time was due to the work of an Anglican minister and missionary, Alf Clint, Tranby's first director, who had a long association with the radical working-class movement dating back to his experiences 'actively supporting pastoral workers during the big 1930s strikes around Brewarrina and Bourke'.[14] Clint's work at Tranby drew also on a progressive Anglican tradition, which had seen programs of adult education and cooperative development established on Queensland missions in the 1950s.[15] The liberal tradition eventually took some interest in the model, as when H. C. Coombs corresponded in 1968 with Stan Davey and Don McLeod, two non-Indigenous leaders in the Federal Council for Aboriginal Advancement (FCAA), seeking information about the Pindan Co-operative that McLeod (a communist) had helped the Pilbara strikers to establish in north-west Western Australia in the 1940s. In his address that same year to the FCAA, Coombs also referred to the Cabbage Tree Island Co-operative, the establishment of which Tranby had supported, calling it one of the organisations that 'may help Aboriginal Australians to cope with the contemporary world by their own efforts'.[16]

In the last three decades of the twentieth century, in NSW as in many other parts of Australia, the independent tradition of adult 'popular' education played a key role in the movement for land rights and self-determination. Tranby was the base from which the first NSW Aboriginal Land Council (NSWALC) was established in 1977; Kevin Cook, a former builder's labourer who took over from Clint as Tranby's director, was the land council's first convenor. The college assisted several NSW communities to prepare land claims well before any legislation was

---

14   Goodall, *Invasion to Embassy*, 299.
15   Loos and Keast, 'The radical promise'; Loos, *White Cross*, 119–24.
16   Boughton, 'The Communist Party'; Rowse, *Obliged*, 31–32.

in place. Tranby played a central role in NSWALC's campaign to get the NSW Labor Government to legislate land rights, which it did in 1983. The college and its supporters were also deeply involved in the campaign against Black Deaths in Custody, which led to the establishment of the Royal Commission into Aboriginal Deaths in Custody in 1988. Some of this history has found its way into accounts of the period, but the direct connection between the kind of adult education that Tranby offered and the growing strength of the social movement for land rights and self-determination is rarely acknowledged.[17] Once the NSW land rights regime was established by legislation in 1983, Tranby continued to provide adult education programs specifically designed to support and strengthen the capacity of Aboriginal communities to win back more of their lands and secure greater control over their own affairs.

The educative work of Tranby and the movement's other organisations occurred against a backdrop of the continuing failure of mainstream formal education to adapt its goals and methods to the policy of self-determination announced by the Whitlam Government in 1973. The Aboriginal Consultative Group's (ACG) report to the Schools Commission in 1975 reflected both the liberal and the independent traditions of adult education:

> We see education as the most important strategy for achieving realistic self-determination for the Aboriginal people of Australia. We do not see education as a method of producing an anglicised Aborigine but rather as an instrument for creating an informed community with intellectual and technological skills, in harmony with our own cultural values and identity. We wish to be Aboriginal citizens in a changing Australia. ...
>
> Our vision of education is not compatible with the current education system with its over emphasis on manpower orientated goals that most Australian people know.[18]

The ACG lamented the fact that, in 1971, out of a population of 'between 106,000 and 150,000', there were only 55 Aboriginal students attending university. It drew specific attention to the lack of administrative expertise, proposing a School of Aboriginal Affairs Administration.

---

17   Norman, 'What Do We Want?', 82–83.
18   Aboriginal Consultative Group, *Education for Aborigines.*

Thirteen years later, the 1988 Aboriginal Education Policy Task Force was more strident, finding that, 'as a result of the lack of education provided for Aboriginal people it can be assumed that at least one half of the Aboriginal population is illiterate or functionally illiterate'. It called on the Commonwealth to negotiate with states and territories to 'develop and implement a national Aboriginal literacy strategy aimed to significantly increase the opportunities available to Aboriginal adults to improve their literacy skills'.[19] The Commonwealth's response, the 1990 National Aboriginal and Torres Strait Islander Education Policy, remains today the only national education policy ever adopted.[20] Two of its 21 goals are relevant to the current analysis:

> Goal 18: To provide community education services which enable Aboriginal people to develop the skills to manage the development of their communities.

> Goal 19: To enable the attainment of proficiency in English language and numeracy competencies by Aboriginal adults with limited or no educational experience.[21]

However, as critics at the time pointed out, responsibility for implementation of the policy was left almost entirely to state education systems, and there was very little government funding for independent Aboriginal-controlled adult education.

The lack of adult education services to support self-determination continued as a major theme of numerous inquiries and academic papers in subsequent years. In August 1990, the House of Representatives Standing Committee on Aboriginal Affairs report *Our Future, Our Selves: Aboriginal and Torres Strait Islander Community Control, Management and Resources* noted that many submissions 'pointed to Aboriginal people's lack of skills – such as English literacy, numeracy, etc – and their lack of

---

19 Hughes, *Report*, 33.
20 The members of the ACG were: David Anderson, NAC, Vic.; Jill Churnside, Pre-School teacher, WA; Roslyn Ella, Teacher, NSW; Walter Fejo, NAC, NT; Rex Granites, Teaching Assistant, NT; Eric Hayward, Community Worker, WA; Nita Koolamatrie, Teacher, SA; Verna Langdon, Community Worker, Tas.; Ted Loban, NAC, Torres Strait Islands; Bruce McGuiness, NAC, Vic.; Natasha McNamara, Lecturer, SA; Michael Miller, Teacher, Qld; George Mye, NAC, Torres Strait Islands; Wiyendji Nunggula, Housefather, NT; May O'Brien, Teacher, WA; James Stewart, Teacher, SA; Margaret Valadian, Social Worker, NSW. Special Advisers: John Moriarty, Department of Aboriginal Affairs; Eric Wilmott, Department of Education. See Australia, Aboriginal Consultative Group, 'Report'.
21 Department of Social Services, 'National Aboriginal and Torres Strait Islander Education Policy, 1989'.

knowledge about how the governmental system works, as major obstacles to the achievement of self-determination or self-management'. It said that 'high levels of adult illiteracy similarly restrict the usefulness of the public exhibition of draft community government schemes'.[22] The final report of the Royal Commission into Aboriginal Deaths in Custody in 1991 similarly recognised the 'historical educational disadvantage which Aboriginal people have experienced' and recommended that governments support 'Aboriginal community controlled education institutions and other institutions which provide a program of courses which have the support of the Aboriginal community' (Recommendation 298). In 2000, Gray, Hunter and Schwab identified 'community development and training including English literacy and numeracy for indigenous adults' as an unmet need 'where attention should be concentrated in attempts to improve outcomes in indigenous education'.[23] In 2004, Diane Smith, writing about governance in the Northern Territory, made the same point:

> Grossly inadequate literacy and numeracy levels, and poor health, mean that Indigenous people will continue to remain reliant upon others for important aspects of their community management and decision-making. Poor outcomes in these areas will continue to substantially impede Indigenous aspirations for self-determination, meaningful participation and effective representation.[24]

A high point

In the 1990s, Tranby began working closely with other independent colleges, including the Institute for Aboriginal Development in Alice Springs and Tauondi College in Adelaide. Together with several smaller organisations, they established the Federation of Independent Aboriginal Education Providers (FIAEP), which lobbied nationally and internationally for the addition of a different model of provision to that offered through state systems, to give people a choice. The Foundation President of FIAEP, Jack Beetson, joined Tranby in the early 1980s, becoming director of studies in 1991. When Kevin Cook became too ill to continue as Tranby's director, Beetson took over and held this position until 2003. Beetson worked with Donna Ah Chee, IAD's director, and Bill Wilson, Tauondi's

---

22   House of Representatives Standing Committee on Aboriginal Affairs, *Our Future, Our Selves*.
23   Gray, Hunter and Schwab, 'Trends in Indigenous', 115.
24   Smith, *From Gove*, 14.

director, to convince the Commonwealth to direct more of its Aboriginal post-school education budget towards the independents, resisting the growing trend at this time towards the 'mainstreaming' of Aboriginal services. In post-school education, mainstreaming would have meant governments funding only public state-run TAFEs and non-Indigenous registered training organisations.

In 1997, Beetson attended UNESCO CONFINTEA V, the Fifth World Conference on Adult Education, the same forum that Rowley had attended in 1949. This was the first time the Australian Government's delegation included an Indigenous representative, and Beetson used the opportunity to call on UNESCO to support the Draft Declaration of the Rights of Indigenous Peoples, referring in particular to Article 15, which declares the right of Indigenous peoples to establish and control their educational systems and institutions providing education in their own languages, in a manner appropriate to their cultural methods of teaching and learning. Addressing the conference, Beetson spoke of the need for Indigenous-controlled education:

> Indigenous education has to mean something different from education FOR indigenous peoples. If our education is conceived as simply something we can get from the non-indigenous mainstream system, by increasing our 'access' and 'participation', then education will remain what it has been for us for over 200 years, a continuation of our colonisation …

> The non-indigenous colonial state has used education as a major arm of its strategy for more effective government administration & control of indigenous peoples, and we have always struggled against this. This struggle has seen the emergence, alongside our informal indigenous educational practices, of a new and now officially-recognised indigenous community-controlled education sector. Today, this sector struggles to survive on inadequate funding and a lack of acknowledgment of its expression of a fundamental right of indigenous peoples, the right to control our own education.[25]

In the late 1990s, the campaigning work of the FIAEP leadership began bearing fruit, due in part to the support of a sympathetic Aboriginal education leader working inside the Department of Education, Employment and Training, Peter Buckskin, who had a long association

---

25   Beetson, 'Address to the UNSECO Confintea'.

through Tauondi with the independent tradition. With increased Commonwealth funding, and responding to the growing need for an educated leadership inside the Aboriginal community-controlled organisations, the independent colleges introduced new courses designed to develop local leaders, courses that included narratives of Australia's colonial history and of the movements of Indigenous resistance, including the land rights campaigns, drawing on movement leaders as guest lecturers and mentors for their students.[26]

By 2004, this independent model of adult education for self-determination was rolled back, as Commonwealth and state governments implemented two articles of neoliberal 'common sense': that post-school education should be 'vocational', endowing students with nothing more than the skills demanded by employers; and that providers of post-school education would be more efficient if they were enterprises responding in a competitive market to student demand for vocational training.[27] While such neoliberal reform initially made it possible for non-government providers, including the independent colleges, to access government funding, all providers soon had to surrender a significant level of control of their curriculum and courses. The colleges were eventually forced to offer, under pain of losing all funding, national 'training packages' with mandated 'competency standards', developed by industry training boards dominated by representatives of employer associations and the training bureaucracy. These uniform 'training packages' were to be utilised by all public TAFEs, and by both non-government and private for-profit registered training organisations.

Aboriginal colleges continued to make some space in their courses for the political, historical and cultural education that had been central to their curriculum in previous decades. Yet the demobilisation of the wider land rights movement that was also occurring at this time made things more difficult. In NSW, the state government introduced much closer supervision of the state's land council, especially the Local Aboriginal Land Councils; in this regime, governance focused much more on compliance with norms of public sector management than on community education and development.[28] As the movement became more defensive, forced to make compromises to protect the gains it had won in the 1980s,

---

26   Durnan and Boughton, *Succeeding Against*; Cook and Goodall, *Making Change*, 390–95.
27   Munro, 'The Indigenous'.
28   Morris, *Protest, Land Rights*, 44–48; Norman, *'What Do We Want?'*, 137.

the education programs that gave the movement its energy and mass support slowly lost their radical edge. At the same time, the increasing professionalisation of community organisation leadership and staffing saw the majority of their 'base', the rural Aboriginal population, become more removed from day-to-day decision-making, as the land councils became more accountable to government than to their social base, a process that the international social movement literature has dubbed 'NGOisation'.[29]

Self-determination, community control and adult literacy

Aboriginal people and their allies rightly claim that Aboriginal community-controlled organisations are the building blocks of self-determination. Megan Davis, writing in the *Indigenous Law Bulletin* about the United Nations Declaration (UNDRIP), asks: 'What does the right to self-determination look like in practice in Australian communities?' Her answer is: 'It looks a lot like "community control"', and her illustration is the Aboriginal Community Controlled Health Organisations (ACCHOs).[30] However, self-determination via community control is not achieved once and for all. As the Aboriginal and Torres Strait Islander Social Justice Commissioner Mick Dodson said in his first report, it is a process, and it develops over time, involving not only the relationships between organisations and government agencies, but also the organisations' relationships with their own communities.[31]

In April 2009, the Lowitja Institute convened a Roundtable on Adult Literacy in Alice Springs. Among the Aboriginal leaders attending were John Liddle (CAAC), Donna Ah Chee (IAD), Pat Anderson (Lowitja), Mick Dodson (The Australian National University/Australian Institute of Aboriginal and Torres Strait Islander Studies), Marcia Langton (Melbourne University) and Jack Beetson. Stephanie Bell, then director of one of Australia's largest ACCHOs, Central Australian Aboriginal Congress (CAAC), outlined the difficulties of achieving effective community control:

---

29   Choudry and Kapoor, *NGOization*.
30   Davis, 'Community Control'.
31   Dodson, 'First Report 1993', 41.

> It is a struggle to find enough people to sit on health boards and to work in clinics – to negotiate with government agencies, and to make decisions and give some leadership about health development. This means it is hard for the community to take control … Moreover, each year, the challenges of service delivery and good governance seem to get more complex, and require even more education and training.[32]

Bell cited the Northern Territory Education Department's own self-critical inquiry (over a decade earlier) to argue that the school system was failing to graduate young people with education sufficient to play an effective role in community governance. In particular, she argued that 'one of the biggest barriers' to Aboriginal control of their own organisations was 'the very low levels of English language literacy we see every day in our communities. People can't read, and don't read'.[33]

However, Bell doubted that the formal system would deliver the kind of education that adults needed:

> The majority of adults never access this system sufficiently to get even a basic education, a basic understanding of how the world works and what you have to do if you want to change things for the better … We see the majority of people continuing to live in intolerable conditions, and no one is helping them learn what they need to know to get out of that situation … non-literate and semi-literate people have got almost no chance of taking control of their health, or of becoming leaders in their communities.[34]

Bell pointed out that, unlike the organised Aboriginal presence in the Territory's health system, 'we don't have a community-controlled education sector'.

The Lowitja Institute subsequently funded another round of work, to secure Commonwealth Government support to pilot an adult literacy campaign in Australia, utilising a Cuban model that was then operating successfully in Timor-Leste. Over two years later, in February 2012, the first campaign was launched in the western NSW town of Wilcannia.[35]

---

32 Bell, 'Opening Address'.
33 Bell, 'Opening Address'.
34 Bell, 'Opening Address'.
35 Boughton et al., 'An Aboriginal Adult'.

Literacy and land councils in western NSW

The campaign has continued for the past seven years, supported by a combination of government and private funding, and much voluntary labour. Having reached eight NSW communities, in 2019 it moved into Central Australia. A key to the model's success is that it requires the local community to provide the leadership to run it, including the people who mobilise the community behind the campaign and the people who teach the classes. It is thus continuing the tradition of independent Aboriginal community-controlled adult education, and the campaign's three national leaders – Jack Beetson, Donna Ah Chee and Pat Anderson – have all had a long association with this tradition. Likewise, many of the community-based campaign activists in NSW have previously been participants in education and political action initiated through Tranby, or are the children and grandchildren of people who were.

There is not space here to tell the story of the campaign over the last seven years in any detail. However, the campaign's action-research, a component of its popular education approach, has confirmed that low levels of adult literacy inhibit people's participation in their community-controlled organisations. In each community, locally recruited researchers conduct household surveys to raise awareness of the campaign and identify people who want help to develop their literacy. At the time of writing, almost 800 adults have been surveyed, of whom more than 70 per cent have self-identified as having difficulty with basic reading and writing tasks. This appalling statistic is confirmed by professional literacy assessments of a sample of the 300 adults who have joined the literacy classes to date. The assessment utilises the national VET system standard known as the Australian Core Skills Framework. On this standard, well over half the adult population in these communities are at Level 1 or below, compared with 14 per cent of the Australian population as a whole.[36] Given that most written texts utilised in workplaces require at least Level 2 and often Level 3 to produce and comprehend, it is not surprising that the majority of the people who join the campaign report that they play little or no role at all in the management of their local community-controlled organisations.[37] As Sullivan has shown in communities in the Kimberley

---

36   Australian Bureau of Statistics, *Programme for the International Assessment of Adult Competencies*.
37   The data in this paragraph are based on research as yet unpublished, from an ARC Linkage project being conducted jointly by UNE, University of NSW, LFLF and the Lowitja Institute.

in Western Australia, the increasing complexity of the accountability and compliance regimes in which local organisations receiving government funding must now operate exacerbates this problem.[38]

The NSW movement for land rights and self-determination must now address low literacy levels. Across NSW, there are about 16,000 members of the Local Aboriginal Land Councils (LALCs) set up under the *Aboriginal Land Rights Act 1983* (NSW). The members elect the directors of their LALC, as well as the councillors who comprise the leadership of the statewide NSW body, NSWALC. Table 7.1, below, traces the membership and voting participation figures for the state body over the period 1991–2015.

Table 7.1: NSW Aboriginal Land Council membership and voting.

	1991	1996	1999	2007	2011	2015
NSW Aboriginal population 18+	42,011	86,886	91,617	110,026	123,371	128,000
NSWALC membership	12,412	19,287	20,539	16,643	16,136	15,718
Memberships as % of adult population (density)	30%	22%	22%	15%	13%	12%
Voters	6,574	7,031	6,148	4,663	4,120	5,106
Participation rate (voters as a proportion of members)	53%	36%	30%	28%	26%	32%
Increase/decrease in participation rate		-17%	-6%	-2%	-2%	7%
Voters as % of 18+ popn	16%	8%	7%	4%	3%	4%

Sources: ABS Census data and relevant NSWALC Election Reports and Annual Reports of the NSW Electoral Commission.

Table 7.1 demonstrates, first, that the NSW Aboriginal adult population grew very rapidly in the first period (1991–96); second, and in part because of this, the proportion of the adult population who are land council members (density) is quite low and falling; and third, that even among members, the participation rate in terms of voting is also very low. Given that both the LALCs and NSWALC were established to lead the movement for land rights and self-determination, the low membership and participation relative to the total Aboriginal population is a serious problem. As one NSWALC councillor said, in a workshop with literacy

---

38   Sullivan, 'The Tyranny'.

campaign participants in Brewarrina: 'The leaders of the movement from the 1970s might have trouble recognising what they fought for in what we now have'.[39]

As people become more literate, they become both more informed and more confident to engage with the local land council and other community organisations, including the ACCHOs. Follow-up surveys conducted as part of a longitudinal study of the campaign's impact show there has also been some increase in membership and participation in land councils and other local Aboriginal organisations among campaign graduates. In one community, Enngonia, where the local Murruwarri Land Council is the only on-site Aboriginal organisation controlled by local community members, the campaign coordinator has now taken on the role of LALC CEO, and is mobilising the campaign graduates to play a greater role in LALC meetings and in developing and implementing small-scale local development projects.[40]

Conclusion

Dealing on equal terms with government in modern Australia requires a level of formal education denied to the majority of the Aboriginal population. The historical movement for self-determination that began with Maynard's Australian Aboriginal Progressive Association in 1924 faced what development theorists call a problem of scale-up when, from the 1970s onwards, governments began to entertain the possibility of increased self-determination. Commonwealth and state government policies that created an expanded role for Aboriginal organisations increased the demand for people to staff and lead these organisations. Each government agency also began to foster the development of their own specific Aboriginal body or bodies to which they could turn for advice, and to partner the provision of their services. The work of such bodies, however, required people in communities to have much more formal education than that to which they had previously had access.

Advisers to governments in the 1960s and 1970s such as Rowley, who had international experience in the political economy of adult education and development, should have seen the problem coming. In UNESCO forums

---

39 Boughton, field notes in author's possession.
40 Lee, 'Remote Disadvantaged'.

at the time, the problem of majority populations in the colonised world having minimal education was already well-known, as was the fact that formal schooling, no matter how much was invested in it, could not, on its own, overcome the problem.[41] There had also to be a systematic system of popular adult education, one that could bring the people who had little formal education into the development process as active participants. This is why, in every decade of the second half of the twentieth century, most newly independent countries mounted mass literacy campaigns, which became the subject of an international literature of research and evaluation.[42]

A more intractable problem, however, faced minority Indigenous populations in modern settler states (the peoples of the Fourth World). Simply increasing Aboriginal peoples' access to formal education was not sufficient, because the formal education system of schools, vocational colleges and universities was so implicated in the colonising practices of the previous decades that it could not simply reinvent itself; such a thorough-going transformation would have to be informed by self-reflective critique. As Paulo Freire had written in his 1972 book, *Pedagogy of the Oppressed*, people oppressed by particular social institutions cannot overcome their situation simply through a process of inclusion in those same institutions. The solution Freire proposed was revolutionary or transformative 'praxis', that is, direct political action to change those institutions, combined with constant critical reflection (i.e. research and theory-building) on what was being learned.[43] In the context of education systems of the Australian settler state, this 'revolutionizing practice' would require what is now commonly called a 'decolonising education'.[44] Because the Literacy for Life campaigns are run with a high degree of local as well as national Indigenous control, the acquisition of literacy is inevitably embedded in, and contextualised to, the life experiences of the Indigenous teachers and students. Literacy is a social practice, never just a technical skill, though acquiring and using it requires one to develop skills (e.g. spelling, reading, writing and so forth). The literacy that people acquire through the Literacy for Life campaign may well turn out to be different from the literacy they did not acquire through the school system.

---

41 Rowley, *The Politics*.
42 Bhola, *Campaigning*; Arnove and Graff, *National Literacy*.
43 Freire, *Pedagogy*.
44 Hickling-Hudson, 'Beyond Schooling'.

This is exactly Paulo Freire's point – people will read the world, from their own standpoint, and what they write and say as they become literate will be informed by their experiences.

In the 1970s, the struggle to decolonise the formal education system in Australia had barely begun, and it would be the work of decades. The formal education system could not, in the form it took in Australia in the late twentieth century, prepare people adequately for the tasks of self-determination, because the social sciences taught within universities, the disciplinary bases of modern theories of governance and organisation, were and still are the intellectual products of twentieth-century colonialism and imperialism.[45] As Torres Strait Islander educator Martin Nakata has argued, the education to be gained within the formal system has to be critiqued from 'an Indigenous standpoint', that is, from the point of view of the knowledges and experiences of Indigenous peoples, rather than simply taken over as a set of neutral ideas and technical skills.[46]

The failure of the formal education system to accommodate a more independent self-determining Aboriginal education has now produced a new contradiction within the movement for self-determination itself. On the one hand, the Aboriginal organisations which set out to become the foundation of self-determination, and the public service agencies with which they must interact to achieve their goals, are increasingly managed, staffed and led by Aboriginal people who have succeeded in formal education. On the other hand, a significant minority of the Aboriginal people from whom these organisation derive their mandate and legitimacy, and the majority of the people whose daily needs are most urgent, struggle to participate in their deliberations, due to their lack of success in formal education and, most importantly, their very low levels of English language literacy.

The policy of self-determination was, for Coombs, 'an experiment', requiring us to view government as 'an activity of knowledge-production'.[47] This chapter has sought to show that the social movement for Aboriginal self-determination in NSW also was, and still is, a process of knowledge creation, of learning-in-action. The Aboriginal adult literacy campaign can thus be seen as a further stage in this movement 'experiment', one which

---

45 Connell, *Southern Theory.*
46 Nakata, *Disciplining.*
47 Rowse, *Rethinking*, 196.

both exposes and clarifies a new contradiction, while at the same time employing an Aboriginal-controlled self-determining education process to move beyond it.

References

Aboriginal Consultative Group. 'Report to the Schools Commission by the Aboriginal Consultative Group – June 1975'. *Aboriginal Child at School* 3, no. 4 (August 1975): 60–64. doi.org/10.1017/s1326011100601473.

Aboriginal Consultative Group. *Education For Aborigines: Report to the Schools Commission*. Canberra: Schools Commission, 2014 [1975].

Arnove, R. F. and H. J. Graff, eds. *National Literacy Campaigns and Movements: Historical and Comparative Perspectives*. New Brunswick and London: Transaction Publishers, 2008. doi.org/10.4324/9781315125077.

Audit Office of New South Wales. *Improving the Literacy of Aboriginal Students in NSW Public Schools: Department of Education and Communities*. Sydney: Audit Office of New South Wales, 2012. Accessed 30 October 2017. www.audit.nsw.gov.au/.

Austin-Broos, Diane. 'Brewarrina: An Australian Story'. *Oceania* 85, no. 2 (2015): 238–42. doi.org/10.1002/ocea.5087.

Australian Bureau of Statistics. *Programme for the International Assessment of Adult Competencies, Australia, 2011–12*. ABS Cat No. 4228.0. Canberra: Australian Bureau of Statistics, 2013.

Beetson, Jack. 'Address to the UNESCO Confintea V Indigenous Education Panel'. 15 July 1997. Transcript. Board of Studies New South Wales, Teaching Heritage Teaching Materials. Accessed September 2018. www.teachingheritage.nsw.edu.au/section07/wd1_beetson.php.

Bell, Sharon. 'Opening Address'. Lowitja Roundtable, Alice Springs. Unpublished manuscript. 2009.

Bhola, H. S. *Campaigning for Literacy: Eight National Experiences of the Twentieth Century, with a Memorandum to Decision-Makers*. Paris: UNESCO, 1984.

Boughton, Bob. 'The Communist Party of Australia's Involvement in the Struggle for Aboriginal and Torres Strait Islander People's Rights 1920–1970'. In *Labour and Community: Historical Essays*, edited by R. Markey, 263–94. Wollongong, NSW: University of Wollongong Press, 2001.

Boughton, Bob. 'Does Popular Education Have a Past?' In *New Directions in Australian Adult Education*, edited by B. Boughton, T. Brown and G. Foley, 1–27. Sydney: University of Technology Sydney (UTS) Centre for Popular Education, 1997.

Boughton, Bob, Donna Ah Chee, Jack Beetson, Deborah Durnan and Jose Chala LeBlanch. 'An Aboriginal Adult Literacy Campaign Pilot Study in Australia using Yes I Can'. *Literacy and Numeracy Studies* 21 no. 1 (2013): 5–32. doi.org/10.5130/lns.v21i1.3328.

Choudry, Aziz. *Learning Activism: The Intellectual Life of Contemporary Social Movements*. Ontario: University of Toronto Press, 2015.

Choudry, Aziz and Dip Kapoor, eds. *NGOization: Complicity, Contradictions and Prospects*. London and New York: Zed Books, 2013.

Connell, Raewyn. *Southern Theory: The Global Dynamics of Knowledge in Social Science*. Sydney: Allen & Unwin, 2007.

Cook, Kevin and Heather Goodall. *Making Change Happen: Black and White Activists Talk to Kevin Cook about Aboriginal, Union and Liberation Politics*. Canberra: ANU E Press, 2013. doi.org/10.26530/oapen_459993.

Davis, Megan. 'Community Control and the Work of the National Aboriginal Community Controlled Health Organisation: Putting Meat on the Bones of the "UNDRIP"'. *Indigenous Law Bulletin* 8, no. 7 (2013): 11–14.

Department of Social Services. 'National Aboriginal and Torres Strait Islander Education Policy, 1989'. Updated 28 May 2015. Accessed 9 September 2018. www.dss.gov.au/our-responsibilities/families-and-children/publications-articles/national-aboriginal-and-torres-strait-islander-education-policy-1989. doi.org/10.1017/9781108123754.004.

Dodson, Mick. 'Aboriginal and Torres Strait Islander Social Justice Commission: First Report 1993'. Canberra: AGPS, 1994 [1993]. Indigenous Law Resources, Austlii. www8.austlii.edu.au/au/other/IndigLRes/1993/3.html.

Durnan, Deborah and Bob Boughton. *Succeeding against the Odds. The Outcomes Obtained by Indigenous Students in Aboriginal Community-Controlled Colleges*. Adelaide: National Centre for Vocational Education Research, 1999.

Dymock, Darryl. *A Sweet Use of Adversity: The Australian Army Education Service in World War II and Its Impact on Australian Adult Education*. Armidale, NSW: University of New England Press in association with AAACE, 1995.

Federation of Independent Aboriginal Education Providers (FIAEP). *Education for Self-determination: A Review of the Implementation of the Recommendations of the Royal Commission into Aboriginal Deaths in Custody in Relation to Aboriginal Community-Controlled Adult Education*. Canberra: FIAEP, 1997.

Fletcher, John J. *Clean, Clad and Courteous: A History of Aboriginal Education in New South Wales*. Carlton, NSW: J. Fletcher, 1989.

Freire, Paulo. *Pedagogy of the Oppressed*. Harmondsworth: Penguin Education, 1972.

Goodall, Heather. *Invasion to Embassy: Land in Aboriginal Politics in New South Wales, 1770–1972*. St Leonards, NSW: Allen & Unwin and Black Books, 1996.

Gray, M. C., Boyd Hunter and R. G. Schwab. 'Trends in Indigenous Educational Participation and Attainment, 1986–96'. *Australian Journal of Education 44*, no. 2 (2000): 101–17. doi.org/10.1177/000494410004400202.

Hickling-Hudson, Anne. 'Beyond Schooling: The Role of Adult and Community Education in Postcolonial Change'. In *Comparative Education: The Dialectic of the Global and the Local*, edited by R. Arnove and C. Torres, 229–51. 3rd ed. Lanham, MD: Rowman & Littlefield Publishers, 2007.

House of Representatives Standing Committee on Aboriginal Affairs. *Our Future Our Selves. Aboriginal and Torres Strait Islander Community Control, Management and Resources*. Report of the House of Representatives Standing Committee of Aboriginal Affairs. Canberra: Australian Govt. Pub. Service, August 1990.

Hughes, Paul. *Report of the Aboriginal Education Policy Task Force*. Canberra: Australian Govt. Pub. Service, 1988.

Inglis, Ken. S. 'Charles Dunford Rowley (1906–1985)'. *Australian Dictionary of Biography*, National Centre of Biography, The Australian National University. adb.anu.edu.au/biography/rowley-charles-dunford-14191/text25203, published first in hardcopy 2012, accessed July 2018.

Lee, Tim. 'Remote Disadvantaged Community Thriving Thanks to Native Bush Food It's Cultivating'. *ABC Landline*, 16 June 2018. Accessed September 2019. www.abc.net.au/news/2018-06-15/native-bush-food-helping-remote-nsw-community-thrive/9870698.

Loos, Noel. *White Cross, Black Cross: The Emergence of a Black Church*, Canberra: Aboriginal Studies Press, 2007.

Loos, Noel and Keast, R. 'The Radical Promise: The Aboriginal Christian Cooperative Movement'. *Australian Historical Studies* 25, no. 99 (1992): 286–301. doi.org/10.1080/10314619208595911.

Maynard, John. *Fight for Liberty and Freedom: The Origins of Australian Aboriginal Activism*. Canberra: Aboriginal Studies Press, 2007.

Morris, Barry. *Protest, Land Rights and Riots: Postcolonial Struggles in Australia in the 1980s*. Canberra: Aboriginal Studies Press, 2013.

Munro, Kate. 'The Indigenous Education (Targeted Assistance) Amendment Bill (2005): A Threat to Self-determination in Indigenous Education?' *Indigenous Law Bulletin* 6, no. 12 (2005): 12–15.

Nakata, Martin. *Disciplining the Savages: Savaging the Disciplines*. Canberra: Aboriginal Studies Press, 2007.

Norman, Heidi. *'What Do We Want?': A Political History of Aboriginal Land Rights in New South Wales*. Canberra: Aboriginal Studies Press, 2015.

Rowley, Charles. D. 'Aborigines and Other Australians'. *Oceania* 32, no. 4 (1962): 247–66. doi.org/10.1002/j.1834-4461.1962.tb01781.x.

Rowley, Charles. D. *The Politics of Educational Planning in Developing Countries*. Paris: UNESCO International Institute for Educational Planning, 1971.

Rowse, Tim. *Obliged to be Difficult: Nugget Coombs' Legacy in Indigenous Affairs*. Oakley: Cambridge University Press, 2000. doi.org/10.1017/cbo978051155 2199.

Rowse, Tim. 'The Reforming State, the Concerned Public and Indigenous Political Actors'. *Australian Journal of Politics & History* 56, no. 1 (2010): 66–81. doi.org/10.1111/j.1467-8497.2010.01542.x.

Rowse, Tim. *Rethinking Social Justice: From 'Peoples' to 'Populations'*. Canberra: Aboriginal Studies Press, 2012.

Smith, Diane. E. *From Gove to Governance: Reshaping Indigenous Governance in the Northern Territory*. Canberra: Centre for Aboriginal Economic Policy Research, ANU, 2004.

Sullivan, Patrick. 'The Tyranny of Neoliberal Public Management and the Challenge for Aboriginal Community Organisations'. In *The Neoliberal State, Recognition and Indigenous Rights. New Paternalism to New Imaginings*, edited by Deirdre Howard-Wagner, Maria Bargh and Isabel Altamirano-Jiménez, 201–15. CAEPR Research Monograph, no. 40. Canberra: ANU Press, 2018. doi.org/10.22459/caepr40.07.2018.11.

8

TAKING CONTROL
Aboriginal organisations and self-determination in Redfern in the 1970s

Johanna Perheentupa[1]

This chapter examines the tensions between some Aboriginal understandings of self-determination and the Whitlam Government's policy of self-determination. These tensions became evident in the context of Aboriginal organisations set up in the inner-Sydney suburb of Redfern in the 1970s: the Aboriginal Legal Service (ALS), Aboriginal Medical Service (AMS), Black Theatre, Murawina preschool and childcare centre, and Aboriginal Housing Company (AHC). These organisations had been founded before the Labor Government came to power. Their central principle was Aboriginal control, which was supported by ideas of Black Power and of Indigenous peoples' right to self-determination. Thus, the organisations' ideas about self-determination differed from the one introduced under the policy of self-determination, which emphasised the need to address Aboriginal disadvantage in order to achieve their equal treatment. In the case of Redfern, the Whitlam Government's self-determination policy reflected the way in which the underlying belief in equal treatment and modernising Aboriginal people remained strong in the Department of Aboriginal Affairs.[2] Accordingly, it treated the self-determination policy ultimately as a temporary solution.

---

1   I would like to thank the editors, the participants of the workshop funded by the Academy of Social Sciences in Australia and Sacha Davis for their generous feedback.
2   Rowse, *Remote*, 131.

Emphasis on Aboriginal control was a continuing aspect of Aboriginal political activism since the establishment of their first political organisations, the Australian Aboriginal Progressive Association, in 1924. Charlie Leon, who was active in Sydney-based Aboriginal rights organisations and the Redfern community, called for Aboriginal-owned cooperatives as well as an Aboriginal-led federal organisation in his article for the Aboriginal Progressive Association journal *Churinga* in 1965.[3] By the 1970s, the objective of Aboriginal control was rearticulated in calls for Aboriginal self-determination.

Although Fred Maynard had already used the concept in Aboriginal politics in the 1920s, Gary Foley, who participated extensively in Aboriginal activism in Redfern, suggested that self-determination became their central goal following the formation of the National Tribal Council (NTC) when it broke away from the Federal Council for the Advancement of Aborigines and Torres Strait Islanders (FCAATSI) in 1970.[4] The NTC had developed as part of a shift in focus from equal rights to Indigenous rights and a growing sense of shared national Aboriginal or pan-Aboriginal identity in the 1960s. Indigenous people from different parts of Australia were able to explore their shared histories under colonisation, as well as common causes such as land rights and the right to self-determination as they got together at the FCAATSI annual general meetings.[5] The Tent Embassy protestors, flying the Aboriginal flag as a symbol of nationhood for the first time, brought Aboriginal claims for self-determination and sovereignty to the awareness of a wider public in 1972.[6]

Even though Aboriginal nationalism was strongly culturally oriented in the 1970s,[7] Aboriginal activists also demanded control over Aboriginal peoples' social, political and economic development within the Australian nation-state, as we can see in the case of Redfern in the 1970s. As Foley defined it in 1975: 'Self-determination means the fundamental right of the Aboriginal people to have at their disposal the facilities and the resources that will enable them to be in full control of their own lives, their own destinies'.[8] The concept of self-determination allowed Indigenous peoples to identify as culturally distinct from the settler colonial societies in which

---

3   Leon, 'Memories', 17, 19.
4   Maynard, *Fight*, 53–54; Foley, 'Self-determination', 18.
5   Anderson, 'Introduction', 18; Attwood, *Rights*, 279, 330.
6   McGregor, *Indifferent*, 163–82; Attwood, *Rights*, 343; Martinez, 'Problematising', 140.
7   McGregor, 'Another', 345.
8   Foley, 'Self-determination', 17.

they lived, and to create political institutions that promoted their specific interests.[9] In Australia, grassroot organisations, or 'self-determination organisations', such as the ALS and AMS, took the role of Aboriginal political institutions in the 1970s.[10]

As Aboriginal articulations of nationhood and arguments for self-determination started to take form as part of Aboriginal political discourse, increasing numbers of Aboriginal people migrated from rural areas to urban centres in New South Wales and elsewhere in Australia. While in 1950 around 3,000 Aboriginal people lived in Sydney, estimates of Sydney's Aboriginal population ranged from 14,000 to over 20,000 by 1976.[11] Many Aboriginal people sought better employment and education opportunities in the city. Yet, they also faced discrimination and problems in health, education and housing, akin to the life they had hoped to escape.

Most Aboriginal people in Sydney lived in the inner-city suburbs of Redfern, Newtown, Glebe and St Peters.[12] In fact, Aboriginal people defined 'Redfern' fluidly to include Waterloo, Alexandria and even Newtown.[13] Inner Sydney, in the vicinity of Central Station, was attractive for its easy access to public transport and its location near the central business district. There was also employment available in local industry, for example at the Eveleigh Railway Yards. Furthermore, many Aboriginal migrants found support and accommodation with family and kin already living in the inner city. Since Aboriginal people were largely excluded from mainstream welfare benefits in Australia until the 1960s,[14] they also relied on the local welfare organisations. One such support base was the Redfern All Blacks Rugby League Club, which symbolised resistance for the whole Aboriginal community and challenged the contemporary discourses of assimilation. As a model of Indigenous self-help it also advanced the welfare of the community.[15]

---

9   Weaver, 'Self-determination', 53.
10   Foley, 'Self-determination', 17.
11   Wait cited in Morgan, *Unsettled Places*, 47; Broome, *Aboriginal Australians*, 173–74; Foley, 'An Autobiographical', 94, 132.
12   Beasley, 'The Aboriginal', 137–39; Department of Health, *Workshop on Aboriginal Medical Services*, 65.
13   Chicka Dixon, interviewed by the author, La Perouse, 26 June 2000.
14   Sanders, 'Citizenship', 142; Cass, 'Contested', 100–101.
15   Hartley, 'Black, White', 154–59.

Although in the middle of an affluent city, Redfern was poverty stricken and even described as a slum in the contemporary media.[16] Local welfare organisation South Sydney Community Aid reported that Redfern had the 'heaviest concentration of Aboriginal population, living in the worst housing conditions'.[17] Finding accommodation was difficult because landlords were hesitant to rent to Indigenous people. The housing they were able to find was poor and crowded; consequently, twice as many people occupied Indigenous residences compared to the regional average. Aboriginal people suffered from diverse health problems; for example, high infant mortality and malnutrition among Aboriginal children.[18] The police maintained an unofficial curfew on the streets of Redfern, and so violent was the harassment that, in the early 1970s, visiting New Zealand anthropologist Leith Duncan deemed it a calculated attempt to break down Aboriginal resistance to assimilation in Redfern.[19] Yet, it had the opposite effect, shaping a stronger sense of a distinct and shared Aboriginal identity in Sydney.

In response to this wide range of socio-economic challenges, Aboriginal activists set up Aboriginal-controlled organisations providing welfare services *by* Aboriginal people *for* Aboriginal people. These organisations provided free, culturally specific services, thereby overcoming the difficulties preventing Aboriginal people from seeking help from mainstream services. As Foley noted, 'since we got started doing things for ourselves, we've got Legal Service, Medical Service, we've got survival programs, we're providing services for the community'.[20]

In establishing their organisations, Aboriginal activists adopted ideas of Black Power, which for Indigenous peoples in the Pacific embodied a form of decolonisation.[21] Gary Williams, co-founder of the Tent Embassy and the first vice-president of the Aboriginal Legal Service, emphasised that Black Power was not about violence, but about reclaiming power to pressure the government to meet demands from Aboriginal people. He further explained Black Power as 'a statement that we are finding our

---

16   'Rats and Water in Aborigines' Homes' Sydney Slums', *Sydney Morning Herald*, 1 September 1964, 4.
17   University of New South Wales (UNSW) Archives, Hollows, 97A48/69.
18   W.D. Scott & Co., *Problems*, 6-37, 8-3, 8-11; Beasley, 'The Aboriginal', 184–86.
19   Duncan cited in Howell, 'Black Power', 68.
20   Cavadini, *Ningla A'Na*.
21   Banivanua-Mar, *Decolonisation*, 197.

own feet and want to control our own lives in our own way'.[22] Black Power helped Aboriginal people to undermine the sense of powerlessness they experienced and to take control of their lives, politically, economically, socially and ideologically.[23]

The Aboriginal Legal Service (ALS), set up in 1970, is perhaps the most famous example of the influence of Black Power ideology in Redfern. Inspired by the Black Panthers' 'pig patrols', young Aboriginal activists such as Gary Foley, Gary Williams and Paul Coe started to record and confront the police for using unnecessary violence and indiscriminately arresting Aboriginal people. Once established with a shopfront office, the ALS, with the support of non-Indigenous volunteer lawyers, made legal representation accessible to Aboriginal people for the first time. The Aboriginal Medical Service (AMS) soon followed in 1971. It was initiated by Gordon Briscoe, a field officer for the ALS, and Shirley Smith, a highly respected member of the Sydney Indigenous community who worked with Aboriginal prisoners. Murawina Preschool and Childcare Service started as the breakfast program run from the AMS in 1972. Aboriginal women took full control of the program in early 1973, forming Murawina to target the disadvantages that Aboriginal children faced in education. The Black Theatre, 'the cultural spearhead' of the Aboriginal movement, had its first performance in 1972.[24] The Aboriginal Housing Company (AHC) answered the desperate need for Aboriginal-controlled housing and strengthened the geographic base for Aboriginal people in inner Sydney. It was set up by Aboriginal activists and their supporters, such as Bob and Kaye Bellear and Father Ted Kennedy from the local St Vincent's Presbytery in 1973.

All these Redfern Aboriginal organisations lobbied for Aboriginal self-determination and argued for their right to have control over their operations. Foley explained in a contemporary newspaper interview: 'We always see ourselves in the context of the political struggle because we're simply an extension of that struggle, working in a positive way to ease the plight of the people we are politically working for'.[25] While access to culturally appropriate services was Aboriginal organisations' initial and central aim, they all also extended their activities beyond service delivery.

22 'Interview with Gary Williams', *Arena* 6, September 1973, 22.
23 Lothian, 'A Blackward', 9, 50.
24 Bob Maza in Cavadini, *Ningla A'Na*.
25 Prokopovich, 'Aboriginal Health', 8.

For example, the members of the AMS emphasised the need to alleviate poverty as it led to poor nutrition and hygiene, substandard housing and lack of clean water, all of which contributed to poor health. They also pointed to police violence and colonisation as causes of ill health and noted the impossibility of taking care of Aboriginal health 'without being drawn in to the many, [v]aried, and serious other problems suffered by the community'.[26] In response to this diversity of problems, the organisations (the Black Theatre included) employed field officers to address social and economic disadvantage in the community.[27] Paul Coe later reflected that Aboriginal field officers were a way to reintroduce Aboriginal cultural structures in their practice.[28]

Community building and strengthening urban Indigenous identity were also important elements of Aboriginal activism for self-determination in Redfern. As Paul Coe stated, the revitalisation of Aboriginal culture was the 'only possible means of counteracting the present government policy of assimilation'.[29] The Black Theatre assumed a central role in this process through its theatre and dance performances as well as workshops and art exhibitions.[30] However, other Aboriginal organisations also affirmed the shared identity of Aboriginal people, who had migrated from different parts of New South Wales and elsewhere in Australia to live in inner Sydney. Murawina women working with Aboriginal children expressed their hope that 'we Aboriginal mothers can at last provide our children with a strong identity and an opportunity for both mothers and children to be part of an Aboriginal dream of self-determination'.[31] The medical service wanted to improve Aboriginal self-esteem by developing their cultural identity and thus improve Aboriginal health. For example, the AMS organised a display of Aboriginal material culture in celebration of Aboriginality.[32] Furthermore, the mere existence of Aboriginal services run and staffed by Aboriginal people affirmed Indigenous identity as they became established in the urban streetscape.

---

26   UNSW Archives, Hollows, 97A48/69.
27   National Archives of Australia (NAA) C1696/10, R76/59 and R76/4; Lester Bostock interviewed by the author, Marrickville, 14 December 2000.
28   Coe, 'The Early', 30.
29   Coe cited in Tatz, *Black Viewpoints*, 105.
30   NAA C1696/10, R76/36.
31   NAA C1696/10, R76/2.
32   NAA C1696/10, R76/59; UNSW Archives, Hollows, 97A48/66.

Although Aboriginal organisations such as the AMS in Sydney drew mainly from pan-Aboriginal identity, rather than a territorial base, in their justification for self-determination, as Maria John discusses elsewhere in this book, there was a territorial element to Aboriginal self-determination in Redfern. The geographic location of the organisations in the heart of Redfern was significant for the developing sense of community among the local Aboriginal people. For example, Coe envisioned in 1972 that he and other Aboriginal people in Redfern were working towards an Aboriginal village in the centre of Sydney. He suggested that this could be achieved with government funding paid as compensation for the effects of colonisation, particularly the loss of land. Coe described 'an Aboriginal type of village, where … you have Aboriginal controlled community, both politically and economically'.[33] The AHC, bordered by Louis, Eveleigh, Caroline and Vine streets, with its design around Aboriginal communal living, was the most salient aspect of this vision of an Aboriginal village and the territorial element of self-determination in Redfern.

Aboriginal activists in Redfern continued to frame their desire for Aboriginal control as self-help in the 1970s, following the earlier approach of organisations such as the Redfern All Blacks.[34] Norma Williams noted in 1975 that 'self-help is our object' when describing the importance of Aboriginal volunteer staff in supporting Murawina's non-Indigenous teaching staff.[35] However, emphasis on Aboriginal self-help now aligned with contemporary social radicalism and a new understanding of self-help designed to empower people on a collective level to manage their own affairs, rather than the older and more conservative idea of self-help that advocated individual and family responsibility as a means of cutting public cost and responsibility.[36] Importantly, a more progressive understanding of self-help supported Aboriginal control and demanded public funding to support Aboriginal empowerment, while at the same time, strategically, the rhetoric of self-help continued to appeal to the potentially more conservative sections of their non-Indigenous support base, such as the 150 barristers who volunteered to roster with the ALS in 1971.[37] After the Tent Embassy protest with its call for self-determination and land rights, and the election of the Whitlam Government, the rhetoric of self-

33 Coe, in Coe and Sykes, 'Monday Conference', 146.
34 NAA C1696/10, R76/4; NAA C1696/10, R76/59.
35 Gare, 'Aboriginal Woman', 50.
36 Lane, 'The History', 7.
37 NAA C1696/10, R76/4.

help, however, started to give way to that of self-determination in Redfern Aboriginal organisations. Murawina had expressed its wish to be part of 'an Aboriginal dream of self-determination' in 1974,[38] while Bobbi Sykes, a Redfern-based Black activist who also worked for the AMS, stated that Aboriginal organisations: 'Have tremendous political function … they are the Blacks working to alleviate their own problems – the power of self-destiny – the power of self-determination'.[39]

In response to Aboriginal calls for control and self-determination, the Whitlam Government introduced a policy of self-determination once it came to power in December 1972. It also established a Department of Aboriginal Affairs (DAA, replacing the Office of Aboriginal Affairs) and boosted its budget by $13 million in early 1973.[40] Aboriginal organisations in Redfern were among the first to experience this new policy in practice. They benefited from the generous funding and from some weaknesses in government oversight during the early stages of the self-determination policy. The DAA, for example, gave advance payments of the entire allocation and policed audits loosely, which allowed Aboriginal activists to take greater control of their organisations and to expand their operations more than was intended by the government and its officials. Thus, Redfern Aboriginal organisations were able to achieve, to a limited extent, self-determination as they defined it under the Whitlam Government.[41]

However, it soon became apparent that the Labor Government and Aboriginal activists in Redfern had different views of the aims and delivery of self-determination policy.[42] The DAA was ultimately accountable to their minister and parliament, rather than to Aboriginal people. Following formal scrutiny of the DAA operations and the auditor-general's supplementary report in 1974, it established funding structures and started to apply stricter financial controls on organisations, such as mandatory quarterly reports.[43] Furthermore, DAA officials saw self-determination as limited to Aboriginal control in service delivery, and already in 1973 criticised the ALS for not limiting their activities to legal

---

38   NAA C1696/10, R76/2.
39   Sykes, 'Bobbi Sykes Talks', 6.
40   Long, 'The Commonwealth', 110.
41   Perheentupa, 'Whitlam'.
42   Gillian Cowlishaw makes similar observation in relations to self-determination as policy and practice in Rembarringa, Northern Territory. Cowlishaw, 'Erasing Culture', 163.
43   Rowse, *Remote*, 6–7.

aid.[44] As the 1970s progressed, the DAA increasingly sought to curtail the organisations' spending and limit their activities to what the DAA considered to be within their field of operations.

DAA officials saw self-determination policy ultimately as a solution to Aboriginal disadvantage that would elevate Aboriginal people to an equal level with the mainstream population. In this they followed their minister's framing of self-determination policy with heavy emphasis on its ability to work towards equality. For Gordon Bryant, 'the basic object of my Government's policy is to restore to the Aboriginal people of Australia their lost power of self-determination in economic, social and political affairs'; he referred to a statement Prime Minister Whitlam had given to a conference of Commonwealth and state ministers in Aboriginal affairs in Adelaide in April 1973.[45] This was to be achieved, Whitlam had stated, by:

> Encouraging and assisting Aboriginal groups and incorporated organisations in the metropolitan areas and groups and communities in the Central Australian and other reserves to develop their own programs and to manage their own affairs.[46]

Whitlam's definition of self-determination had the potential to align with Indigenous views. However, his statement did not clearly frame 'self-determination' in the context of Indigenous rights and, when executing the policy, as Bryant explained in July 1973:

> Our programs are designed to restore to the Aboriginal people their lost power of self-determination, their self-respect and dignity. They are designed to eliminate their handicaps in health, housing, education and vocational training and to promote their enjoyment of civil liberties and remove remaining laws discrimination against them.[47]

Thus, even if self-determination policy was clearly a shift from the policy of assimilation, in that it supported the continuity of Aboriginal cultures and Aboriginal people as distinct from the settler colonial population with different needs, it was set up as a policy with a strong emphasis on elimination of disadvantage, rather than to assure the right of Indigenous peoples to self-determination.

44   Aboriginal Legal Service, *Conference*.
45   *Commonwealth Parliamentary Debates*, House of Representatives, 10 April 1974, Question no. 437, Gordon Bryant.
46   Whitlam, 'Aboriginals', 3.
47   Bryant, 'Government Policy', 899.

Framing self-determination in the context of Aboriginal disadvantage rather than Indigenous rights made it vulnerable to being viewed as temporary in the inner city, where Indigenous people could not demand self-determination on a territorial or linguistic basis. Bryant likened self-determination policy to pre-existing policies and legislation that targeted disadvantage, such as those governing aged pensions, widowed pensions and child endowment.[48] He also justified the establishment of the Department of Aboriginal Affairs on the high level of need of Aboriginal people, whom he considered special citizens, similar to veterans, needing departmental advocates.[49] However, unlike the financial support required by pensioners or persons with disability, Aboriginal disadvantage could arguably cease to exist, and thus would end the rationale for supporting Aboriginal self-determination policy.

The tendency to see self-determination policy as temporary, and as one of several possible policy approaches, was reflected in the early threats to mainstream the services under the Whitlam Government. Jim Cavanagh, Minister for Aboriginal Affairs after Bryant, raised the possibility of an alternative service to the ALS in New South Wales in November 1974.[50] Barrie Dexter, Secretary of the DAA, in his letter to Kevin Martin, Regional Director of the DAA, in November 1975, considered that the Australian Legal Aid Office could provide an alternative to the ALS. He wrote:

> Even if the Aboriginal Legal Service were, as it threatened, to close down when funds run out, I have no doubt that we could provide an adequate service to NSW Aboriginals without it – and indeed such a situation would be advantageous to us.[51]

Dexter noted in 1975 that the self-determination policy's rationale was to allow Aboriginal communities to decide the pace and nature of their development within the government framework, but this development was to take place within 'the legal, social and economic restraints of Australian society'.[52] Dexter's definition of self-determination emphasised the way in which he felt accountable to the Australian public for administering the policy of self-determination and defining its limits.

---

48   Bryant cited in Nettheim, *Aborigines Human Rights*, 156.
49   Rowse, *Obliged*, 111.
50   NAA C1696/10, R76/4.
51   NAA C1696/10, R76/4.
52   Dexter, *Pandora's Box*, 320.

Redfern activists felt that 'the Labour [sic] Government has betrayed the Black Community', and they protested against the government's interpretation of self-determination policy and control by the DAA in 1974, when they re-established the Aboriginal Tent Embassy on the Lawns of Parliament House.[53] For Aboriginal people, the crucial areas of policy were 'self-determination and land rights', according to a statement released by a Redfern-based Organisation for Aboriginal Unity at the time.[54] The statement further claimed that neither 'Black people nor their representatives have any say in the funding or its allocations', and demanded a greater role for Aboriginal people in making decisions. Gordon Briscoe, who had been involved with both the ALS and the AMS, criticised the restrictiveness of government policy in 1975: 'anything that has the slightest suggestions of policies of "a nation within a nation", or "self-determination", or "Black Power", or "separation", is rejected' by governments.[55] As far as the Indigenous activists were concerned, their organisations were an avenue towards a lasting Aboriginal self-determination, not merely a pathway to equality with the mainstream population. In his memoir, Briscoe reflected that: 'In the 1920s [self-determination] meant "the rights of nations" and in the 1970s it meant the "rights of Indigenous peoples and decolonised groups"'.[56] Accordingly, the Redfern organisations took part in the continuing Aboriginal resistance to colonisation and were accountable to Aboriginal people.[57]

In their correspondence with government, Redfern organisations emphasised their demand for Aboriginal control of their operations. The ALS 1974 submission underlined the role of government in funding the organisation, while asserting full independence in its operations:

> We see the venture as a joint enterprise in which the Government contributes the necessary funds and the ALS contributes the necessary organisation, know-how, experience, professional expertise, drive, enthusiasm, identification with Aborigines, and independence.[58]

---

53   UNSW, Hollows, 97A48/69.
54   UNSW, Hollows, 97A48/69. Organisation for Aboriginal (or Black) Unity comprised of AHC, Black Theatre, the AMS and ALS (NAA C1696/10, R76/4).
55   Briscoe cited in Tatz, *Black Viewpoints*, 100.
56   Briscoe, *Racial Folly*, 177.
57   Briscoe, 'Aboriginal Health', 16.
58   NAA C1696/10, R76/4.

Accordingly, Aboriginal organisations in Redfern resisted DAA officials' attempts to supervise and monitor spending; for example, by not submitting all reports required by the DAA. They treated government funding as compensation for colonisation and thought of it as Aboriginal money.[59] Redfern organisations also resisted government attempts to limit their operation to service delivery and continued to pursue a wider role in serving their community.

The DAA under the Whitlam Government was not entirely opposed to the idea of the revitalisation of Aboriginal culture in the city. It saw, for example, the development of the Black Theatre and an urban arts program as vital to Aboriginal people in Redfern. Barrie Dexter specifically hoped that a cultural centre would help to solve problems of alcohol abuse and violence in the inner-city area.[60] Thus, the DAA's emphasis was on alleviating social disadvantage via cultural revitalisation, effected only through the operation of a cultural centre. Meanwhile, from the government's perspective the AHC provided solutions to Aboriginal housing problems, but it also fitted the popular rhetoric of 'slum clearance' that the government had adopted.

While sharing a struggle for self-determination, the Aboriginal organisations in Redfern differed in the way they responded to the opportunities and challenges of the DAA's self-determination policy. The ALS had a unique position compared to the other organisations in Redfern. Together with other Aboriginal legal services in Australia, it had responsibility for providing free legal representation for Aboriginal people as pledged by the Whitlam Government.[61] However, as the government did not yet have funding structures in place, the ALS in Redfern seized the opportunity to expand its operations to other parts of New South Wales. It refused to seek government permission for the resulting expenses, submit to government conditions or negotiate the limits of its activities with government.

The medical service, like the ALS, expanded the kinds of services it offered under the government's self-determination policy. However, the DAA rejected its plans to operate statewide, preferring to fund separate medical services in different parts of New South Wales. Members of the AMS

---

59   NAA C1696/10, R76/4; NAA C1696/10, R79/16.
60   NAA C1696/10, R76/36.
61   Attorney-General's Department, 'Aboriginal Legal Service'.

protested at the way the DAA controlled its activities. Naomi Mayers, the administrator of the AMS, wrote in her correspondence to the DAA in May 1975: 'I feel that the AMS seems to be banging its head against a brick wall whenever we submit for funds to enlarge our activities'.[62] There were at least two possible reasons why the DAA opposed AMS plans to expand outside Redfern, while it funded the ALS's statewide operations. First, the AMS competed for funding with the state's mainstream health services that also arguably serviced Aboriginal people, while the ALS was the only legal service available to Aboriginal people. Second, the DAA perhaps wanted to limit the influence of the Sydney-based Aboriginal activists in other parts of New South Wales. Thus, the DAA also prevented the AMS from becoming as powerful an organisation as the ALS, which DAA officials had difficulty in making comply with government requirements and regulations.

The DAA also expected the AMS, unlike the ALS, to do voluntary fundraising to support its activities. The AMS became very efficient at fundraising and used the independent funding to set up medical services elsewhere in New South Wales, thus circumventing DAA control. In 1975, the AMS financed the opening of a clinic at Mt Druitt and was also directly involved in setting up a medical service at Kempsey.[63]

Reliance on donations and non-Indigenous supporters who volunteered their time and expertise, however, made the AMS dependent on its non-Indigenous supporters, doctors and other medical practitioners, to a different degree than the ALS. Thus, it was important that AMS members defined Aboriginal control in such a way that it allowed cooperation with non-Indigenous people. Individual non-Indigenous supporters, such as Fred Hollows, who respected the principles of Aboriginal control and the AMS's desire for self-determination, remained active members of the AMS throughout the 1970s. Hollows, a professor of ophthalmology at the University of New South Wales, assisted in setting up the service and became its medical director. The ALS, however, did not rely on donations or volunteer lawyers and legal practitioners once it started to receive funding under the Whitlam Government. It decided to exclude non-Indigenous people from its council membership in 1974 and, later, in 1975, they were also excluded from attending council meetings.[64]

---

62   NAA C1696/10, R76/59.
63   NAA C1696/10, R76/59; *AMS Newsletter*, no. 16, June 1975, 3.
64   ML MSS 6222/1, Vivienne Abraham papers.

With the election of the Liberal Government in December 1975, and in line with its principle of small government, federal Aboriginal affairs policy shifted from self-determination to 'self-management'. Once DAA officials started to further emphasise accountability, Aboriginal activists strengthened their call for self-determination while opposing the changes in government policy. However, as before, the organisations responded differently to the challenges presented by the changes to government policy. The ALS continued to refuse to provide the DAA with financial reports or report on its activities. Nor did it follow its budget or the DAA guidelines. The ALS was able to maintain this position for two more years, as there were no alternative legal services available for Aboriginal people and the DAA was unwilling to fund breakaway Aboriginal legal services. Coe reflected confidence in the ALS's position in his letter to Ian Viner, then minister for Aboriginal affairs, in 1977: 'your depriving us of funds leaves us no option other than to close office immediately leaving the Aboriginal community to your tender mercies. All clients of the service will be referred to you personally'.[65] However, later in 1977 the government decided to fund three breakaway legal services in different parts of New South Wales, thus limiting the ALS's power to decide its own agenda and to resist DAA control.

The AMS, unlike the ALS, provided the DAA with the minimum necessary information to fulfil government requirements of accountability and to assure continued funding. In their negotiations with government, the AMS, like the other Aboriginal organisations, ultimately tried to maximise their level of funding and the level of Aboriginal control under changing government policies, maintaining the argument that funding for Aboriginal organisations was compensation. Bobbi Sykes stated in the *Aboriginal Medical Service Newsletter* in 1977: 'funding of Black organizations should not be considered an act of charity – compensating the Black community for historical land loss would merely be an act of JUSTICE'.[66] The same year, the DAA listed the AMS, together with the ALS and Murawina, among the most politically sensitive organisations with which the DAA Area Office had dealings. DAA officials disapproved of the way these organisations employed 'radical' Aboriginal activists who used the organisations for political purposes.[67] The government's views

---

65   NAA C1696/10, R76/4.
66   *AMS Newsletter*, October 1977, 2.
67   NAA C1696/10, R76/59.

about the management of Aboriginal affairs had drifted even further away from the idea of self-determination advocated by Redfern Aboriginal organisations.

Although the Aboriginal organisations in Redfern started as 'self-help' organisations relying on non-Indigenous support, self-determination became their defining principle once the Whitlam Government came to power. However, the Aboriginal view of self-determination differed from that introduced by the Whitlam Government and its Department of Aboriginal Affairs. Aboriginal activists in Redfern argued for Aboriginal control of their organisations based on their rights as Indigenous peoples and, with the means available and in their multiple ways, strove to establish the organisations as long-term elements of community governance and platforms for political activism. They tended to see government funding as compensation for colonisation. Meanwhile, the government ultimately saw self-determination policy as a way to address Aboriginal disadvantage and achieve equal opportunity. Its framing of self-determination policy in the context of Indigenous disadvantage, rather than as Indigenous rights, set it up as reliant on public funding and opinion, and thus as potentially temporary. While the Liberal Government's shift to a policy of self-management further undermined the organisations' autonomy, they nonetheless continued to fight for their own views of self-determination and to maintain control over their operations.

References

Archival sources

Attorney-General's Department. 'The Aboriginal Legal Service Program'. In 'Aboriginal Legal Service of New South Wales – An Outline Documentary History and Description of ALS Operations 1971–1975', Vol. 2, edited by P. Tobin, 1976. Unpublished manuscript, UNSW Library, Sydney.

Mitchell Library (ML). ML MSS 6222, Vivienne Abraham papers, reports and minutes of Council meetings, 1972–1975.

National Archives of Australia (NAA). NAA C1696, General correspondence files, annual single number series with 'S' (Sydney) prefix.

University of New South Wales (UNSW) Archives, 97A48/69, Hollows, F. C., Aboriginal Legal Service; Aboriginal Health Committee; Loose in box, Organisation for Aboriginal Unity.

Other sources

Aboriginal Legal Service. *Conference of Members and Delegates Held at Lakeside International Hotel, Canberra on 3–4 December 1973.* Canberra: Department of Aboriginal Affairs (DAA), 1973.

Anderson, Ian. 'Introduction: The Aboriginal Critique of Colonial Knowledge'. In *Blacklines: Contemporary Critical Writing by Indigenous Australians,* edited by M. Grossman, 17–24, Melbourne: Melbourne University Press, 2003.

Attwood, Bain. *Rights for Aborigines.* Crows Nest, NSW: Allen & Unwin, 2003.

Banivanua-Mar, Tracey. *Decolonisation and the Pacific. Indigenous Globalisation and the Ends of Empire.* Cambridge: Cambridge University Press, 2016. doi.org/10.1017/cbo9781139794688.

Beasley, Pamela. 'The Aboriginal Household in Sydney'. In *Attitudes and Social Conditions,* edited by Ronald Taft, John L. M. Dawson and Pamela Beasley, 133–89, Canberra: Australian National University Press, 1975.

Briscoe, Gordon. 'Aboriginal Health and Land Rights'. *Identity* 3, no. 3 (July 1977): 14–15.

Briscoe, Gordon. *Racial Folly: A Twentieth Century Aboriginal Family.* Canberra: ANU E Press and Aboriginal History, 2010. doi.org/10.22459/RF.02.2010.

Broome, Richard. *Aboriginal Australians: Black Response to White Dominance 1788–1980.* Sydney, London: George Allen & Unwin, 1987.

Bryant, Gordon. 'Government Policy Towards Aborigines'. *Australian Government Digest,* 1 July–30 September 1973, 899–904.

Cass, Bettina. 'Contested Debates about Citizenship Rights to Welfare: Indigenous People and Welfare in Australia'. In *Culture, Economy and Governance in Aboriginal Australia,* edited by Diane Austin-Broos and Gaynor Macdonald, 95–108. Sydney: Sydney University Press, 2005.

Cavadini, Alessandro, prod. and dir. *Ningla A'Na: Hungry for Our Land.* Documentary. Sydney: Australian Film Institute, 1972.

Coe, Paul and Bobbi Sykes. 'Monday Conference' (interview with Robert Moore, Brian White and Dominic Nagle, ABC Television 20 March 1972). In *The Aboriginal Tent Embassy: Sovereignty, Black Power, Land Rights and the State* edited by Gary Foley, Andrew Schaap and Edwina Howell, 144–57. Abingdon [Oxon]: Routledge, 2014.

Coe, Paul. 'The Early History of the Aboriginal Legal Service in New South Wales'. *Duran-Duran* (Aboriginal Education Council (NSW) Newsletter), May 1991, 28–31.

Commonwealth Parliamentary Debates. House of Representatives, 10 April 1974, 1376. Aborigines: Power of Self Determination (Question No. 437), Gordon Bryant. Accessed 29 March 2019. parlinfo.aph.gov.au/parlInfo/search/display/display.w3p;query=Id%3A%22hansard80%2Fhansardr80%2F1974-04-10%2F0140%22.

Cowlishaw, Gillian. 'Erasing Culture and Race: Practising Self-determination'. *Oceania* 68, no. 3 (1998): 145–69. doi.org/10.1002/j.1834-4461.1998.tb02663.x.

Department of Health. *Workshop on Aboriginal Medical Services: Albury, NSW, 5–7 July 1974*. Parliamentary Paper no. 249. Canberra: Australian Government Publishing Service, 1974.

Dexter, Barrie. *Pandora's Box: The Council for Aboriginal Affairs 1967–1976*, edited by Gary Foley and Edwina Howell. Southport, Qld: Keeaira Press, 2015.

Foley, Gary. 'An Autobiographical Narrative of the Black Power Movement and the 1972 Aboriginal Embassy'. PhD thesis, University of Melbourne, 2015.

Foley, Gary. 'Self-determination'. In *Report of a Seminar on Aborigines in Australian Society*, edited by H. R. Kelly, 17–20. Vic.: Monash University, 16–19 November 1975.

Gare, Shelley. 'Aboriginal Woman: The Power Behind the Man'. *Cleo*, no. 29, March 1975, 49–51.

Hartley, Jackie. 'Black, White … and Red? The Redfern All Blacks Rugby League Club in the early 1960s'. *Labour History*, no. 83 (November 2002): 149–71. doi.org/10.2307/27516887.

Howell, Edwina. 'Black Power – by Any Means Necessary'. In *The Aboriginal Tent Embassy: Sovereignty, Black Power, Land Rights and the State*, edited by Gary Foley, Andrew Schaap and Edwina Howell, 67–83. Abingdon, New York: Routledge, 2013. doi.org/10.4324/9780203771235-15.

Lane, Mary. 'The History of Community Work in NSW'. In *Community Work: Current Issues, Future Directions. Proceedings from Summer Studies Program*, edited by Mary Lane and Glenn Lee, 1–21. Sydney: Department of Social Work, University of Sydney, 1987.

Leon, C. L. 'Memories of the Past and Work of the Present and Future'. In *Churinga: Official Journal of the Aborigines' Progressive Association,* December 1965, 15, 17, 19.

Long, Jeremy. 'The Commonwealth Government and Aboriginal Housing, 1968–81'. In *Settlement: A History of Australian Indigenous Housing,* edited by Peter Read, 103–17. Canberra: Aboriginal Studies Press, 2000. Accessed 22 November 2019. search.informit.com.au/documentSummary;dn=333473 693821171;res=IELIND.

Lothian, Kathleen. '"A Blackward Step Is a Forward Step", Australian Aborigines and Black Power, 1969–1972'. MA thesis, Monash University, 2002.

Martinez, Julia. 'Problematising Aboriginal Nationalism'. *Aboriginal History* 21 (1997): 133–47.

Maynard, John. *Fight for Liberty and Freedom: The Origins of Australian Aboriginal Activism.* Canberra: Aboriginal Studies Press, 2007.

McGregor, Russell. 'Another Nation: Aboriginal Activism in the Late 1960s and Early 1970s'. *Australian Historical Studies* 40 (2009): 343–60. doi.org/ 10.1080/10314610903105217.

McGregor, Russell. *Indifferent Inclusion: Aboriginal People and the Australian Nation.* Canberra: Aboriginal Studies Press, 2011. doi.org/10.1017/jie.2013.1.

Morgan, George. *Unsettled Places: Aboriginal People and Urbanisation in New South Wales.* Kent Town, SA: Wakefield Press, 2006.

Nettheim, Garth, ed. *Aborigines, Human Rights and the Law.* Sydney: Australia and New Zealand Book Company, 1974.

Perheentupa, Johanna. 'Whitlam and Aboriginal Self-determination in Redfern'. In 'Taking "a Rightful Place in Our Own Country": Indigenous Self-determination and the Australian People: A Symposium'. Special issue, *Australian Journal of Public Administration* 77, no. 1 (December 2018): 13–18. Accessed 17 October 2019. doi.org/10.1111/1467-8500.12354.

Prokopovich, Olga. 'Aboriginal Health in Our Hands'. *Black National Times,* 31 July 1975.

Rowse, Tim. *Obliged to be Difficult: Nugget Coombs' Legacy in Indigenous Affairs.* Cambridge, New York: Cambridge University Press, 2000. doi.org/10.1017/ cbo9780511552199.

Rowse, Tim. *Remote Possibilities: The Aboriginal Domain and the Administrative Imagination*. Darwin: North Australia Research Unit, The Australian National University, 1992.

Sanders, Will. 'Citizenship and the Community Development Employment Projects Scheme: Equal Rights, Difference and Appropriateness'. In *Citizenship and Indigenous Australians: Changing Conceptions and Possibilities,* edited by Nicolas Peterson and Will Sanders, 141–53. Cambridge, New York: Cambridge University Press, 1998. doi.org/10.1017/cbo9780511552243.008.

Sykes, Bobbi. 'Bobbi Sykes Talks about the Aboriginal Medical Service, Redfern'. 'Health', *Aboriginal Issues* (Centre for Research into Aboriginal Affairs, Monash University), no. 1 (1976): 6–11.

Tatz, Colin, ed. *Black Viewpoints: The Aboriginal Experience*. Brookvale, NSW: Australia and New Zealand Book Company, 1975.

W.D. Scott & Co. *Problems and Needs of the Aboriginals of Sydney: A Report to the Minister for Youth and Community Services*. Sydney: NSW Department of Youth and Community Services, March 1973.

Weaver, Sally. 'Self-determination, National Pressure Groups, and Australian Aborigines: The National Aboriginal Conference, 1983–1985'. In *Ethnicity and Aboriginality: Case Studies in Ethnonationalism*, edited by Michael D. Levin, 53–74. Toronto, Buffalo, London: University of Toronto Press, 1993. doi.org/10.3138/9781442623187-006.

Whitlam, Gough. 'Aboriginals and Society', Press Statement no. 74, Department of the Prime Minister and Cabinet, 6 April 1973. Accessed 29 March 2019. pmtranscripts.pmc.gov.au/release/transcript-2886.

9

BEYOND LAND
Indigenous health and self-determination in an age of urbanisation

Maria John

This chapter examines how Indigenous peoples in the United States and Australia worked out the potential for their self-determination beyond claims to land or territory – that is, in the pursuit of self-governance over two interconnected realms: health services and individual bodily health. In doing so, the chapter seeks to make a case for the significant role played by urban Indigenous health struggles in reframing and reshaping the broader project of Indigenous self-determination in the twentieth and twenty-first centuries.

In the context of past and continuing colonisation, the political projects of sovereignty and self-determination have long been touchstones for Indigenous communities. One might assume, however, that these terms have come to hold special (and potentially new) significance over the last 30 years or so. Within Indigenous political discourse, the language of sovereignty was invoked almost exclusively in relation to legal and territorial claims until around the 1990s, but even a cursory glance at recent protest placards from Indigenous political rallies across the globe, or at new monograph titles containing the word 'sovereignty' within Indigenous studies, reveals a vastly broadened discourse around this term. Diverse conceptual sovereignties including cultural, intellectual, visual and sexual, to name a few, have now become prevalent within Indigenous studies. For instance, in her important work theorising 'visual sovereignty', Michelle Raheja (Seneca) defines this as a 'creative act of self-representation that has the potential to both undermine stereotypes of Indigenous peoples and to strengthen … the intellectual "health" of communities in the wake of genocide and colonialism'.[1] In one of the fastest growing research areas within Indigenous studies, scholars and communities are defining 'food sovereignty' as 'the right of peoples to healthy and culturally appropriate food produced through ecologically sound and sustainable methods, and their right to define their own food and agriculture systems'.[2]

In part, I think these changes reveal that, in recent decades, there has been some blending of the terms 'sovereignty' and 'self-determination'. They are often used interchangeably. More than this, however, we are also seeing that what increasingly is meant by 'sovereignty' *is* self-determination because *self-determination* can refer to matters of ownership, control and access. Within Indigenous politics, self-determination is commonly understood as a right Indigenous communities and individuals have to determine their economic, social and cultural development. Illustrating the ways in which self-determination has become central to Indigenous peoples' ideas about, and practices of, sovereignty, we might note that a seminal 2005 monograph edited by Indigenous Studies scholar Joanne Barker (Lenape) blends the terms sovereignty and self-determination even within the book's title: *Sovereignty Matters: Locations of Contestation and Possibility in Indigenous Struggles for Self-Determination.*[3] In her Introduction Barker explains:

> Following World War II, sovereignty emerged not as a new but as a particularly valued term within indigenous political discourses to signify a multiplicity of legal and social rights to political, economic, and cultural self-determination … It has come to mark the complexities of global indigenous efforts to reverse ongoing experiences of colonialism as well as to signify local efforts at the reclamation of specific territories, resources, governments, and cultural knowledge and practices.[4]

While Barker is also rightly at pains to emphasise that not all Indigenous peoples share 'the same understanding of what sovereignty is or how it matters', her discernment that sovereignty has come to encompass both legal and social rights to self-determination in multiple realms

---

1   Raheja, 'Reading Nanook's', 1161.
2   Nyéléni, 'Declaration of Nyéléni', Forum for Food Sovereignty, 27 February 2007, accessed 15 August 2020, nyeleni.org/spip.php?article290.
3   Barker, *Sovereignty.*
4   Barker, *Sovereignty*, 1.

(economic, cultural, etc.) and, crucially, to refer to the conjoined projects of *reversing* (ongoing experiences of colonialism) and *reclaiming* (specific resources, lands, practices, etc.), underscores not only the very broad contexts in which sovereignty is now a meaningful concept and project for Indigenous peoples, but also the very central role that a principle of self-determination plays within this expanded pursuit of sovereignty.

And while it would be another two years before the United Nations Declaration on the Rights of Indigenous Peoples (UNDRIP) was signed in 2007, given the centrality of the language of 'self-determination' within that document, it is important to clarify here that the model of self-determination established by the declaration sits at odds with the much broader visions of sovereignty and self-determination to which I refer in this chapter, and which are discussed by Barker (and by others). As many critics of the declaration point out, a close reading of the rights protected by the UNDRIP shows that they are both less powerful than they appear and that they are limited and superseded by the human rights framework in which they are embedded. Legal scholar Karen Engle expresses this last problem succinctly when noting that the Indigenous right to self-determination recognised by the UNDRIP takes the form of 'a collective human rights demand rather than a claim for statehood'.[5] While the document has been lauded by many for its recognition of collective rights, the right to culture, and self-determination for Indigenous peoples, it is also heavily critiqued for not doing enough. Most problematically, it was clear the UN system actively sought to adopt a stance of ambiguity towards the meaning of self-determination as specifically applied to Indigenous peoples. The result has been that the declaration is clear in limiting its recognition of Indigenous self-determination to 'internal' matters only, stating: the right to self-determination guarantees only 'the right to autonomy or self-government in matters relating to their internal and local affairs'.[6] This language makes it clear that strong forms of Indigenous self-determination, which might threaten the sovereignty and territorial integrity of nation-states, would not be recognised or protected by the United Nations.

In contrast, the melding of the political language and goals of sovereignty and self-determination, which I seek to address in this chapter, includes within the wider purview of an 'expanded' sovereignty, the goals of *reversing* and *reclaiming* as described above. While the sovereignty and

5   Engle, 'On Fragile', 148.
6   United Nations, *United Nations Declaration on the Rights of Indigenous Peoples*, at Article 4.

self-determination of which Barker speaks are not exclusively or even primarily about these two goals (goals that certainly might be seen to more explicitly challenge the sovereignty of nation-states), the fact that *reversing* and *reclaiming* are a part of Indigenous peoples' projects of sovereignty and self-determination means we must understand this in a different light to the kind of self-determination expressed within the UNDRIP. One might even speculate that the recent rise in the use of the language of 'sovereignty' has been a strategy to escape the limitations of the UNDRIP. Within this chapter, I distill the strengthening conceptual tie between sovereignty and self-determination into the idea that both concepts have become increasingly interchangeable, since both are increasingly used, most crucially, to refer to the ability to be self-governing (understood broadly). This is the core of the many different ways in which Indigenous political actors and theorists are invoking sovereignty in new ways and in new contexts.

The shift towards something more closely resembling self-determination when speaking of sovereignty, and the frequent interchange we now see between these terms, should also be understood against another key development. That is, a critique that argues for the necessity of rewriting or 'decolonising' the concept of sovereignty within Indigenous political discourse. As the critique goes, the concept of sovereignty (and the modern nation-state) is rooted in European monarchies, hierarchical power structures and traditions of jurisprudence. As such, because these kinds of governing structures were typically foreign to Indigenous peoples, sovereignty is said to be ill-suited to their political conceptions of community. Mohawk activist and scholar Taiaiake Alfred is an oft-cited proponent of this critique, calling for the rejection of state sovereigntist discourse in Indigenous politics because of its connection to European colonialism:

> The next phase of scholarship and activism, then, will need to transcend the mentality that supports the colonisation of Indigenous nations, beginning with the rejection of the term and notion of Indigenous sovereignty.[7]

In this sense, one might again speculate that the recent rise in the use of the language of self-determination when discussing 'sovereignty' has also been a strategy to escape the colonial implications of traditional 'sovereigntist' discourse.

---

7   Alfred, 'Sovereignty', 39–40.

Although such critiques might help us understand the supplanting, or at least the converging of sovereignty talk with the language and goals of self-determination, this shift has not been universally accepted. Influential scholar and activist Vine Deloria Jr (Standing Rock Sioux), for instance, memorably critiqued the growing ubiquity of the concept of sovereignty within Indigenous politics and its straying from non-legal matters: 'Today the definition of sovereignty covers a multitude of sins, having lost its political moorings, and now is adrift on the currents of individual fancy'.[8]

My interest in this convergence and expansion of the ways in which Indigenous peoples, scholars and communities are engaging with concepts of sovereignty and self-determination is, in the first instance, less about what has been gained or lost in this endeavour. As a historian, I seek to bring to light the lived experiences and historical contexts out of which this discursive and political reconfiguring has emerged. In particular, my attention is drawn to a neglected context in which the language of self-determination has always been central to Indigenous political struggles: health. Health and medical contexts also emerge as a logical place to look for the political configurations around contemporary Indigenous claims to self-determination and sovereignty once we recognise the potent ways in which health statistics have steadily become one of the starkest means of illustrating levels of historical and continuing injustice experienced by Indigenous peoples in places like the United States, Canada and Australia. This chapter considers recent rearticulations of Indigenous self-determination and sovereignty within health contexts by Indigenous communities in settler states. In particular, I ask what the example of urban Indigenous community-controlled health services in the United States and Australia can tell us about a new and distinctly urban, non-territorial form of Indigenous self-determination that emerged in these nations during the 1970s. What happens to our understanding of self-determination if we attempt to decentre, or if we look beyond, land claims?

I compare the establishment of the Seattle Indian Health Board (Seattle) and the Aboriginal Medical Service (AMS) (Sydney) in this chapter, as these clinics were among the first Indigenous community-controlled health services in their respective national contexts, and formed in response to similar struggles. Although they did embrace a diasporic and

---

8   Deloria, 'Intellectual', 26–27.

multiethnic vision of the future (marking a distinct departure from forms of Indigenous political community that formed the basis of sovereignty claims in the past), I argue that the ideals of self-determination these clinics represented were not inconsistent with forms of sovereignty pursued by Indigenous communities tied to traditional homelands. By considering the political discourse and the events from which these clinics emerged, we see that the activists who created these health services, and who advocated for a model of self-determination distinct from land claims, stood in solidarity with rural and urban traditional landowners, even as they argued for the urgency of reimagining the project of Indigenous self-determination as governance over social services. The history and legacy of these two health organisations becomes, I argue, a vivid example of how Indigenous people reconfigured the terrain upon which their claims to sovereignty and self-determination (understood as self-governance) could be pursued.

In the remaining sections of this chapter, I will first trace the origins of the Seattle Indian Health Board and the AMS. Though having little direct connection to each other at the time of their founding, I suggest these clinics might nonetheless be understood within the same historical frame given the political struggles and health crises that led to their development. Finally, by making a case for the importance of recognising the simultaneous emergence of these separate clinics as markers of a shared historical and political experience, this chapter uses their histories to foreground a view of Indigenous self-determination as a non-territorial project, and a transnational Indigenous response to government policies of urbanisation and assimilation pursued across settler states.

A catalyst for change: Indigenous urbanisation and a crisis of health care access

Beginning in 1970, in major US and Australian cities, urban Indigenous communities in places like Seattle, Minneapolis, Sydney and Melbourne, started establishing their own grassroots, community-controlled health services. These clinics aimed to provide free medical care by Native people, for Native people. To this day, Indigenous community-controlled health services are still operational. Health experts agree this model of healthcare delivery has been transformative for the Indigenous communities they serve.[9] Indeed, evidencing this, Indigenous community-controlled health services have grown steadily since the 1970s.[10]

Two of the first such clinics were established in Seattle and Sydney: the Seattle Indian Health Board in 1970 and the AMS just six months later, in 1971. In both cases urban Indigenous people faced a common issue of structural invisibility that prevented them from accessing mainstream health services. Two factors worked symbiotically to exclude urban Indigenous people in Seattle and Sydney from accessing medical care in all but emergency cases before 1970. On the one hand, free government healthcare afforded to Indigenous people as part of historic agreements applied only to Indigenous residents of reserves or reservations; a person thus effectively 'lost' their Indigenous rights to healthcare as soon as they moved off the reserve or reservation. On the other hand, mainstream doctors in cities often refused to treat Indigenous patients, either assuming they were entitled to free government services or on the basis of blatant racism and indifference. So common was this experience, a well-known joke referenced it in the American Indian community in Seattle during the 1960s. It concerned an urban Indian seeking a room at a hospital: 'Did you hear the one about the Indian who couldn't get a room? He didn't have a reservation'.[11] In short, in the postwar period, Indigenous people who relocated from rural to urban settings in both the United States and Australia (often at the government's encouragement) were simultaneously forced into mainstream healthcare on the one hand while they were actively excluded from it on the other. By the 1950s and 1960s, Indigenous people in cities were thus growing increasingly wary of mainstream health services because they were proving to be fruitless and inhospitable – often outright discriminatory – environments.

A comparison of this shared struggle across two different national contexts reveals a much larger political challenge faced by pan-Indigenous urban communities at this time: they were unable to gain federal government support and recognition *as* Indigenous peoples. As a result of moving into cities (and thereby 'assimilating'), it was argued they had forfeited any

---

9   Panaretto et al., 'Aboriginal', 650.

10   For example, 41 urban Indian health clinics now exist across the United States. In Australia, Indigenous community-controlled health services now serve both rural and urban populations, and thus a significantly higher number exist than in the US. There are 141 clinics currently operational in Australia.

11   *Indian Center News*, American Indian Women's Service League (AIWSL), 3, no. 1, February 1963.

rights to special treatment *as* Indigenous peoples. Put simply, when urban Indigenous communities in these cities tried to make their grievances and health struggles heard in the late 1960s, they were told by municipal and federal authorities alike that they could and should access mainstream health services like all other citizens, or else they should access resources set aside for other 'minorities'. Not satisfied with being told they had essentially 'lost' their Indigenous rights and identities simply by virtue of relocating into cities, and not content to let the health issues of their communities worsen, activists in Seattle and Sydney alike were compelled by the early 1970s to take measures into their own hands. Pan-Aboriginal and pan-Indian activists therefore created their own free grassroots medical clinics run by, and exclusively for, their own people.

The stories of how these clinics got off the ground and eventually won government support are fascinating and inspiring, but too lengthy to be reproduced here. Instead, I turn to what these clinics stood for, what they hoped to create and/or change, and how we might be able to read them as evidence of a political vision that enlarges the traditional scholarly focus on the history of Indigenous self-determination as a land-centric political project.

Beyond land

In 1967, Seattle resident and Indigenous activist Pearl Warren (Makah) told a reporter from the *Seattle Post-Intelligencer* that, in striving to create a place where urban Indians could receive free social services from their own people, the city's Indian community did not desire 'a reservation right in the middle of town'. All they wanted was a place 'where in our most vulnerable times of feeling unwell, we could feel free and proud to be ourselves'.[12] Warren expressed a special regard for the importance of Indigenous people's freedom simply to be Indigenous at all times and places, but most especially when they were not in good health. Rather than seek jurisdictional control over territory, Warren asserted they were pushing back an assimilationist agenda that encroached into even the most vulnerable and private moments in an Indigenous person's life. The creation of their own social services was seen to be essential in achieving this political goal. Soon after the opening of their Indian

---

12   Pearl Warren in Bryant, 'Loneliness Is the White Man's City', 51.

(Cultural) Center, in 1965 Warren again underscored the significance of their own community services in a lengthy message to members of the Seattle Indian community: 'For too long we have depended upon the non-Indians to do for us, the time has come when we must start doing more for ourselves and each other'.[13]

Compare Warren's comments here with those made in Australia by celebrated Aboriginal activist Ruby Hammond (Ngarrindjeri). During the 1980s, Hammond wrote an op-ed for the *Sydney Morning Herald* reflecting on the close relationship between Aboriginal land rights and community-run health services. She lamented the difficulties encountered by Aboriginal activists and communities across Australia who were struggling to achieve land rights: 'We are adapting every day. We have to adapt because we are living in a changing society'. And yet, precisely because of these challenges, she underscored the vital necessity of the work being done by Aboriginal health activists in cities: 'But the only way we will survive is if we have community-based services'.[14]

Warren and Hammond both underscored a subtle but important difference between the politics of territorial sovereignty (or 'land rights' in Australian parlance) and the model of Indigenous sovereignty that I suggest urban Indigenous health activists were striving to create with their medical services. Hammond's and Warren's comments call our attention to the ways we might read the actions of Indigenous activists in both nations as attempts to make an important distinction within the political project of Indigenous sovereignty, even if they were not yet using the language of self-determination. In their respective efforts to articulate and create a means by which their communities could start living in accordance with their own political, cultural and social goals and needs, Warren and Hammond shared a commitment to the idea that Indigenous peoples in their respective communities had to be in charge of their own affairs – that is, be self-determining. Yet, the strategy each advocated for achieving this was not the acquisition of territory, but rather the creation of their own community-controlled services. In their focus on self-governance, self-control and self-reliance through their community services, Warren and Hammond both challenged the statist assumption

---

13   Warren, 'Pearl's Message', 2.
14   Hammond, 'Land Rights: Key to Aboriginal Health', *Sydney Morning Herald*, 1982. (Precise date unknown, but newspaper clipping can be found in Hannah Middleton Papers, ML MSS 5886, Box 7, New South Wales State Library, Sydney.)

that legal monopoly over a territory must necessarily be the only or even most effective way by which a group collectively governs itself or, as we might say, achieves self-determination. In fact, the innovative character of their political ambitions is evident in how Warren and Hammond each proposed a new and different social mechanism that would allow Indigenous people who had no recourse to nationhood status or to land claims as a group (such as many people in cities), to nonetheless find ways to exist as a recognisable community, exercise self-governance and, eventually, make claims on the federal government for financial support. In Warren's words, this could be achieved, not by creating a reservation in the middle of town, but by creating another kind of space that would allow Native people to practise their culture freely and to feel a sense of community, especially during difficult times. In Hammond's words, this could be achieved explicitly by creating community-controlled organisations.

This move serves as an important reminder that many urban Indigenous people *do* have a claim to nationhood status in cities. For some, fighting for recognition of urban communities as authentic Indigenous communities with rights as such, thus *can* be about demanding urban territory as Indigenous territory. Second, it underscores that, in the case of the activism that created Indigenous health clinics, it is clear these claims were pressed on the basis of a pan-Indigenous identity rather than a national or tribal one. Third, Warren's and Hammond's comments might be read in ways that suggest the irrelevance of particular location to the status of these 'non-reservation' spaces as Indigenous, and thus they evinced the non-territorial basis of the underlying rights they were meant to uphold.

It is important to note in both examples that urban Indigenous health activists made a distinction between, on the one hand, what we might regard as the right of the community to be self-determining, and on the other hand, the right of the community to be able to be self-determining on a specific piece of territory under their control. For ease, we can refer to the former as recognising the right to 'self-governance' or 'self-determination', and to the latter as the right to 'territorial sovereignty' (although, both ideas still fall under the broad concept of sovereignty in the sense I have been using the term). As a practical matter, by seeking the right to be self-governing as opposed to the right to territorial sovereignty, urban Indigenous health activists made a substantive claim about the goals of Indigenous sovereignty as a whole. Their efforts supported the idea that securing territory, rather than being the only goal of Indigenous sovereignty, was just one aspect of it – to be sure, an undeniably important one. But, as their actions demonstrate, they believed a meaningful form of self-determination could be realised for peoples who did not seek territorial control or claims to nationhood.

In pressing for forms of de-territorialised control over their own affairs, urban Indigenous health activists did not seek to displace the importance of land claims (it was never an 'either/or' argument), they simply intended to make room for other political endeavours. Their goals were thus ultimately expansive; they sought to extend the reach of Indigenous self-determination such that it could be realised by Indigenous people in all contexts at all times, not only when they were within the bounds of recognised Indigenous territories.

Understanding how postwar urbanisation and the ensuing growth of an Indigenous diaspora in cities brought on these changes in the political goals of those Indigenous communities means reframing the history of Indigenous political activism in the 1960s and 1970s. Although at this time urban Indigenous communities led the way in political and social movements to protect sovereign homelands (Red Power, Alcatraz, Aboriginal Tent Embassy), these experiences only sharpened a collective realisation among urban communities that their pan-Indigenous political and cultural life in cities was neither represented nor protected by territorial sovereignty. They imagined a common terrain linking separate reservations/reserves with the growing urban Indigenous communities hailing from diverse origins. They imagined their community this way because it actually represented how many of them lived – with family members split across rural and urban locales, and with many urban migrants travelling back and forth. Indeed, a continuing connection with rural homelands was, for many urban people, an important reason to stand in solidarity with struggles for land rights and territorial sovereignty in the first place. That is, even though territorial sovereignty may not have benefited them directly in cities, urban pan-Indigenous activists fought for it since territorial sovereignty benefited their families, friends and communities. Indeed, they saw urban and reserve/reservation populations as part of the same community, and as sharing in the same political struggle. Bearing this out, in the 1960s, Aboriginal urban migrants in Australia came to speak of themselves and of all Aboriginal people as 'Black'.[15]

---

15   Jones and Hill-Burnett, 'Political Context of Ethnogenesis'; McGregor, 'Another Nation'; McGregor, *Indifferent Inclusion*.

Similarly, as urban Indian communities grew in US cities in the late 1950s, community members initially made contact with other Indians in the city via pre-existing networks from reservations, tribal nations and boarding schools. Gradually, these contacts combined with the exigencies of urban life to create a pan-Indian or what sociologist Stephen Cornell calls a 'supra-Indian' identity: a 'pan-ethnic' identity based on shared histories of responding to racist federal Indian policies and on a syncretic culture of tribally specific, intertribal and newly invented traditions.[16] Much like the language of 'Black Power' in Australia, the language of 'Red Power' in the United States drew little distinction between how this politics and a generalised 'Indian' identity applied to urban versus rural communities. By speaking generally of Red Power, urban Indian activists also asserted their communities and rural Indian communities were linked; in fact, they were the very same community.

In both the Indigenous Red Power and Black Power movements, a vocal anti-colonialism with ties to the global decolonising struggles of the postwar era blended with a new awareness of local constructions of race ('Black' and 'Red'). Activists in Seattle and Sydney used their community-run clinics to assert ideas about their identity and rights as Indigenous peoples that provided alternative plot lines to the fiction of assimilation that falsely dichotomised rural and urban Indigenous communities and erased the realities of continuing political, social, cultural, familial and economic ties between them. Remembering back to their strategising in the 1970s, Dr Walt Hollow (Assiniboine-Sioux), one of the Seattle Indian Health Board's first physicians, recalled the emphasis the early founders of the clinic placed on their treaty rights, even as urban Indians living off-reservation: 'The treaty said we were to get healthcare. And here we could demonstrate that there were a group of Indians living in Seattle, who were not getting regular healthcare'.[17] Drawing little distinction between the political struggles of urban and rural communities, urban Aboriginal activists often spoke up on behalf of rural communities, referring to people within those communities as 'our brothers and sisters'.[18] And, in defending territorial sovereignty even when it did not directly stand to benefit their pan-Indigenous communities in cities, activists in the postwar period pursued a pan-Indian and pan-Aboriginal politics that connected cities and reservations, as a counter-narrative to the romances of assimilationist

---

16   Cornell, *The Return*, 33.
17   Walt Hollow, interviewed by the author, Seattle, WA, 18 August 2013.
18   *Black News Service* 3, no. 3 (1977).

'melting pots' imagined by Australian and American national history and federal policy. Ruby Hammond, for example, in her work advocating for the importance of Aboriginal health as a political priority, often spoke of how 'land rights is fundamental to any improvements in the health of Aboriginal people'.[19]

Ironically, the visibility of the territorial struggles urban activists fought for on behalf of rural communities in the 1960s and 1970s often obscured efforts to protect their own (non-territorial) sovereignty in cities. The shift towards imagining Indigenous self-determination in forms that could exist apart from territorial politics also took place slowly, which made it harder to observe. However, the community-controlled health clinics (and the political struggles that built them) were key contexts in which this vision took shape, and hence I suggest that these clinics ultimately became an expression and embodiment of this de-territorialised politics. Even when the clinics later pushed for federal funds as a means of more explicitly advancing their claim that their communities had a right to government support, they insisted they would only take government funds free of restrictions. This was a reiteration of their concern for autonomy from government control but was simultaneously a means to assert the government's obligation to support their communities given the special obligations owed to Indigenous peoples by the US and Australian federal governments.

With the clinics themselves embodying the ideal of a 'de-territorialised' form of sovereignty, they might also be considered as mobile mini sovereign zones or 'hubs', where Indigenous people were in control of their own affairs and free to gather and associate as a community on terms they set. In using this language of the 'hub', I draw from the work of anthropologist Renya K. Ramirez, who writes:

> The hub suggests how landless Native Americans maintain a sense of connection to their tribal homelands and urban spaces through participation in cultural circuits and maintenance of social networks, as well as shared activity with other Native Americans in the city and on the reservation.[20]

---

19 Hammond, 'Land Rights: Key to Aboriginal Health'.
20 Ramirez, *Native*, xx.

As a cultural, social and political concept, for Ramirez the hub ultimately has the potential to 'strengthen Native identity and provide a sense of belonging, as well as to increase the political power of Native peoples'. She also describes 'hub-making activities' as practices that 'bridge tribal differences so Native Americans can unify to struggle for social change'.[21] I borrow this language of the hub, with its emphasis on urban and rural mobility, diasporic Indigenous identity and connection, as well as political and social innovation, to conceptualise the social, cultural and political significance of urban Indigenous health clinics as a kind of 'native hub'. On this reading, referring to the clinics as 'health hubs' (indexing a shift away from specific land/territories), and which in theory could be located anywhere, registers how they freed the project of Indigenous sovereignty considerably and provided Indigenous peoples a capacious means to exercise their self-determination wherever they lived.

If this constitutes one way in which urban health activists de-territorialised the project of Indigenous sovereignty through their clinics, their health activism also served to drastically reconfigure the political goals of Indigenous sovereignty by directing the concern for self-determination to the level of individual bodies. (Here, arguably, we can trace the most direct line of connection to ways in which the language of sovereignty now functions with increasing frequency in twenty-first-century Indigenous political discourse.) In a certain sense, of course, this concern that individual Indians/Aboriginals exhibit agency and control over their bodies and medical affairs looks similar to the liberal concern that individuals have sovereign control over their own bodies. I contend, however, that the health activists' concern with the bodily sovereignty of their respective community members was distinctive in a number of important respects.

First, in the case of Indigenous peoples, health activists did think Indigenous bodily sovereignty required a particular social, political and cultural context in order to be fully realised. Namely, it was believed what was needed, instrumentally speaking, to ensure the self-determination of Indigenous individuals, was precisely the kind of social and political environment provided by services run by and for Indigenous people. In other words, the dignity and autonomy of Indians and Aboriginals in their medical affairs, and their concomitant capacity to exercise bodily

---

21   Ramirez, *Native*, 3–8.

integrity, required a set of institutions that catered to their Indigenous identity. Thus activists were concerned to ensure their community members could enjoy individual dignity and bodily control in their medical affairs as Indians and as Aboriginals. This is perhaps what Pearl Warren meant, when she said all the Seattle Indian community wanted was a place 'where in our most vulnerable times of feeling unwell, we could feel free and proud to be ourselves'.

Second, while many activists no doubt shared the 'liberal' aspiration that individual Indigenous persons enjoy autonomy over their own bodies and medical care qua individual subjects, I contend the activists' concern with the bodily integrity and sovereignty of their communities' members manifested a distinct set of Indigenous normative concerns. Structures of colonial governance decimated and undermined Indigenous communities in the United States and Australia, and, importantly, this was often manifested most acutely at the level of individual Indigenous bodies. In this context, ensuring the health and integrity of individual Indigenous persons became a form of resistance to continuing colonisation in the twentieth century (assimilation) that worked to undermine the integrity of Indigenous communities. In other words, the health of the Indigenous community and its own capacity for self-direction was predicated on ensuring the health and bodily sovereignty of its individual members, just as the concern for the self-determination of individuals within that group was also advanced by the health of the group as a whole. Hammond expressed precisely this when she extolled the work of the AMS in 1980, writing:

> The Redfern Service, however, offers an impressive example of the advantages of such community run organisations – their total commitment to the task [of self-determination], their acceptance by the target population and their vital role in the total development of the Aboriginal community by supporting individual people and the larger community.[22]

Providing for the health of individual members in the way specified – through Indigenous-run organisations – was thus thought to be necessary to the self-determination of the community. Seeing the clinics in this light points to the important role health issues played as part of the wider narrative sweep of Indigenous activism in Australian and United

---

22   Hammond, 'Land Rights and Aboriginal Health', 13.

States history. Many scholars have recently recognised that, as Indigenous people in both the United States and Australia moved off reserve or rural land in the second half of the twentieth century and started living in ways that complicated and defied a simple binary between urban and rural communities, the meanings of Indigenous sovereignty were reconfigured in response to these demographic and geographic changes. Typically, the imprint of these social and political shifts has been recognised in advocacy for self-determination that came to be associated with land rights or territorial claims and associated efforts to prove ongoing attachment to specific lands and waterways in the late 1960s and 1970s. Scholars have already noted how, as Indigenous communities became more diasporic in the postwar period, the need arose to protect ongoing attachments to specific territories. By contrast, I argue the concurrent efforts to protect Indigenous health in cities put forward a new and different set of ideas about Indigenous self-determination both in response to and to expand upon the limited reach of a territorial model of Indigenous sovereignty. Rather than developing in separate and isolated ways, ideas about Indigenous sovereignty were multifaceted, responsive and contested in the postwar world. In particular, Indigenous migration and mobility in Australia and the United States in the 1950s and 1960s raised all sorts of questions – for the newly transplanted in particular – about the status of any rights and recognitions enjoyed by Indigenous peoples in their new settings. Did Indigenous rights travel along with the people? Was Indigenous identity lost outside of the reserve and traditional territories?

I argue here and elsewhere that urban Indigenous communities' fight for healthcare as Indigenous peoples in the 1960s and 1970s elevated the significance of self-governance and articulated a politics of the body that offered alternative foundations for Indigenous sovereignty to what they perceived as a limiting and limited focus on land and jurisdiction, both of which, the federal governments of Australia and the United States sought to enforce. In their struggle to assert urban Indigenous rights to healthcare, and to be recognised in the cities as communities that were culturally continuous with reserve and reservation communities, pan-Indigenous urban activists in Seattle and Sydney grappled head-on with the reality that the project of colonisation and assimilation was never only about land. In postwar cities, where Indigenous people lost even the modicum of territorial sovereignty they had on reserves and reservations, resisting colonisation and defending Indigenous sovereignty turned on defying assimilation and asserting the continuities of their cultural and political identities regardless of where they resided. They aimed to show that Indigenous communities remained cohesive even if they lived in ways that cut across geographic borders and even if their cultures changed (became 'pan-Indigenous') in new settings. These health activists made the argument that, by moving off recognised Indigenous lands, urban migrants were not forfeiting their Indigenous rights but, rather, were expanding the boundaries of Indigenous life and thus of Indigenous rights. Urban Indigenous health activists recognised the extension of assimilationist and colonial pressures into even their most private spaces (seeing a doctor), and thus pressed a case for reconceptualising the 'terrain' through which, and on which, Indigenous sovereignty could be asserted. They de-emphasised territory and elevated the significance of their own organisations and their own bodies in the struggle for Indigenous self-determination. In setting their sights beyond land in these specific ways, it is unsurprising health struggles became a key site for the political reconfiguration of Indigenous sovereignty and self-determination in the twentieth, and into the twenty-first centuries.

References

Alfred, T. 'Sovereignty'. In *Sovereignty Matters: Locations of Contestation and Possibility in Indigenous Struggles for Self-determination*, edited by J. Barker, 33–50. Lincoln: University of Nebraska Press, 2005. doi.org/10.2307/j.ctt1dnncqc.5.

Barker, J. 'For Whom Sovereignty Matters'. In *Sovereignty Matters: Locations of Contestation and Possibility in Indigenous Struggles for Self-determination*, edited by J. Barker, 1–32. Lincoln: University of Nebraska, 2005. doi.org/10.2307/j.ctt1dnncqc.4.

Bryant, H. 'Loneliness Is the White Man's City'. In *The Red Man in America*, 50–52. Olympia: Office of the State Superintendent of Public Instruction, 1970.

Cornell, S. *The Return of the Native: American Indian Political Resurgence*. New York: Oxford University Press, 1988.

Deloria, V., Jr. 'Intellectual Self-determination and Sovereignty: Looking at the Windmills in Our Minds'. *Wicazo Sa Review* 13, no. 1 (1998): 25–31. doi.org/10.2307/1409027.

Engle, K. 'On Fragile Architecture: The UN Declaration on the Rights of Indigenous Peoples in the Context of Human Rights'. *European Journal of International Law* 22, no. 1 (2011): 141–63. doi.org/10.1093/ejil/chr019.

Hammond, R. 'Land Rights and Aboriginal Health' Lecture. Hannah Middleton Papers, ML MSS 5866. Mitchell Library, Sydney.

Hannah Middleton Papers, ML MSS 5866, State Library of New South Wales, Sydney.

Jones, D. J. and J. Hill-Burnett. 'The Political Context of Ethnogenesis: An Australian Example'. In *Aboriginal Power in Australian Society*, edited by Michael C. Howard, 214–46. St Lucia, Qld: University of Queensland Press, 1982.

McGregor, Russell. 'Another Nation: Aboriginal Activism in the Late 1960s and Early 1970s'. *Australian Historical Studies* 40, no. 3 (2009): 343–60. doi.org/10.1080/10314610903105217.

McGregor, Russell. *Indifferent Inclusion: Aboriginal People and the Australian Nation*. Canberra: Aboriginal Studies Press, 2011. doi.org/10.1017/jie.2013.1.

Panaretto, K., M. Wenitong, S. Button and I. Ring. 'Aboriginal Community Controlled Health Services: Leading the Way in Primary Care'. *Medical Journal of Australia* 200, no. 11 (2014): 649–52. doi.org/10.5694/mja13.00005.

Raheja, M. 'Reading Nanook's Smile: Visual Sovereignty, Indigenous Revisions of Ethnography, and "Atanarjuat (The Fast Runner)"'. *American Quarterly* 59, no. 4 (2007): 1159–85. doi.org/10.1353/aq.2007.0083.

Ramirez, R. K. *Native Hubs: Culture, Community, and Belonging in Silicon Valley and Beyond*. Durham: Duke University Press, 2007. doi.org/10.1215/9780822389897.

United Nations. *United Nations Declaration on the Rights of Indigenous Peoples*. Resolution adopted by the General Assembly, 13 September 2007. March 2008. Accessed 28 November 2019. www.un.org/esa/socdev/unpfii/documents/DRIPS_en.pdf. doi.org/10.1163/2211-4394_rwilwo_sim_032185.

Warren, Pearl. 'Pearl's Message'. *Indian Center News* 4, no. 25 (19 February 1965): 1–2.

10

SELF-DETERMINATION'S LAND RIGHTS
Destined to disappoint?

Jon Altman[1]

Introduction

The Commonwealth's *Aboriginal Land Rights (Northern Territory) Act 1976* (ALRA) is a statutory instrument designed to deliver a form of social justice – that is, to arrest and even reverse the illegal land dispossession that occurred in Australia since British colonisation. The ALRA was developed and passed during the same period (1972–77) in which the Australian Government established a policy of Indigenous self-determination; as Justice Woodward stated when presenting the framework of the ALRA, 'Aborigines should be free to choose their own manner of living'.[2] Both conservative and Labor governments expected that land title would be a means for remote living Aboriginal people in the Northern Territory to eventually attain economic and social equality with other Australians.

The ALRA remains the most progressive and comprehensive land rights law in Australia. It has delivered a form of inalienable collective title over an estimated 48–50 per cent of the Northern Territory (635,000–650,000 sq kms) – with exact acreage remaining difficult to calculate because some claims are still being legally resolved. Ownership of land has afforded many

---

1   I would like to thank Sana Nakata, Melinda Hinkson, Shino Konishi, Michael Dillon, Karrina Nolan and the editors of this book for critical engagement with an earlier version of this chapter.
2   Woodward, *Commission*, 10.

Aboriginal people in the Northern Territory the choice to live differently in accord with diverse elements of their traditions and customs. I use the term differently here in two senses: differently to mainstream Western ways, and differently to how they had lived on government settlements and missions. However, the expectations that the ALRA raised are fundamentally contradictory. On the one hand, traditional owners may wish to live differently on Aboriginal-owned land. Such 'difference', from an Indigenous standpoint, might emphasise the protection of sacred sites in a sentient ancestral landscape and the use of the land's natural resources for sustenance and wellbeing. On the other hand, individuals might aspire to attain socio-economic equality; to strive for equality as sameness – assessed from a political or bureaucratic standpoint using conventional social indicators and statistics – that might make it impossible to live on one's ancestral land. Assessment of whether the ALRA has met its objectives is thus relative to one's choice of a wide spectrum of standpoints – ranging from that of a recognised traditional owner of land who might be focused on maintaining difference to that of a member of Australia's political, corporate or bureaucratic elites who often emphasise sameness.

By all statistical accounts, the ALRA has failed to deliver socio-economic equality between the Northern Territory's Aboriginal and non-Aboriginal people, measured as two distinct populations. Could land title ever have simultaneously satisfied the Aboriginal aspiration to live differently and any aspiration to be equal, in socio-economic terms, to non-Aboriginal people? This is a complex question that I look to address in my conclusion. This question matters to me personally because, since the late 1970s, I have worked at various times with and/or on behalf of traditional owners, Aboriginal groups, governments, statutory authorities and non-government organisations to strengthen the ALRA and to resist the dilution of its provisions.

The ALRA's immediate antecedents: 1972

Ruling on a case brought by residents of Yirrkala mission in the Northern Territory Supreme Court, in April 1971 Justice Blackburn found that Australian law did not recognise Aboriginal title to land; this meant that the Commonwealth Government was under no legal obligation to consult with Aboriginal residents about a massive bauxite mine on Crown land reserved for their exclusive use. The Australian Government had to respond to the public perception that while the ruling was correct in law it was unfair in its effect on the plaintiffs' community. On Australia Day 1972, Prime Minister McMahon announced that the Australian Government would create a new form of tenure – a lease, lasting 50 years, available to individuals, groups or communities who could demonstrate to a Land Board their intention and ability to make economic and social use of the land.[3] As in other leases, mineral and forest rights would be reserved for the Crown. It was assumed by the McMahon Government (and more widely) that the interest of Aboriginal people themselves would be served by mineral exploration and development on Aboriginal reserves.

The prime minister's Australia Day statement angered Aboriginal activists; they immediately set up the 'Aboriginal Tent Embassy' on the lawns of Parliament House. By early February activists associated with the Embassy had drawn up a five-point plan for land rights: Aboriginal control of the Northern Territory as a state within the Commonwealth, legal title and mining rights to all reserves throughout Australia, the preservation of all sacred sites throughout Australia, legal title and mining rights to areas in and around all Australian capital cities, and compensation (6 billion dollars, worth about $200 billion in 2019) for lands not returnable and an annual percentage of gross national income.[4] According to John Newfong, 'the figure of six billion was chosen in order to establish in the minds of the white men and their governments not only this right of prior ownership but also our right to compensation'.[5] Like the McMahon statement, the demands of the Aboriginal Tent Embassy encompassed competing logics: a call for social justice and compensation for past wrongs, and for land as the economic base for self-sufficiency as well as for its spiritual and sacred importance.

On 8 February 1972 a delegation of activists met Opposition leader Gough Whitlam who gave partial endorsement of the five-point plan and made a commitment to Aboriginal land rights that was widely reported in the media.[6] In his election speech of November 1972 Whitlam stated:

> We will legislate to give aborigines land rights – not just because their case is beyond argument, but because all of us as Australians are diminished while the aborigines are denied their rightful place in this nation.[7]

---

3   McMahon, *Australian Aborigines Commonwealth Policy*.
4   Newfong, 'Aboriginal Embassy', 139.
5   Newfong, 'Aboriginal Embassy', 142.
6   Robinson, 'Aboriginal Embassy', 8; Foley, 'Reflection', 36.
7   Whitlam, 'It's Time'.

At the same time Whitlam, like McMahon, promoted northern development: 'Labor's objective is to develop the vast and valuable resources of Northern Australia for the benefit of the Australian nation and future Australians'.

From Woodward's royal commission to land rights: 1972–77

Exactly 12 months after Whitlam met with Aboriginal activists on the lawns of Parliament House, his government (elected 2 December 1972) commissioned Mr Justice Woodward, who had represented the Yolngu plaintiffs in the Gove case, to advise how to recognise in legislation the traditional land rights of the Aboriginal people of the Northern Territory. Woodward's inquiry was limited to the Northern Territory in part because his commission was a direct political response to the Blackburn decision, but also because the Territory was administered from Canberra and the Australian Constitution empowered the Commonwealth to make laws there.[8]

Woodward produced a template for land rights law. The 20 per cent of the Northern Territory that had been reserved for Aboriginal use was to be transferred to land trusts to be managed by statutory land councils as instructed by the owners of that land. All unalienated Crown lands were to be open to claim by people who could demonstrate before an Aboriginal land commissioner that they were a local descent group with primary spiritual responsibility for land and associated sacred sites and were entitled 'as a right to forage over the land claimed'.[9]

Woodward was determined to complete his inquiry quickly and so chose an approach that he assessed as measured, 'taking into account financial and political realities'.[10] Woodward did not engage with, or receive submissions from, the Black activists from the Aboriginal Tent Embassy; he may have assessed their more radical demands as unrealistic.

---

8   Neate, *Land Rights Law*, 3.
9   Section 3 of *Aboriginal Land Rights (Northern Territory) Act 1976* (Cwlth).
10   Woodward, *One Brief Interval*, 141.

Woodward's 'measured' approach had shortcomings. Although the Letters Patent of his commission directed him to include 'rights in minerals and timber', he did not recommend that landowners be vested with property rights in subsurface minerals.[11] The question of mineral rights probably caused Woodward the most difficulty and concern.[12] But in the end, he was persuaded by mining industry submissions that Aboriginal traditional owners should be treated no differently from other Australians. This decision undoubtedly reduced the economic potency of land rights. Instead, he recommended a right of veto, so that Aboriginal landowners would have the legal authority to determine what happens on their land: 'I believe that to deny Aborigines the right to prevent mining on their land is to deny the reality of their land rights'.[13] Woodward thought it 'likely, particularly in the long term, that consent will generally be given'.[14] On the 'difficult question'[15] of how to distribute money paid by miners, he recommended that:

> All statutory payments for permits and leases be paid over by the Government to the regional Land Council for distribution among traditional owners; all royalty payments be paid over by the government to the regional Land Council for distribution as follows: two tenths to be retained by the Land Council, two tenths to be paid to the other regional Land Council, three tenths to be paid to the local community, and three tenths to be paid to the A.B.T.F [Aborigines Benefits Trust Fund].[16]

Passed by the Australian Parliament in 1976, the ALRA established Aboriginal land councils as statutory authorities to represent traditional owners with a degree of independence from governments. In other respects, Woodward's recommendations had been diluted. For example, the ALRA excluded the possibility that land could be claimed based on need or in towns. Some responsibilities that Woodward had imagined for the Commonwealth were delegated to the new Northern Territory Government, effective 1 July 1978, so that Aboriginal people have found themselves in a politically fraught tripartite arrangement. Mining royalties that were to be paid to land councils were now to be paid to the Northern Territory Government. The Commonwealth was to pay

11 Woodward, *Commission*, 1.
12 Woodward, *Commission*, 103–04.
13 Woodward, *Commission*, 104.
14 Woodward, *Commission*, 104.
15 Woodward, *Commission*, 108.
16 Woodward, *Commission*, 109.

an equivalent amount to the newly established Aboriginals Benefit Trust Account that superseded the existing Aboriginal Benefits Trust Fund. This changed the way that the use of royalties was to be accountable. Because these Commonwealth payments were now from consolidated revenue, royalty-equivalents were not the 'private' income that Aboriginal people might derive from consenting to the commercial use of their property but 'public moneys' subject to ministerial directions and scrutiny.[17]

Woodward's hope was that 'Aboriginal communities should have as much autonomy as possible in running their own affairs'.[18] As a law enabling self-determination, the ALRA's version of land rights goes beyond any land or native title laws passed since. However, while Aboriginal people own considerable tracts of land, most of what happens on that land where Aboriginal people are invariably in the clear majority is legally subject to external governance, not local Aboriginal regulation. Political jurisdiction over Aboriginal lands, mineral exploration aside, remains almost exclusively with mainstream forms of government. Both Woodward's proposals and the ensuing the ALRA combine the visions of becoming equal and remaining different, though Woodward seemed to privilege difference over sameness. While 'Aborigines should be free to choose their own manner of living', their land rights would be 'a first essential step for people who are economically depressed and who have at present no real opportunity for achieving a normal Australian standard of living'.[19] He warned that 'the granting of land rights can only be a first step on a long road towards self-sufficiency and eventual social and economic equality for Aborigines' and that 'there is little point in recognising Aboriginal claims to land unless the Aboriginal people concerned are also provided with the necessary funds to make use of that land in any sensible way which they wish'.[20]

17 Altman, *Mining Royalties*, 42–47.
18 Woodward, *Commission*, 10.
19 Woodward, *Commission*, 10, 2.
20 Woodward, *Commission*, 133, 9.

Equality and difference as a practical research problem

Almost on the day the ALRA was proclaimed, my Aboriginal economic policy research commenced at the University of Melbourne collaborating with John Nieuwenhuysen. Our project, funded by the Commonwealth Department of Aboriginal Affairs, was to document the economic situation of Indigenous people across Australia.[21] We were aware of the postcolonial optimism of those with newly acquired property rights in land, especially among those people who had moved to outstations or homelands from the government settlements and missions where they had been centralised, voluntarily and involuntarily, under colonial regimes. We were no less aware of an emerging tension between the rights of groups to enjoy their land rights, a form of difference, and a government goal shared by many Aboriginal people for socio-economic sameness. Like Woodward, we were careful to argue that it would be difficult, and in some situations perhaps impossible, to achieve socio-economic equality. We sought to reduce expectations that land rights would enable economic independence from government, especially for remote outstation communities.[22]

Shifting from the academic discipline of economics to anthropology, in 1979 I was granted permission by the late Anchor Kulunba and his family to live with them at an outstation called Mumeka located on their Kurulk clan estate in western Arnhem Land. I wanted to understand how Kuninjku people made their living and what they thought about development.

Kuninjku-speaking people had moved to the government settlement of Maningrida, established in 1957 under the policy of assimilation. In the early 1970s, when rights to land were emerging as a national issue, they returned to live on their ancestral lands at outstations, including Mumeka, as 'an experiment in self-determination' assisted administratively and logistically by unusual and sympathetic officials like the enigmatic John Hunter in their particular situation (see Haynes chapter).[23] Kuninjku people who had maintained only vestiges of their pre-colonial hunter-gatherer way of living in Maningrida went back to live on their land as 'modern hunter-gatherers'.[24]

---

21 Altman and Nieuwenhuysen, *Economic Status*.
22 Altman and Nieuwenhuysen, *Economic Status*, 195–96.
23 Peterson and Myers, *Self-determination*.
24 Altman, *Hunter-Gatherers*.

My research showed that people were sustained from three sources. First, they worked consistently to self-provision, exploiting the resources on their country; much of their dietary intake was from bush foods. When I quantified the value of this food, I found that most of their 'income' (cash and non-cash) came from hunting and fishing. At the same time, Kuninjku engaged with market capitalism. Assisted by a community-controlled arts centre based at Maningrida, they produced art for sale. Over time they became increasingly adept at refiguring their artistic traditions using local materials and references to sacred places and mythology. Their third source of support was the social security benefits to which they had recently become entitled as Australian citizens. Inequitably, as poor Australians, they received very little else from the state in terms of health or education or community services. The plural (or hybrid) economy they fashioned for themselves fundamentally challenged evolutionary thinking, dominant in policy circles, about the superiority of capitalism in remote regions such as Arnhem Land.

This was land rights and self-determination at work. Kuninjku people were taking primary spiritual responsibility for their clan lands, protecting sacred sites while exercising their economic right to make a living off their land and resources. In 1985, when a mining company sought permission to explore their land for minerals, the Northern Land Council mediated, as required by law, to identify and consult traditional owners. Key landowners had observed the nearby Nabarlek and Ranger uranium mines and had talked to these mines' beneficiaries, so they were aware of the potential monetary benefits of consenting to exploration and mining.[25] However, their experience of the ALRA was that it secured their access to their lands and resources, and Kuninjku people were now relatively economically and politically autonomous. Vetoing exploration, they implicitly accepted a social compact that enabled them to lead a materially modest, but spiritually rich and socially cohesive, lifeway.

Over a two-year period from 1985 to 1987 I used my Mumeka research in submissions to two national inquiries. In each case I advocated for policies to support people who chose to live at outstations on their ancestral lands. The Miller Committee on Aboriginal Employment and Training Programs saw economic value in people living off the land and recommended the rapid expansion of the Community Development Employment

---

25   Altman, *Mining Royalties*.

Projects (CDEP) scheme as a form of unconditional income support for outstation residents.[26] While the ensuing Aboriginal Employment Development Policy (AEDP) partly implemented this recommendation, the AEDP also aimed to deliver economic equality between Indigenous and other Australians by 2000, which I had advised was impossible to achieve in very remote Australia.[27] The second inquiry – a national review of outstations – was conducted by the House of Representatives Standing Committee on Aboriginal Affairs. The committee's report *Return to Country* not only lauded the relative autonomy of outstation residents but also recommended the flexible delivery of citizenship entitlements such as education and health and municipal services to these small and remote communities.[28] The committee also endorsed the Miller recommendations for investment in appropriate forms of income support and economic development. In my view, it is an enduring indictment of Australian fiscal federalism and of the lack of intergovernmental cooperation and accountability that the Commonwealth and Northern Territory governments never properly implemented the recommendations from these national inquiries. Policy innovation and its implementation might well have ameliorated the emerging tensions and conflicted logics of simultaneously supporting forms of difference and sameness that continue to undermine the aspirations of many traditional owners today.

Defending land rights and self-determination from equality as sameness

Twenty years after the ALRA's passage, and with the election of a conservative government in March 1996, self-determination's land rights were subject to increasing criticism as an obstacle to socio-economic equality. Policy thinking swung to focus more on the socio-economic status of individuals and households and less on collective rights and Indigenous-specific approaches to governance and development. In the period since 1996, governments have revisited assimilationist goals – adopting Western norms

---

26 Miller, *Aboriginal Employment*.

27 Australian Government, *Aboriginal Employment*. The Miller Committee also endorsed capital programs to build an economic base and new industries in Aboriginal-owned remote Australia. This recommendation resonated with the Aboriginal Tent Embassy's claim for compensation in 1972 but, as Dillon's chapter in this book argues, implementation of this idea has been disappointing.

28 House of Representatives Standing Committee on Aboriginal Affairs, *Return to Country*.

and values in judging wellbeing and in comparing Indigenous people living remotely on their land with all other Australians.[29] In 1993, many of the conservative parliamentarians who now made up the Howard Government (1996–2007) had opposed the *Native Title Act 1993*. Pandering to populism, the incoming Prime Minister John Howard represented native title as endangering national economic development.[30] Because the ALRA's free prior and informed consent provisions conferred stronger negotiating rights on traditional owners than the Native Title Act, the ALRA was in the new government's sights for reform.[31]

To describe my own engagements in these policy debates I will focus on two episodes of attempted reform before revisiting Mumeka to outline what this has meant on the ground.

In 1997, the Howard Government commissioned John Reeves QC to review the ALRA. His report *Building on Land Rights for the Next Generation* sought to make the ALRA an instrument to secure economic and social advancement for all Aboriginal people in the Northern Territory, not only for Aboriginal landowners.[32] In this respect, Reeves's vision resonated with McMahon's in 1972. Reeves proposed diluting the rights of traditional owners and the political power of their representative land councils. The Territory government, having consistently opposed land claims made under the ALRA since 1978, welcomed Reeves's reforms as strengthening its territorial and political jurisdictions. The land councils fought back, armed with activist expertise and – reminiscent of the Aboriginal Tent Embassy in 1972 – support from a substantial section of national public opinion. Aboriginal people in several Central Australian communities burned copies of the Reeves Report. John Herron, Minister for Aboriginal Affairs, referred the review and its recommendations to the public scrutiny of a parliamentary inquiry. Sir Edward Woodward, now in his late 70s, was so disappointed with the Reeves Report that he made submission to the inquiry highlighting the shortcomings of its recommendations.[33]

---

29 Sullivan, *Belonging Together*; Strakosch, *Neoliberal Indigenous*.
30 John Howard, television interview with Kerry O'Brien, 7.30 Report, ABC, 4 September 1997, transcript, PM Transcripts, Department of the Prime Minister and Cabinet, accessed 26 February 2019, pmtranscripts.pmc.gov.au/release/transcript-10469.
31 McKenna 'Assessing the Relative'. In 1984, the Hawke Government had similarly proposed to weaken the ALRA's right of veto as an element of its unsuccessful plan for a 'preferred national land rights model'. Libby, *Hawke's Law*.
32 Reeves, *Next Generation*.
33 Woodward, *One Brief Interval*, 150.

I was among a group of academics at The Australian National University that collaborated with the Northern Territory land councils to convene a conference whose proceedings were quickly published.[34] Among the conference contributors were Nicolas Peterson, who had been Woodward's expert anthropological adviser, Ian Viner, the government minister who had chaperoned the ALRA through parliament in 1976, and John Reeves. My own contribution took aim at Reeves's proposal that the land councils and royalty associations be replaced by a Northern Territory Aboriginal Council (NTAC). NTAC's function would be to receive and redistribute money earned from the agreed commercial use of Aboriginal land. I argued that this mechanism would blur an important distinction: between money coming to Aboriginal people as owners who had consented to others' extraction of mineral resources from their land and money coming to Aboriginal people, at the discretion of the minister, via the Aboriginals Benefit Trust Account. One likely effect of implementing NTAC, I argued, was that it would greatly reduce any incentive for traditional owners to negotiate royalty-generating agreements counter to Reeves's purported intention.[35]

In *Unlocking the Future: The Report of the Inquiry into the Reeves Review* the parliamentary standing committee unanimously rejected Reeves's recommendations.[36] The unanimity of this rejection, given that the Reeves inquiry was government-initiated, was surprising, as was the committee's lead recommendation that the ALRA should not be amended without the free, prior and informed consent of traditional Aboriginal owners in the Northern Territory.[37] Unlike Woodward in 1974, Reeves in 1998 clearly underestimated the support for what the ALRA had achieved: political representation and property rights in land.

The conservatives' desire to reform the ALRA re-emerged in 2005, during the fourth Howard Government. This government was emboldened by its control of both houses of parliament; by the bipartisan abolition of the Aboriginal and Torres Strait Islander Commission (ATSIC), leaving the

---

34 Altman, Morphy and Rowse, *Land Rights*. By 1999 there were four land councils, the original Northern and Central Land Councils augmented by the Tiwi Land Council (established in 1978) and the Anindilyakwa Land Council (established in 1991).

35 Altman, 'The Proposed'.

36 House of Representatives Standing Committee on Aboriginal and Torres Strait Islander Affairs, *Unlocking the Future*.

37 House of Representatives Standing Committee on Aboriginal and Torres Strait Islander Affairs, *Unlocking the Future*, xvii.

ALRA politically exposed with only land councils as its defenders; and by intensifying assault on the institutions of Indigenous Australia.[38] To replace ATSIC, the Howard Government appointed a National Indigenous Council (NIC). The NIC called for Indigenous Australians to have more opportunity for private home ownership and for business development. Warren Mundine, a New South Wales Aboriginal member of the NIC, was mistaken in describing tenure over Aboriginal land as 'communal' but his label was endorsed by powerful officials and the government. Mundine and others argued that the 'communal' title conferred by the ALRA inhibited both private home ownership and business development on Aboriginal land. Some commentators also managed to link the need for better security for women and children – widely acknowledged – with the need to reform 'communal' land tenure. In June 2007, the Howard Government exploited the *Little Children Are Sacred* report of the Board of Inquiry into the Protection of Aboriginal Children from Sexual Abuse, and seeming inaction by the Northern Territory Government, to launch the Northern Territory Intervention and harness public outrage to attack the ALRA by suggesting the permit system provided a protective umbrella for child sexual abusers.[39] The government judged that it had public support to intervene in the Territory's remote communities, including by changing the ALRA, for the good of Aboriginal people.

Under the Howard Government's Northern Territory Intervention, entire townships located on Aboriginal land were leased compulsorily by the Australian Government for a five-year period. In response, the traditional owners of Maningrida brought an action in the High Court of Australia. The court ruled in 2009 that such unilateral acquisition of property was constitutionally legal only if the government paid just terms compensation.[40] After protracted legal negotiations the Gillard Government paid. This incident was a clear reminder about power relations in Australia – the settler state retains radical land title. Self-determination's land rights are qualified, a gift that can be withdrawn. The ALRA is vulnerable to deleterious amendment, even abolition, by the same parliament that conferred the rights, as long as it meets its constitutional obligation to compensate.

---

38   Sullivan, *Belonging Together.*
39   Hinkson, 'Introduction'.
40   Brennan, '*Wurridjal v Commonwealth*'.

The 'national emergency' amendments to the ALRA abolished the need for a permit to enter public areas of Aboriginal-owned townships and promoted new arrangements for 99-year leasing of land within townships (under a new Section 19A of the ALRA) to implement earlier NIC and government proposals. The leases were to be managed by a Canberra-based executive director of township leasing appointed by the minister and funded from royalties raised on Aboriginal land. This last reform was an ironic reversal of McMahon's (1972) proposal that Aboriginal people hold leases over Crown land; now Aboriginal landowners could issue a lease over their land to a government agency that in turn would issue subleases. Few land trusts have embraced the Section 19A leasing option. To transfer ultimate control of their land to the executive director of township leasing has had very limited appeal.

To understand what these struggles over land tenure have meant to those pursuing their lifeways on Aboriginal land, let us return to the Kuninjku. They have remained committed to their country for decades in the face of deepening ambivalences and underfunding by Commonwealth and Territory governments. Until the Northern Territory Intervention, Kuninjku had maintained what I have described as a plural economy in which minimal, unconditional state support facilitated self-provisioning and engagement with the extremely limited market opportunities available in remote Australia.[41] In this adaptive economy, they enacted Woodward's freedom 'to choose their own manner of living' and 'freedom to change traditional ways as well as a freedom to retain them'.[42]

Wary that fundamental reform of the ALRA would be politically difficult and could incur high compensation costs, Australian governments since 2007 have instead amplified a project of improvement to reform the people. A suite of paternalistic measures has been introduced seeking to convert the norms and values of remote living Aboriginal people to match those of some imagined responsible neoliberal subject. These measures are not about land rights per se, but about the owners' commitment to live on the land. Kuninjku, like homelands people everywhere, have been under enormous administrative pressure to recentralise to larger townships. Some wish to do so, but to the extent that traditional owners cease to live on their land, their territorial rights have little meaning.

41　Curchin, 'Economic Hybridity'.
42　Woodward, *Commission*, 10.

Kuninjku are aware of the strategies designed to recentralise them, to eliminate their mobile way of living, and to inculcate them with Western norms and values ostensibly to close statistical gaps via enhanced engagement with market capitalism. They understand that they are losing the right to sustain themselves with a 'hybrid' economy dependent on continuing connection to their traditional lands and resources. They are deeply frustrated and angered that if they resist this second wave of colonisation they will be punished with impoverishing loss of the welfare payments on which their adapted economy has been dependent since the 1970s. The government is also coopting their regional support organisation, the Bawinanga Aboriginal Corporation, to assist delivery of programs, like compulsory work for the dole and income management, that close rather than open on-country possibilities.[43]

The recent actions of government have not extinguished all possibility of on-country living. For example, traditional owners in western Arnhem Land residing within the Warddeken Indigenous Protected Area have garnered support for living on country by voluntarily committing their biodiverse lands to the Australian conservation estate. These same lands have also been committed to a carbon farming commons, the Arnhem Land Fire Abatement project that extends over most of Arnhem Land's 100,000 sq kms. Managing wild fires contributes to the abatement of greenhouse gas emissions, and such abatement is sold. By attracting payments from diverse public, private and philanthropic sources to conserve biodiversity and reduce carbon emissions, some groups have managed to maintain enough independence from the state to successfully exercise their ongoing desire to live at outstations and make a living. This replicable example might prove a harbinger of how proactive members of remote communities might refigure their relations with the state and capitalism to be more politically and economically autonomous.

Conclusion

Was self-determination's land rights destined to disappoint? Did the ALRA deliver simple justice to people unfairly dispossessed and betterment to people who are economically depressed? At the start of this chapter, I identified twin logics embedded in the ALRA: to deliver simple justice

---

43   Altman, 'Raphael Lemkin'.

by returning ancestral lands and to encourage the utilisation of this land to improve socio-economic marginality. I have argued that the tension between these logics has been exacerbated in the last two decades by policy settings that measure the wellbeing of Aboriginal people (and thus the success or failure of policy) by assessing only the degree to which they live in the same way as non-Aboriginal people. In such assessment, no value is accorded to people's self-determining choice to live in accord with elements of their customs and traditions.

The ALRA has contributed to simple justice by assuring legal title to vast tracts of ancestral land. However, by excluding the mineral rights that the land councils had argued were of fundamental importance to achieving full land rights, both Woodward's recommendations and the ALRA failed Aboriginal expectations. The ALRA's concession to the enduring influence of the mining industry in capitalist Australia marked the limits of settler state recognition.[44]

And why only in the Northern Territory? A request was made to Woodward to expand his inquiry to cover all Australia.[45] He declined because he believed this would take six years and he considered it preferable to treat the Northern Territory as a pilot study. In its limited spatial coverage and lack of political empowerment and compensation, the ALRA did not meet the demands made by Black activists in Canberra in 1972. The ALRA applies only to the Northern Territory, less than one-fifth of the Australian continent; the Territory's Indigenous population, the ALRA's potential beneficiaries, constitute less than 10 per cent of the total Indigenous population estimated from the 2016 Census (compared to 20 per cent in 1971). From the perspective of those at the Aboriginal Tent Embassy, the early commitment to national land rights made by Whitlam soon turned to bitter disappointment. As Gary Foley, one of the Black activists now a professor of history notes, the young Black radicals got their first major lesson about 'political deceit and duplicity' owing to the failure of Whitlam to deliver on his promises.[46]

Perhaps there has been unrealistic expectation that land rights would deliver too much too quickly? Woodward cautioned that 'the granting of land rights can only be a first step on a long road towards self-sufficiency

---

44 Altman, *Mining Royalties*, 39.
45 Woodward, *One Brief Interval*, 138; Woodward, *Commission*, 130.
46 Foley, 'A Reflection', 41.

and eventual social and economic equality for Aborigines'. He went on: 'it is an essential step even though its outcome may not be apparent for many years'.[47] While some tentative steps forward were taken in the early years of the ALRA, in the last two decades the steps have been backward. Those living on Aboriginal land in the Northern Territory are not only the most impoverished people in Australia, but also they are becoming relatively poorer.[48] This trend is the result of policy to discourage and even financially penalise those who live on their country. The most recent estimates from a Centre for Appropriate Technology (2016) survey indicated that there are over 600 homelands in the Northern Territory.[49] People may have land rights, but because the Commonwealth and Northern Territory governments fail to support living at outstations, people are leaving their ancestral lands. To pressure Aboriginal people for whom connection to country, sacred sites and ancestors in the landscape are paramount values to live in the same way as non-Aboriginal people is a form of cultural genocide.[50]

According to Woodward, one of the aims of land rights was to remove, as far as possible, the legitimate grievance of an important minority group within the community.[51] After nearly half a century, we can see that this aim has failed. The Aboriginal Tent Embassy stills stands in Canberra as a potent symbolic reminder of outstanding Aboriginal claims against the settler state. Gary Foley predicts that 'the Embassy can only be removed when Aboriginal people achieve their goals of land rights, self-determination and economic independence'.[52]

This chapter makes two broad arguments. First, that the ALRA was initially designed as an innovative and progressive institution. However, as Commonwealth law, the ALRA is always vulnerable to change, especially if a government controls both houses of parliament. The ALRA has been increasingly poorly applied, adversely amended and associated with other increasingly misconceived policies of betterment. Second, the twin logics of the land rights agenda – to enable both difference and equality – are in so much tension that the ALRA, as a settler colonial project, must always fail to some degree irrespective of how it is attempted. The underlying

---

47   Woodward, *Commission*, 133.
48   Markham and Biddle, 'Income'.
49   Centre for Appropriate Technology, *Northern Territory Homelands*.
50   Altman, 'Raphael Lemkin'; see also Short, *Redefining Genocide*.
51   Woodward, *Commission*, 2.
52   Foley, 'A Reflection', 41.

principle of land rights policy should be to align with and support the aspirations of traditional owners and to assure them the resources they need. Government policy must acknowledge that Aboriginal people in some regions have very limited possibilities of becoming the same in statistical terms as the other Australians with whom they are so often compared. Informed by such realism, steps along Woodward's long road can yet again be forwards, not backwards.

References

Altman, Jon C. *Aborigines and Mining Royalties in the Northern Territory*. Canberra: Australian Institute for Aboriginal Studies, 1983.

Altman, Jon C. *Hunter-Gatherers Today: An Aboriginal Economy in North Australia*. Canberra: Australian Institute for Aboriginal Studies, 1987.

Altman, Jon C. 'The Proposed Restructure of the Financial Framework of the Land Rights Act: A Critique of Reeves'. In *Land Rights at Risk: Evaluations of the Reeves Report*, edited by J. Altman, H. Morphy and T. Rowse, 109–122. Canberra: Centre for Aboriginal Economic Policy Research, ANU, 1999.

Altman, Jon C. 'Raphael Lemkin in Remote Australia: The Logic of Cultural Genocide and Homelands'. *Oceania* 88, no. 3 (2018): 336–59. doi.org/10.1002/ocea.5204.

Altman, Jon C., F. Morphy and T. Rowse, eds. *Land Rights at Risk: Evaluations of the Reeves Report*. Canberra: Centre for Aboriginal Economic Policy Research, ANU, 1999.

Altman, Jon C. and J. Nieuwenhuysen. *The Economic Status of Australian Aborigines*. Cambridge: Cambridge University Press, 1979.

Australian Government. *Aboriginal Employment Development Policy Statement: Policy Paper No 1*. Canberra: Australian Government Publishing Service, 1987.

Brennan, S. '*Wurridjal v Commonwealth*: The Northern Territory Intervention and Just Terms for the Acquisition of Property'. *Melbourne University Law Review* 33, no. 3 (2009): 957–84.

Centre for Appropriate Technology. *The Northern Territory Homelands and Outstations Assets and Access Review: Final Report*. Alice Springs: Centre for Appropriate Technology, 2016.

Curchin, K. 'Economic Hybridity in Remote Indigenous Australia as Development Alterity'. In *Postdevelopment in Practice: Alternatives, Economies, Ontologies*, edited by E. Klein and C. E. Morreo, 176–189. New York: Routledge, 2019. doi.org/10.4324/9780429492136-13.

Foley, G. 'A Reflection on the First Thirty Days of the Embassy'. In *The Aboriginal Tent Embassy: Sovereignty, Black Power, Land Rights and the State*, edited by G. Foley, A. Schaap and E. Howell, 22–41. New York: Routledge, 2014.

Hinkson, M. 'Introduction: In the Name of the Child'. In *Coercive Reconciliation: Stabilize, Normalise, Exit Aboriginal Australia*, edited by J. C. Altman and M. Hinkson, 1–12. Melbourne: Arena Publications, 2007.

House of Representatives Standing Committee on Aboriginal Affairs. *Return to Country: The Aboriginal Homelands Movement in Australia*. Canberra: Australian Government Publishing Service, 1987.

House of Representatives Standing Committee on Aboriginal and Torres Strait Islander Affairs. *Unlocking the Future: The Report of the Inquiry into the Reeves Review of the Aboriginal Land Rights (Northern Territory) Act 1976*. Canberra: The Parliament of the Commonwealth of Australia, 1999.

Libby, R. T. *Hawke's Law: The Politics of Mining and Aboriginal Land Rights in Australia*. Perth: University of Western Australia Press, 1989.

McMahon, W. *Australian Aborigines Commonwealth Policy and Achievements, Statement by the Prime Minister, 26 January 1972*. Canberra: W.G. Murray, Government Printer, 1972.

Markham, F. and N. Biddle. 'Income Poverty and Inequality'. *CAEPR 2016 Census Paper*, no. 2. Canberra: Centre for Aboriginal Economic Policy Research, ANU, 2018.

McKenna, S. L. 'Assessing the Relative Allocative Efficiency of the Native Title Act 1993 and the Aboriginal Land Rights (Northern Territory) Act 1976'. *CAEPR Discussion Paper*, no. 79. Canberra: Centre for Aboriginal Economic Policy Research, ANU, 1995.

Miller, M. (chair). *Report of the Committee of Review of Aboriginal Employment and Training Programs*. Canberra: Australian Government Publishing Service, 1985.

Neate, G. *Aboriginal Land Rights Law in the Northern Territory*. Sydney: Alternative Publishing Cooperative Limited, 1989.

Newfong, J. 'The Aboriginal Embassy: Its Purposes and Aims' [1972]. In *The Aboriginal Tent Embassy: Sovereignty, Black Power, Land Rights and the State*, edited by G. Foley, A. Schaap and E. Howell, 139–43. New York: Routledge, 2014. doi.org/10.4324/9780203771235-20.

Peterson, N. and F. Myers, eds. *Experiments in Self-determination: Histories of the Outstation Movement in Australia*. Canberra: ANU Press, 2016. doi.org/10.22459/esd.01.2016.

Reeves, J. *Building on Land Rights for the Next Generation: The Review of the Aboriginal Land Rights (Northern Territory) Act 1976*. Canberra: Aboriginal and Torres Strait Islander Commission, 1998.

Robinson, S. 'The Aboriginal Embassy: An Account of the Protests of 1972'. In *The Aboriginal Tent Embassy: Sovereignty, Black Power, Land Rights and the State*, edited by G. Foley, A. Schaap and E. Howell, 1–21. New York: Routledge, 2014. doi.org/10.4324/9780203771235-11.

Short, D. *Redefining Genocide: Settler Colonialism, Social Death and Ecocide*. London: Zed Books, 2016.

Strakosch, E. *Neoliberal Indigenous Policy: Settler Colonialism and the 'Post-Welfare' State*. New York: Palgrave Macmillan, 2015.

Sullivan, P. *Belonging Together: Dealing with the Politics of Disenchantment in Australian Indigenous Policy*. Canberra: Aboriginal Studies Press, 2011.

Whitlam, G. 'It's Time: Whitlam's 1972 Election Policy Speech'. Policy Speech for the Australian Labor Party delivered by Gough Whitlam at the Blacktown Civic Centre, Sydney, 13 November 1972. WhitlamDismissal.com. Accessed 26 February 2019. whitlamdismissal.com/1972/11/13/whitlam-1972-election-policy-speech.html.

Woodward, A. E. *The Aboriginal Land Rights Commission: Second Report, April 1974*. Canberra: Australian Government Publishing Service, 1974.

Woodward, E. *One Brief Interval: A Memoir by Sir Edward Woodward*. Melbourne: The Miegunyah Press, 2005.

11

'ESSENTIALLY SEA-GOING PEOPLE'[1]

How Torres Strait Islanders shaped Australia's border

Tim Rowse

As an Opposition member of parliament in the 1950s and 1960s, Gough Whitlam took a keen interest in Australia's responsibilities, under the United Nations' mandate, to develop the Territory of Papua New Guinea until it became a self-determining nation. In a chapter titled 'International Affairs', Whitlam proudly recalled his government's steps towards Papua New Guinea's independence (declared and recognised on 16 September 1975).[2] However, Australia's relationship with Papua New Guinea in the 1970s could also have been discussed by Whitlam under the heading 'Indigenous Affairs' because from 1973 Torres Strait Islanders demanded (and were accorded) a voice in designing the border between Australia and Papua New Guinea. Whitlam's framing of the border issue as 'international', to the neglect of its domestic Indigenous dimension, is an instance of history being written in what Tracey Banivanua-Mar has called an 'imperial' mode. Historians, she argues, should ask to what extent decolonisation was merely an 'imperial' project: did 'decolonisation' not also enable the mobilisation of Indigenous 'peoples' to become self-determining in their relationships with other Indigenous

---

1   H. C. Coombs to Minister for Aboriginal Affairs (Gordon Bryant), 11 April 1973, cited in Dexter, *Pandora's Box*, 355.
2   Whitlam, *The Whitlam Government*, 4, 10, 26, 72, 115, 154, 738.

peoples?[3] This is what the Torres Strait Islanders did when they asserted their political interests during the negotiation of the Australia–Papua New Guinea border, though you will not learn this from Whitlam's 'imperial' account.

In this chapter, after describing the border that resulted from Australia's negotiations with Papua New Guinea from 1973 to 1978 under the Whitlam and Fraser governments, I will describe how the Torres Strait Islanders' interests shaped the Australia–Papua New Guinea border. I will conclude by discussing how this passage of events illustrates the possibility of a history of the decolonising of *peoples* and not merely of *territories*.

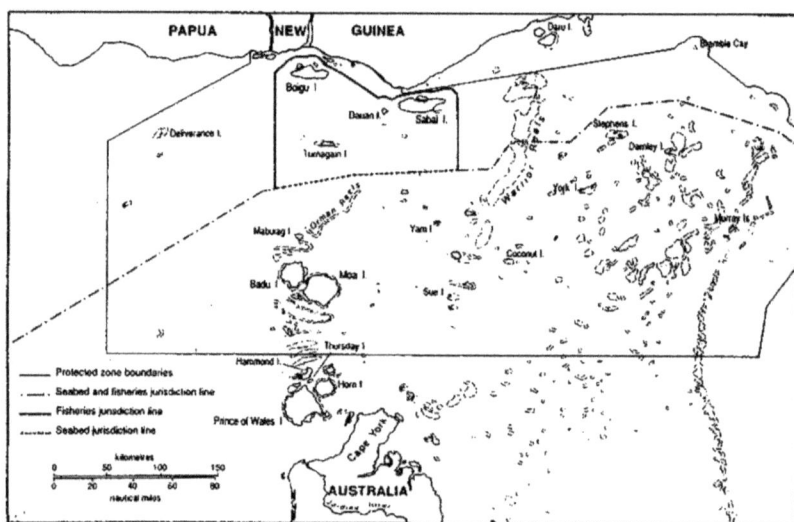

Map 11.1: The Australia–Papua New Guinea boundary.

Source: Annex 7 to the treaty between Australia and the independent state of Papua New Guinea concerning sovereignty and maritime boundaries in the area between the two countries, including the area known as Torres Strait, and related matters. Prepared by the Division of National Mapping, Canberra, and the National Mapping Bureau, Port Moresby.

---

3   Banivanua-Mar, *Decolonisation*, 8–9.

The Australia–Papua New Guinea border

The Torres Strait Treaty[4] was signed on 18 December 1978 and became effective in 1985, expressing the agreement by Australia and Papua New Guinea that the border between them should have the following features:

- Distinct seabed and fisheries jurisdictions. While a fisheries jurisdiction line and a seabed jurisdiction line are in exactly the same position over much of their lengths – that is, running approximately halfway between the Australian and the Papua New Guinea mainlands – they diverge, so that the fisheries line includes the islands Saibai, Dauan and Boigu within Australian fisheries jurisdiction. In this area between the divergent seabed and fishery lines (known as the 'top hat' or 'box') Papua New Guinea has jurisdiction in matters relating to the seabed (such as sedentary fisheries, minerals and petroleum), while Australia has fisheries jurisdiction and jurisdiction over the inhabitants of Saibai, Dauan and Boigu and over uninhabited islands and reefs that are sometimes visited by both Papuans and Torres Strait Islanders.

- A 'protected zone'. This area overlaps both seabed and fisheries jurisdiction lines, covering most of Torres Strait, excluding Thursday Island (the administrative centre of the Torres Strait region). According to Article 10 of the Treaty, what the 'protected zone' protects are 'the marine environment and indigenous fauna and flora' and 'the traditional way of life and livelihood of the traditional inhabitants' living in the Torres Strait and in 13 villages on the Papuan coast. 'Protection' has included an embargo on oil drilling.

- Provision for the 'traditional inhabitants' of the Strait. The 'traditional inhabitants' are understood to include certain citizens of both Australia and Papua New Guinea, so that each set of persons may move about within the protected zone as if there were no national boundaries running through it. That is, the protected zone has the effect of suspending, in ways significant to these people, the operation of the border between the two nation-states, so that relationships between Papuans and Torres Strait Islanders are governed by evolving custom.

---

4   'Treaty between Australia and the Independent State of Papua New Guinea concerning sovereignty and maritime boundaries in the area between the two countries, including the area known as Torres Strait, and related matters, 18 December 1978' (15 February 1985): Department of Foreign Affairs, *Australian Treaty Series* 1985 No. 4.

- A governing body. A Joint Advisory Council, with members from both Australia and Papua New Guinea, contributes to both nations' practices of implementation of the treaty.

This was not what the Australian Government initially intended. Whitlam came to power in December 1972 believing that Australia's border with the soon to be independent Papua New Guinea was too far north, and that shifting the border to a point halfway (latitude 10° south) between the two nations (giving more of the Torres Strait to Papua New Guinea) would respect the new nation's legitimate interests. However, Whitlam's advisers told him that the Torres Strait Islanders passionately opposed any change in a boundary that – since colonisation – had placed all Torres Strait Islanders within the same jurisdiction – first Queensland's (1879–1900) and then Australia's (from 1901). The Torres Strait Islanders persuaded both the Whitlam and Fraser governments to honour their territorial unity as a sea-going people.

Notwithstanding that the Torres Strait Islanders, throughout negotiations from 1973 to 1978, opposed *any* boundary that bisected the Strait – begrudging even the median line that now apportions only 'seabed' sovereignty – the treaty makes major concessions to Torres Strait Islanders that I will underline. First, *all* inhabitants and all fisheries of the islands of the Torres Strait remain within Australia's jurisdiction and thus within Australia's duty of care, as Islanders continue to expect it. Second, marine resources that continue to form a significant part of their livelihood are under protection against threatening 'development'. Third, the treaty makes space for customary jurisdiction: Papuans and Torres Strait Islanders behave towards each other according to their evolving protocols, as they use the seas and lands of the Torres Strait.

How the wishes of Torres Strait Islanders came to matter

In 1901, when the Australian colonies confederated to form the Commonwealth, the new nation's border in the Torres Strait was where the colony of Queensland had drawn it in 1879, thus including within Queensland (and consequently Australia) all residents of 17 inhabited islands (out of 100 islands in total) in the Torres Strait. Three of these islands are very close to the Papuan coast: Saibai, Dauan and Boigu.

Under the federal compact, Queensland controlled the Strait's seaways and sea bottom. Some of this power shifted to the Commonwealth when the Whitlam Government passed the *Sea and Submerged Lands Act 1973*, but Queensland retained authority over the fishing rights of the entire Strait. Queensland also administered the lives of those living on Torres Strait's 13 reserves. The 1967 referendum had given the Commonwealth concurrent power over these people, but by the time the Whitlam Government was elected in December 1972, the Commonwealth had declined to use this new power, respecting Queensland's continuing legal and administrative supremacy over Aboriginal and Torres Strait Islander peoples.

The imminence of Papua New Guinea's independence forced the Commonwealth to rethink its relationship to the Torres Strait. Australians who wished to deal equitably with Papua New Guinea saw the boundary as unjustifiably favouring Australia. Whitlam had hypothesised in May 1972 that, if the future nation of Papua New Guinea were to litigate the International Court of Justice, Australia would not be able to defend a border that enlarged Australia at the expense of the new nation. Whitlam would have been aware of a motion passed by Papua New Guinea's House of Assembly in May 1972, moved by Ebia Olewale and Naipura Maina, that the border be moved south to latitude 10° south. Olewale continued in the next few years to press this view, asserting that 'the people are Papuans, and my elders can trace the history of how these people migrated down to those islands'. While Olewale conceded that 'they might be rightful owners', he thought it relevant that:

> They have relatives on the Papuan coast, who also claim that they own those islands. There are relatives living on those islands and there are relatives living on the Papuan coast … these same people have got to be brought together, and the only solution is to move this border south.[5]

The Queensland Government understood itself to be in a strong position to block such a change because, under Section 123 of the *Colonial Boundaries Act* (passed by the British Parliament in 1895, but binding the Commonwealth from 1901), the Commonwealth Parliament may alter the boundary of a state only with the consent of the parliament of that state and the approval, by referendum, of the majority of the electors

---

5   Quoted in Griffin, *The Torres Strait*, xxii; and see Griffin, 'Impasse'.

of that state. The Premier of Queensland, Joh Bjelke-Petersen, told Canberra that he would not give a portion of his state to another country. Queensland's conservative government was confident that Queenslanders would support standing up to 'Canberra'. Over the next five years, the government of Queensland presented itself to the public (and especially to the Torres Strait Islanders) as if it should be a third party to a border negotiation that was, strictly speaking, a matter for Australia and Papua New Guinea only. The tactics of Queensland were always to claim to be the only legitimate representative of the Torres Strait Islanders.

The Torres Strait had long had structures of political representation enabled by colonial government – the closest that Australia's domestic colonial administration has come to 'indirect rule'.[6] The policy of the London Missionary Society (from its arrival in the Strait in 1871) had included the formation of Indigenous enterprises from 1897. In 1899, 'without precedent anywhere in the Pacific', the Government Resident John Douglas (on Thursday Island) had initiated elected councils to advise administrators on each island.[7] Against the advice of Douglas, the Queensland Government in 1904 subjected the Islanders to the *Aboriginals Protection and Restriction of the Sale of Opium Act 1897*; however, the councils continued. They were among a series of secular and religious institutions through which the Islanders participated actively in their own governance throughout the twentieth century. The Islanders staffed and, to a significant extent, managed the marine industries initiated by mission and government – the collection of trochus, trepang, pearls and pearl-shell. These industries were effectively subsidised by a continuing Indigenous economy of gardening and fishing, for the declaration of the islands as reserves left natural resources in Islander hands. In 1936, angered by officials' control over their earnings, they demonstrated the strength of this Indigenous economy when they withdrew their labour from the commercial fishing fleet for four months. The Queensland Government response eventually included allowing each elected council authority over police and courts. A meeting of councillors in 1937 cancelled certain state by-laws, and the state government wrote these changes into the *Torres Strait Islanders Act 1939*, which differentiated the Islanders' governance from the administration of Queensland Aboriginal people's lives. Wartime

---

6   Silverstein, *Governing Natives* has recently argued that reforms proposed in the Commonwealth's administration of the Northern Territory in 1939 would have produced 'indirect rule' had they been implemented.

7   Beckett, *Torres Strait Islanders*, 45.

service further confirmed the Islanders' sense of worth and entitlement. Over 700 Islanders served, most of them in the Torres Strait Light Infantry Battalion or the Torres Strait Pioneer Company (in contrast, there was no distinct 'Aboriginal' corps in the Second World War). From 1949, the state's system of 'indirect rule' included recognising a trio of Strait representatives – those elected from the Western, Central and Eastern island reserves. Beckett has pointed out the continuity of representative personnel, each man's community standing sustained by his job – boat captain, local official, store-manager. The Islanders were also proud of the persistence of the Strait's two languages, Miriam and Mabuiag, and their fervent adherence to Christianity did not extinguish reverence for the ancestors of their pre-colonial cosmology. Their mainland contact with Aboriginal people told them that Islanders were a comparatively well-treated colonised people. Most Islanders residing in the Strait were not restless for change, but anxious to continue the security that Queensland's hegemony afforded.[8] The Queensland premier was therefore building confidently on a long tradition of government-solicited Islander politics in his February 1973 tour of the island reserves, when he endorsed the formation of a 'Border Action Committee'.

For the Whitlam Government to develop a border policy, it had either to accept what amounted to a Queensland/Islander veto on any change in the border's position (a hopeless start to any conversation with the leaders of Papua New Guinea) or to open its own line of communication with the Torres Strait Islanders, so that its public negotiating position (when talks with Papua New Guinea began) would be safe from the Torres Strait Islanders' denunciation. Once in power, Whitlam was advised to be less specific about where he would like the boundary. The Chair of the Council for Aboriginal Affairs (CAA), Dr H. C. Coombs, warned Whitlam in January 1973 that he must take seriously not only that the Islanders felt 'genuine anxiety and concern' about the possible border change, but also that they were evidently pleased that the Queensland Government was voicing their opposition to it. In the same memorandum, Coombs recommended that Whitlam set up a series of meetings between the CAA and the Islanders, between the Islanders' representatives and members of Whitlam's Cabinet (Whitlam, Bill Morrison, Foreign Minister, and Gordon Bryant, Minister for Aboriginal Affairs), and between representatives of Papua New Guinea and the Islanders.

---

8   Fisk and Tait, 'Rights'.

Perhaps, from such meetings, the Islanders would assent to the border change in exchange for security of land tenure, joint citizenship and the continuation of Australia's social service and other benefits. 'It would be important that Islanders' representatives see [the solutions resulting from these meetings] as successes won by their personal efforts. They would then be more likely to advocate them among their own people.'[9] In a joint statement with Michael Somare (Chief Minister of Papua New Guinea) on 17 January 1973, Whitlam declared that Australia was willing to negotiate the relocation of the border with Papua New Guinea, and that the Queensland Government and the Islanders would be consulted.

What could the Whitlam Government offer Torres Strait Islanders that they were not already getting from Queensland's patronage? The national government, at that time, had little first-hand knowledge of a people that had long been administered exclusively by the Queensland Government. The 1971 Australian Census had counted 9,664 people of Torres Strait Islander descent. Of the 3,926 living on the islands of the Strait, 2,348 were residents of reserves administered by the Queensland Government. If we add the residents of Bamaga Reserve, on the tip of Cape York, we can say that there were 2,932 Islanders living under the Queensland Government's direct supervision in 1971. More than half (59 per cent) of those identifying as Torres Strait Islanders in 1971 did not live on the islands of the Strait but on the mainland: 37 per cent in Queensland, the other 22 per cent in the other states and territories of Australia. Islanders were numerous on the mainland because they were confident that they could improve their lot by selling their labour in the wider Australian economy. This diaspora maintained a sense of connection with the land, seas and people of the Strait, despite long absences, but they were not the subjects of Queensland Government patronage, and indeed some had left the reserves because they had fallen foul of the Queensland Government and of Torres Strait Islanders to whom the state had delegated a degree of power. Was their estrangement from the reserves an opportunity for the Whitlam Government to (in Coombs's words to Bryant) 'break the nexus between the Torres Strait Islanders and the Queensland government'?[10] Could transactions between the Commonwealth and the Islanders form a new public version of the Islanders 'interest', removing a domestic political obstacle to negotiating a new border?

---

9   Coombs to Whitlam, 10 January 1973, cited in Dexter, *Pandora's Box*, 360–61.
10   Coombs to Whitlam, 16 March 1973, cited in Dexter, *Pandora's Box*, 363.

The Whitlam Government did not tackle this question in a unified way in 1973; the Minister for Aboriginal Affairs, Gordon Bryant, competed with the CAA in finding a way to talk to the Islanders. Since 1970, the Office of Aboriginal Affairs (OAA), the executive arm of the CAA, had been reaching out to the people of the Strait in an exploration of possible paths of regional economic development. The OAA had funded a zoologist from The Australian National University (ANU), Dr Robert Bustard, to experiment in the farming of turtles in the Strait. When Bustard left ANU in 1971, the OAA recommended further funding for his project – now known as Applied Ecology. Bustard was necessarily in continuous dialogue with turtle-farming Islanders about how they saw their future. The CAA was also briefed by Jeremy Beckett, an anthropologist who had started to visit the Strait in 1958, leading to his 1964 PhD thesis and to ongoing visits. Initiating their own contact in Cairns on 14 February 1973, the CAA (Coombs, Barrie Dexter and William Stanner) met with Tanu Nona, Getano Lui (Snr) and George Mye (who currently represented the Western, Central and Eastern island reserves), confirming that the Islanders wished to send a delegation to Canberra.

Bryant did not want the CAA to be the only source of his government's knowledge of Strait politics; he sought to establish his own 'task force' for consultations, but this was quickly vetoed by Whitlam, acting on Coombs's advice.[11] Bryant sent a staff member to the Strait in March 1973 to prepare the Islanders for a visit from Bryant himself in April. Believing the council chairmen to be too beholden to the state government, Bryant and his staff paid a lot of attention to Islanders not living on the reserves (i.e. to politically articulate Islanders on Thursday Island). These two visits made the councillors on the reserves uneasy; their coolness towards Bryant confirmed his assessment of them as no more than 'favoured sons of the Queensland government', unlike the progressive Islanders he had been able to speak to on Thursday Island.[12] Bryant's visit placed Barrie Dexter, Secretary of the Department of Aboriginal Affairs, in an awkward position. Formally responsible for carrying out his minister's plans, Dexter had become convinced that they were ill-conceived. The cardinal rule guiding Commonwealth diplomacy in the Strait must be to avoid offending the men who were powerful in the reserve councils and who were, for the moment, supporting the Border Action Committee; Bryant's overtures

---

11   Dexter, *Pandora's Box*, 364.
12   Bryant to Whitlam, 29 May 1973, cited in Dexter, *Pandora's Box*, 293–94.

had broken that rule. This tension within the Whitlam Government's early diplomacy towards the Islanders reflected not only wider tensions between Bryant's and the CAA's approach to 'Aboriginal affairs', they also were rooted in the differentiating impact of Queensland's years of indirect rule. Some Islanders had flourished under Queensland reserve supervision and others had found it better to escape the reserves (to Thursday Island or the mainland). Those who had left were apt to be regarded as exiles by those who stayed, their claims to political participation sometimes contested by the reserve chairmen and by Queensland's officials.

Between February and June 1973, the Department of Aboriginal Affairs was arranging to bring Islander representatives to Canberra for a face-to-face meeting with Prime Minister Whitlam, and the department felt it had no choice but to respect the wishes of the Island Advisory Council chairmen about who could speak for the Torres Strait Islanders. Bryant sought to include an additional 12 Islanders whom he judged less compliant with Queensland Government wishes. When the official delegation of 42 gathered in Canberra on 12 and 13 June, it voted to exclude Bryant's 12. This and other missteps by Bryant led to Whitlam replacing him with James Cavanagh on 9 October 1973. Cavanagh trusted the CAA's approach to giving Islanders voice to Canberra, and so his appointment confirmed that the Torres Strait Islanders to whom the Whitlam Government would listen were those established leaders with whom both the Queensland Government and (increasingly) the CAA felt comfortable.

The Torres Strait Islands as a Commonwealth territory?

Before describing what the Whitlam Government learned from its June 1973 meeting with Torres Strait Islanders, we should note the wider context of the Australian Government's Strait diplomacy: the Whitlam Government's aspiration to end the Queensland Government's control over Aboriginal and Islander lives.

To 'break the nexus between the Torres Strait Islanders and the Queensland government', as the CAA advised Whitlam on 16 March (and substantially repeated to Bryant on 11 April 1973), the Australian Government should legislate Commonwealth control over all reserves in all states, and then give Aboriginal residents title 'in accordance with traditional native law and practice'.[13] The government could then establish the Torres Strait reserve islands as a separate Commonwealth territory, governed by a council representing the former island reserves. To legitimise such an intervention, the government should conduct a referendum among Islanders 'to ratify (a) the relocation of the border, (b) the establishment of the Commonwealth Torres Strait Territory, (c) the legislation to confirm traditional land tenure, [and] (d) the measure to protect Islanders' fishing rights within the Torres Strait area'.[14] This would remove the Queensland Government from the politics of negotiating a new boundary with Papua New Guinea and give Australia an explicit Islander mandate to negotiate a border change with Papua New Guinea. In such negotiations with Papua New Guinea, the CAA further advised, Australia should seek agreement that Australia would continue to be sovereign over the islands, rocks and reefs to the north of the new boundary. Repeating this advice to Bryant on 11 April 1973, the CAA gained Bryant's support.[15]

Barrie Dexter later acknowledged that one of the CAA's greatest political failures was not persuading the Whitlam or Fraser governments to take over Queensland's reserves.[16] Although Whitlam and Bryant announced in September 1973 that they would do so, and that they would fight Queensland in the High Court if necessary, Whitlam referred the policy to an interdepartmental committee that took until April 1975 to make a submission to Cabinet. Cabinet sent the idea back to this committee for reconsideration of the policy's administrative complexities and financial costs. By the time the Whitlam Government fell on 11 November 1975, Cabinet had still not agreed to a workable course of action.

There is no doubt that some Torres Strait Islanders supported the idea of making the Torres Strait a territory of the Commonwealth. At a Townsville seminar to discuss the border issue, held under the joint auspices of the Townsville College of Advanced Education and the North Queensland branch of the Australian Institute of International Affairs on 29–31 October 1976, Murray Island–born Eddie Mabo endorsed the proposal as a step towards Torres Strait Islanders' autonomy – first within Australia and then (possibly) outside Australia:

13   Coombs to Whitlam, 16 March 1973, cited in Dexter, *Pandora's Box*, 363.
14   Coombs to Whitlam, 16 March 1973, cited in Dexter, *Pandora's Box*, 363.
15   Dexter, *Pandora's Box*, 356.
16   Dexter, *Pandora's Box*, 477.

> We are a people of unique identity and we should work towards an ultimate goal of independence. We want to be recognised separately from our Papuan brothers and from our Australian brothers. We are <u>the</u> Islanders ... I would like to suggest that the Federal Government take over all the Torres Strait region from Queensland and then negotiate with the Islanders themselves to vest their administration in their own hands. The area could then be declared an autonomous region within the Commonwealth of Australia with its own sovereign rights and the right to secede.[17]

Australian Government caution about taking over all Aboriginal and Islander reserves in Queensland meant that a referendum was never held to test Islander support for making the Torres Strait a Commonwealth territory. More pertinent to this chapter is that the idea of such a territory quickly became irrelevant to solving the specific political problem of securing an Islander mandate for border negotiation, because another solution emerged from the June 1973 meeting between the Australian Government and the Islander delegation.

Towards the protected zone

In the June 1973 meeting, Islanders rejected a border change, asserting that 'everything that is contained within the [current] border – land and waters – are ours by tradition'.[18] According to the CAA's notes, they rejected as misconception that, historically and culturally, they were linked with the Papuans. They did not acknowledge Papuan fishing rights in the Strait, though they admitted to tolerating Papuans fishing at Warrior Reef. They spoke proudly of establishing their supremacy over Papuans in nineteenth-century battles. The representatives were unanimous also in rejecting oil drilling in the Strait: 'any spills would destroy everything that means life for our people'.[19] When questioned on the possibility of petroleum royalties, they insisted that they were interested in survival, not in wealth. They said that they wanted their Australian citizenship to continue, and they wished Australia to retain the uninhabited islands close to the Papuan coast, seeing them as belonging to residents of islands nearby.[20] When

---

17   Mabo, 'Perspectives', 35. Emphasis in original.
18   George Mye cited in Dexter, *Pandora's Box*, 367.
19   Mye cited in Dexter, *Pandora's Box*, 367.
20   The DAA notes on this meeting are included in H. C. Coombs's Minutes to Whitlam, H. C. Coombs Papers, National Library of Australia (NLA) MS 802, Box 46, between Minutes 135/73 and 136/73.

Whitlam joined this meeting (welcomed by the Islanders' hymns), he made it clear that he wanted them to consider a border change. He cited United Nations' interest in the border issue since 1971, and foreshadowed that Papua New Guinea would get self-government on 1 December 1973 and full independence 12 or 15 months after that.

Assessing these discussions for Whitlam, Coombs summarised what he understood to be the Islanders' position:

> 1. the land and sea is all one region owned by them; 2. they are ethnically distinct from Papuans; 3. they opposed any oil or mineral development of the seabed, at any price; 4. they feared PNG control over the seas, as Japanese interests would be given permission to fish; 5. they did not like the proposal to move the border, and nor did their Papuan friends see any point in the change.[21]

The meeting made it possible for the Australian Government to discern differences among the Islanders' hopes and fears. Not only were they fearful that parts of the Strait would be ceded to Papua New Guinea (a point already being made effectively by the Queensland premier), but they were worried that their seas would be despoiled by oil drilling (which the Queensland Government was more likely to permit). The prime minister told the Islander representatives in June that Queensland, not the Commonwealth, had been promoting off-shore oil drilling in the Strait.[22] Thus was revealed a point of leverage for the Commonwealth: perhaps the Commonwealth could distinguish itself as the Islanders' better champion by linking the change in the border with a promise of environmental protection?

At the June meeting in Canberra, Whitlam persuaded the Islanders to meet with Papuans from the coastal villages and discuss border change. They did so on Yam Island on 19 and 20 September 1973. Getano Lui (Snr) said of this discussion:

> We told the Papuan people we did not want our border changed. They said they did not ask for it to be changed either. The Papuan people asked about fishing – they wanted to know if they could go on fishing in the Torres Strait. We said we were happy to share the

---

21 Coombs to Whitlam, 12 June 1973, Minute 127/73, NLA MS 802, Box 46.
22 The 28-page transcript of the 12–14 June meeting of the Torres Strait Islander delegation in Canberra is in NLA MS 802, Box 11, folder 81.

fishing. Both peoples said they were worried about the damage to our fishing grounds and islands if there was oil drilling or mining and we decided to ask for protection against this. Out of the conference there came an agreement between us – and we are the people directly involved.[23]

Coombs, who also attended the meeting, was quick to convey its resolutions to Whitlam:[24]

That the waterways between the Torres Strait and the coastal area of the western district of Papua New Guinea be reserved wholly and solely for the use of our two peoples, namely the coastal people of the villages of the western district of Papua New Guinea and the Islander inhabitants of the Torres Strait Islands as was tradition practised by our forebears; drilling for oil in such waters which could result in possible oil spillage and the consequent threat of pollution to the environment be banned; fishing by outside interests should also be banned.[25]

In combination, the Canberra and Yam Island meetings gave the CAA confidence that the border change proposal could be reformulated so that environmental protection would be its central feature, a regime acknowledging the customary fishing practices of both Torres Strait Islanders and coastal Papuans. Referring to the 'unique and integrated environment on which the livelihood and the culture and traditions of the Islanders and the peoples of the South-western coast of Papua-New Guinea depend', the earliest draft of this proposal (in October 1973, shortly after Cavanagh succeeded Bryant as minister) outlined possible government guarantees of residents' free movement and fishing. The Islanders and Papuans would have the benefit of scientific scrutiny of future 'economic projects' before any were submitted for approval by the chairmen of the councils of the Torres Strait Islands and of the coastal communities of south-western Papua New Guinea. In this proposal, the licensing of marine harvesting would be restricted to locals and to companies in which locals had at least 85 per cent equity. The Torres Strait would be administered 'as a National Park in accordance with internationally accepted practices for such Parks'. If the governments of Australia and Papua New Guinea could agree to administer jointly a marine park in the Strait, perhaps they would not need to plot a precise

---

23 As reported in the *Courier Mail*, 10 May 1976, and cited by Griffin, 'Impasse', 230.
24 Coombs to Whitlam, 24 September 1973, cited in Dexter, *Pandora's Box*, 369.
25 Resolutions of the Yam Island meeting are cited in Dexter, *Pandora's Box*, 369.

boundary between the two nations. Referring to permanent residents of the Torres Strait Islands and the south-western coast of Papua New Guinea, the draft recognised 'traditional and customary practices of the local inhabitants with respect to the taking of fish and other living marine products' and the right of 'traditional and customary freedom of movement of local inhabitants' including navigation.[26]

Negotiations by the Fraser Government

Although in 1974 and 1975 the concept of a jointly administered protected zone without boundary found favour among some of the departments that were determining the Whitlam Government's approach to negotiating with Papua New Guinea, the negotiations had not commenced by the time the Whitlam Government was sacked in November 1975. Champions of the Torres Strait Islander interest now had to pitch the protected zone model within an interdepartmental committee that would advise a government led by Malcolm Fraser. Their advocacy succeeded. On 26 February 1976, Cabinet (in Dexter's summary) 'endorsed the concept of a Protected Zone, preferably with no seabed boundary through it, and the concept of no prospecting or mining initially'.[27] What remained in dispute, within the Fraser Government, was how closely the Australian Government should involve the Islanders in the consideration of its tactics once the negotiations started. As the Australian Government was anticipating pressure from Papua New Guinea to concede a hard border bisecting the Strait, it had to consider at what point to make tactical concessions to Papua New Guinea's expectations. Unless there were close communications between Canberra and the Islander leaders, it was possible for the Queensland Government, not party to the border negotiation, to embarrass the Australian Government by telling the Islanders that Canberra was about to sell them out by allowing a new line to be drawn through the Strait.[28]

---

26 In this paragraph I draw on two documents drafted by Coombs: 'Drafting notes on Torres Strait Border', 8 October 1973, NLA MS 802, Box 11, folder 81; and 'Draft Agreement', 29 October 1973, NLA MS 802, Box 12, folder 88.

27 Dexter, *Pandora's Box*, 451.

28 Dexter gives a detailed account of the battles within the Australian Government in *Pandora's Box*, 450–60.

Islander leaders such as Getano Lui (Snr) were quick to warn the Fraser Government that, were the negotiators to concede such a new border, the Islanders would complain to the International Court and the United Nations; the Queensland Government said it would support them.[29] Within the Australian Government, some officials were more willing than others to take this risk; they saw justice in Papua New Guinea's wish for a hard border bisecting the Strait, and they thought that there was a good chance that international adjudicators would agree. In this perspective, Australia's tactics should be to signal early in the negotiations that it was sympathetic to pressure from Papua New Guinea to draw a hard median border. In April 1976, Commonwealth departments (Aboriginal Affairs and Attorney-General's) that continued to present the Torres Strait Islander interest in a borderless protected zone found themselves standing between Australian officials preparing to concede a new border and those, outside the negotiations, opposed to this concession. Trying to persuade the Torres Strait Islanders not to turn back to the Queensland Government as their champion, the departments of Aboriginal Affairs and Attorney-General's struggled against the Department of Foreign Affairs, seeking to maintain the Torres Strait Islander perspective within the Australian negotiating position.

In the ensuing negotiations, a compromise position emerged. A seabed resources line bisecting the Strait gave Papua New Guinea something of what it wanted, partly satisfying those who had thought it equitable between nation-states that the people and resources of the Strait be bisected, and partly satisfying those who wanted Australian sovereignty to continue over all the lands and seas that the Torres Strait Islanders understood to be their customary territory. The seabed resources boundary was a line of potential, not immediate, significance because the protected zone disallowed mining and drilling of the seabed for 10 years after the treaty's commencement (and this embargo has since been extended).

Concluding reflections

This story would have made an apt case for the kind of history of decolonisation practised by Tracey Banivanua-Mar – a perspective on decolonisation made possible, she once wrote, by 'the angle of vision offered from the Pacific'.[30] That is, instead of supposing that the only

---

29   Dexter, *Pandora's Box*, 452.
30   Banivanua-Mar, *Decolonisation*, 8.

significant territorial results of decolonisation have been clearly bounded independent nation-states, historians of decolonisation should look for evidence of what the colonised peoples wanted and considered themselves entitled to have. If we 'refocus on people rather than territory, as agents of decolonisation', then we may notice Pacific Indigenous 'formations of decolonisation' that have 'exceeded the nation'. Banivanua-Mar's framework sensitises the historian to Pacific peoples' aspirations to devise political structures that correspond with their own evolving sense of who the Pacific's peoples are and how they want to relate to each other; such a history would note the distinctions that such peoples would make among themselves and the relationships that they wish to sustain. Such histories 'may learn of the innovative means by which independence and self-determination were practised in the absence of it being gifted by administering states'.[31]

I have puzzled over why Banivanua-Mar did not see the possible richness of the Torres Strait case for her 2016 book; perhaps she would have tackled it had her productive life not ended so early. But her professed interest in what she calls 'stateless forms of decolonisation' may be a clue to the absence of the Torres Strait border story from her work.[32] For Torres Strait Islander agency in the period 1973–78 was hardly 'stateless'. On the contrary, the historical conditions of their awkward force (awkward from the point of view of the governments of Australia and Papua New Guinea) included the fact that Australia is a federation with a long heritage of states (Queensland, at least) jealously preserving their patronage over *their* Indigenous people. Torres Strait Islander intransigence was amplified by Queensland's insistence on its rights as a state. It is partly an effect of the politics of Australian federalism that two nation-states had to consider what Banivanua-Mar calls the 'primarily transnational lateral connections and networks throughout the peripheries' – in this case, the customary relationships between the Torres Strait Islanders and their nearest Papuan neighbours.[33]

The Torres Strait Islanders, in the story that I have told, were simultaneously Queenslanders, Australians and familiar neighbours of coastal Papuan villagers. As Queenslanders they had long experience of indirect rule. As Australians they had recently become fully eligible

---

31   Banivanua-Mar, *Decolonisation*, 8.
32   Banivanua-Mar, *Decolonisation*, 20.
33   Banivanua-Mar, *Decolonisation*, 9.

for welfare payments that were generous by the standards of their region. As sea-going peoples of the Strait, they saw value in state protection of shared marine resources. In 1973 they began to announce themselves as critics of a particular instance of what Banivanua-Mar calls the 'imperial' assumption that decolonisation is a two-party transaction – in this case, between Australia and Papua New Guinea. Such an 'imperial' view of the border issue persists in Donald Denoon's 2009 remark: 'a deal could perhaps have been struck much sooner, if not for the Islanders stubborn resistance.'[34] His words express both 'imperial' frustration that a two-sided transaction became devilishly three-sided and admiration for Torres Strait Islander gumption.

The resulting Torres Strait Treaty hopefully expresses a community of interest among those living partly on the marine resources of the Torres Strait. Olewale represented this community of interest as 'Papuan', but in the September 1973 Yam Island meeting it was possible to represent the people of the Strait without such singular ethnicity. Before that meeting, when briefing Canberra in June 1973, Torres Strait Islanders had clearly stated their longstanding sense of distinction from, and even superiority over, the coastal Papuans who also used parts of the Strait's fisheries. Political circumstances generated a search for common interests. The resulting protected zone is not only an agreed jurisdictional overlap between two nation-states, but also the continuing commons of these sea-going peoples. With the emergence of Papua New Guinea from Australia's mandate, and with the currency of the idea that equitable dealing required Australia to cede seas and islands to the new nation, it became politically necessary for the Papuans and the Torres Strait Islanders to state joint opposition to nation-state partitioning and economic development of a region of their customary mingling. The Papua New Guinea independence process and the politics of Australian federalism were the contexts in which the Strait's 'primarily transnational lateral connections and networks throughout the peripheries' could be simultaneously Papuan and Torres Strait Islander.[35]

---

34   Denoon, *The Hundred*, 12.
35   Banivanua-Mar, *Decolonisation*, 9.

References

Banivanua-Mar, Tracey. *Decolonisation and the Pacific: Indigenous Globalisation and the Ends of Empire*. New York: Cambridge University Press, 2016.

Beckett, Jeremy. *Torres Strait Islanders: Custom and Colonialism*. Melbourne: Cambridge University Press, 1987.

Denoon, Donald. *The Hundred Fathers of the Torres Strait Treaty*. R.G. Neale Lecture, 5 November 2009. Canberra: National Archives of Australia and the Department of Foreign Affairs and Trade, 2009.

Department of Foreign Affairs, *Australian Treaty Series* 1985 No. 4. Canberra: Australian Government Publishing Service, 1995.

Dexter, Barrie. *Pandora's Box: The Council for Aboriginal Affairs 1967–1976*. Edited by Gary Foley and Edwina Howell. Southport, Qld: Keeaira Press, 2015.

Fisk, Ernest K. and M. Tait. 'Rights, Duties and Policy in the Torres Strait'. *New Guinea* 8 (1973): 1–27.

Griffin, James. 'Impasse in Torres Strait'. *Australian Outlook* 31 (1977): 217–40.

Griffin, James, ed. *The Torres Strait Border Issue: Consolidation, Conflict or Compromise?* Townsville, Qld: Townsville College of Advanced Education, 1976.

Mabo, Edward. 'Perspectives from Torres Strait'. In *The Torres Strait Border Issue: Consolidation, Conflict or Compromise?*, edited by James Griffin, 34–35. Townsville: Townsville College of Advanced Education, 1976.

National Library of Australia. MS 802, Coombs Papers.

Silverstein, Ben. *Governing Natives: Indirect Rule and Settler Colonialism in Australia's North*. Manchester: Manchester University Press, 2019.

Whitlam, E. Gough. *The Whitlam Government 1972–1975*. Ringwood, Vic.: Penguin, 1985.

PART THREE: SELF-DETERMINATION AS PRINCIPLE OF INTERNATIONAL LAW AND CONCEPT IN POLITICAL THEORY

12

SELF-DETERMINATION UNDER INTERNATIONAL LAW AND SOME POSSIBILITIES FOR AUSTRALIA'S INDIGENOUS PEOPLES

Asmi Wood

Introduction

Indigenous peoples in Australia are not seeking full political independence (or external self-determination) but rather the right of Indigenous self-determination as spelled out in articles 3–15 of the United Nations Declaration on the Rights of Indigenous Peoples (UNDRIP).[1] This chapter explores how this notion of self-determination has developed in international law and how it applies to Indigenous peoples in Australia. I have written this chapter from the standpoint that self-determination could and should apply in a regionally differentiated way as determined freely by each group in accordance with their own customs and traditions.[2] I will illustrate ways that Australia's approach to Indigenous self-determination has been and is still affected by the institutions of Australia's federation.

---

1   UN General Assembly, *United Nations Declaration on the Rights of Indigenous Peoples.*
2   See also, Wood, 'Constitutional Recognition', 104–13.

First, I show how Australia's dualistic approach to international legal obligations influences the domestic implementation of self-determination. Second, I examine the legal lacuna that have arisen from the interactions between Australia's constitutionally entrenched notion of terra nullius and Australia's common law and legislative recognition of Indigenous people.[3] Third, I will examine the evolution of the concept of self-determination, with particular attention to the meanings of 'peoples' and 'self-determination' in international law. I will conclude by considering the prospects for self-determination for Indigenous peoples in Australia.

Dualism: International law in Australia

'Dualism', as it applies in Australia, can be explained by citing High Court of Australia Justice Anthony Mason:

> It is a well settled principle of the common law that a treaty not terminating a state of war has no legal effect upon the rights and duties of Australian citizens and is not incorporated into Australian law on its ratification by Australia.[4]

International law is not self-effecting. After Australia ratifies an instrument of international law, the Parliament of Australia must then decide whether to incorporate this instrument to give domestic effect to its provisions. For example, Australia signed the International Convention on the Elimination of All Forms of Racial Discrimination on 13 October 1966, but it was not until 1975 that the Australian Parliament legislated the *Racial Discrimination Act* to implement Australia's obligations under that convention. Below, I will describe Australia's approach to instruments of international law that codify the right of self-determination. First, it is necessary to examine the implications of 'dualism'.

Dualism affects the analysis of self-determination in this chapter in two ways. First, self-determination is largely a creature of international law, but Australian law does not automatically recognise international law concepts deriving in the international plane. For international law that is not already a part of the broader common law or unambiguously

---

3   *Mabo v Queensland (No 2)* (1992) 175 CLR 1.
4   *Koowarta v Bjelke-Petersen* (1982) 153 CLR 168, 224–25 (per Mason J).

part of customary international law to be binding under Australian law, the parliament must decide whether to incorporate these international obligations into domestic law, as I have explained.[5]

Second, Australia is not a unitary legal or political entity but a federation, so the six states retain plenary power, and Section 106 of the Australian Constitution preserves state constitutions. States' plenary powers include jurisdiction over land and inland waters, likely to be material to self-determination for Indigenous people for whom land is significant. If the Australian Government wishes to bind state governments to take a certain approach to land rights that originate in the international plane, it has the power to do so. Under Section 51(xxix), the federal parliament has primary responsibility for external affairs, and it is empowered by the Constitution to enter into and incorporate international obligations into laws that could be made binding on the states and territories. Further, the Australian Constitution was amended by referendum in 1967 to give the Australian Government power to pass law in respect of 'the people of any race'; in the recent past, only Aboriginal and Torres Strait Islander people have been subject to laws enacted under this provision. If an Australian government has the constitutional power to make a law and thinks it is necessary to invalidate state law, to the extent of any inconsistency with federal laws, it has that power to do so under Section 109, thus enabling it to create national laws, including treaty-based laws with respect to land.[6] While the Australian Capital Territory and the Northern Territory have been self-governing since 1989 and 1978, respectively, under Section 122, the federal parliament 'may make laws for the government of any [Australian] territory' – a very broad power that can negate territory laws, in effect allowing the federal parliament domestically to incorporate international obligations that can then apply nationally.[7]

Australian common law and this model of federation affect the way that Australia acts on its international obligations. A decision by the national government to act in accordance with an international instrument on

---

5   That is, *opinio juris* or that Australia must believe that it is legally bound (by a law through custom): *Military and Paramilitary Activities in and against Nicaragua (Nicaragua* v *United States of America)*, Merits, International Court of Justice (ICJ) Reports 1986, 14, para. 176, 194, 237. Customary international law is binding on all nations: *North Sea Continental Shelf*, Judgment, ICJ Reports 1969, 3, para. 39, 77. See Higgins, *Problems*, 204.

6   Australian Constitution, s. 109, and s. 122 for matters related to territories.

7   For example, the rights created under the *Rights of the Terminally Ill Act 1995* (NT) were negated by the federal parliament's *Euthanasia Laws Act 1997* (Cth).

Indigenous self-determination (such as the UNDRIP) could trigger political negotiations among Australian governments. This mediation of international law through Australia's domestic, intergovernmental politics may affect how self-determination will operate in practice. Conversely, and to avoid the heavy hand of the parliament, Indigenous people would like to ensure that the principles of the UNDRIP will frame future negotiations and would seek to maintain the integrity of the instrument and the spirit in which the UNDRIP was formulated.

The interaction between such a federal system and self-determination 'models' for Indigenous peoples in Australia is likely to give rise to separate agreements between Indigenous groups and between the different jurisdictions in the federation. Consequently, a number of different self-determination models may emerge from the interplay between the various Indigenous groups and federal, state, territory and international laws. Further, Indigenous traditional territories do not necessarily fall neatly within state or territory boundaries, potentially creating a conflict of laws between different Australian jurisdictions.

Australian sovereignty: A legal question yet to be resolved

At Possession Island, Cape York, on 22 August 1770, Captain James Cook claimed possession of what he called 'New South Wales' for the British Crown. Colonisation began in January 1788, with Britain's formation of a penal colony at Port Jackson. When the British Crown asserted sovereignty over the Australian continent, international law provided three separate grounds for the acquisition of territory: (a) conquest, (b) cession or (c) the settlement of an uninhabited tract of land.[8]

Apart from 'treaty' negotiations in 1835 between the Kulin people and settlers led by John Batman – the outcome of which the Crown refused to recognise as legitimate – Indigenous peoples have never negotiated with a view to possibly ceding territory.[9] Further, in Australian legal doctrine, the British did not win sovereignty over the continent by conquest, even though at certain times the colonial governors in New South Wales

---

8   *Mabo v Queensland (No 2)* (1992) 175 CLR 1; Dodson, Bailey and Wood, 'Australia and International Protection'.
9   Attwood (with Doyle), *Possession*, 13–101.

(in 1824) and in Van Diemen's Land (1828–32) declared martial law in response to armed Aboriginal resistance.[10] If neither cession nor conquest was the basis of Britain's sovereignty, Australian law developed on the basis of what Andrew Fitzmaurice calls the 'enlarged notion of terra nullius' (that the continent, while not strictly uninhabited, was not populated by people capable of exercising sovereign power over it).[11] British control over the continent was consistent with (c): the doctrine that the Aboriginal inhabitants did not live under a system of government and law. That is, Australian federal law until 1992 implicitly or explicitly denied the prior existence of a civilised human population on the continent, denying 'visibility' (or legal personality) to Indigenous peoples as the original sovereigns; instead, colonial law had treated Aboriginal and Torres Strait Islander peoples as British subjects whose rights could be (and were) limited by legislation. That Australia's colonial law was based on the legal fiction of 'terra nullius' was explicitly enunciated and rejected by the High Court in 1992, as factually and morally flawed and as a 'narrow and ... rigid' doctrinal basis for Australia's sovereignty.[12]

Although the High Court recognised that Australia was not terra nullius (negating 'settlement' as a lawful means of acquiring inhabited lands), it did not declare a substitute legal basis for Australia's claim of sovereignty, saying that the question of sovereignty was a matter outside the competence of a municipal court.[13] This posture leaves no further domestic legal avenues for plaintiffs wanting to test the legality of Australian claims of sovereignty. Litigation and/or negotiations on questions of sovereignty and self-determination should be conducted on the international plane.

Further, in the absence of a treaty between Australia and the Indigenous peoples of Australia, the principle of *uti possidetis* holds that territory remains with its (original) possessor (i.e. Indigenous people, at the end of a conflict).[14] Therefore, in the absence of an Australian common law theory as to how sovereignty was acquired, at international law Australia arguably remains under its original possessors. Their common law rights became 'visible' to Anglo-Australian law in 1992 when the High Court recognised customary law as a source of law for Indigenous peoples

---

10 Connor, *The Australian*, 58, 91. And see Reynolds, *Aboriginal*.
11 Fitzmaurice, *Sovereignty*, 328.
12 *Mabo v Queensland (No 2)* (1992) 175 CLR 1. See paragraph 12 of the joint judgment of Justices Deane and Gaudron.
13 *Mabo v Queensland (No 2)* (1992) 175 CLR 1, 2.
14 Steiner and Alston, *International*.

in Australia. As the legal question of Australia's sovereignty remains unresolved, there is both an opportunity and a space for negotiations and discussions on self-determination without preconditions. Because there is no doctrinal answer to the question of how sovereignty was acquired, the principle of *uti possidetis* puts Indigenous Australians in a position to negotiate under international law.

Although this is not a relevant consideration for Indigenous peoples who have never ceded sovereignty, one objection by the Australian state to allowing disputes over Australian sovereignty to be resolved in the international plane is that such negotiations would diminish the Crown's own claim to sovereignty. However, and again while this is not directly relevant from an Indigenous perspective, there are other domains of law in which UN member states have voluntarily agreed to weaken their claims to absolute sovereignty – such as multilateral commercial treaties that give rights to corporations to litigate the policies and laws of nation-states.[15] While acknowledging that claims over sovereignty and self-determination are complex matters, it is particularly for this reason that I suggest that these discussions are better if conducted under international law and that negotiations take place in the international plane.[16]

Legal personality: Domestic and international

Indigenous people have always maintained their own sense of who they are as sovereign peoples. This chapter is a critique of the common law in Australia and consequently does not examine the question of the recognition of the Australian state by Indigenous peoples. Australia, while initially denying their existence through the legal fiction of terra nullius has recently recognised their 'legal personality' that would now lawfully (under the common law) enable the Australian state to engage in such negotiations. The constitutive theory of recognition broadly holds in the realm of sovereigns, such that *legal personality* and its rights and obligations can only occur through *mutual recognition*.[17] Recognition is a branch

---

15   See, for example, UNCITRAL (United Nations Commission on International Trade Law) Arbitration Rules, as revised in 2010, www.uncitral.org/uncitral/en/uncitral_texts/arbitration/2010 Arbitration_rules.html.

16   Wood and Gardiner, 'Identifying'.

17   See Lauterpacht, *Recognition*, xxxi.

of international law administered by the executive.[18] 'Recognition' of a 'People' in international law, however, is a complex issue with a broader technical discussion outside the scope of this chapter.[19] How might recognition be effected under Australian law?

'Indigenous recognition' in Australia has gradually, over time, been effected under the law. The rescission, by referendum, of Section 127 of the Australian Constitution in 1967 is a striking example of a slow recognition of Indigenous people under Australian law. While Aboriginal people have been enumerated by various colonial administrations since the early nineteenth century, an administrative practice continuing under every federal census, the population data so generated could not be used (in the words of Section 127) to 'reckon the numbers of the people of the Commonwealth, or of a State or other part of the Commonwealth'. This section had not stopped governments from counting and estimating an 'Aboriginal population', but it had stopped them from including those numbers in the published tables of the 'Australian population'; their exclusion materially affected the calculation of the number of House of Representatives electorates in each state. One effect of the rescission of Section 127 was that, from 1968, when authorities compiled tables of the 'Australian population' the people known as 'Aborigines' and as 'Torres Strait Islanders' were now added to the nation's total; at the same time, governments continued to publish figures on the 'Aboriginal population'.[20] Many Indigenous people welcome this revised approach (combining inclusion and distinction) as Australia's recognition of them as distinct populations within the Australian population – a step towards the recognition in the common law of their peoplehood in 1992.

From time to time, Australian prime ministers have used words that arguably recognise Aboriginal peoples and Torres Strait Islanders as 'peoples'. In 1988, Prime Minister Bob Hawke attended the annual Barunga Sport and Cultural Festival, hosted by the Jawoyn community. Galarrwuy Yunupingu and Wenten Rubuntja, chairs of the Northern and Central land councils, there presented Hawke with 'The Barunga Statement', a painted declaration of the aspirations of 'the Indigenous owners and occupiers of Australia'; the statement requested that the

---

18   Lauterpacht, *Recognition*, xxv. Alternatives, such as the declarative theory of recognition, are not considered here.
19   Lauterpacht, *Recognition*.
20   For the Australian Government's and others' reasoning in making these changes see Rowse and Smith, 'The Limits'.

Australian Government and people 'recognise our rights'. Hawke's speech at the festival agreed to the statement's request for a treaty-making process. Prime Minister John Howard's government reiterated this recognition of Aboriginal and Torres Strait Islander peoples as the first inhabitants of the continent, and articulated it in an ultimately unsuccessful referendum in 1998.[21]

Under international law, prime ministers' words are significant. In the *Eastern Greenland Case* (1933), the Permanent Court of International Justice (PCIJ) held that a country is bound by the undertakings given by its Minister of Foreign Affairs (in this case, a Norwegian minister) speaking in his official capacity.[22] Thus, the words used by a head of government must also have significant, if not binding, effect on the international plane, even if subsequent words (including from some of the leader's successors) do not explicitly reiterate that recognition. That is, even if these Australian leaders' actions do not honour their words, the utterance of the words of recognition reinforces their sense of obligation and hence *opinio juris* on Indigenous recognition under international law. Determining the exact point at which custom crystallises into law is now a matter for the International Court of Justice (ICJ), which replaced the PCIJ in 1946. Further, while precedent does not strictly apply in the ICJ, the PCIJ's decision in the 1933 *Eastern Greenland Case* is strongly indicative that, if litigated, the ICJ is likely to hold Australian leaders to their word. How such a case would be mounted is, however, a different issue. Fortunately, the existence of the notion of *opinio juris* allows groups such as Indigenous peoples with an emerging international legal personality to apply these concepts to states and to hold their leaders to their words even when litigation is not possible.

The executive (through parliament) has explicitly *recognised* Indigenous peoples in legislation – the *Aboriginal and Torres Strait Islander Peoples Recognition Act 2013*. The Act acknowledges that Aboriginal and Torres Strait Islander people are the first inhabitants of this nation; it includes a broad timeframe for the holding of the referendum on recognition in the Constitution, without anticipating what forms such recognition will take. This law confirms the common law notion that Indigenous

---

21   McKenna, 'The Need'. The fact that the referendum was not successful is not relevant to international law.

22   *Legal Status of Eastern Greenland (Norway v Denmark)*, Judgement, 1933 Permanent Court of International Justice (PCIJ) (ser. A/B) No. 53 (5 April).

peoples are 'peoples' for purposes of domestic Australia law, permitting the parliament lawfully to enter into negotiations with Indigenous peoples.[23] However, under Australia's Westminster system, the parliament (at the executive's will) can also rescind this legislation. This is an issue for Indigenous people, as the various parties here live on the same land but only one of these parties – the Australian state – possesses military capacity to enforce its will.

Constitutional amendment would be a more secure and lasting way to recognise Aboriginal people and Torres Strait Islanders as 'peoples', and there is a 'recognition process' currently in train. Without constitutional recognition there is a significant gap between the common law, legislation and the Constitution. The significance of this lack of a comprehensive legal recognition of Indigenous Australian peoples under Australia's *domestic* law is that Indigenous people are vulnerable to the whims of the executive. These deficiencies in the domestic law have a minimal impact for international law considerations.[24]

Notwithstanding the absence of constitutional recognition of Aboriginal peoples and Torres Strait Islander peoples as 'peoples', which, as mentioned above, can have practical implications for Indigenous peoples, legislative recognition by the parliament and executive clearly and unambiguously satisfies the technical test of mutual recognition according to international law. That is, Australia has recognised that Aboriginal and Torres Strait Islander peoples have legal personality; consequently, each of these groups is 'a people' in the meaning of the Charter of the United Nations ('UN Charter').[25] As the ICJ said:

> What [legal personality] does mean is that it [the body, in that case the UN but here Indigenous people] is a subject of international law and capable of possessing international rights and duties, and that it has capacity to maintain its rights by bringing international claims.[26]

---

23 *Aboriginal and Torres Strait Islander Peoples Recognition Act 2013* (Cth).

24 Wood, 'Constitutional Recognition: A Case'; Wood, 'Constitutional Recognition and Racial Equality'. See also Article 27 (Internal law and observance of treaties) of the *Vienna Convention on the Law of Treaties*, 1155 UNTS 331, which prohibits states from using their domestic laws to avoid their international obligations.

25 United Nations, *Charter of the United Nations*. Approval by the Australian parliament: *Charter of the United Nations Act 1945* (Cth).

26 *Reparation for Injuries Suffered in the Service of the United Nations (Advisory Opinion)* [1949] ICJ Rep, 180,183.

For the purposes of Australian law and thus the Australian state, Indigenous Australians have the legal standing to negotiate treaties and to pursue self-determination in both the domestic and international planes. This chapter examines the notion of self-determination only. The broader content of these treaties is outside the scope of the chapter and is examined elsewhere.[27] With international supervision, perhaps through the UN's Human Rights Commission or (preferably, but less likely) the ICJ, Indigenous Australians could pursue self-determination.[28] Internationally supervised treaty processes, including the rights to self-determination, are the better, more secure option for Indigenous people because they offer a degree of protection from the absolute, unilateral control of the executive, the parliament and the perils of trusting a dualistic legal system.[29]

The development of the putative 'right' to self-determination in international law

The right of Indigenous peoples to self-determination has developed in international law since the Second World War. There was no reference to 'self-determination' in the Dumbarton Oaks proposals for the draft UN Charter in late 1944.[30] As a result of pressure from the Soviet Union, however, the charter accepted at San Francisco in June 1945 refers to self-determination:

> To develop friendly relations among nations based on respect for the principle of equal rights and self-determination of peoples, and to take other appropriate measures to strengthen universal peace.[31]

Further, with reference to promoting international economic and social cooperation, the charter says:

> With a view to the creation of conditions of stability and well-being which are necessary for peaceful and friendly relations among nations based on respect for the principle of equal rights and self-determination of peoples, the United Nations shall promote:

---

27 Wood and Gardiner, 'Identifying'.
28 Wood, 'Constitutional Recognition: A Case'.
29 Article 2 of the *Vienna Convention on the Law of Treaties*, 1155 UNTS 331. While this Convention refers to states as parties, it is arguable that these provisions could by agreement between the parties apply to 'the Peoples' entering into and concluding the treaty.
30 Hula, 'Dumbarton'.
31 Article 1(2) UN Charter.

a. higher standards of living, full employment, and conditions of economic and social progress and development;

b. solutions of international economic, social, health, and related problems; and international cultural and educational cooperation; and

c. universal respect for, and observance of, human rights and fundamental freedoms for all without distinction as to race, sex, language, or religion.[32]

The UN Charter does not refer to a '*right* to self-determination' nor does it clarify who, beyond the charter's broad reference to 'Peoples' (i.e. a group right), is the subject referred to by the word 'self'.

After the UN commenced, the Soviets continued to present 'self-determination' as a 'right'. At the second session of the General Assembly, the Soviet delegation proposed that the following words be included in the Universal Declaration of Human Rights:

> Each people and each nation has the right to national self-determination. A state which has *responsibility for the administration of self-determining territories*, including colonies, must ensure the realisation of that right, guided by the principles and goals of the United Nations in relation to the peoples of such territories.[33]

However, the members of the UN that were still colonial powers opposed these words, and so the *Universal Declaration of Human Rights* (1948) does not mention 'self-determination' of peoples.

In the 1940s, the concept of 'self-determination' was understood to apply to the anticipated process of decolonisation. That is, it was understood to refer to the 'external self-determination' that would be enabled by the formal withdrawal of imperial dominion from colonised territories. As the European empires receded and enabled the formation of new nations, this concept of 'self-determination' was reinforced. Seventeen newly independent states were present at the opening of the Fifteenth Session of the General Assembly in 1960. The effect was to intensify the UN's attention on the right of external self-determination, resulting in the 'Declaration on the Granting of Independence to Colonial Countries

---

32 Article 55 UN Charter.
33 Quoted by Bowring, 'Positivism', 159.

and Peoples' in December 1960.[34] The Preamble and Article 2 of this declaration had a broad reference to self-determination and required all states to 'end colonialism in all its forms and manifestations'.[35] This declaration did not receive unanimous support. Nine colonial member states, including Australia, abstained from this vote. Although Australia was an independent state, it cherished colonial connections, with a deep and enduring commitment to Britain, as demonstrated in its founding documents, language, parliamentary processes and conventions, and the judicial system that invokes the prayer of 'God save the Queen' (albeit the Queen of Australia).[36] However, the anti-colonial mood was powerful within the UN in the 1960s, resulting in General Assembly Resolution 1803 (XVII) of 14 December 1962, 'Permanent Sovereignty Over Natural Resources' and Resolution 1514 of 14 December 1965, 'The Declaration on the Granting of Independence to Colonial Countries and Peoples'. In such resolutions, the General Assembly reaffirmed colonised peoples' right to self-determination.

In tracking the rapid evolution of international law, we must note the significance of some member nations' dissent from such resolutions: dissent means that the resolution ranks lower in the hierarchy of the sources of international law as set out in the *Statute of the International Court of Justice*.[37] Unanimous adoption arguably reflects that a resolution codifies international custom and state practice, and so unanimous resolutions rank higher as a source of law.[38] Conventions and covenants (when ratified or when they become customary law), on the other hand, are binding at international law. So it was significant that, in 1966, the UN General Assembly expanded the human rights regime founded on the Universal Declaration on Human Rights by producing new international agreements that included the International Covenant on Civil and Political Rights (ICCPR) and the International Covenant on Economic, Social

34   UN General Assembly, Resolution 1514 (XV) of 14 December 1960, UN Doc. A/RES/1514(XV). Adom Getachew has emphasised the *discontinuity* between the UN's 1945 agreement that 'self-determination' is a 'principle' and the 1960 resolution declaring 'self-determination' to be a 'right'. In Getachew's account, the 'reinvention' of self-determination as a 'right' was a hard-won victory for global (particularly African) anti-colonial diplomacy as it faced the persistent strength of the colonial powers in League of Nations and then United Nations affairs in the 1940s. Getachew, *Worldmaking*, Chapter Three.

35   UN General Assembly, Resolution 1514 (XV).

36   Wilson, *International Law*, 68.

37   Article 38 of the *Statute of the International Court of Justice*, the citation, 33 UNTS 993.

38   Article 38(1)(b) of the *Statute of the International Court of Justice*, the citation, 33 UNTS 993.

and Cultural Rights (ICESCR).[39] Article 1 of the ICCPR is identical to Article 1 of the ICESCR and they are known as Common Article 1. It declares the right to self-determination for all peoples:

> Article 1.
>
> 1. All peoples have the right of self-determination. By virtue of that right they freely determine their political status and freely pursue their economic, social and cultural development.
>
> 2. All peoples may, for their own ends, freely dispose of their natural wealth and resources without prejudice to any obligations arising out of international economic co-operation, based upon the principle of mutual benefit, and international law. In no case may a people be deprived of its own means of subsistence.
>
> 3. The States Parties to the present Covenant, including those having responsibility for the administration of Non-Self-Governing and Trust Territories, shall promote the realization of the right of self-determination, and shall respect that right, in conformity with the provisions of the Charter of the United Nations.

Steiner and Alston refer to the right to self-determination in Common Article 1 as 'one of the most influential, debated and contested provisions'.[40] Member states sought to limit the meaning and scope of self-determination in Common Article 1 so that it applied only to countries under 'foreign domination' and so that the words did not apply to independent states. Their efforts strengthened the concept of the territorial integrity of nation-states recognised by the UN.[41] Thus, in the evolution of the concept of self-determination, it has become both possible and important to distinguish external self-determination (the right of a people to independent statehood) from internal self-determination that does not challenge the territorial integrity of the nation-state (the right of peoples to self-determination in the UNDRIP). Indigenous peoples are relatively weak politically and demographically and, consequently, settle pragmatically for internal self-determination only.

---

39   UN General Assembly, *International Covenant on Civil and Political Rights*, 16 December 1966, United Nations Treaty Series, vol. 999, p. 171, accessed 29 August 2018, www.refworld.org/docid/3ae 6b3aa0.html. UN General Assembly, *International Covenant on Economic, Social and Cultural Rights*, 16 December 1966, United Nations Treaty Series, vol. 993, p. 3, accessed 29 August 2018, www.ref world.org/docid/3ae6b36c0.html.

40   Steiner and Alston, *International*, 527.

41   Hannum, *Autonomy*, 41.

Fear of internal fracturing by states is understandable as the drafting of the covenants goes back to the mid-1950s, a time when many states had just received independence and others were still to become independent of the colonising power. For example, India had received political independence from Britain in 1949 and then immediately experienced the breakup of its territory as West Pakistan (renamed Pakistan from 1971) and East Pakistan (renamed Bangladesh from 1971). Sensitive to the threat of further fragmentation, India declared in 1979 that the words 'the right of self-determination' 'apply only to the peoples under foreign domination and that these words do not apply to sovereign independent States or to a section of a people or nation – which is the essence of national integrity'.[42] More recently, the situation in ex-Yugoslavia is a reminder that the UN's member states do not want international law to be used to promote a general 'Balkanisation' of the globe.[43] There remain instances of the tension between the principle of the territorial integrity of a member state and the principle of external self-determination, as distinct and relatively large minorities in some nation-states (such as the Catalan in Spain) seek political and/or economic independence.

As international law has developed, the UN has produced further statements that support the self-determination of peoples. In 1970, the Declaration on Principles of International Law Concerning Friendly Relations and Co-operation among States in Accordance with the Charter of the United Nations (Friendly Relations Declaration) imposed on states the authoritative interpretation of seven charter principles. Principle 5 of this declaration is 'the principle of equal rights and self-determination of peoples'.[44] In 1970, the UN General Assembly adopted the Friendly Relations Declaration without vote and so this decision represents consensus on the interpretation of these principles.[45] Professor James Crawford includes self-determination in a list of *jus cogens* (peremptory) norms.[46] The significance of the inclusion of this particular right by a judge of the ICJ is that, in his view, no derogation is possible from the right to self-determination.

---

42   India's Reservation to the Common Article 1 [Dated 10 April 1979], United Nations Treaty Collection, Status of Treaties, treaties.un.org/Pages/ViewDetails.aspx?src=TREATY&mtdsg_no=IV-3&chapter=4&clang=_en.

43   Tomuschat, *Modern*.

44   *Declaration on Principles of International Law Concerning Friendly Relations and Co-operation among States in Accordance with the Charter of the United Nations,* Adopted on 24 October 1970, A/RES/25/2625(XXV).

45   Lowe, *International*, 100.

46   United Nations, International Law Commission, *The International*, 246–47.

The development of the UNDRIP

The UNDRIP is the result of years of diplomacy and research by the UN's Working Group on Indigenous Populations.[47] The UN Human Rights Committee noted in 1982 that 'the precise contours under international law of the right of self-determination remain in a state of flux'.[48] One reason for this flux, by then, was that new answers were being given to the question of who could be recognised as a 'minority'. In the 1970s, an international 'indigenous' lobby emerged within the broader UN bureaucracy, encouraged by the interest that the ECOSOC's (Economic and Social Council's) Sub-Commission on Prevention of Discrimination and Protection of Minorities expressed in 1971 in the problem of discrimination against Indigenous populations. While commissioning research, the subcommittee in 1982 also established a Working Group on Indigenous Populations (WGIP). The flexible working methods adopted by the WGIP enabled many Indigenous people to present their historical experiences as distinguishing them from ethnic, religious and other minorities. The WGIP produced a draft declaration that was referred to the Commission on Human Rights, which established another working group. This second working group met on 11 occasions. Progress was slow because of certain states' concerns regarding some key provisions of the declaration, such as Indigenous peoples' right to self-determination and the control over natural resources existing on Indigenous peoples' traditional lands. The final version of the declaration was adopted on 29 June 2006 by the 47-member Human Rights Council (the successor body to the Commission on Human Rights), with 30 member states in favour, 2 against, 12 abstentions and 3 absentees. The declaration was then referred to the General Assembly, which voted on the adoption of the proposal on 13 September 2007.[49] Through these episodes in international diplomacy, the idea that there were specifically 'indigenous' groups with legitimate claims to self-determination became thinkable.[50]

---

47   While the issues of Indigenous and Tribal peoples were originally considered by the International Labour Organization (ILO) this chapter will not examine the resulting Conventions, as Australia refused to ratify both Convention 107 'Indigenous and Tribal Populations' (1957) and Convention 169 'Indigenous and Tribal Peoples' (1989).

48   UN Human Rights Commission, 'Civil and Political Rights: The Human Rights Committee: Fact Sheet no. 15 (rev. 1)', www.ohchr.org/Documents/Publications/FactSheet15rev.1en.pdf; Pomerance, *Self-determination*.

49   Adopted by the General Assembly on 13 September 2007 with four states voting against and 11 abstentions, www.un.org/press/en/2007/ga10612.doc.htm.

50   Pritchard, 'Working'; Reed, *Indigenous*.

Australia had actively participated in the drafting of the UNDRIP and, along with some other colonial states, it significantly slowed the draft's evolution. When the resolution was put to vote in 2007, Australia voted against the UNDRIP and did so with three other countries: Canada, the United States of America and Aotearoa/New Zealand (all states that have a very similar colonial history to Australia). Australia subsequently endorsed the UNDRIP on 3 April 2009, reiterating that, as a declaration (as opposed to a convention or covenant) the UNDRIP was not binding.[51] This claim is technically true in Australia on two grounds. As a declaration, in effect a resolution of the General Assembly, the instrument is not binding.[52] Further, the instrument is not binding in Australia, as a dualistic nation, until incorporated into domestic law.[53]

Incorporating the UNDRIP into domestic law would provide a level of certainty and a collective understanding, including to legal terms related to self-determination when treaty negotiations within Australia begin. Constitutional recognition of Indigenous people would also remedy the defect of the inconsistency of 'recognition' between the common law and the Constitution as discussed above. Domestic incorporation of the UNDRIP in its original form would provide recognition of internationally framed rights of Indigenous peoples in Australian courts.

---

51 Endorsed by the Australian Government on 3 April 2009; 'Chart of Australian Treaty Ratifications as of May 2012 – Human Rights at Your Fingertips', Australian Human Rights Commission, 14 December 2012, www.humanrights.gov.au/chart-australian-treaty-ratifications-may-2012-human-rights-your-fingertips-human-rights-your.

52 Öberg, 'Legal'.

53 Indigenous people have argued that the UNDRIP codifies already existing international custom, which is binding on all nations. Australia does not accept this position as indicated by its vote against the adoption of the UNDRIP (Australia would not be able to vote against internationally accepted customary law). Further, while Indigenous peoples have a strong moral claim to their position the fact that the instrument (the UNDRIP) is a declaration and not a convention gives strength to the position of countries such as Australia, Canada, the US and Aotearoa/New Zealand.

The prospects for Australia

It took about 10 years for the ICESCR and the ICCPR to receive the required number of ratifications and to enter into force in the international plane.[54] Australia ratified the ICESCR in 1975 and the ICCPR in 1980.[55] Australia included the ICCPR as a schedule to the *Australian Human Rights Commission Act 1986* and so the ICCPR forms part of Australian domestic law.[56] The ICCPR arguably provides a broad but untested legal basis for the pursuit of self-determination. The UN's Human Rights Commission says of the group right to self-determination granted in Common Article 1 that:

> This right differs from the other Covenant rights in that it is a right expressly ascribed to 'peoples' rather than to individuals … [I]t can safely be taken that a precondition for a full and genuine expression of self-determination on the part of a people is the enjoyment by its members in whole measure of the rights contained in the Covenant.[57]

However, actions by Australian governments both domestically and in the international plane have given reason to doubt Australia's commitment to self-determination. For example, after legislating the Aboriginal and Torres Strait Islander Commission (ATSIC) in 1989, the Australian Government extinguished it in two steps in 2004 and 2005. ATSIC – a body with specific executive powers, elected by Aboriginal and Torres Strait Islander adults – had been a substantial step towards self-determination. Further, in 1998, the Australian Government amended the *Native Title Act 1993*

---

54 ICESCR entered into force on 3 January 1976; Australia ratified the ICESCR on 10 December 1975: humanrights.gov.au/our-work/commission-general/international-covenant-economic-social-and-cultural-rights-human-rights.

55   Department of Foreign Affairs, 'International Covenant on Economic, Social and Cultural Rights (New York, 16 December 1966), Entry into force generally: 3 January 1976; Entry into force for Australia: 10 March 1976', *Australian Treaty Series* 1976 No. 5 (Canberra: Australian Government Publishing Service).

Department of Foreign Affairs and Trade, 'International Covenant on Civil and Political Rights (New York, 16 December 1966), Entry into force generally (except Article 41): 23 March 1976; Entry into force for Australia (except Article 41): 13 November 1980; Article 41 came into force generally on 28 March 1979 and for Australia on 28 January 1993', *Australian Treaty Series* 1980 No. 23 (Canberra: Australian Government Publishing Service).

56   In Section 3 of the *Australian Human Rights Commission Act 1986* (Cth), 'Covenant' is defined as the International Covenant on Civil and Political Rights. A copy of the English text of that Covenant is in Schedule 2, as that International Covenant applies in relation to Australia.

57   UN Human Rights Commission, Fact Sheet no. 15 (rev. 1).

in ways that were calculated to appease non-Indigenous critics of native title. In 1998, the High Court held that the Australian Government's use of the 'race' power was not limited to legislation that parliament judged to be beneficial.[58] In 2006–07, the Australian Government amended the *Aboriginal Land Rights (Northern Territory) Act 1976* unilaterally.[59] The parliament's unilateral, lawful power to act against Indigenous interests within Australia, coupled with some examples of Australia's current record on self-determination above, show that Indigenous rights are not likely to improve without at least some general international supervision. Further, and without resiling from the broader call for international supervision, since Indigenous peoples will exercise this specific right to internal self-determination under the umbrella of domestic law and domestic courts, domestic incorporation of the international definitions of self-determination is crucial.

The UNDRIP's vision of self-determination does not fragment the nation-state; rather it explicitly articulates what internal self-determination means. If Australia is reluctant to incorporate the whole UNDRIP, incorporating into domestic law the provisions quoted below would arguably provide a reasonable, internationally accepted basis and common understanding for self-determination negotiations between Indigenous peoples, the Commonwealth and the states and territories (and not discounting other legal entities, which may wish to participate).

The UNDRIP preamble reiterates that:

> The Charter of the United Nations, the International Covenant on Economic, Social and Cultural Rights and the International Covenant on Civil and Political Rights, as well as the Vienna Declaration and Programme of Action, *affirm the fundamental importance of the right to self-determination of all peoples*, by virtue of which they freely determine their political status and freely pursue their economic, social and cultural development, Bearing in mind that nothing in this Declaration may be used to deny any peoples their right of self-determination, exercised in conformity with international law…[60]

---

58   *Kartinyeri v Commonwealth* [1998] HCA 22; (1998) 195 CLR 337, 355.
59   *Aboriginal Land Rights (Northern Territory) Amendment Act 2006* (Cth).
60   UN General Assembly, *United Nations Declaration on the Rights of Indigenous Peoples*.

The UNDRIP then provides substance to the notion of self-determination:

> Article 3
>
> Indigenous peoples have the right of self-determination. By virtue of that right they freely determine their political status and freely pursue their economic, social and cultural development.
>
> Article 4
>
> Indigenous peoples, in exercising their right to self-determination, have the right to autonomy or self-government in matters relating to their internal and local affairs, as well as ways and means for financing their autonomous functions.
>
> Article 5
>
> Indigenous peoples have the right to maintain and strengthen their distinct political, legal, economic, social and cultural institutions, while retaining their rights to participate fully, if they so choose, in the political, economic, social and cultural life of the State.

Articles 3–5 provide a useful legal content to the expression of self-determination. Incorporated into domestic legislation, they would provide a common internationally recognised legal basis and a touchstone for the negotiation of self-determination for Indigenous peoples. Any possibility of domestic incorporation depends on the parliament taking an interest in the principle of Indigenous self-determination as defined by international law and, at present, this seems unlikely.

Conclusion

The international community and international law have come some way in recognising the group rights of Indigenous peoples to self-determination and to 'freely determine their political status and freely pursue their economic, social and cultural development'.[61] For the right fully to be realised in Australia, there is a further barrier: the necessity to incorporate the international obligations into domestic law.

The complexities of Australia's federal structure mean that the various treaties that result through different groups' expressions of self-determination will likely form a complex web of rights and obligations.

---

61   UNDRIP Preamble.

On the other hand, the Australian political elite fears, as it did with native title, that potential litigation will clog up the courts, and that Australia's claims to sovereignty will be subject to the jurisdiction and supervision of international bodies.

Australia's dualistic approach has a detrimental effect on Indigenous peoples. The hierarchy of sources is mentioned here to highlight the weakness of Indigenous arguments in domestic law. Further, Australia has ratified very little of the international law *explicitly* spelling out Indigenous rights.[62] On the other hand, Indigenous people can also rely upon general human rights instruments, which are part of Australian law, to strengthen their claims to a right to self-determination under international law. That is why I have argued for negotiations taking place in the international plane. Domestic incorporation of the relevant international law provisions on self-determination will also allow the higher domestic courts to help adjudicate disputes, having regard to the vast international law and literature on this matter. Failure to resolve matters within Australia in the first instance will still leave open the possibility of a resolution of the disputes in the international plane.

While international law in the eighteenth century enabled the British Crown to claim sovereignty over the Australian continent, as a colony of settlement, this claim has resulted in great historical wrongs. Contemporary international law and norms, as they have evolved over the last two centuries, are legal and political resources for arresting and reversing the processes of colonisation. It is possible for parliament to take steps in this direction by working in good faith with Indigenous peoples to identify and resolve the problems of self-determined groups.

Since 1949, Australian governments have slowly dismantled the statutory discriminations against Indigenous peoples, and in recent years more and more Indigenous peoples have acquired formal education, making the fight for Indigenous rights and equality a little more practical and realistic than has been the case in the past.

This has made it possible for Indigenous people to acquire the skills and knowledge to negotiate and slowly recover their lost rights dating back for two centuries or more. They are getting to the point where they can do this almost as equals (although without the vast financial resources available to the state and with the parliament's ability still, in the domestic plane, to

---

62   For example, the ILO's *C169 – Indigenous and Tribal Peoples Convention, 1989.*

discriminate explicitly against them under the law and the Constitution). Nonetheless, the law and public opinion are slowly evolving to recognise the truth of the existence and survival of First Nations Peoples in Australia.

Since the graduation of the first Indigenous person through an Australian university about 50 years ago, Indigenous people have gradually been receiving tertiary and post-tertiary education in Western and international laws and ways, although there is still a long way to go in achieving population parity in this regard. Nonetheless, there is a critical mass of Indigenous Australians able to assert their rights as peoples. Subject to a few, very significant, remaining legal and constitutional barriers, they are on the threshold of being able to achieve their aim of exercising their peoplehood under the law.

Parties entering into good faith negotiations could right some of the most egregious wrongs of history. Recognising Indigenous peoples' rights truly and fully to self-determine and to evolve their cultures alongside the majoritarian Anglo-Australian law and culture will enrich, rather than diminish, our broader community.

References

Attwood, Bain (with Helen Doyle). *Possession: Batman's Treaty and the Matter of History*. Melbourne: The Miegunyah Press, 2009.

Bowring, Bill. 'Positivism versus Self-determination: The Contradictions of Soviet International Law'. In *International Law on the Left: Re-examining Marxist Legacies*, edited by Susan Marks. Cambridge: Cambridge University Press, 2008.

Connor, John. *The Australian Frontier Wars, 1788–1838*. Sydney: University of New South Wales Press, 2002.

Department of Foreign Affairs, *Australian Treaty Series* 1976 No. 5. Canberra: Australian Government Publishing Service, 1976.

Department of Foreign Affairs and Trade, *Australian Treaty Series* 1980 No. 23. Canberra: Australian Government Publishing Service, 1980.

Dodson, Michael, Peter Bailey and Asmi Wood. 'Australia and International Protection of Indigenous Rights'. In *International Law in Australia*, edited by D. Rothwell and E. Crawford, 139–64. Pyrmont, [NSW]: Thomson Reutuers, 2017.

Fitzmaurice, Andrew. *Sovereignty, Property and Empire, 1500–2000.* Cambridge: Cambridge University Press, 2014.

Getachew, Adom. *Worldmaking after Empire: The Rise and Fall of Self-determination.* Princeton: Princeton University Press, 2019.

Hannum, Hurst. *Autonomy, Sovereignty, and Self-determination: The Accommodation of Conflicting Rights.* Philadelphia: University of Pennsylvania Press, 1966.

Higgins, Rosalyn. *Problems and Process: International Law and How We Use It.* Oxford: Clarendon Press; New York: Oxford University Press, 1994.

Hula, Erich. 'The Dumbarton Oaks Proposals'. *Social Research* 12, no. 2 (1945): 135–56.

International Labour Organization (ILO). *C169 – Indigenous and Tribal Peoples Convention, 1989.* Jakarta: International Labour Office, 2007. Lauterpacht, Hersch, Sir. *Recognition in International Law.* Cambridge: Cambridge University Press, 1948.

Lowe, A. V. *International Law.* Oxford: Oxford University Press, 2007.

McKenna, Mark. 'The Need for a New Preamble to the Australian Constitution and/or a Bill of Rights'. Research Paper 12, 1996–97, Law and Bills Digest Group, Australian Parliament.

Öberg, Marko Divac. 'The Legal Effects of Resolutions of the UN Security Council and General Assembly in the Jurisprudence of the ICJ'. *European Journal of International Law* 16, no. 5 (1 November 2005): 879–906.

Pomerance, Michla. *Self-Determination in Law and Practice.* The Hague: Martinus Nijhoff, 1982.

Pritchard, Sarah. 'Working Group on Indigenous Populations: Mandate, Standard-Setting Activities and Future Perspectives'. In *Indigenous Peoples, the United Nations and Human Rights,* edited by S. Pritchard, 40–62. Annandale: the Federation Press, 1998.

Reed, Bradley. *Indigenous Peoples and the State: The Struggle for Native Rights.* DeKalb: Northern Illinois University Press, 2003.

Reynolds, Henry. *Aboriginal Sovereignty: Three Nations, One Australia.* Sydney: Allen & Unwin, 1996.

Rowse, T. and L. Smith. 'The Limits of "Elimination" in the Politics of Population'. *Australian Historical Studies* 41, no. 1 (March 2010): 90–106.

Steiner, Henry and Phillip Alston. *International Human Rights in Context: Law, Politics, Morals.* Oxford: Clarendon, 1996.

Tomuschat, T. Christian. *Modern Law and Self Determination.* Dordrecht/Boston: Martinus Nijhoff Publishers, 1993.

United Nations. *Charter of the United Nations*, 1945. 1 United Nations Treaty Series XVI, 24 October 1945.

United Nations General Assembly. *International Covenant on Civil and Political Rights*, 16 December 1966, United Nations, Treaty Series, vol. 999, p. 171. Accessed 29 August 2018. www.refworld.org/docid/3ae6b3aa0.html.

United Nations General Assembly. *International Covenant on Economic, Social and Cultural Rights*, 16 December 1966. United Nations, Treaty Series, vol. 993, p. 3. Accessed 29 August 2018. www.refworld.org/docid/3ae6b36c0.html.

United Nations General Assembly. Resolution 1514 (XV) of 14 December 1960. UN Doc. A/RES/1514(XV).

United Nations General Assembly. *United Nations Declaration on the Rights of Indigenous Peoples: Resolution / Adopted by the General Assembly*, 2 October 2007. UN Doc. A/RES/61/295.

United Nations International Law Commission. *The International Law Commission's Articles on State Responsibility: Introduction, Text, and Commentaries*, compiled by James Crawford, 246–47. Cambridge: Cambridge University Press, 2002.

Wilson, Heather. *International Law and the Use of Force by National Liberation Movements.* New York: Clarendon Press, 1988.

Wood, Asmi. 'Constitutional Recognition: A Case for Less is More'. In *It's Our Country: Indigenous Arguments for Meaningful Constitutional Recognition and Reform*, edited by Marcia Langton and Megan Davis, 104–13. Melbourne: Melbourne University Press, 2016.

Wood, Asmi. 'Constitutional Recognition and Racial Equality'. In *Constitutional Recognition*, edited by Jennifer Nielsen, Simon Young and Jeremy Patrick, 103–28. Annandale, NSW: Federation Press, 2016.

Wood, Asmi and C. M. Gardiner. 'Identifying a Legal Framework for a Treaty between Australia's First Peoples and Others'. In *Indigenous Governance, Indigenous Development: International Case Studies of Common Futures and Common Pathways*, edited by D. E. Smith, A. Wighton, S. Cornell and R. Joseph, forthcoming 2020.

13

SELF-DETERMINATION WITH RESPECT TO LANGUAGE RIGHTS

Jane Simpson

Introduction

In 1788 the whole of Australia was covered with people speaking one or more of at least 300 languages. In well-watered areas there were many languages; elsewhere one language (with different dialects) was spoken across more than a quarter of the continent. People were often multilingual, speaking the language of their community and those of neighbouring communities. There was no need for a common language across Australia, because people in each area spoke the language of their neighbours and perhaps those of their neighbours' neighbours. If they moved to another area, they generally expected to learn the language of the other area.

At the start of colonisation, the British colonists often made use of interpreters, but warfare, dispossession and new diseases resulted in an immediate and rapid decline in the number of people speaking the languages of the regions around the colonies. Once the British had become well established in an area, they imposed English as the language of government and as the language in which to access services (e.g. shops, paid work, medical help, justice and schooling). They saw no need to learn or recognise the languages of Aboriginal and Torres Strait Islander peoples, who then had to learn some English. A few missionaries encouraged literacy in Aboriginal languages and promoted mother-tongue medium instruction ('bilingual education') in schools.

In 1972, when Australia's policy of self-determination for Indigenous people was proposed, nearly 200 years of colonisation had resulted in many Aboriginal and Torres Strait Islander groups with different aspirations, and whose opinions were rarely considered. The policymakers were not Indigenous, and were trying to implement a policy of self-determination at a time when everyone was struggling to understand what self-determination actually meant.

Internationally, the right to self-determination had been adopted a few years earlier by the United Nations General Assembly in 1966. It was Article 1.1 of two covenants: the International Covenant on Civil and Political Rights (ICCPR) and the International Covenant on Economic, Social and Cultural Rights (ICESCR):

> All peoples have the right of self-determination. By virtue of that right they freely determine their political status and freely pursue their economic, social and cultural development.[1]

ICCPR included rights related to language, the right not to be discriminated against on the basis of language (Articles 2.2, 24, 26), the right when charged to be given information in a language one can understand, and the right to an interpreter (Article 14.3a, f). But most significant was Article 27:

> In those States in which ethnic, religious or linguistic minorities exist, persons belonging to such minorities shall not be denied the right, in community with the other members of their group, to enjoy their own culture, to profess and practise their own religion, or to use their own language.[2]

The ICESCR became part of Australian law in 1976, but it was not until 1986 that the ICCPR, with its stronger emphasis on language rights as individual liberties, became part of Australia's law.

---

1   UN General Assembly, *International Covenant on Civil and Political Rights*; UN General Assembly, *International Covenant on Economic*, 3.
2   UN General Assembly, *International Covenant on Civil and Political Rights*, 3.

One thing missing in 1972 was the recognition that language rights are essential for effective self-determination. As primarily monolingual speakers of English, the policymakers had difficulty in imagining the needs and wants of people who did not speak English, and found it hard to realise that language rights, which they took for granted, might not be shared by others. For example, as Australian English speakers, they took it for granted that they could use English to talk with government officials, and that their children would be educated through their mother-tongue, English. These rights were not enjoyed by speakers of Indigenous languages in remote communities in 1972.

As language is both an individual and a social phenomenon, language rights are complex, bringing in both the rights of individuals and the rights of groups. Language is used both to communicate ideas (*communicative rights*) and to express associations (*identity rights*). The *identity right* to speak one's mother-tongue language or heritage language is guaranteed by ICCPR Article 27. *Communication right*s include the right to access information in a language one understands. ICCPR Article 14 guarantees this only for court proceedings, not for other important information such as health, education and government services. People cannot make the most of self-determination if they do not have access to the best information to make the best decisions for themselves and their family, because it is only presented in a language they do not understand. This was certainly the case in 1972 for many Indigenous people in remote communities.

Apart from the right to an interpreter, the language rights mentioned in ICCPR were basically individual liberties; they did not guarantee positive support for languages. For example, they do not mention the communication right for children to receive an education in a language they understand, as well as being taught effectively the language of wider communication. In the Australian context this was known as 'bilingual education'. When self-determination became policy in 1973, 'bilingual education' was given new legitimacy by the Whitlam Government. I will discuss the gradual acceptance and implementation of these rights from the start of the self-determination policy, focusing mostly on the literature and reflections of people involved in Indigenous education in the Northern Territory[3] and, to a lesser extent, South Australia.[4]

---

3   Black and Breen, 'The School of Australian Linguistics'; Devlin, Disbray and Devlin, *History of Bilingual*; Hoogenraad, 'Critical Reflections'; Huijser et al., *Finding Common Ground*.
4   Simpson, Amery and Gale, 'I Could Have Saved You'.

Twentieth century

A step towards recognising identity and communication rights came with the establishment of the Presbyterian mission at Ernabella in 1937. It had a strong policy of using the local language in preference to English,[5] as part of a general policy of 'no compulsion or imposition of our way of life', which could be seen as an earlier recognition of the right to self-determination.[6]

In 1950, missionary organisation the Summer Institute of Linguistics (SIL) began work in Australia. Teams of SIL linguists worked with Indigenous people in remote Australia on Bible translation and language documentation. The linguistic and cultural insights gained in this translation work gave both Indigenous and non-Indigenous people better understanding of each other's languages and societies. Some other missionaries performed similar roles in the 1950s and 1960s: Beulah Lowe (Methodist Overseas Missions, Milingimbi) documented Yolŋu varieties and helped communication between Yolŋu and non-Aboriginal people, and Judith Stokes (Church Missionary Society, Groote Eylandt) learned Anindilyakwa and taught some Anindilyakwa people to read and write in their own language. But, as Rademaker shows, the attitudes of missionaries towards Indigenous languages and towards communicative rights was nuanced, in part because of the tension between assimilation, self-determination, and the uncertainty of the place of missionaries if they were not needed as brokers between Indigenous people, the wider Australian populace and the state.[7]

For non-Indigenous people, cross-cultural understanding received a boost when, in 1966, Presbyterian missionaries collaborated with the University of Adelaide to teach Pitjantjatjara as a university course.[8] Another major step was taken in 1969 when the Uniting Church established the Institute for Aboriginal Development (IAD) in Alice Springs and then, in 1971, transferred it to an Aboriginal-controlled board of management.[9] Its aim was to 'assist community development for Aboriginal people and provide cross-cultural education between Aboriginal and non-Aboriginal society'.[10]

---

5   Trudinger, 'Converting Salvation'.
6   Pybus, 'We Grew Up This Place', 10.
7   Rademaker, *Found in Translation*.
8   Simpson, Amery and Gale, 'I Could Have Saved You'.
9   Zoellner, *Vocational Education*, 77.
10 Institute for Aboriginal Development (Aboriginal Corporation) website, 2018, iad.edu.au/.

These two-way exchanges through community development and attempts to learn Aboriginal and Torres Strait Islander languages were essential for Indigenous people gaining information that they needed in order to make the choices that the later policy of self-determination required.

The communication right of children to be educated in a language they understood also gained some traction when, in 1950, the Commonwealth Office of Education adopted a policy recognising that in some circumstances Indigenous languages should be used in education:

> The language of instruction in Native schools shall be English, except where local conditions (e.g., where natives are still in a tribal or semi-tribal state) render bilingual instruction desirable.[11]

In practice, while education for Indigenous children in remote communities was greatly expanded, an assimilation drive promoted English above Indigenous languages.[12] Rademaker discusses the implementation of this among Anindilyakwa children at a mission school on Groote Eylandt.[13]

Mother-tongue medium instruction was put forward as an ideal in 1964 with the Watts-Gallacher report on curriculum and teaching methods used in Aboriginal schools in the Northern Territory.[14] Watts and Gallacher saw the importance of reducing the cultural divide between home and school. But they deemed bilingual education impractical at the time, given the lack of teachers who could speak Indigenous languages, among other factors. Other consequences of the Watts-Gallacher report included the establishment in 1967 of Kormilda College, a post-primary boarding school in Darwin for Indigenous children from remote areas. Once schooling for Indigenous children expanded, the importance of Indigenous teaching assistants as interpreters and classroom support was soon recognised, and so Kormilda College also ran short courses for Indigenous teaching assistants. This teacher training grew into an Indigenous tertiary institute, which was moved to Batchelor, Northern Territory, renamed Batchelor College, and established as a teacher training college in 1975.[15] It is now called Batchelor Institute of Indigenous Tertiary Education (BIITE).

---

11   Quoted in Brian Devlin, 'Government Support for NT Bilingual Education after 1950: A Longer Timeline', 12, FOBL: Friends of Bilingual Learning, last revised 7 March 2019, accessed 2 June 2019, www.fobl.net.au/index.php/au-TI/history/71-government-support-for-nt-bilingual-education-after-1950-a-longer-timeline.
12   Devlin, 'A Glimmer of Possibility'; Sommerlad, *Kormilda*.
13   Rademaker, *Found in Translation*, 70–84.
14   Watts and Gallacher, *Report on an Investigation*.
15   Reaburn, Bat and Kilgariff, 'Looking for a New Common Ground'.

Self-determination policy

Access to information for Indigenous people was greatly expanded following the election in 1972 of the Labor Government, the adoption of the policy of self-determination and the great expansion of educational opportunities for Aboriginal and Torres Strait Islander people.

In 1972 at Nhulunbuy, Northern Territory, Dhupuma College was established as a bicultural/bilingual high school, with Gumatj as a school language. The seeds of 'both-ways' or 'two-way' education were sown.[16] Many Indigenous people gained access to better English literacy, spoken Standard Australian English (SAE), numeracy and an increased understanding of non-Indigenous society through education at Indigenous high schools like Dhupuma, and through BIITE.[17] However, the great gulf between the residential colleges and the home communities caused severe stress for many Indigenous students who felt they belonged nowhere.[18]

With the election of a Labor Government on 2 December 1972 there was a major push for mother-tongue medium instruction, spearheaded by the minister for education, Kim Beazley Senior, and the new Prime Minister, Gough Whitlam.[19] The first five pilot programs began in 1973. While the initial programs were imposed from above, some programs were later established at community request.[20] The bilingual educational approaches were informed by two reports, the Watts-McGrath-Tandy report by educators,[21] and the O'Grady-Hale report by linguists.[22] Both reports recognised the importance of Indigenous teachers. The O'Grady-Hale report also highlighted local control by Indigenous communities of education as a goal of bilingual education.[23]

The bilingual programs were not limited to traditional languages. Educators and missionary linguists also spearheaded a movement for bilingual education using Kriol (a new contact language that had developed

---

16   White, 'Finding the Common Ground'.
17   Huijser et al., *Finding Common Ground.*
18   Sommerlad, *Kormilda.*
19   Hoogenraad, 'Critical Reflections'.
20   Vaarzon-Morel and Wafer, '"Bilingual Time"'.
21   Watts, McGrath and Tandy, *Recommendations.*
22   O'Grady and Hale, 'Recommendations Concerning'.
23   O'Grady and Hale, 'Recommendations Concerning', 2.

in the Katherine and Roper River area). They recognised the importance of using in classrooms a language that children felt comfortable with,[24] regardless of whether it was a traditional Indigenous language or a new language. The O'Grady-Hale report endorsed this view, which departed from the widespread view that contact languages like Kriol were to be discouraged as broken, inferior English.[25]

The new bilingual programs faced many obstacles: lack of models, lack of trained teachers, lack of materials (all foreshadowed in the reports), as well as opposition from senior education department officials. But the school workers were enthusiastic.[26] Highlights of the bilingual education programs were the collaborations between Indigenous and non-Indigenous people in team teaching and in producing stories and materials in Indigenous languages through Literature Production centres. The team teaching approach was strongly supported by Beth Graham, an experienced teacher in Aboriginal schools who became an adviser in bilingual education in the Northern Territory Education Department in 1979. As she said, 'if children are to learn effectively, teachers have to teach together, plan together and learn together'.[27] Team teaching produced much greater understanding between Indigenous and non-Indigenous people, and affirmed the role of Indigenous teachers in the classroom.

The need for more Indigenous teachers led the federal government to establish a Remote Area Teacher Education (RATE) program in 1976 through Batchelor College, as well as the School of Australian Linguistics (SAL) in Batchelor, Northern Territory (later the Centre for Australian Languages and Linguistics and part of BIITE).[28] Both SAL and RATE students acquired skills in language documentation, literature production and translation expertise. An example is one of the first linguistics papers co-authored by an Indigenous person, the Ngalkbun and Kriol linguist David Nangan:golod Jentian, and a non-Indigenous linguist, John Sandefur:

> David Jentian began the compilation of the wordlist and gave invaluable help in the analysis because of his knowledge of elementary linguistics gained while at the Aboriginal teacher Trainees course in Darwin.[29]

---

24 Meehan, 'Starting Out at Bamyili'; Sandefur, *Kriol of North Australia*.
25 Rademaker, *Found in Translation*, 54, 59.
26 Gale, 'Lessons Learned'; Gale, 'Boom and Then Bust'.
27 Graham, 'Reflecting on Team', 31.
28 Black and Breen, 'The School of Australian Linguistics'.
29 Sandefur and Jentian, 'A Tentative Description', 57.

Meanwhile, in Western Australia, from 1975, around 600 people living at Strelley speaking mostly Nyangumarda and Manjiljarra began moves towards having their own independent school, the Strelley Community School. They wanted an Aboriginal-controlled school, a bilingual curriculum that was not purely for transition to English, a focus on adults as well as children and a curriculum that reflected their priorities. Liberman has described the community's belief that this type of school would 'guarantee Aboriginal self-determination in the future'. He quotes an elder: 'When the whitefellas come to this country, he bin kill 'em blackfella. Now we learn all this literacy, we win the country back'.[30]

Communication between many Indigenous people and governments was still poor. In 1979 the Aboriginal linguist and anthropologist Gloria Brennan published a research report for the Department of Aboriginal Affairs pointing out the need for interpreters for Indigenous people, especially in the Northern Territory.[31] In Alice Springs, IAD began training Indigenous people as interpreters and as language teachers, teaching Indigenous languages such as Warlpiri and Arrernte, often to people who were working in Indigenous communities. Then, when mother-tongue medium instruction programs started, school staff sometimes organised language learning programs, which were seen as exciting and empowering.[32] IAD staff also worked on major resources for communication, learners' guides, handbooks and dictionaries of Central Australian languages.[33] Although IAD trained interpreters and provided free interpreting services, they had difficulty persuading courts and hospitals to make much use of them.[34]

Self-determination policy, with respect to language, addressed both identity rights and communication rights. Assertion of identity rights received bipartisan support in 1972 when the then Prime Minister William McMahon said on Australia Day that Aboriginal people 'should be encouraged and assisted to preserve their own culture, languages, traditions and arts so that these can become living elements in the diverse culture of the Australian society'.[35]

---

30 Liberman, 'Aboriginal Education', 141.
31 Brennan, *The Need for Interpreting*.
32 Ross and Baarda, 'Starting Out at Yuendumu'.
33 Simpson, Amery and Gale, 'I Could Have Saved You'.
34 John Henderson pers. comm. to J. Simpson.
35 McMahon, *Australian Aborigines*, 1.

Respect for identity rights also grew concomitantly with respect for communication rights. The first person to make a speech in an Indigenous language in parliament was Neil Bell who had learned Pitjantjatjara as a schoolteacher working at Areyonga School. In 1981, as Labor member for MacDonnell, he made his maiden speech in Pitjantjatjara in the Northern Territory Legislative Assembly. It was a statement of respect for his constituents, and an important symbolic use of an Indigenous language in a parliament. For the first time also, the government began to have access to information about Aboriginal and Torres Strait Islander languages, with the introduction of a question on language into the 1976 Census.

The self-determination policy of the 1970s both supported and was supported by the assertion of communication rights, both in the education sector and in the interpreting domain. The new access to secondary school education and tertiary training, the bringing together of Indigenous people from across the Northern Territory for classes at Batchelor, and the training and placement of Indigenous teachers in schools, created a new generation who could share ideas and understandings about the changes that the self-determination policy could make possible. The new bilingual education programs provided a springboard for demands for more local Indigenous control of education.

Beginning of reversal of self-determination

In 1978 the Northern Territory was granted self-government, and the Northern Territory Government pushed back against the mother-tongue medium instruction model. Without warning, in 1980 the government closed down Dhupuma College in the midst of the school year.[36] This was deeply shocking to the students, to their communities and to other schools across the Northern Territory. Bilingual education programs continued after self-government in the Territory, but always under threat.[37]

However, the 1980s provided much greater access to tertiary education for Indigenous people, access for non-Indigenous people to learn Indigenous languages and increased job opportunities for Indigenous people particularly in the school sector. A major achievement was the

---

36   Amagula and McCarthy, 'Red Ochre Women'.
37   Hoogenraad, 'Critical Reflections'; Nicholls, 'Death by a Thousand Cuts'.

expansion and establishment of remote area teacher training schemes, so that Indigenous people living in remote communities could study at least part of the time based in their home community. By 1985 the number of campus-based students (80+) at Batchelor College was close to the number of RATE students (75).[38] These included Indigenous people from bilingual schools as well as from English-medium instruction schools. South Australia began the Anangu Teacher Education Program (AnTEP) in 1984,[39] which provided similar training and opportunities for Aboriginal Education Workers in the APY (Anangu Pitjantjatjara Yankunytjara) Lands. At this time, the APY Lands schools, under South Australian education policy, were still bilingual.

Many Indigenous people saw higher education as a chance for taking control of their lives and communities:

> Through RATE, we Yolngu see our chance of getting loose and getting rid of the harness and the bridle that the Balanda has long used to steer us in the direction that they wanted us to go and that is the way of Balanda. Through this type of teacher training we have a chance of getting educational skills so that we can work in our communities and put our qualification and what we've learnt into use in our own Homeland communities. We Yolngu would like to gather enough understanding and knowledge about Balanda law and system so as to understand and live with both laws and worlds. ... This will also make communications better between Yolngu and Balanda.[40]

The new cohort of Indigenous educators looked beyond presence in the classroom for presence in the curriculum. They proposed a 'both-ways' or 'two-ways' curriculum, to incorporate Indigenous perspectives in school education.[41] It was most famously described by the late Dr Marika in her Wentworth Lecture when she talked about the 'both-ways' maths curriculum that staff at Yolŋu schools had developed:

> *Ganma* is a still lagoon. The water circulates silently underneath, and there are lines of foam circulating across the surface. The swelling and retreating of the tides and the wet season floods can be seen in the two bodies of the water. Water is often taken to

---

38   Reaburn, Bat and Kilgariff, 'Looking for a New Common Ground'.
39   Underwood, *Response to: Achieving Equitable*.
40   Ngurruwutthun, cited in Marika-Mununggiritj et al., 'The History', 43–44.
41   Keeffe, *From the Centre to the City*; Reaburn, Bat and Kilgariff, 'Looking for a New Common Ground'; White, 'Finding the Common Ground'.

represent knowledge in Yolŋu philosophy. What we see happening in the school is a process of knowledge production where we have two different cultures, Balanda and Yolŋu, working together. Both cultures need to be presented in a way where each one is preserved and respected. This theory is Yirritja.[42]

There was a continued push for greater Aboriginal control of schools and, in 1983, Yipirinya School, an independent school in Alice Springs, finally achieved registration. Arrernte language was a medium of instruction.

The desire for Aboriginal control extended beyond running schools to other related matters. In 1982 David Wilkins, a linguist working for the Yipirinya School Council, prepared a draft research policy for Central Australia. Its first article was:

> 1.1 a) All research in Central Australia involving Aboriginal people must be approved, controlled and monitored by a body representing, and chosen by, the Aboriginal community, or communities, in which the research will take place.[43]

Wilkins's call for responsible linguistics was echoed in other work, as linguists and communities began to understand the devastating effect of English on the Indigenous language ecologies of Australia. *Keeping Language Strong: Report of the Pilot Study for the Kimberley Language Resource Centre* appeared in 1984 and made the case for establishing Indigenous-run language centres to help Indigenous people maintain their languages.[44]

Nationally, an important step forward in identity rights and for preservation of languages came with the first national policy on languages 'to recognize, value and take action to enhance the survival of Aboriginal languages and promote an appreciation and an awareness of them among non-Aborigines'.[45]

From 1987 onwards, the Commonwealth Government began providing funds for Indigenous language maintenance and revival, through a grants scheme operated by the National Aboriginal Languages Program. Language centres were set up, along with many out-of-school initiatives, since school education is a state responsibility.

---

42 Marika, 'The 1998 Wentworth Lecture', 7.
43 Wilkins, 'Linguistic Research', 189.
44 Hudson and McConvell, *Keeping Language Strong*.
45 Lo Bianco, *National Policy*, 7.

In terms of communication rights, reflections by Indigenous people involved in the schools of the 1970s and 1980s reveal the benefits that they saw in the new approaches to schooling, and the hopes they held for the future,[46] although there was continued suspicion of formal schooling, especially when it seemed to be controlled by non-Indigenous people.[47]

Generally, understanding and communication was strengthened among Indigenous people and non-Indigenous people working with Indigenous people. Indigenous politicians, such as Bess Price and Alison Anderson, trained at Batchelor College and/or SAL, as did Indigenous leaders such as the late Jeannie Nungarrayi Egan, Mandawuy Yunupingu, John Joshua, Norma Nangali Joshua, Alice Limbiari Nangala/Napurrula Nelson, Michael Jampin Jones, Valda Napurrula Shannon and Geoffrey Jupurrula Shannon. Inspired by working in Indigenous schools, several non-Indigenous teachers became politicians, such as Neil Bell, Trish Crossin, Peter Toyne and Warren Snowdon.

When non-Indigenous authorities were mindful of the principle of self-determination, Indigenous people were consulted more often about their wishes. But it was often hard for people who did not speak English well to make truly informed decisions when there was little information accessible in their own languages. Complex concepts conveyed by the English words 'right', 'freedom' and 'non-discrimination' do not have one word equivalents in most Indigenous Australian languages. Holcombe describes the difficulties and length of time it took to unpack such concepts when translating the Universal Declaration of Human Rights into Pintupi-Luritja.[48] That project took two years and involved two Pintupi-Luritja speakers, Lance Macdonald, an experienced interpreter, and Sheila Joyce Dixon, a Papunya local authority member; an anthropologist, Sarah Holcombe; and a missionary linguist, Ken Hansen, who had worked out of Papunya since 1966. It was published in 2015, more than 40 years after the self-determination policy was launched.[49] The fact that in 2015 these ideas were still so hard to convey in an Indigenous language shows how far short Australia has fallen in protecting the communicative right of access to information in an understandable form.

---

46 Devlin, 'A Glimmer of Possibility'; Huijser et al., *Finding Common Ground.*
47 Keeffe, *From the Centre*; Liberman, 'Aboriginal Education'.
48 Holcombe, *Remote Freedoms.*
49 Macdonald et al., *Universal Declaration of Human Rights: Pintupi-Luritja.*

Increasing awareness of Indigenous languages

Throughout the 1990s the identity rights of Indigenous people were strengthened. The National Aboriginal Languages Program funded more language centres and language revival programs. Renaming or restoring Indigenous placenames began.[50] The ritual of 'welcome to country' increased,[51] and began to contain words or sentences in the relevant local Indigenous languages. Using Indigenous languages in parliament has continued: in 2016, for the first time, a prime minister, Malcolm Turnbull, spoke in parliament in Ngunnawal.[52]

The communicative right to receive information in a language one understands was gradually strengthened, but with opposition. While a full-time free interpreter service was available for immigrant languages, only in 1997 was an interpreter service for Indigenous languages trialled in the Top End of the Northern Territory. According to Senator Trish Crossin (who spoke on this matter in 1999), Denis Burke, the then Territory's chief minister, had rejected the need for an Aboriginal interpreter service, saying that it was a disgrace that Aboriginal people still needed them: 'to my mind (that) is akin to providing a wheelchair for someone who should be able to walk'.[53]

Only in 2008 did TAFE SA begin operating an interpreter training program on the APY Lands. Before that, two elderly people – Mona Tur and Bill Edwards – did much of the interpreting for Pitjantjatjara people in Adelaide, covering high stakes legal and medical interpreting.[54]

This lack of awareness of communicative language needs continued to cause serious problems for Indigenous people. It also caused problems for the federal government during the Northern Territory National

---

50   Amery and Williams, 'Reclaiming Through'; Committee for Geographical Names in Australasia, 'Guidelines for the Recording'; Reid, 'Creating Aboriginal Placenames'.

51   Merlan, 'Recent Rituals'.

52   Jacqueline Battin, 'Indigenous Languages in Australian Parliaments', *AIATSIS* (blog), *Australian Institute of Aboriginal and Torres Strait Studies*, 21 May 2018, accessed 2 June 2019, aiatsis.gov.au/news-and-events/blog/Indigenous%20Australian%20Languages.

53   *Commonwealth Parliamentary Debates*, Senate, Matters of Public Interest, 8 December 1999, 11416.

54   House Standing Committee on Aboriginal and Torres Strait Islander Affairs, *Our Land, Our Languages*; Bill Edwards pers. comm. to Jane Simpson. See also Simpson, Amery and Gale, 'I Could Have Saved You', 100.

Emergency Response (the 'Intervention') of 2007: how to convey the unpleasant information that Indigenous people's freedoms would be curtailed in the name of improving their general welfare. In 2008, the head of the federal government Intervention taskforce, Major General David Chalmers, said that a major and unforeseen challenge had been the difficulty of communicating with Aboriginal people.[55] The responsible policymakers simply had not understood that many Northern Territory Aboriginal people did not speak English well, and the taskforce had not made effective use of interpreters.

Finally, with respect to the communicative right to mother-tongue medium education, the promise and hopes of the 1970s and 1980s faded in the 1990s and 2000s. Right from the start, 'bilingual education' programs had suffered from public conflation of different language rights: the identity right to preserve Indigenous languages, the communicative right to learn the language of wider communication (SAE) and the communicative right of children to be taught in a language they understand. Opponents of mother-tongue medium education argued that its supporters simply had a romantic desire to preserve Indigenous languages at the expense of the children learning English. They did not realise that children could grow up bilingual with proper teaching of English and maintenance of their first languages.

Some Indigenous people also argued against mother-tongue medium instruction as they were convinced of the importance of learning SAE, and they blamed a mother-tongue medium instruction program for the poor English language skills of their children. The longstanding Pitjantjatjara program fell victim to this argument in 1990 when the Indigenous-controlled Pitjantjatjara/Yankunytjatjara Education Committee recommended an English-only approach, asserting that schools should focus on teaching children English and that families could maintain Pitjantjatjara at home.[56] The results did not bear out their hopes, and older teachers began calling for a return to mother-tongue medium instruction. In 2018 the state government announced a return to mother-tongue medium instruction.[57]

55   Smiles, 'Five Years'.
56   Anangu coordinators, 'Submission 116'.
57   Department of Education South Australia, *Aboriginal Education Strategy*.

A major blow to bilingual education and, indirectly, to real self-determination was caused by changes to BIITE's and SAL's funding and educational frameworks[58] that made it hard for remote area Indigenous people to gain teacher qualifications. While BIITE expanded its student numbers in the early 2000s, reaching over 3,000 in 2003,[59] the numbers of Indigenous students from remote communities declined rapidly, due in part to the abolition of in-community training. In 2008 only two Aboriginal teachers graduated from BIITE.[60] By 2017 BIITE had stopped operating a teacher training program. The Institute for Aboriginal Development had had to wind down its vocational training role and, in 2019, it went into voluntary administration. Because these decisions have choked off the source of young trained Indigenous teachers and other professionals, the consequences are terrible for communities, with the loss of support for the plans, hopes and enthusiasm of this generation.

Conclusion

The language ecologies of Indigenous Australians are changing rapidly. Fewer people are speaking traditional Indigenous languages as their first language, while more are speaking new Indigenous languages as their first languages.[61] At the same time, the diaspora of speakers of Indigenous languages in cities such as Darwin, Alice Springs and Adelaide is growing, as people seek better access to services. This means that the chances for communities to maintain their traditional Indigenous languages are rapidly diminishing.

Since the beginning of the self-determination policy, identity rights have been strengthened. Governments and communities are investing in Indigenous language revival, and in emblematic gestures such as naming places with Indigenous names and using Indigenous languages at public events. However, with respect to communication rights, the picture is patchier.[62] Major polices, such as the Intervention, were implemented

---

58   Black and Breen, 'The School of Australian Linguistics'; Reaburn, Bat and Kilgariff, 'Looking for a New Common Ground'.

59   Gilbey and McCormack, 'Telling Histories'.

60   Devlin, Disbray and Devlin, *History of Bilingual*, 206.

61   Simpson and Wigglesworth, 'Language Diversity'.

62   See papers in Jane Simpson, Samantha Disbray and Carmel O'Shannessy, eds, 'Teaching and Learning Australian Aboriginal and Torres Strait Islander Languages', special issue *Babel* (Journal of the Australian Federation of Modern Language Teachers' Associations) 54, no. 1–2 (2019).

without proper consideration of communication needs. Subsequently, interpreter services in Indigenous languages have expanded, and governments have made more effort to put information in Indigenous languages. But children still have only limited access to education in their mother-tongue along with proper explicit teaching of English. The move to monolingual English immersion education has been accompanied by the reduction of opportunities for remote Indigenous communities to obtain tertiary training (whether as teachers, interpreters or health workers) in their home communities. These two factors have greatly reduced the opportunities for people living in remote Indigenous communities to access information in order to make the best decisions for themselves and their families. At the same time, the aims of giving children good access to English, and to the content of education, have not so far been achieved.

In 1981 Kenneth Liberman wrote:

> The problem, as the Aboriginal people view it, is that too many of the important everyday decisions in their remote communities are being made by European officials who work for one of these three government bureaucracies. At each Aboriginal central settlement, European officials live in a mini-suburb of portable houses, surrounded by high fences. The majority of Europeans do not speak the Aboriginal language and know little about Aboriginal life. In most cases, they remain for only one or two years, and yet they are actively involved in setting administrative policies for the settlements.[63]

The policy of self-determination was supposed to change that perception. In 2019 it seems that not much has changed for Indigenous people in remote communities.

References

Amagula, Jacqueline and Helen C. D. McCarthy. 'Red Ochre Women: Sisters in the Struggle for Educational Reform'. In *Finding Common Ground: Narratives, Provocations and Reflections from the 40 Year Celebration of Batchelor Institute*, edited by Henk Huijser, Robyn Ober, Sandy O'Sullivan, Eva McRae-Williams and Ruth Elvin, 62–68. Batchelor, NT: Batchelor Press, 2015.

---

63   Liberman, 'Aboriginal Education', 140.

Amery, Rob and Georgina Yambo Williams. 'Reclaiming through Renaming: The Reinstatement of Kaurna Toponyms in Adelaide and the Adelaide Plains'. In *The Land Is a Map: Placenames of Indigenous Origin in Australia*, edited by Luise Hercus, Flavia Hodges and Jane Simpson, 255–76. Canberra: Pacific Linguistics and Pandanus Press, 2002. doi.org/10.22459/lm.03.2009.18.

Anangu coordinators. 'Submission 116'. In *Our Land, Our Languages: Language Learning in Indigenous Communities*, edited by the House Standing Committee on Aboriginal and Torres Strait Islander Affairs. Canberra: Commonwealth of Australia, 2012.

Black, Paul and Gavan Breen. 'The School of Australian Linguistics'. In *Forty Years On*, edited by Jane Simpson, David Nash, Mary Laughren, Peter Austin and Barry Alpher, 161–78. Canberra: Pacific Linguistics, 2001.

Brennan, Gloria. *The Need for Interpreting and Translation Services for Australian Aboriginals, with Special Reference to the Northern Territory: A Research Report.* Canberra: Research Section, Department of Aboriginal Affairs, 1979.

Committee for Geographical Names in Australasia. 'Guidelines for the Recording and Use of Aboriginal and Torres Strait Islander Place Names'. In *The Land Is a Map: Placenames of Indigenous Origin in Australia*, edited by Luise Hercus, Flavia Hodges and Jane Simpson, 276–81. Canberra: Pacific Linguistics and Pandanus Press, 2002. doi.org/10.26530/oapen_459353.

Commonwealth Parliamentary Debates. Senate. 'Matters of Public Interest: Aboriginals: Interpreter Service', 8 December 1999, 11414–17.

Department of Education South Australia. *Aboriginal Education Strategy 2019– 2029.* Adelaide: Government of South Australia, 2018.

Devlin, Brian. 'A Glimmer of Possibility'. In *History of Bilingual Education in the Northern Territory: People, Programs and Policies*, edited by Brian Devlin, Samantha Disbray and Nancy Regine Friedman Devlin, 11–24. Singapore: Springer, 2017. doi.org/10.1007/978-981-10-2078-0_2.

Devlin, Brian, Samantha Disbray and Nancy Regine Friedman Devlin, eds. *History of Bilingual Education in the Northern Territory: People, Programs and Policies*. Singapore: Springer, 2017. doi.org/10.1007/978-981-10-2078-0_5.

Gale, Kathryn. 'Lessons Learned from Bilingual Education'. In *History of Bilingual Education in the Northern Territory: People, Programs and Policies*, edited by Brian Devlin, Samantha Disbray and Nancy Regine Friedman Devlin, 49–60. Singapore: Springer, 2017. doi.org/10.1007/978-981-10-2078-0_1.

Gale, Mary-Anne. 'Boom and Then Bust: Lessons Learnt from My Time Teaching in Three Bilingual Schools in the Northern Territory'. In *History of Bilingual Education in the Northern Territory: People, Programs and Policies*, edited by Brian Devlin, Samantha Disbray and Nancy Regine Friedman Devlin, 73–84. Singapore: Springer, 2017. doi.org/10.1007/978-981-10-2078-0_7.

Gilbey, Kathryn and Rob McCormack. 'Telling Histories: Performing History, Becoming History'. In *Testimony, Witness, Authority: The Politics and Poetics of Experience*, edited by Tom Clark, Tara Mokhtari and Sasha Henriss-Anderssen, 130–43. Newcastle upon Tyne, UK: Cambridge Scholars Publisher, 2014.

Graham, Beth. 'Reflecting on Team Teaching'. In *History of Bilingual Education in the Northern Territory: People, Programs and Policies*, edited by Brian Devlin, Samantha Disbray and Nancy Regine Friedman Devlin, 27–33. Singapore: Springer, 2017. doi.org/10.1007/978-981-10-2078-0_3.

Holcombe, Sarah E. *Remote Freedoms: Politics, Personhood, and Human Rights in Aboriginal Central Australia*. Stanford, CA: Stanford University Press, 2018.

Hoogenraad, Robert. 'Critical Reflections on the History of Bilingual Education in Central Australia'. In *Forty Years On*, edited by Jane Simpson, David Nash, Mary Laughren, Peter Austin and Barry Alpher, 123–50. Canberra: Pacific Linguistics, 2001.

House Standing Committee on Aboriginal and Torres Strait Islander Affairs. 2012. *Our Land, Our Languages: Language Learning in Indigenous Communities*. Canberra: Commonwealth of Australia.

Hudson, Joyce and Patrick McConvell. *Keeping Language Strong: Report of the Pilot Study for the Kimberley Language Resource Centre*. Halls Creek, WA: Kimberley Language Resource Centre, 1984.

Huijser, Henk, Robyn Ober, Sandy O'Sullivan, Eva McRae-Williams and Ruth Elvin, eds. *Finding Common Ground: Narratives, Provocations and Reflections from the 40 Year Celebration of Batchelor Institute*. Batchelor, NT: Batchelor Press, 2015.

Keeffe, Kevin. *From the Centre to the City: Aboriginal Education, Culture and Power*. Canberra: Aboriginal Studies Press, 1992.

Liberman, Kenneth. 'Aboriginal Education: The School at Strelley, Western Australia'. *Harvard Educational Review* 51 (1981): 139–44. doi.org/10.17763/haer.51.1.v93x127q438k160p.

Lo Bianco, Joseph. *National Policy on Languages*. Canberra: Australian Government Publishing Service, 1987.

Macdonald, Lance, Sheila Dixon, Sarah Holcombe and Ken Hansen. *Universal Declaration of Human Rights: Pintupi-Luritja*. UN Human Rights (Office of the High Commissioner for Human Rights), 2015.

Marika, Raymattja. 'The 1998 Wentworth Lecture'. *Australian Aboriginal Studies* 99, no. 1 (1999): 3–9.

Marika-Mununggiritj, Raymattja, Banbapuy Maymuru, Multhara Mununggurr, Badang'thun Munyarryun, Gandalal Ngurruwutthun and Yalmay Yunupingu. 'The History of the Yirrkala Community School: Yolngu2 Thinking about Education in the Laynha and Yirrkala Area'. *Ngoonjook*, no. 3 (September 1990): 32–52.

McMahon, William. *Australian Aborigines: Commonwealth Policy and Achievements. Statement by the Prime Minister, The Rt Hon. William McMahon, C.H., M.P.* W.G. Murray, Government Printer, 1972.

Meehan, Dorothy. 'Starting Out at Bamyili: Factors Specific to the Development of the Kriol Program'. In *History of Bilingual Education in the Northern Territory: People, Programs and Policies*, edited by Brian Devlin, Samantha Disbray and Nancy Regine Friedman Devlin, 61–71. Singapore: Springer, 2017. doi.org/10.1007/978-981-10-2078-0_6.

Merlan, Francesca. 'Recent Rituals of Indigenous Recognition in Australia: Welcome to Country'. *American Anthropologist* 116 (2014): 296–309. doi.org/10.1111/aman.12089.

Nicholls, Christine. 'Death by a Thousand Cuts: Indigenous Language Bilingual Education Programmes in the Northern Territory of Australia, 1972–1998'. *International Journal of Bilingual Education and Bilingualism* 8 (2005): 160–77. doi.org/10.1080/13670050508668604.

O'Grady, Geoff and Ken Hale. 'Recommendations concerning Bilingual Education in the Northern Territory July 1974'. Parliamentary Paper No. 329. Canberra: The Parliament of the Commonwealth of Australia, 1975.

Pybus, Carol Ann. '"We Grew Up This Place": Ernabella Mission 1937–1974'. PhD thesis, University of Tasmania, 2012.

Rademaker, Laura. *Found in Translation: Many Meanings on a North Australian Mission*. Honolulu: University of Hawai'i Press, 2018.

Reaburn, Sue, Melodie Bat and Claire Kilgariff. 'Looking for a New Common Ground: A Reflection on Batchelor Institute's Teacher Education Training Programs for Remote Aboriginal Education Professionals in the Northern Territory'. In *Finding Common Ground: Narratives, Provocations and Reflections from the 40 Year Celebration of Batchelor Institute*, edited by Henk Huijser, Robyn Ober, Sandy O'Sullivan, Eva McRae-Williams and Ruth Elvin, 31–42. Batchelor, NT: Batchelor Press, 2015.

Reid, Nicholas. 'Creating Aboriginal Placenames: Applied Philology in Armidale City'. In *The Land Is a Map: Placenames of Indigenous Origin in Australia*, edited by Luise Hercus, Flavia Hodges and Jane Simpson, 241–54. Canberra: Pacific Linguistics and Pandanus Press, 2002. doi.org/10.22459/lm.03.2009.17.

Ross, Tess and Wendy Baarda. 'Starting Out at Yuendumu School — Teaching in Our Own Language'. In *History of Bilingual Education in the Northern Territory: People, Programs and Policies*, edited by Brian Devlin, Samantha Disbray and Nancy Regine Friedman Devlin, 247–57. Singapore: Springer, 2017. doi.org/10.1007/978-981-10-2078-0_20.

Sandefur, John R. *Kriol of North Australia: A Language Coming of Age*. Work papers of SIL-AAB. Series A, vol. 10. Darwin: Summer Institute of Linguistics, Australian Aborigines Branch, 1986.

Sandefur, John R. and David N. Jentian. 'A Tentative Description of the Phonemes of the Ngalkbun Language (including a Small Word List)'. In *Five Papers in Australian Phonologies*, edited by Joyce Hudson, 57–96. Darwin: Summer Institute of Linguistics, 1977.

Simpson, Jane, Robert Amery and Mary-Anne Gale. 'I Could Have Saved You Linguists a Lot of Time and Trouble: 178 Years of Research and Documentation of South Australia's Indigenous Languages, 1826–2004'. In *Encountering Aboriginal Languages: Studies in the History of Australian Linguistics*, edited by William B. McGregor, 85–144. Canberra: Pacific Linguistics, 2008.

Simpson, Jane and Gillian Wigglesworth. 'Language Diversity in Indigenous Australia in the 21st Century'. *Current Issues in Language Planning*, 19 (2018): 67–80. doi.org/10.1080/14664208.2018.1503389.

Smiles, Sarah. 'Five Years "Too Short" for NT Intervention'. *The Age* (Melbourne), 2008.

Sommerlad, Elisabeth. *Kormilda: The Way to Tomorrow? A Study in Aboriginal Education*. Canberra: Australian National University Press, 1976.

Trudinger, David. 'Converting Salvation: Protestant Missionaries in Central Australia, 1930s–40s'. PhD thesis, The Australian National University, 2011.

United Nations General Assembly. *International Covenant on Economic, Social and Cultural Rights*, 16 December 1966. United Nations, Treaty Series, vol. 993, pp. 3–12. doi.org/10.18356/f95a34ca-en-fr.

United Nations General Assembly. *International Covenant on Civil and Political Rights*, 16 December 1966. United Nations, Treaty Series, vol. 999, pp. 171–86. doi.org/10.18356/b703d8a8-en-fr.

Underwood, Bruce. *Response to: Achieving Equitable and Appropriate Outcomes – Indigenous Australians in Higher Education [Backing Australia's Future, DEST]*. AnTEP, University of South Australia, 2002.

Vaarzon-Morel, Petronella and Jim Wafer. '"Bilingual Time" at Willowra: The Beginnings of a Community-Initiated Program, 1976–1977'. In *History of Bilingual Education in the Northern Territory: People, Programs and Policies*, edited by Brian Devlin, Samantha Disbray and Nancy Regine Friedman Devlin, 35–48. Singapore: Springer, 2017. doi.org/10.1007/978-981-10-2078-0_4.

Watts, Betty H. and James D. Gallacher. *Report on an Investigation into the Curriculum and Teaching Methods Used in Aboriginal Schools in the Northern Territory to C. E. Barnes, Minister of State for Territories*. Darwin: Australian Department of Territories, 1964.

Watts, Betty H., William McGrath and James Linsley Tandy. *Recommendations for the Implementation and Development of a Program of Bilingual Education in Schools in Aboriginal Communities in the Northern Territory*. Canberra: Department of Education, 1973.

White, Leon. 'Finding the Common Ground with Indigenous and Western Knowledge Systems and Seeking the Common Good for All Present and Future Australians – Where Is the Common Ground if We Are Going to Find It?' In *Finding Common Ground: Narratives, Provocations and Reflections from the 40 Year Celebration of Batchelor Institute*, edited by Henk Huijser, Robyn Ober, Sandy O'Sullivan, Eva McRae-Williams and Ruth Elvin. Batchelor, NT: Batchelor Press, 2015.

Wilkins, David. 'Linguistic Research under Aboriginal Control: A Personal Account of Fieldwork in Central Australia'. *Australian Journal of Linguistics* 12 (1992): 171–200. doi.org/10.1080/07268609208599475.

Zoellner, Don. *Vocational Education and Training: The Northern Territory's History of Public Philanthropy*. Canberra: ANU Press, 2017.

14

SELF-DETERMINATION THROUGH ADMINISTRATIVE REPRESENTATION

Insights from theory, practice and history

Elizabeth Ganter

Introduction

In the period of Indigenous 'self-determination', Aboriginal and Torres Strait Islander representatives have moved between the public service and Indigenous organisations. In this chapter, I will draw on normative political theory to argue that such movements have contributed to self-determination in a way that was anticipated by a neglected source of advice on Indigenous administration and representation: the 1974–76 Royal Commission on Australian Government Administration ('the Royal Commission'), chaired by H. C. Coombs.[1] The Royal Commission commenced one year after the Whitlam Government had announced a policy to 'restore to the Aboriginal people of Australia their lost power of self-determination in economic, social and political affairs' on 6 April 1973.[2] Although the Royal Commission did not use the term 'self-determination', its recommendations on how to encourage Aboriginal participation in government, I will argue, canvassed the central issues that

---

1   Phillips, *Politics of Presence*; Mansbridge, 'Should Blacks Represent Blacks'; Dovi, 'Preferable Descriptive Representatives'; Dovi, *The Good Representative*.
2   Whitlam, 'Aborigines and Society'.

have been raised by political theorists about 'descriptive representation'. That is, the Royal Commission's reflections on an unrepresentative public service and its 10 recommendations to address that problem were about how to constitute and then draw upon Indigenous voices to build the means of Indigenous self-determination.

The concept 'descriptive representation' is central to my argument. Political theorists use this term to refer to the possibility that political systems will be more democratic if minorities and politically marginal sections of society (such as women) are enabled to be visibly present in positions of power. Political parties, legislatures and bureaucracies enact descriptive representation when they ensure that a certain proportion of their personnel are members of constituencies (e.g. women, ethnic minorities and disabled people) that are considered to be (unjustifiably) marginal to, and lacking influence over, decisions that affect them. Those who have debated the worth of descriptive representation have argued that it is not sufficient for members of historically disadvantaged groups to be visibly *present* in positions of power. To gain strength and legitimacy in the processes of government, descriptive representatives need also to *speak and act* in ways that are accountable to their people – some have argued, through robust mutual relationships with members of the communities for which they speak.

Self-determination by Indigenous Australians needs descriptive representation. The normative political theory outlined above was implicit (and sometimes explicit) in the words of some Aboriginal and Torres Strait Islander senior public servants in the Northern Territory of Australia whom I interviewed in the period 2006–8. Unwilling to accede to the tokenistic 'any Indigenous person will do', some Aboriginal and Torres Strait Islander officials were applying stricter criteria to their representation of communities. Oscillating between jobs in the public service and in Indigenous organisations, they were searching for roles that both grounded them in their communities and empowered them in government decision-making. Their ambivalence about upward career mobility implied a standard by which they judged 'good' representation: maintaining community connection. Some found this standard hard to meet while they remained in government settings, though I do not mean to suggest that long-term Aboriginal and Torres Strait Islander public servants apply a different standard, as my research found them similarly motivated. I characterised Aboriginal and Torres Strait Islander officials as 'reluctant representatives' when their work neither connected them to their communities nor empowered them within the public service, but still made demands of their Indigeneity.[3]

'Reluctant representatives'

In interviews in the Northern Territory in 2007, I invited 76 Aboriginal and Torres Strait Islander senior public servants to reflect on whether they believed the Northern Territory Government's claim, in regularly published Indigenous employment statistics, that the Northern Territory Public Service was becoming an increasingly representative bureaucracy.

The interviewees described not only their family connections and their workplace experience, but also their motivations for entering and leaving the public service. The snowballing effect of my word-of-mouth recruitment had brought me into contact with nearly as many former employees as current employees, suggesting a high level of movement between the public service and Indigenous organisations. More than half the interviewees had worked in Indigenous sector organisations before becoming a public servant, or were still working in these organisations having left the public service. Of the 33 interviewees who were in senior government positions at the time of their interview, three years later, 10 or nearly one-third had moved into Indigenous servicing roles outside government, and one had already returned to government service. In response to these intriguing statistics, I observed that 'a professionally mobile group was in some kind of orbit between the public service and its publicly funded, arm's length organisations'.[4]

To understand the significance of this mobility, we need to appreciate the relationship between the public service and the 'Indigenous sector' – 'the most important product of the policy era known as "self-determination"'.[5] The publicly funded Indigenous representative and service organisations are 'neither the "state" … [nor] "civil society"' but a 'third thing created out of the interaction … of government and the Indigenous domain'.[6] In 2011, anthropologist Patrick Sullivan argued that recent policy reform

---

3 Ganter, *Reluctant Representatives*.
4 Ganter, *Reluctant Representatives*, 48-49.
5 Rowse, *Indigenous Futures*, 1; see also Rowse, 'Indigenous Sector'.
6 Rowse, *Indigenous Futures*, 13.

had glossed over important distinctions between this 'unacknowledged community sector' and other not-for-profit organisations.[7] Indigenous organisations are like other not-for-profits in their reliance on public funding, but unlike other not-for-profits, Indigenous organisations incorporated under what was now the *Corporations (Aboriginal and Torres Strait Islander) Act 2006* (or its state equivalents) are the 'institutional framework of Aboriginal civil society' and, for many communities, the main source of civic engagement, political identity and material security.[8]

Indigenous organisations are also like other not-for-profits in the larger sense of providing government 'at a distance'.[9] As I have noted elsewhere, they are 'government' in the sense that they are part of government's outsourced service delivery arm and comply with the government's terms of reference and rules of contracting.[10] Indeed, a department and its funded providers may have more in common than that which divides them. One interviewee's career illustrated this well. After having been in the public service in a role servicing Indigenous communities earlier in his career, this interviewee had taken on a leadership position in an Indigenous representative organisation dealing with similar issues. He recalled having been actively recruited back into the public service to manage the government's side of an agreement he had helped set up while leading the organisation. This agreement required the government to match funding that had been granted to his former organisation with an in-kind contribution. This interviewee had agreed to the new public service role so he could follow up on the project from the inside or, as he put this to his recruiters, 'to know exactly what sort of in kind they were giving'.[11] At the time of his interview, he was again working for Aboriginal and Torres Strait Islander people from the outside; by the conclusion of the research, he was back in the government in a more senior role. He would later leave this position for an even more senior role as an external Indigenous representative spokesperson.

For this interviewee, as for others, the public service and the Indigenous sector were co-dependent and formed a combative relational space. Mobility within this space provided not only employment but also political identity. As I observed:

---

7   Sullivan, *Belonging Together*, 48–66.
8   Sullivan, *Belonging Together*, 50, 55–57.
9   Rose and Miller, 'Political Power', 180–81.
10   Ganter, 'Representatives in Orbit'; Ganter, *Reluctant Representatives*.
11   Ganter, *Reluctant Representatives*, 107.

> The interviewees did not describe a purely external political identity, but an orbital one in which Aboriginal and Torres Strait Islander participants were courted by both sectors as an asset in the government's engagement with [its] people. As long as Aboriginal and Torres Strait Islander participants were respectful of the concerns and priorities of their employers, they could move easily across sectors, and through this mobility forge an identity that was relatively autonomous of both.[12]

The public service was the employer of choice for many interviewees, as they found it better resourced and closer to decision-making. So why did some become frustrated and leave? If representation 'makes something present', descriptive representatives do this by the degree to which they resemble their group. In the same way, when Indigenous employment programs identified and selected Aboriginal and Torres Strait Islander public servants, they did so on the basis of their likeness to, or identity with, the 'under-represented' Indigenous population. Yet, Aboriginal and Torres Strait Islander public servants have been selected by the public service because they have skills and capacities other members of their group may not have. To participate in the public service was to accede to the construction of their people as the subjects of remedial policies and programs, which also distanced them from communities. Working in Indigenous organisations took Aboriginal and Torres Strait Islander officials closer to communities but further away from government decision-making. When in government, they clearly brought their identity to their work. But it was not this that distinguished them from other public servants: all public servants bring their identity into their work. It was their difference that made Aboriginal and Torres Strait Islander public servants distinct, or, in the words of political philosopher Charles Taylor, the fact that 'only the minority or suppressed cultures are being forced to take alien form'.[13] That is, while the identity of public servants from majority populations was mostly unacknowledged, Indigenous employment programs marked Aboriginal and Torres Strait Islander recruits as different. Many interviewees commented that they felt singled out as Aboriginal and Torres Strait Islander public servants, perceived as representatives whether or not they sought that role or felt comfortable speaking for their communities. The interviews suggested that Aboriginal and Torres Strait Islander public servants saw the need to be more than

---

12   Ganter, *Reluctant Representatives*, 113.
13   Taylor, 'Politics of Recognition', 43.

just statistics, or the passive representatives of their population; yet they were mindful of public service ethics, which made them unwilling to call themselves representatives in any other sense. 'Reluctant representatives' have no clear mandate to engage in the active representation of their people, yet they look to respond to invitations to speak up.[14] To do otherwise is to begrudge their people a source of assistance. Not all interviewees had left the public service, but it was a possibility in the mind of all of them.

Indeed, to resist the formalistic, principal-agent view of representation, most interviewees were 'reluctant' to call themselves 'representatives' in any sense. They did not see themselves as acting on direct instruction from their constituency as a 'delegate', nor did their accounts suggest it. Their accounts more commonly suggested the 'trustee' relationship, bringing their own judgement to the role. When governments invite Aboriginal and Torres Strait Islander people into their bureaucracies, they are often not just seeking the passive, or descriptive, representation of their population, but their substantive judgements and advice as Indigenous people. To accept a job in Indigenous affairs, which my research showed is the most likely area in which a job will be available to an Aboriginal and Torres Strait Islander person, is to field calls on one's empathy, knowledge and connections – but represent who, how?[15] What if a program is not working well in a community, and providing that advice appears subjective or rubs against unacknowledged public service norms? Public administration scholars long ago expressed doubts about how well administrative structures could reflect communities, arguing that the institutional norms of the public service would always prevail over the social identity of those recruited from under-represented sections of society,[16] and some scholars have more recently observed that the link between passive and active representation had never been proven.[17] In other words, minority personnel did not necessarily mediate between the government and the communities from which they were recruited.

A paradox of representative bureaucracy bedevils every public sector employment strategy that invites Aboriginal and Torres Strait Islander people to bring their Indigeneity to bear on Indigenous policies and programs. If identity is *not* important, why seek Indigenous contributions?

---

14 Ganter, *Reluctant Representatives*, 155.
15 Ganter, *Reluctant Representatives*, 59–70.
16 See, for example, Mosher, *Democracy and the Public Service*.
17 Meier and Hawes, 'Ethnic Conflict', 274.

If identity *is* important, how can Aboriginal and Torres Strait Islander public servants be accountable to their communities and to government at the same time? To tease out these tensions, we need to look beyond the public administration account.

'Good' representatives – developments in normative political theory

When political theorist Hanna Pitkin in 1967 questioned the accountability of descriptive representatives who seek to act for their people, she initiated a prolonged and continuing defence of the descriptive representation of historically disadvantaged groups.[18] Originally focusing on electoral representatives, scholars have gradually come to consider the role of informal descriptive representatives in a wider range of democratic contexts, including bureaucracies.[19]

Scholars have agreed that descriptive representation risks 'essentialising' – that is, assuming that all members of the group have the same view of its interests. In the process of descriptive representation, divisions within the group are likely to become evident and may be exacerbated. Descriptive representation also creates the expectation that the point of view attributed to a group is unique to that group, forcing representatives to speak only for that bounded group, and leaving them 'isolated and marginalized at the representational level'.[20] The interviewees' many stories about meeting invitations, corridor conversations and job interviews illustrated these problems. Yet, as political theorist Virginia Sapiro highlighted and my interviewees also theorised through their reflections, even if it is not easy to get right, descriptive representation is still necessary for the accountability of democratic government.[21]

The historical circumstances of the Northern Territory resemble the conditions that Jane Mansbridge has described as justifying descriptive representation: an extended history of distrust necessitating repairs to communication; the group's interests not 'crystallized' into a known

---

18   Pitkin, *Concept of Representation*.
19   For an excellent genealogy of the literature, see Suzanne Dovi, 'Political Representation', *The Stanford Encyclopedia of Philosophy* (Fall 2018 edition), edited by Edward N. Zalta, last updated 29 August 2018, accessed March 2019, plato.stanford.edu/archives/fall2018/entries/political-representation/.
20   Young, *Inclusion and Democracy*, 150.
21   Sapiro, 'When Are Interests Interesting'.

agenda of reform; and the dominant group's 'fitness to rule' in question, so that the polity is seen to have a low level of legitimacy.[22] Not all Australian Indigenous communities are in such circumstances, but it is common for Australian governments to underestimate Indigenous political capacities, despite the sophistication of some interlocutors. The Turnbull Government's rapid dismissal of Indigenous Australians' carefully prepared and executed 'Statement from the Heart' in 2017 is an illustration.

Among the models of descriptive representation that have emerged, Anne Phillips's 'politics of presence' comes the closest to justifying Indigenous public sector employment as a strategy for the descriptive representation of Aboriginal and Torres Strait Islander people in Australian bureaucracies. Phillips argues that it is better for minorities to be present in, than absent from, the corridors of power – even if, as she acknowledged, being in high places can seem elitist. The members of disadvantaged or dispossessed groups are likely to be better trustees of their group interests than individuals from more advantaged groups. As well, she argues, descriptive representatives provide role models, contribute 'overlooked' perspectives and increase democratic legitimacy.[23] The interviewees mentioned these benefits, role modelling in particular. However, Phillips's theory does not explain other concerns of the interviewees: their exit rate and their wariness of *substituting* themselves for their absent people. Their accounts suggested that the 'politics of presence' sometimes worked against 'good' representation by making it easier for governments not to communicate directly with Aboriginal and Torres Strait Islander constituencies.[24]

By what standards should descriptive representatives be judged? Suzanne Dovi offered a single criterion: that 'preferable descriptive representatives possess strong *mutual* relationships with *dispossessed* subgroups of historically disadvantaged groups'.[25] Dovi later argued the importance of this demanding criterion for any 'good representative', not just for descriptive representatives.[26] Dovi's norm seems to go to the heart of the matter for the 'reluctant representatives' who spoke to me. They were reluctant to represent their people without authority or accountability;

22 Mansbridge, 'Should Blacks Represent Blacks', 644, 646, 649.
23 Phillips, *Politics of Presence*, 167–68.
24 Ganter, *Reluctant Representatives*, 97–103, 184–85; and see Young, *Inclusion and Democracy*, 123, 126–28.
25 Dovi, 'Preferable Descriptive Representatives', 729. Emphasis in original.
26 Dovi, *Good Representative*.

yet, applying Mansbridge's conditions, their circumstances justified them trying. Political theory identifies the conditions under which descriptive representatives may substitute for the absent: when it would be remiss *not* to do so, because there would be a clear situational benefit to absent constituencies who in that particular instance could not possibly speak for themselves.[27]

Those interviewees who were in orbit between the public sector and Indigenous organisations were judging themselves more harshly; feeling that they were merely token was the most agonising of their concerns. What they really cared about was not their relationship with government, but *how their communities would judge them*. They wanted to sustain strong mutual relationships, to be recognised by disadvantaged members of their group as belonging to the same group and sharing the same aims or vision. Descriptive representatives ideally have 'a sense of sharing their fate with a historically disadvantaged group'.[28] The 'good representative' must have this relationship with 'dispossessed subgroups' (Indigenous communities), who might otherwise be excluded twice – once by being a member of the historically disadvantaged group (Indigenous Australians), and a second time by the routine substitution of their own representative. It was in order to address this problem of connection and disconnection that many interviewees were moving between the public sector and Indigenous organisations. The careers of Aboriginal and Torres Strait Islander public servants who are seeking to influence the lives of their people are legitimately unsettled. The public sector positions them in places where they believe they can make a substantial difference to policies and programs, but where it is more difficult to have a robust interactive relationship with communities. The Indigenous sector positions them back with their dispossessed subgroup. Here they feel more grounded, but less empowered. Their mobility supplies the missing elements of each, and authenticates their efforts to be descriptive representatives with something to say.

---

27 Alcoff, 'Problem of Speaking'; see also Spivak, 'Can the Subaltern Speak'.
28 Dovi, 'Preferable Descriptive Representatives', 736.

The Royal Commission on Australian Government Administration

In 1976, the Australian Government received good advice from the Royal Commission on Australian Government Administration. The Royal Commission's central task was 'to adapt the national public administration to the needs of contemporary government' through a 'fundamental rethinking of administrative principles and practices'.[29] One of the Royal Commission's aims was to make the public service more representative of, and responsive to, sections of Australian society that had recently emerged as politically significant – for example, women, Indigenous Australians and non-English speaking migrants. The Royal Commission report was released under the Fraser Government in 1976. By then, 'self-determination' had been replaced by that government's preferred term 'self-management' for its policy approach in Indigenous affairs. Notwithstanding this change in language, the Fraser Government was in broad sympathy with the Whitlam Government's policy towards Indigenous Australians. Acknowledging 'the persistence of attitudes based on now rejected policies of assimilation and "protection"', the Royal Commission endorsed 'respect for Aboriginal aspirations' as an objective of reformed government practice.[30] The Royal Commission saw Aboriginal aspirations as twofold: to 'restore a distinctive Aboriginal culture' and to 'seek significant authority in the determination of policies and the management of programs concerned with their affairs'.[31] The commissioners deliberated at length over how to respond so that Aboriginal people would be involved in both 'the processes of decision and ... the decisions themselves', that is, in both administration and policymaking.[32]

Ten recommendations of the Royal Commission, many of them multi-part, touched on Aboriginal administration and representation, spread over two chapters of the report:[33]

---

29   Royal Commission on Australian Government Administration (Royal Commission), *Report*, 3.
30   Royal Commission, *Report*, 336.
31   Royal Commission, *Report*, 336.
32   Royal Commission, *Report*, 337.
33   In government writing, Torres Strait Islander people were not referenced as a separate people until the 1980s.

- In Chapter 8, 'Staffing the Administration – I Efficiency and Equity', under the heading 'equal opportunity and equity', Recommendation 136 (a–g) outlined 'a 5–10 year program of special recruitment and training'.[34]
- In Chapter 10, 'Special problems of Administration', under the heading 'the administration of Aboriginal affairs', recommendations 289–97 covered external representation, the coordination of programs, processes for ministerial advice and the growth of Aboriginal institutions.[35]

The opening paragraphs of Chapter 8 outlined two concepts framing the Royal Commission's approach to Aboriginal and Torres Strait Islander participation in the public service: first, the government as an 'enlightened employer' and, second, 'government employment as a community instrument of policy'.[36] The first concept encouraged the government to open the public service to diverse social categories, and the second suggested a broad channel of ideas between society and government. Without using the term, the two recommendations effectively proposed 'descriptive representation', which challenged conventional ideas of bureaucratic neutrality. Even though it is the basic premise of representative bureaucracy that people bring their identity into their work, the notion that this affects the judgements they make troubles the conventional presumption that executive government is the neutral instrument of policymaking, and that the legislature is policy's authoritative source. The Royal Commission did not see the bureaucracy as having been politically neutral: 'procedures for selection and the choice of the tests of merit' had introduced 'effective, if unintentional, discrimination against members of particular groups'.[37] The Royal Commission was clear in its warning that the under-representation of any significant citizen group in government employment 'must be regarded as *prima facie* evidence of discrimination or disadvantage or, at the very least, of a matter deserving investigation'.[38] The report announced 'a bold and imaginative program of special recruitment, training and experience' towards the aim of achieving 'substantial Aboriginal participation in departmental work within a few years'.

---

34 Royal Commission, *Report*, 184–89.
35 Royal Commission, *Report*, 335–42.
36 Royal Commission, *Report*, 165–66.
37 Royal Commission, *Report*, 170–71.
38 Royal Commission, *Report*, 185.

Recommendation 136 outlined 'a 5–10 year program of special recruitment and training of Aboriginals' – not only in the Department of Aboriginal Affairs (DAA), which had been established by the Whitlam Government in December 1972, but also in 'other departments with significant Aboriginal to total client ratios' as well as in 'the administration generally'.[39] What was 'bold and imaginative' here? Recommendation 136 was a systematic effort to equip Aboriginal people to meet their own aspirations by respecting and supporting their social identity and community grounding. Recommendation 136 required that:

> Appropriately designed programs of general education, specialised training and graduated experience be developed to equip different categories of trainees to enter, at various levels, Commonwealth Government employment *and Aboriginal incorporated organisations* [emphasis added] (Recommendation 136d).[40]

The Royal Commission was here including Aboriginal organisations, the locally incorporated structures of self-determination for Aboriginal and Torres Strait Islander communities, in the proposed program of recruitment and training. By recommending further that 'formal educational programs required for this purpose be provided as far as possible by institutions *outside the government service* [emphasis added]' (Recommendation 136e), the Royal Commission sought to prevent the public service from monopolising training.[41] Not only was the Royal Commission seeking to raise the number of Aboriginal public servants (to be at least population proportionate), it was trying to breathe fresh air into the public service by asking it to embrace Indigenous public sector employment as a 'community instrument'.

During the Royal Commission hearings, Aboriginal rights activist, Arrernte man and DAA Assistant Secretary Charles Perkins publicly questioned his public service seniors' commitment to his people's self-determination. Perkins had a wide public and media following, and must have provided the commissioners with a constant reminder of the risk of unrestrained internal representation by Aboriginal senior public servants. In *A Bastard Like Me*, the autobiography Perkins published during the time of the Royal Commission, he warned government seniors that Aboriginal public

---

39   Royal Commission, *Report*, 188.
40   Royal Commission, *Report*, 188.
41   Royal Commission, *Report*, 188.

servants were no longer their 'black messenger boys'.[42] Did respecting Aboriginal aspirations mean accepting such challenges to public service authority? While Coombs was open to individual challenges to public service authority, his vision for Indigenous self-determination encouraged widely representative voices. Coombs heard Perkins as a witness to the Royal Commission, but he listened to other Aboriginal and Torres Strait Islander people and communities as well. Wisely, Recommendation 136 recognised that Aboriginal and Torres Strait Islander participation in government would grow both outside and inside government. The Royal Commission sought to support individual careers not only to improve government, but also to advance communities' self-determination.

Chapter 10's 'administration of Aboriginal affairs' recommendations (recommendations 289–97) took 'inside' administrative skills *outside* into Indigenous representative bodies and corporations. The first three recommendations (recommendations 289–91) focused on political expression, or building the skills and effectiveness of the Aboriginal elected body, the National Aboriginal Consultative Committee (NACC).[43] The remaining recommendations (recommendations 291–97) followed four points of reform in the administration of Aboriginal affairs. The first point of reform faced inward. This recommendation asked the DAA to explore in centres with significant Aboriginal populations the feasibility of combining Aboriginal programs, while affirming continued responsibility by functional departments (Recommendation 292). Like the NACC recommendations, the remaining three points and associated recommendations faced outward. These were:

- *To support 'the increasing participation, at the policy level, of representatively chosen Aboriginals'*: appoint a Ministerial Council comprising relevant department heads and NACC members, to be mirrored by regional and community committees reporting to the Ministerial Council half-yearly (Recommendation 293a–e), including on the evaluation of DAA programs (Recommendation 297) and informed by research on welfare indicators through collaboration between the DAA and the Australian Institute of Aboriginal Studies (as it was then known) (Recommendation 296).

---

42 Perkins, *A Bastard Like Me*, 172.
43 Royal Commission, *Report*, 337–38.

- *To support the 'growth of Aboriginal institutions':* confirm the policy of 'steadily shifting responsibility for appropriate local and community tasks to Aboriginal institutions' (Recommendation 294) and conduct 'systematic study of the prerequisites of success for emerging institutions' through collaboration as above (Recommendation 295).

- *To support 'the increasing participation of Aboriginals in administration and service delivery':* implement Recommendation 136's 5–10 year recruitment and training program. Without this, the report explains, the recommendations for the administration of Aboriginal affairs would increase Aboriginal participation but would not meet the equal opportunity requirement.[44]

These recommendations sought to build Aboriginal capacity outside the public service because the commissioners did not view the Australian Public Service as constituted so as to listen to Aboriginal and Torres Strait Islander people. In taking this position, the commissioners may have been influenced by Charles Rowley, a consultant to the Royal Commission, who advised that Aboriginal policy input should come only from external representatives through a 'bargaining process' and not through Aboriginal public servants at all.[45] This was consistent with Rowley's earlier argument that Aboriginal people needed a protective 'carapace' within which to build their own leadership and coalesce their political interests.[46] Rowley was deeply sceptical of Aboriginal people's ability to participate in the bureaucracy without losing their identity, stating, '"Aboriginality" has to be a significant qualification; this also must conflict with the Weberian values of the service in general'.[47] Rowley was not opposed to recruiting Aboriginal public servants; he recommended a recruitment target of population-proportionate Aboriginal representation (1 per cent), across the entire public service.[48] However, he had no faith that the channels of advice inside the government would serve them well, and he recommended replacing the DAA over time with a more representative 'Aboriginal Commission'.[49]

---

44   Royal Commission, *Report*, 339–42.
45   Royal Commission, *Report*, 361.
46   Rowley, *The Remote Aborigines*, 11.
47   Royal Commission, *Report*, 362.
48   Rowley, 'Aboriginals and the Administration', 363.
49   Rowley, 'Aboriginals and the Administration', 360.

While the Royal Commission rejected Rowley's Aboriginal Commission and recruitment target, it adopted his other advice to build skill sharing, career mobility and external representation into the recommendations on the administration of Aboriginal affairs. Coombs must have hoped that narrow attitudes within the Australian Public Service would be challenged by more contact with Aboriginal public servants and organisations. Coombs's strategy for Indigenous political development was dual: providing for the sharing of 'inside' administrative skills with outside representative bodies, while at the same time bringing 'outside' personnel into the public service through employment and training.

It is possible to express this strategy in terms of the political theory outlined above: the Royal Commission saw descriptive representation through the inclusion of Aboriginal and Torres Strait Islander people as public servants as necessary but not sufficient for their inclusion in the democratic process. The Royal Commission appreciated the importance of Indigenous public sector employment, both for equal opportunity and to ensure that there was some Indigenous trusteeship of Indigenous policies and programs, but it also saw the risk of obliging Aboriginal and Torres Strait Islander public servants to serve political authorities other than the communities they were supposed to be representing. The Royal Commission's outward-facing recommendations for Aboriginal affairs administration – strengthen external representation, support Aboriginal institutions and mobilise Indigenous administrators – supported robust connections by building relationships between Indigenous administrators on the inside and their communities and organisations on the outside. Addressing both the internal and external dimensions of government, the Royal Commission's 10 recommendations on Aboriginal administration and representation urged the Australian Public Service to respond to a complex social and political circumstance. Aboriginal and Torres Strait Islander people had been promised self-determination, and the Royal Commission was empowering the public service by insisting that it reach out to Aboriginal and Torres Strait Islander communities.

Concluding comments

As a package, the recommendations of the Royal Commission on Australian Government Administration have been all but forgotten. While the Commonwealth, state and territory public sectors put considerable effort into employing Aboriginal and Torres Strait Islander public servants, they have been content with merely the passive representation afforded by such social diversity, and they have struggled to understand the job mobility of these recruits.[50] Experiments in building representative institutions external to the Australian Government have faltered. We have seen the demise of the NACC in 1977, the formation and dissolution of the National Aboriginal Conference (NAC, 1977–85) and the Aboriginal and Torres Strait Islander Commission (ATSIC, 1989–2005). There has been some investment in capacity building, including by training people to be functionaries in the many continuing Indigenous corporations, but this partial fulfilment of the Royal Commission recommendations has been offset by creating markets for public services in which Indigenous organisations must tender competitively for public money. The impact of this managerialism is still playing out in Indigenous affairs, where an Australian Public Service that has been hollowed out by decades of outsourcing has overlooked the importance of encouraging Aboriginal and Torres Strait Islander voices through external representation, and of keeping direct connections with service delivery.

Some Aboriginal and Torres Strait Islander people are participating in government by working beyond its conventional boundaries. They are operating in a more permeable, fluid and responsive zone of service delivery and representation than the public service, because their operational zone includes locally incorporated Indigenous organisations. They are drawing on public sector employment opportunities, taking their skills into the Indigenous sector and bringing their grounded knowledge and experience back into the public service. They are seeking robust mutual relationships that acknowledge that, as members of a people, they share fates with all Indigenous communities. Wherever they are positioned on the governmental spectrum, they are enriching the Indigenous polity. In these respects they are fulfilling the vision of the Royal Commission on Australian Government Administration. But they are doing this on their own initiative and at their own financial cost, not through good public policy, so the public service is not the meaningful player and instrument of Indigenous self-determination that it could be. If Indigenous career mobility is an indicator, many key players would prefer to speak through properly constituted representative voices than through the substitutive administrative voices that the public service currently encourages.

---

50 Biddle and Lahn, *Understanding Decisions to Exit*; Lahn, 'Being Indigenous'; Lahn and Ganter 'Representation, Recognition and Relationships'; see also Smith, 'Representative Bureacracy'.

Aboriginal and Torres Strait Islander people's participation in the administration of Indigenous affairs is a matter of the utmost importance for their self-determining future and their right to be heard – but their participation in the public service will remain compromised while they have to leave it in order to speak and act in ways that meet their own standards of authenticity as representatives.

An opening observation of this chapter was that self-determination needs descriptive representation, and that both self-determination and descriptive representation need Indigenous Australians to be present in politically relevant and efficacious ways. Career mobility is building political efficacy for Indigenous representatives. They are crossing over the inside and outside dimensions of government to realise their ambitions and their people's ambitions. Through their movement between the public service and Indigenous organisations, they are presenting a model of Indigenous self-determination through administrative representation and applying performance criteria to themselves as descriptive representatives. Some Aboriginal and Torres Strait Islander people stay in the public service and try to improve its connection with external organisations. Some leave to work for similar agendas from the outside, where they often work in inadequately supported organisations. Of course, some never join the public service – but theirs would be a different story. Whatever their strategy of participation, when Aboriginal and Torres Strait Islander people are striving for an ethic of service and a standard of connection that involves mutual recognition with their disadvantaged communities, they are within reach of being 'good' representatives in political theory. And whatever else it needs, Indigenous self-determination must surely need good representatives.

References

Alcoff, Linda. 'The Problem of Speaking for Others'. In *Who Can Speak?: Authority and Critical Identity*, edited by J. Roof and R. Wiegman, 97–119. Urbana: University of Illinois Press, 1995.

Biddle, Nicholas and Julie Lahn. *Understanding Aboriginal and Torres Strait Islander Employee Decisions to Exit the Australian Public Service*. CAEPR Working Paper no. 110. Canberra: Centre for Aboriginal Economic Policy Research, The Australian National University, 2016.

Dovi, Suzanne. *The Good Representative*. Oxford: Blackwell Publishing, 2007.

Dovi, Suzanne. 'Preferable Descriptive Representatives: Will Just Any Woman, Black, or Latino Do?' *American Political Science Review* 96, no. 4 (2002): 729–43. doi.org/10.1017/s0003055402000412.

Ganter, Elizabeth. 'Representatives in Orbit: Livelihood Options for Aboriginal People in the Government of the Australian Desert'. *Rangeland Journal* 33, no. 4 (2011): 85–93. doi.org/10.1071/rj11027.

Ganter, Elizabeth. *Reluctant Representatives: Blackfella Bureaucrats Speak in Australia's North*. Canberra: ANU Press, 2016. doi.org/10.1002/ajs4.32.

Lahn, Julie. 'Being Indigenous in the Bureaucracy: Narratives of Work and Exit'. *International Indigenous Policy Journal* 9, no. 1 (2018): 1–17. doi.org/10.18584/iipj.2018.9.1.3.

Lahn, Julie and Elizabeth Ganter. 'Aboriginal and Torres Strait Islander People in Public Service Roles: Representation, Recognition and Relationships in Australian Government Bureaucracies'. Special Issue on 'Aboriginal and Torres Strait Islander Employment: Key Issues for Policy, Practice and Research', *Journal of Australian Political Economy* 82 (2018): 133–48.

Mansbridge, Jane. 'Should Blacks Represent Blacks and Women Represent Women? A Contingent "Yes"'. *Journal of Politics* 6, no. 3 (1999): 628–57. doi.org/10.2307/2647821.

Meier, Kenneth J. and Daniel P. Hawes. 'Ethnic Conflict in France: A Case for Representative Bureaucracy?' *American Review of Public Administration* 39, no. 3 (2009): 269–85. doi.org/10.1177/0275074008317844.

Mosher, Frederick C. *Democracy and the Public Service* [1968]. New York: Oxford University Press, 1982.

Perkins, Charles. *A Bastard Like Me*. Sydney: Ure Smith, 1975.

Phillips, Anne. *The Politics of Presence*. Oxford: Clarendon Press, 1995.

Pitkin, Hanna F. *The Concept of Representation*. Berkeley: University of California Press, 1967.

Rose, Nikolas and Peter Miller. 'Political Power beyond the State: Problematics of Government'. *British Journal of Sociology* 43, no. 2 (1992): 173–205. doi.org/10.2307/591464.

Rowley, Charles D. 'Aboriginals and the Administration: Royal Commission on Australian Government Administration', Appendix 3.1. *Parliamentary Paper* 188/1976. Canberra: The Government Printer of Australia, 1976.

Rowley, Charles D. *The Remote Aborigines: Aboriginal Policy and Practice. Volume 3*. Canberra: Australian National University Press, 1971.

Rowse, Tim. *Indigenous Futures: Choice and Development for Aboriginal and Islander Australia*. Sydney: University of New South Wales Press, 2002.

Rowse, Tim. 'The Indigenous Sector'. In *Culture, Economy and Governance in Aboriginal Australia*, edited by D. J. Austin-Broos and G. Macdonald, 207–24. Sydney: Sydney University Press, 2005.

Royal Commission on Australian Government Administration. *Report – Royal Commission on Australian Government Administration*. Canberra: Australian Government Publishing Service, 1976.

Sapiro, Virginia. 'When Are Interests Interesting? The Problem of Political Representation of Women'. *American Political Science Review* 75, no. 3 (1981): 701–16. doi.org/10.2307/1960962.

Smith, Rodney. 'Representative Bureaucracy in Australia: A Post-colonial, Multicultural Society'. In *Representative Bureaucracy in Action: Country Profiles from the Americas, Europe, Africa and Asia*, edited by P. von Maravić, B. G. Peters and E. Schröter, 217–30. UK: Edward Elgar Publishing, 2013. doi.org/10.4337/9780857935991.00022.

Spivak, Gayatri. C. 'Can the Subaltern Speak?' In *Marxism and the Interpretation of Culture*, edited by C. Nelson and L. Grossberg, 271–313. Urbana: University of Illinois Press, 1988. doi.org/10.1007/978-3-658-13213-2_84.

Sullivan, Patrick. *Belonging Together: Dealing with the Politics of Disenchantment in Australian Indigenous Affairs*. Canberra: Aboriginal Studies Press, 2011.

Taylor, Charles. 'The Politics of Recognition'. In *Multiculturalism and 'The Politics of Recognition': An Essay*, edited by Amy Gutmann. Princeton, NJ: Princeton University Press, 1992.

Whitlam, E. Gough. 'Press Statement: Aborigines and Society, 6 April 1973'. *Australian Government Digest* 1, no. 2 (1973): 696–98.

Young, Iris M. *Inclusion and Democracy*. Oxford, UK: Oxford University Press, 2000.

15

WHO IS THE SELF IN INDIGENOUS SELF-DETERMINATION?

Sana Nakata

Introduction

In Australia, as in other settler colonial states, self-determination could not be practised as a process of decolonisation in which the coloniser exits the territory of the Indigenous sovereign. Rather, Indigenous self-determination in Australia from the 1970s to the turn of the twenty-first century was focused upon the transformation of an ongoing Indigenous–settler relationship, in which the settler state might be compelled or persuaded to transfer some decision-making powers to Aboriginal and Torres Strait Islander peoples. As other chapters in this book illustrate, these transfers took many forms with different effects in different parts of the continent. However, in this century, we have seen a rhetorical and substantive shift away from self-determination towards constitutional recognition – particularly since the 2010 establishment of the Expert Panel on Recognising Aboriginal and Torres Strait Islanders in the Constitution and through to the 2017 delivery of the Referendum Council report (inclusive of the Uluru Statement from the Heart). Constitutional recognition would be a structural reform, a pathway towards Indigenous justice in the context of ongoing colonisation.

This chapter explores the history of the *idea* of self-determination in an effort to understand the difference between the discourse of self-determination and the discourse of constitutional recognition. While they are clearly related, I will argue that they place differentiated emphasis and demands upon processes of self-identification.

Self-identification has been an important element of self-determination, connecting the formation of individual identity to the collective assertion of nationhood. Internationally, policies that have enabled self-identification have enabled Indigenous nation-building and decolonisation. In the settler colonial context of Australia, however, self-determination has been associated not so much with nation-building and more with increasing Indigenous control of policy design, implementation and service provision; self-determination practised in this way has resulted in less than fully independent governance. As a result, the question of who is the 'self' in self-determination has been answered through the implementation of publicly verifiable criteria, through a three-part definition, allowing for clear delineation between those individuals to whom Indigenous policy applies and those to whom it does not.[1] With the emergence of a politics of constitutional recognition, this delineation has become less important because specific material benefits are less immediately at stake in constitutional recognition discourses; thus the politics of constitutional recognition do not require the state or Indigenous communities and organisations to police Indigenous identities in the same way, or for the same purpose. Instead, constitutional recognition attends to the historical fact of colonisation as a foundation of the nation-state, and recognises the ongoing presence of First Australians *generally*, rather than through individual-level identification processes.

In being less prescriptive, this politics of recognition allows more complexity of historically emergent Indigeneities to be expressed by Aboriginal and Torres Strait Islander peoples. Any transfers of political power that might flow from such recognition are less immediately dependent upon the question: who is the self in Indigenous self-determination?

The chapter will first place Indigenous self-determination in its historical and local context. It will then consider the 'recognition' turn in political theory, and the academic debates this has produced with respect to Indigenous politics. In the third part, I engage with the ways Indigenous

---

1   See Gardiner-Garden, *Defining Aboriginality*.

Australians describe their identity as a site of contestation through Bronwyn Carlson's book *The Politics of Identity*. My purpose is not to expand our understanding of 'who' the Indigenous self is in Indigenous self-determination; rather I seek to understand how the *question* of Indigenous identity became a site of both personal and political contestation. This contestation persists even as discourses of Indigenous claims to justice are shifting from the language of self-determination to constitutional recognition and beyond.

Indigenous self-determination in historical context

From the perspective of Western law and politics, self-determination can be considered a longstanding principle that relates the sovereignty of individual selves to the political legitimacy of state power. The principle of self-determination was evident in both the American Declaration of Independence (1776) and the French Declaration of the Rights of Man and Citizen (1791). In both, the consent of the governed underpinned the political legitimacy of the sovereign. As an organising principle of international relations on the European continent, self-determination can be dated back further, to at least the Peace of Westphalia in 1648. It was an expression of a much more longstanding commitment in Western moral and political philosophy: Autonomy. Freedom. Sovereignty. These are Western concepts that attach as much to individual human beings as they attach to nations and states. Thus, self-determination operates not only at the level of institutions and organised political communities but also at the level of autonomous individuals. Sovereign states are self-determining, but only because they are constituted of sovereign, individualised, selves. Discourses of self-determination then come to focus on the postcolonial formation of Indigenous individuals and their identity claims, not only on formations of self-determination in Indigenous institutions and governing bodies. Indeed, the normative value of these concepts of autonomy, freedom and sovereignty as they relate to individuals underpins the whole premise of a legitimate political order in the West: the people are sovereign, and the power of the state is legitimate only insofar as it commands the willing consent of the people.

Asmi Wood, in his chapter for this book, has told how 'self-determination' acquired new significance in the twentieth century as the European and Ottoman empires came to an end and as norms of international conduct issued from first the League of Nations and later the United Nations. Self-determination is now a keystone in the new international order – present not only in the UN Charter, but also in the International Covenant on Civil and Political Rights and in the International Covenant on Economic, Social and Cultural Rights. In the Declaration on the Rights of Indigenous Peoples (UNDRIP), the General Assembly in 2007 attached Indigenous peoples' claims for justice to that principle. Australia endorsed UNDRIP in 2009 as a non-binding framework for better recognising and protecting the rights of Aboriginal and Torres Strait Islander Australians. As other chapters of this book show, the Australian Government began to label its approach to Indigenous affairs as 'self-determination' in 1973 – a framework that guided policy on land rights, native title and Indigenous political rights, including on questions of representative structures and organisations.[2]

The 'idea' of self-determination can produce different forms of politics and political claim-making. Internationally, the discourse of Indigenous self-determination initially and primarily emerged as a framework for decolonisation following the vacating of colonised territories by diminished empires, in which the legitimacy of state claims to sovereignty is put under external examination. Domestically, in the context of ongoing settler colonial governance, self-determination has necessarily operated as a framework for Indigenous governance within a context of contested but near invincible state sovereignty. Internationally, the principle of self-determination allows the question: is the state's claim to sovereignty legitimate? Domestically, the principle of self-determination asks a different kind of question: what forms of policy and governance can legitimately be enacted over Indigenous peoples by the colonial state?

Dylan Lino helpfully expresses an important distinction in the literature on the right to self-determination between its *external* and *internal* aspects: 'the former generally being conceived of as the right of a people to be free from external domination, the latter as the right of a people to freely choose their political regime and to be autonomous'.[3] He describes the internal register as an 'appropriation' of self-determination, as a way

---

2   Lino, 'Towards', 840; Hunt, 'Between', 27.

3   Lino, 'The Politics', 846.

Indigenous Australians have been able to 'frame' their political claims.[4] The language of peoplehood – and its corollary, self-determination – is a language of international law, and this too has bolstered Indigenous demands. When the collective right of peoples to self-determination became prominent in the decolonisation era, Indigenous minorities in settler colonies were not seen to be among the right's beneficiaries (at least not independently of the settler states in which they resided). But especially from the 1970s onwards, Indigenous advocates globally, including in Australia, appropriated the linked ideas of peoplehood and self-determination to frame their political struggles.[5]

As a framework for decolonisation and as an appropriated framework for Indigenous people within settler colonies, self-determination operates to transfer power and resources from the coloniser to the colonised, giving rise to critical questions and challenges about policy, institutions and their governance. In both registers, self-determination operates as a practice or a mechanism to facilitate this transfer between political communities.

It is in this second 'internal' mode that self-determination has predominantly operated in Australia, superseding policies of 'protection' and 'assimilation' in which there had been 67 definitions, descriptions and classifications of Aboriginality written into over 700 pieces of legislation across the states and federal government to 1986.[6] Just before the official inception of self-determination as a national policy in 1973, Section 127 of the Australian Constitution was deleted by the 1967 referendum so that the exclusion of Aboriginal and Torres Strait Islanders from Australia's total official population was no longer justified. This encouraged the Australian Bureau of Statistics (ABS) to publish national population totals that included Indigenous Australians. At the same time, the ABS sought to improve the accuracy of its counting by changing the census question so that it no longer asked respondents to differentiate themselves as 'full-bloods', 'half-castes' and 'quarter castes'. Official recognition that 'Aboriginal identity' was a social and not a biological construct was part of a wider shift in Australians' thinking of which the rise of the land rights movement in the 1960s and 1970s was another example. The land rights movement encouraged Aboriginal and Torres Strait Islander peoples to assert their diverse forms of social and political practice across

---

4   Lino, 'Towards', 121.
5   Lino, 'Towards', 121.
6   McCorquodale, 'The Legal', 9.

the continent in ways that have produced recognition of their humanity, their rights and their social and political identities. Another effect of the 1967 referendum was that it empowered the Australian Government to develop national policies, and this encouraged the Australian Government to produce a nationwide definition of 'Aboriginal' that conceded that Aboriginal identity was not determined by descent but by subjective identification and social recognition. The new three-part definition of 'Aboriginal' – formulated in 1968 and confirmed after a review in 1981 – was composed of (1) descent, (2) self-identification and (3) community recognition.[7] This three-part definition was adopted by governments as a way to determine which Australians were eligible to benefit from targeted government programs, and it remains the dominant definition of Indigeneity in Australia today.[8] A positive result from what is known as the Confirmation of Aboriginality process is recorded as an official written document in which an incorporated Aboriginal or Torres Strait Islander organisation endorses an individual's claim to Aboriginal or Islander identity; this is the operational form of 'community recognition'.[9]

Self-determination was a departure from assimilatory policies; it operated by developing legal and administrative devices to recognise and manage the 'Aboriginal domain'.[10] This included changes to land title from the late 1960s onwards, and the statutory encoding of 'native title', as well as the creation of statutory bodies in the form of land councils that are ongoing. As well, self-determination included the (now defunct) Aboriginal and Torres Strait Islander Commission, and a range of other incorporated Indigenous bodies and organisations that deliver services to Indigenous peoples and communities, including forms of Indigenous local government that have superseded old missions and settlements. The proliferation of community-controlled health organisations, land councils, legal services and housing cooperatives indicates the transformative impact of self-determination in Australia. Nonetheless, the self-governing capacity of Indigenous communities has emerged without serious engagement with the complexities and multiplicities of Indigenous Australian's identity.

---

7   Department of Aboriginal Affairs, *Report*. For a description of the circumstances in which the Australian government reformed its definition, see Rowse and Smith, 'The Limits'.
8   See Gardiner-Garden, *Defining Aboriginality*.
9   Carlson, *The Politics*, 7.
10   Rowse, *Remote*.

The recognition turn – within and beyond self-determination

To understand the similarities and the differences between the discourses of self-determination and of constitutional recognition we need to see how recognition is a requisite for justice.[11] Recognition theory takes up a Hegelian master/slave dialectic to emphasise that identities are constructed in relational, rather than autonomous terms: constituted by a self-consciousness that allows us to understand who we are, in terms of who we are not. Identity is, in short, intersubjectively produced and takes shape especially in relation to our 'significant other'. Our significant others are those whose acts have a strong bearing on our sense of self. This might be immediate members of family and community, who may have positive or negative views of you. It is also those who hold positions of authority, and wield control, influence and power over us whether for good or for bad. As a site of justice, recognition produces an alignment between our sense of self and the sense with which our significant others understand us. As a site of injustice, *non-recognition* and *mis-recognition* risks the diminishment of self-esteem, self-respect and self-confidence in ways that do harm and violence to individuals and communities.[12] Such accounts are compelling, but Indigenous political theorists Glen Coulthard and Audra Simpson remind us that not all slaves seek recognition of their master: Indigenous peoples are not necessarily looking to the settler colonial state to recognise or affirm our existence. On the contrary, Coulthard and Simpson remind us, in different ways, that, for many, justice lies in turning away from the coloniser's gaze, refusing the right of the coloniser to know us at all.

It is relevant to understand that issues of identity and recognition have been grappled with from *within* the self-determination discourse. For example, the 1986 report of UN Special Envoy Martinez Cobo identifies:

> Indigenous communities, peoples and nations [as] … those which, having a historical continuity with pre-invasion and pre-colonial societies that developed on their territories, consider themselves distinct from other sectors of the societies now prevailing in those territories.[13]

---

11   See Taylor, 'The Politics'; Honneth, *The Struggle*; cf. Coulthard, 'Subjects' and *Red Skin*; Simpson, *Mohawk*.
12   See Honneth, *The Struggle*.
13   Martinez Cobo cited in Daadaoui, 'The Western', 154.

Daadaoui's social constructivist critique of Cobo highlights the disjuncture between two elements of this definition: the need for historical continuity in Indigenous identities and the need to acknowledge that colonisation has produced 'divergent self-perceptions and political discourses of groups and national societies, and diverse state-society relations'.[14] The colonising process had the effect of dislocating Indigenous peoples from country; it reordered their social and family lives, and it deployed disciplinary practices that allowed the coloniser to know the colonised. Against this process, the requirement that Indigenous peoples must be able to assert pre-colonial identities, practices and knowledge systems against the colonial state as a condition for either self-determination or recognition is problematic.

In both self-determination and constitutional recognition, the importance of identity and the 'self' (individuated or collective) is easily displaced because it is so difficult to *comprehend* the multiplicities of being and subjectivities that produce Indigenous identity. Instead of grappling with the question of *who* is the self in Indigenous self-determination or of asking *who* seeks recognition from the Australian settler order, it is understandable that both the self-determination and constitutional recognition discourses must get on with the urgent and essential task of *how* we can develop mechanisms for the transfer of power from the settler order to Indigenous peoples, even if we cannot comprehend who those peoples are.

Both discourses maintain a focus on the transfer of power and resources, with attendant focus on issues of policy, governance and institutions, and both discourses continue to return to questions of identity. As Dylan Lino observes:

> Australia's recent politics of Indigenous constitutional recognition can be seen as contests over Indigenous identity – over who Aboriginal and Torres Strait Islander peoples are – and what it means to respect that identity within the constitutional norms of the settler state.[15]

---

14 Daadaoui, 'The Western', 154.
15 Lino, 'Towards', 119.

By the late twentieth century, Australian political discourse had shifted from a language of self-determination predominantly pursued through the domain of policy to one of 'constitutional recognition': for example, the 2012 report of the Expert Panel on Constitutional Recognition of Indigenous Australians, the 2014 Aboriginal and Torres Strait Islander Peoples Act of Recognition Review Panel, and the 2015 Parliamentary Joint Select Committee on Constitutional Recognition of Aboriginal and Torres Strait Islander Peoples. Most recently, the 2017 Referendum Council report has emphasised constitutional reform demanding deep structural change beyond mere symbolic recognition.[16] This points to a shift to constitutional reform *beyond the politics of recognition*: constitutional reform demands the rewriting of the Australian Constitution not only to 'recognise' Aboriginal and Torres Strait Islander peoples but also to provide a constitutionally protected representative body that gives Aboriginal and Torres Strait Islander First Nations a Voice to Parliament, including the ability to monitor the use of the heads of power in Section 51(xxvi) (the 'race' power) and Section 122. While recognition is a dimension of this proposed reform, and while matters of identification are relevant in understanding representativeness, questions of who the Indigenous self is are less acute than the question of who the Australian state is constituted for in the first place.

The discourse of constitutional recognition presents different terrain upon which we might make sense of the relation between identity and justice. Recent efforts to mobilise towards constitutional recognition are in some ways a response to the limits of self-determination. Glen Coulthard described in the Canadian context in 2007 that 'self-determination efforts and objectives … have been increasingly cast in the language of "recognition"'.[17] On the one hand, recognition can be understood as an effort to better capture the plurality of identities within and across groups and nations. On the other hand, as Coulthard makes clear, recognition offers up relational configurations between the coloniser and Indigenous peoples that risk reproducing rather than transcending historical oppression.[18] If one is to turn towards recognition to take more seriously the constituting role of a sovereign self in claims for justice, then one will also find they are turned towards their coloniser (their master), their significant other, asking – indeed, begging – to be recognised.

---

16 See Davis and Langton, 'Introduction'.
17 Coulthard, 'Subjects', 437.
18 Coulthard, 'Subjects', 439.

In Australia, this problematic politics of recognition played out in the efforts of the 'Recognise' campaign (2012–16), which sought to create a public movement in support for constitutional recognition of Australia's First Peoples.[19] Megan Davis and Marcia Langton, in 2016, made clear that the gap between substantive reform desired by most Indigenous Australians and the public messaging required for a 'Yes' vote, 'explains why the ambiguity of the word recognition has led to a dissonance between the campaign to recognise and the Aboriginal political domain'.[20] This dissonance was evident in two competing surveys on constitutional recognition in 2015: the first by Recognise suggested 87 per cent of Aboriginal and Torres Strait Islander peoples supported a symbolic form of constitutional recognition. *IndigenousX* initiated its own survey and found support for this was much lower at 25 per cent.[21] The *IndigenousX* survey, which also returned more than 50 per cent support for an Indigenous parliamentary body being included in a referendum for constitutional change, highlighted the unwillingness of Aboriginal and Torres Strait Islanders to accept mere recognition of their ongoing presence in the Constitution and their insistence that substantive, structural reform of representation and political decision-making processes was necessary. Megan Davis also emphasises that there are many competing meanings of 'recognition' that are deployed in public conversation and debate about constitutional reform from the shallow and symbolic to substantive, structural reform.[22] These competing meanings risk its operation as an 'empty signifier' in contexts in which precise details matter most. The relevance to this paper is to complicate assumptions surrounding a singular, unified, potentially essentialist understanding of Indigenous identities and political claim-making in discourses that are ever-preoccupied with the need to determine who the 'self' in Indigenous self-determination is, to determine who it is that seeks recognition from whom.

These two discourses can be usefully understood as having shared purpose: to remedy the injustice of dispossession and disempowerment enacted through historical and ongoing practices of colonisation. But this produces

---

19   Maddison, 'Recognise', 9.
20   Davis and Langton, 'Introduction', 5.
21   Celeste Liddle, '87% of Indigenous People Do Not Agree on Recognition. You'd Know if You Listened'. *The Guardian*, 19 June 2015, accessed 16 December 2019, www.theguardian.com/comment isfree/2015/jun/19/87-of-indigenous-people-do-not-agree-on-recognition-youd-know-if-you-listened.
22   Davis, 'Competing Notions'; see Davis, 'Correspondence'.

a shared problem: the *incomprehensibility* of Aboriginal and Torres Strait Islander identity.[23] In the discourse of Indigenous self-determination, the Indigenous 'self' has persistently sought expression and recognition within the Australian settler order, not only as individual human beings but also as a coherent collectively – a 'peoples'.

Comprehending the politics of Indigenous identity in the settler colonial order

For all that distinguishes self-determination from constitutional recognition, they are united by this shared purpose and shared problem. There is a *historical continuity* between the idea of self-determination (from the 1970s onwards) and efforts towards constitutional recognition (2006–16) and it is grounded in the incomprehensibility of Indigenous peoples within ongoing colonial contexts. In Australia, 'Aboriginal' is little more than the projection of a coloniser's taxonomy of the natural world. But the Aboriginal person has always been a real, embodied, human being – an individual nestled into family, kin, clan and nation – named by themselves, in their own languages, for their own needs. The 'Torres Strait Islander' is a specific invention of the Queensland legislature of 1939. Yet, here I am: both a fiction brought into being by the colonial order and also something else. This is the incomprehensibility of Aboriginal people.[24] And it is to this incomprehensibility that I now turn.

In *The Politics of Identity*, Bronwyn Carlson expresses the deep plurality of Indigenous Australian identities and provides some insight into why the question of 'who' is so difficult in settler colonial contexts. She writes that, 'Aboriginal identity, whether we think of it in individual, local community or pan-Aboriginal terms, is a product of our position within and our relationship to the nation-state'.[25] Here, she is not only

---

23   The turn toward recognition was partly a response to the limits of self-determination to engage seriously with the politics of identity alongside the politics of territory. However, constitutional recognition (and recognition theory more broadly) are also gravely limited in their capacity to comprehend Indigenous identities (Coulthard, 'Subjects of Empire'; Coulthard, *Red Skin*; Simpson, *Mohawk Interruptus*). This historical continuity of the incomprehensibility of Indigenous peoples suggests that what distinguishes self-determination from constitutional recognition may be less significant than sometimes suggested.

24   See Langton, *Well*; Langton, 'Aboriginal Art', 122.

25   Carlson, *The Politics*, 269.

referring to colonial impact in its generic, all-encompassing sense, she is making quite specific reference to the three-part test for Confirmation of Aboriginality.[26]

This presents a central perversion of the principle of self-determination. The establishment of Aboriginal councils and community-controlled organisations is a key outcome of the self-determination effort in the early 1970s, allowing for the material transfer of some power and resources back to Indigenous Australian communities. Alongside this, the *Racial Discrimination Act 1975* was crucial in making it illegal for Aboriginal and Torres Strait Islanders to be discriminated against, while still allowing for Aboriginal and Torres Strait Islanders to be positively discriminated towards in order to redress the inequitable distribution of resources and opportunities due to historical, structural and ongoing practices of colonisation. As with many things in Indigenous affairs, the perversion arises from 'good' intentions. If some people are to receive positive discrimination on account of their group identity, then it becomes necessary for those people to prove their membership to the group. However, it becomes incumbent upon Aboriginal communities and organisations themselves to act as the arbiters of Indigenous identity claims for reasons that have less to do with their own nationhood and more to do with the need to accommodate the settler order of things. As Carlson explains:

> Any government, agency, employer, service or benefit provider which requires proof of Aboriginal identity to allocate a government benefit or service can accept a Confirmation of Aboriginality document from an individual only if it has been verified by an Aboriginal organisation, and only if that organisation has been formally incorporated under State or Territory legislation ... The Confirmation of Aboriginality is accepted as a pseudo-legal document by institutions and their officers, and demonstrates due diligence.[27]

The dislocation of people from their families, land, language and cultural practices is colonisation's defining characteristic wherever and whenever it occurs in the world. This means that supporting the self-determination of communities to provide them with the right to control and make decisions with respect to membership (producing and maintaining the

26 Carlson, *The Politics*, 7.
27 Carlson, *The Politics*, 133.

self) also makes it exceptionally difficult for some Indigenous peoples to meet the three-part test (eliminating and diminishing the self). This is an uneasy tension from the perspective of self-determination. On the one hand, it is a form of self-determination. On the other hand, it is the devolvement of the very same colonial administrative regime that 'sorted' Aboriginal and Islander peoples for the purpose of implementing policies of family separation, education and employment to Aboriginal communities themselves. As Carlson concludes:

> My study indicates that this wider picture [of the complexity of Indigenous identities] is a necessary one for us, the Aboriginal community, to understand how we are complicit agents of oppressive practices that restrict the creative regeneration and production of Aboriginal identities.[28]

Carlson persuasively sets out how this concern is not one of mere principle. The substantive contribution of her research is to detail the experiences of those Aboriginal people whose identity status might be ambiguous – whether due to family disconnection, or those of mixed heritage who may or may not be recognisably Aboriginal – with respect to the Confirmation of Aboriginality process. That some speak positively, and others negatively, is less significant than the way in which the process operates to keep 'colonial binaries alive', not only in terms of the significance of being able to distinguish between Indigenous and non-Indigenous peoples within the settler colonial context, but also in terms of a colonial binary between the power of the 'identifier' and the 'identified'.[29] The binary here refers to the power relation between the institution who 'knows' and the individual who must be 'known'. That is, here it becomes evident that the question of *who* is the self in Indigenous self-determination is not the only question we should be asking. The other question is: how do the politics of identity come to be contested in the pursuit of the Indigenous 'self'? What power relations between institutions and individuals are taking place to sustain self-determination as a practice for Indigenous governance? And what are the effects of these relations on those subject to those power relations? This is not about the tension produced towards individual identity and selfhood and the legitimacy of collective Indigenous authority: the individual self and the self as a collective 'peoples' will always sit in relation to one another, sometimes

---

28 Carlson, *The Politics*, 269.
29 Carlson, *The Politics*, 122.

easily and sometimes uneasily. What is of core concern from a perspective of law and politics is to understand how the 'self' – individual or collective – is transformed from an embodied, lived expression to a politically strategic manoeuvre necessary for ontological existence.

Whether the people she talks to have always known or only recently discovered their Aboriginal heritage, Carlson is able to describe diverse experiences and ways that people make sense of their Indigenous selves. In the cases of those who have always known, there is a sense that 'recognition' through Confirmation of Aboriginality is disconnected from one's actual identity:

> It's not just about that piece of paper. I think to be Aboriginal you need to identify with a group of people. Actually, that could be really hard to identify too because you don't know that family.[30]

For some, it does not necessarily mean connection to community:

> I think it means acknowledging ... my ancestry and just knowing who I am in that respect. Not necessarily being what I am doing or where I live ... not necessarily being part of community involvement and all that stuff.[31]

For others, it does:

> [Aboriginality] means basically belonging to here and family. I guess association to the land and culture as well as knowing where I come from ... It's the search of wanting to know that deep meaning of where they've come from.[32]

> So I am endeavouring to get connection back with culture. I was brought up in a white society, a white culture and I probably relate more to white society than Aboriginal society. But yeah, I feel there is an imbalance now, and I want to get a balance in my life with my Aboriginal side of the family.[33]

While for another, 'a part of that Diaspora of almost lost and forgotten Aboriginal Australians', the effect of colonisation means that his identity *cannot* be connected to land or community:

---

30 P10 [anonymised interviewee] quoted in Carlson, *The Politics*, 183.
31 P1 [anonymised interviewee] quoted in Carlson, *The Politics*, 186.
32 P7 [anonymised interviewee] quoted in Carlson, *The Politics*, 189.
33 P16 [anonymised interviewee] quoted in Carlson, *The Politics*, 193.

I live in a world in which I don't belong in the sense that I was born in Leichhardt [suburb of Sydney] which is in Gadigal country but I have no connection to Gadigal people [apart from growing up there].[34]

But for some, this is part of the injustice that defines Aboriginal identity:

Aboriginal people have had it hard and that is what makes us Aboriginal in some way, we all know about our past and what it means to be Aboriginal. So that is why, when people aren't really Aboriginal because they haven't faced these things, it isn't right they can say they are Aboriginal.[35]

In this context, it is unsurprising that Carlson's research showed that many Aboriginal people spoke about the 'gaps in their knowledge about what it means to be Aboriginal'.[36] Thus, for many this means seeking out opportunities to learn and perform their identity, all the while having diverse experiences of how to do so:

I'm at a loss at the moment. I just find it really hard to find culture and I want to learn language.[37]

To my knowledge being Aboriginal was what I was taught at school as a whitefella. They lived in the bush a long time ago, wore loin cloths and speared roos and that was my understanding of being Aboriginal. So I was lost and just had no idea of who I was after that.[38]

I've changed the way I talk and everything ... I don't know ... have to be on the same level as people in the community so I don't look upper-class or I don't look like or I don't identify.[39]

We are still in limbo, don't know which world to fit in... I don't know when I should start saying 'cuz' or 'bruz', yeah, I don't know when I should start acting Aboriginal.[40]

---

34 P13 [anonymised interviewee] quoted in Carlson, *The Politics*, 192.
35 P23 [anonymised interviewee] quoted in Carlson, *The Politics*, 190.
36 Carlson, *The Politics*, 226.
37 P10 [anonymised interviewee] quoted in Carlson, *The Politics*, 230.
38 P8 [anonymised interviewee] quoted in Carlson, *The Politics*, 231.
39 P10 [anonymised interviewee] quoted in Carlson, *The Politics*, 236.
40 P10 [anonymised interviewee] quoted in Carlson, *The Politics*, 247.

I labour these personal expressions of Aboriginal identities here to demonstrate the diverse experiences that Indigenous Australians have in comprehending, or making sense, of the 'self' in the modern settler colonial context. What comes through so strongly in Carlson's work is that this process of comprehension takes place at a 'cultural interface'.[41] She writes that:

> There was evidence in the transcripts of the interviews of the push-pull of the discourses of Aboriginality. A push against them as they operated to exclude some subjectivities, and the pull of them for the newly identifying trying to enter into the world of Aboriginal meaning or those wanting to belong and work as a member of the collective community.[42]

What Carlson exposes through these diverse experiences is the manner in which Indigenous Australian communities themselves have taken on the surveillance required for the settler colonial order to determine which persons count as Aboriginal today.[43] Carlson's task is not to resolve these tensions but to:

> Suggest there is room for Aboriginal people [as individuals] to reflect on and examine our own practices and our compliance with a de facto government regime that insists on applying definitional criteria for access to government resources as the complete 'truth' of what it also means to be Aboriginal in all aspects of our daily lives.[44]

Conclusion

In this chapter I have attempted to place the recommendations of the 2017 Referendum Council, which call for constitutional and structural reform, in a historical and theoretical context. The proposed reforms offer a move beyond 'the politics of identity' in Indigenous affairs potentially displacing the question of 'who' is the Indigenous self in Indigenous self-determination with a new question: how can the Australian state be made to hear the many voices of Aboriginal and Torres Strait Islander people on the issues that affect them? The determination of who is and who is

---

41 See Nakata *Disciplining*; Carlson, *The Politics*, 239–50.
42 Carlson, *The Politics*, 239.
43 Carlson, *The Politics*, 273.
44 Carlson, *The Politics*, 273.

not an Aboriginal or Torres Strait Islander person should and could never become redundant. But the question of who we are, as individuals and collectives, ought to be reclaimed as a question for our many selves, as we navigate the complexities of being First Nations in a settler colonial order. The question of our identity needs no longer be a question for the state's organisation of our lives. Who is the 'self' in Indigenous self-determination matters less than understanding how and why and under what conditions that 'self' must be produced.

This is an effort to present a problematisation: an effort to reframe the ways in which we seek to understand who Indigenous Australians are and instead to focus upon why we ask for Indigenous expressions of self and sovereignty in the ways that we do. The final lines of Carlson's book ask:

> In what other ways can we express ourselves and conduct a community discourse that is open to all Aboriginal experiences? What can we achieve in our relations with the wider nation-state if we are not so preoccupied in our community with regulating and surveilling each other for a few crumbs thrown under the master's table?[45]

My argument is a simple one: the question of who is the self in self-determination is a question that reveals the ways in which the politics of Indigenous identity helps to organise the settler colonial state's organisation of our lives, families and justice claims. In self-determination, the politics of our identities must produce a coherent and organised social and political community as a basis for our justice claims. In constitutional recognition, particularly in its symbolic form, our justice claims are predicated upon receiving recognition of the very master whose authority we refuse. In both, the politics of identity deepen our entanglements with the state in ways that risk deepening tensions within and between our many, diverse, 'Indigenous' selves. Problematising this is an effort to find space outside of the discourses that bind us.

The self in Indigenous self-determination is an idea: both a colonial idea and a colonising idea. A necessary fiction, and also a real body: educatable, incarcerable, governable. The self in Indigenous self-determination is also an ideal: that something past can be recovered, and that something new will be made. Having grappled with the history of self-determination, and as we turn towards future debate about deep, structural, constitutional

---

45 Carlson, *The Politics*, 273.

reform, the answer to the question *who is the self in Indigenous self-determination* ought to begin to matter far less than an answer to the question: *will Australia finally hear our many voices?*

References

Carlson, Bronwyn. *The Politics of Identity: Who Counts as Aboriginal Today?* Canberra: Aboriginal Studies Press, 2016.

Coulthard, Glen S. 'Subjects of Empire: Indigenous Peoples and the "Politics of Recognition" in Canada'. *Contemporary Political Theory* 6, no. 4 (2007): 437–60.

Coulthard, Glen Sean. *Red Skin, White Masks: Rejecting the Colonial Politics of Recognition.* Minneapolis: University of Minnesota Press, 2014.

Daadaoui, Mohamed. 'The Western Sahara Conflict: Towards a Constructivist Approach to Self-determination'. *Journal of North African Studies* 13, no. 2 (2008): 143–56.

Davis, Megan. 'Competing Notions of Constitutional "Recognition": Truth and Justice or Living "Off the Crumbs That Fall Off the White Australian Tables"?' *Papers on Parliament*, no. 62. Department of the Senate, Parliament of Australia. October 2014. Accessed 6 January 2020. www.aph.gov.au/About_Parliament/Senate/Powers_practice_n_procedures/~/~/link.aspx?_id=4B5E02CC60064C6080B5ECBCACB5533D&_z=z.

Davis, Megan. 'Correspondence: The Status Quo Ain't Working'. *Quarterly Essay* 70 (2018): 81–91.

Davis, M. and Langton, M. 'Introduction'. In *It's Our Country: Indigenous Arguments for Meaningful Constitutional Recognition and Reform*, edited by M. Davis and M. Langton, 10–34. Melbourne: Melbourne University Press, 2016.

Department of Aboriginal Affairs. *Report on a Review of the Administration of the Working Definition of Aboriginal and Torres Strait Islander.* Canberra: Commonwealth of Australia, 1981.

Gardiner-Garden, John. *Defining Aboriginality in Australia.* Current Issues Brief, no. 10 2002–2003. Canberra: Australian Parliamentary Library, 2002.

Honneth, Axel. *The Struggle for Recognition: The Moral Grammar of Social Conflicts.* Cambridge, MA: The MIT Press, 1992.

Hunt, Janet. 'Between a Rock and a Hard Place: Self-determination, Mainstreaming and Indigenous Community Governance'. In *Contested Governance: Culture, Power and Institutions in Indigenous Australia*, edited by J. Hunt, D. E. Smith, S. Garling and W. Sanders, 27–54, Canberra: ANU E Press, 2008.

Langton, Marcia. 'Aboriginal Art and Film: The Politics of Representation'. In *Blacklines: Contemporary Critical Writings by Indigenous Australians*, edited by Michele Grossman, 109–24. Carlton, Vic.: Melbourne University Press, 2003.

Langton, Marcia. *Well, I Heard It on the Radio and I Saw It on the Television…* Sydney: Australian Film Commission, 1993.

Lino, Dylan. 'The Politics of Inclusion: The Right of Self-determination, Statutory Bills of Rights and Indigenous People'. *Melbourne University Law Review* 34, no. 3 (2010): 839–69.

Lino, Dylan. 'Towards Indigenous–Settler Federalism'. *Public Law Review* 28, no. 2 (2017): 118–37.

Maddison, Sarah. 'Recognise What? The Limitations of Settler Colonial Constitutional Reform'. *Australian Journal of Political Studies* 52, no. 1 (2017): 3–18.

McCorquodale, John. 'The Legal Classification of Race in Australia'. *Aboriginal History* 10, no. 1/2 (1986): 7–24.

Nakata, Martin. *Disciplining the Savages: Savaging the Disciplines*. Canberra: Aboriginal Studies Press, 2007.

Rowse, Tim. *Remote Possibilities: The Aboriginal Domain and Administrative Imagination*. Darwin: North Australia Research Unit, The Australian National University, 1992.

Rowse, T. and L. Smith. 'The Limits of "Elimination" in the Politics of Population'. *Australian Historical Studies* 41, no. 1 (March 2010): 90–106.

Simpson, Audra. *Mohawk Interruptus: Political Life across the Borders of Settler States*. Durham: Duke University Press, 2014.

Taylor, Charles. 'The Politics of Recognition'. In *Multiculturalism: Examining the Politics of Recognition*, edited by Amy Gutmann, 25–73. Princeton, NJ: Princeton University Press, 1994.

CONTRIBUTORS

Jon Altman – School of Regulation and Global Governance, The Australian National University

Bob Boughton – School of Education in the Faculty of Humanities, Arts, Social Sciences and Education, University of New England

Katherine Curchin – Centre for Social Research and Methods, The Australian National University

M. C. Dillon – Centre for Aboriginal Economic Policy Research, The Australian National University

Elizabeth Ganter – Centre for Aboriginal Economic Policy Research, The Australian National University

Chris Haynes – Honorary Research Fellow, Anthropology and Sociology, University of Western Australia

Maria John – Director of the Native American and Indigenous Studies Program, College of Liberal Arts, University of Massachusetts

Sana Nakata – Indigenous-Settler Relations Collaboration, Faculty of Arts, University of Melbourne

Johanna Perheentupa – Nura Gili Indigenous Studies, UNSW Sydney

Laura Rademaker – School of History, The Australian National University

Tim Rowse – Institute for Culture and Society, Western Sydney University; National Centre for Biography, The Australian National University

Will Sanders – Centre for Aboriginal Economic Policy Research, The Australian National University

Jane Simpson – ARC Centre of Excellence for the Dynamics of Language, The Australian National University

Charlie Ward – Collection Development Co-ordinator, Library & Archives Northern Territory and Visiting Fellow at the School History, The Australian National University

Asmi Wood – National Centre for Indigenous Studies, The Australian National University

www.ingramcontent.com/pod-product-compliance
Lightning Source LLC
Chambersburg PA
CBHW040146270326
41929CB00025B/3391